A Music Business Primer

A Music Business Primer

By
Diane Rapaport

A Jerome Headlands Press Book

Prentice
Hall

Upper Saddle River, New Jersey
Needham, Massachusetts

Library of Congress Cataloging-in-Publication Data

Rapaport, Diane Sward.
    A music business primer / by Diane Rapaport.
       p.cm
    Includes bibliographical references and index.
    ISBN 0-13-034077-4 (pbk.)
    1. Music trade. I. Title.

ML3790 .R38 2002
338.4'778--dc21

2002027441

 A Division of Pearson Education
Upper Saddle River, NJ 07458

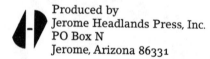 Produced by
Jerome Headlands Press, Inc.
PO Box N
Jerome, Arizona 86331

Cover and book design-Sullivan Santamaria Design, Inc.
Cover illustration and interior spot illustrations-Mark Hemleben
Editor and copyeditor-George Glassman
Index-Rebecca R. Plunkett Indexing Services

10 9 8 7 6 5 4 3 2 1

ISBN 0-13-034077-4

Prentice Hall International (UK) Limited, London
Prentice-Hall of Australia Pty. Limited, Sydney
Prentice-Hall Canada Inc., Toronto
Prentice-Hall Hispanoamericana, S.A., Mexico
Prentice-Hall of India Private Limited, New Delhi
Prentice-Hall of Japan, Inc., Tokyo
Pearson Education Asia Pte. Limited, Singapore
Editora Prentice-Hall do Brasil, Ltda., Rio de Janeiro

CONTENTS

ACKNOWLEDGEMENTS

Thank you to Christopher Johnson, senior editor at Prentice-Hall for suggesting I write this book and supporting the project.

Thank you to all who graciously granted me interviews: artist, producer and businessman, Will Ackerman, cofounder of Windham Hill Records; Wendy Day, founder of Rap Coalition; independent recording artist Marco "Magic" Cardenas, founder of Nasty Boy Records; publisher Michael Eames, cofounder of PEN Music Group, Inc.; entrepreneur and musician Peter Gotcher, cofounder of Digidesign; artist manager Stan Hertzman, founder of Umbrella Artist Management; talent agent and artist manager Edna Landau of IMG Artists; businessman Michael Laskow, founder of TAXI; concert promoter Julie Lokin, cofounder of New Audiences Productions; Leslie Ann Jones, Director of Music Recording and Scoring at Skywalker Sound, a division of Lucas Digital, Ltd. LLC; songwriters, publishers and songwriting educators, Pete and Pat Luboff, founders of Pea Pod Music; and Steven Wlson, Director of Sales and Marketing, Music Sales, Omnibus Press and Schirmer Trade Books.

Thank you to all the photographers, recording labels and businesses that graciously provided photographs.

I especially want to thank people that read over chapters and provided needed clarifications. They include, Henry Vincent, CPA; John Braheny, author, *The Craft and Business of Songwriting*; Patrick Sullivan (NMPA); Amanda Collins (RIAA); Jim Donio (NAMM); Matt Graves of *www. Listen.com*; Edward Hearn, attorney; Marty Polon, independent music business and audio consultant; Professor Roy Pritts, University of Colorado, Denver; Neville Johnson, attorney; Clay Pasternak, AFIM

Thank you to *Music Biz Magazine*, which first published portions of the interviews with Wendy Day, founder of Rap Coalition and Marco "Magic" Cardenas of NB Ridaz. The magazine folded in August 2002.

Thank you to the people that helped keep me on a professional track, particularly my editor George Glassman and production assistant, Susan Tillman. Both have given Jerome Headlands Press stellar work since 1990.

Thank you to Julie Sullivan, cofounder Sullivan Santamaria Design for cover, interior design and production. Since 1990, Julie and her staff have designed all Jerome Headlands Press books and their many revisions.

Thank you to Mark Hemleben, fine artist in Jerome, Arizona, for the cover illustrations and spot illustrations that are seen throughout the book.

Thank you to my husband Walter for his continuing support and patience.

Thank you to the nurturing artists' community of Jerome, Arizona, my home since 1979.

PERMISSIONS

The author gratefully acknowledges permission to use the following articles:

"Collaborator/Songwriter Agreements" by Mark Halloran and Edward R. Hearn, Esq. From The Musician's Business and Legal Guide, ©) 2000 Beverly Hills Bar Association.

"When There are No Written Partnership Agreements" by Edward R. Hearn from The Musician's Business and Legal Guide,© 2000 Beverly Hills Bar Association.

"Sampling" by Gregory T. Victoroff, from The Musician's Business and Legal Guide, ©) 2000 Beverly Hills Bar Association.

"Creating A Story: The Radio Air Play Bandwagon" by Bryan Farrish from his Web site www.radio-media.com (© 2001 Bryan Farrish).

Thank you to the Recording Industry Association of America (RIAA) and the National Association of Recording Merchandisers (NARM) for permission to reprint statistics and information from their publications and Web sites.

Permission to use selected graphics and photographs was graciously granted by Bread & Roses, Bob Brozman, Digidesign, IMG Artists, Inner Peace Music, Limp Bizkit, Music Sales Corporation, Nasty Boy Records, New Audiences Productions, Inc., New West Records, The New Yorker's Cartoon Bank, PEN Music Group, Skywalker Sound, Sugar Hill Records, TAXI, Umbrella Management and Young Concert Artists,

Notice About Trademarks
Designations used by companies to distinguish their products are often claimed as trademarks. Rather than list the names of entities that own the trademarks or insert a trademark symbol with each mention of trademarked names, Jerome Headlands Press, Inc. states that it is using the names only for editorial purposes with no intention of infringing upon any trademark.

The Ecology of the Music Business

Welcome to the 500 billion dollar global entertainment industry. According to Michael J. Wolfe, in his book *The Entertainment Economy,* "Entertainment—not autos, not steel, not financial services—is fast becoming the driving wheel of the new world economy… and, in many parts of the world, the fastest—growing sector of the economy."

Where does music fit? It is found in music products, television programs, videos, movies and video games. It is an integral part of retail store environments, spectator sports, theme parks, casinos, advertising, political and business conventions, fundraising events, etc. It is an integral part of the cultural arts community, which includes classical and choral music, opera, dance and musical theater. The sounds of music are everywhere and integral to the diversity of our culture.

There is a symbiotic partnership between music businesses and the creativity and talent of musicians and performers. Without the contributions of each, there is no music industry.

Artists need support businesses to help their talent flourish and profit. These include attorneys, artist managers, talent agents, concert promoters, record companies and music publishers that help artists market and sell their creativity. In turn, these businesses need a constant supply of creative material, which means they must help artists to nurture and develop their careers.

Artists must learn the craft of their art—how to play, perform, compose, record and widen those abilities with the innovative tools that are available. A good education is the foundation of the music industry and this is provided by music educators, songwriting teachers and music business and audio technology instructors.

ENTERTAINMENT CONGLOMERATES

Entertainment conglomerates have engulfed many companies that manufacture, create and promote entertainment products. These include AOL-Time Warner, Bertelsmann AG, Sony International and Vivendi Universal. They own music manufacturing and other technology companies; record, film, book and music publishing companies; distribution systems; and television, Internet and print media companies. They unite artistic content with communications platforms that can deliver it to billions of people worldwide.

Other entertainment giants—EMI International, VIACOM and Walt Disney Company—do not have such a broad span. EMI owns record and music publishing companies, but not television and print media companies. VIACOM and Walt Disney Company own theme parks, television networks, book, magazine, radio and film companies, but not record and music publishing companies. AT&T and General Electric

AN ARTIST'S SUPPORT ON THE ROAD TO SUCCESS

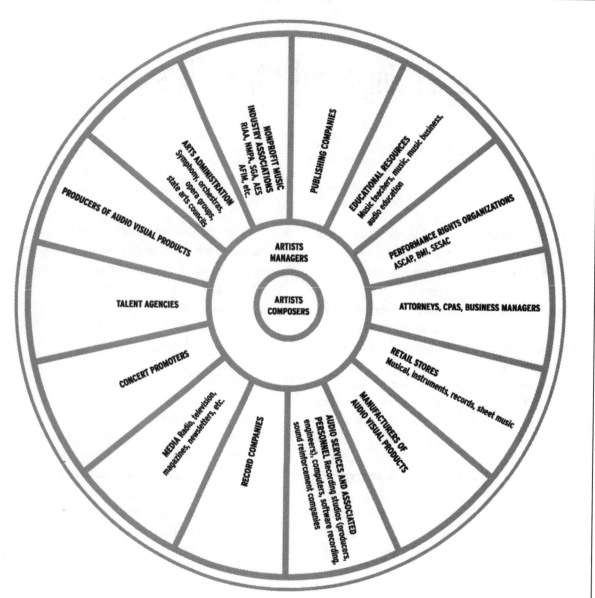

ILLUSTRATION: SUSAN PEARCE

Picture a wagon wheel. At the very center is the axle. The axle is the performing artist around which everything revolves. The hub protects and supports the axle. That is the personal manager. The rim of the wheel is the artist's career, which travels on what can often be a bumpy, long, winding road. Connecting the hub with the rim are many spokes which give the wheel support in different directions. These are the agents, publicists, attorneys, business managers and other industry professionals that support an artist on the road to success. When the wheel is well-constructed, the artist's journey can be smooth, speedy and successful.
Courtesy: National Conference of Personal Managers, www.ncopm.com

own partnerships with other entertainment conglomerates in television stations, radio stations, movie companies, etc.

The integration of compatible companies under single entities enables those entities to effectively market their products, such as best-selling novels and simultaneously market other products based on them—films, audiobooks, music videos, music sound tracks and merchandise—and provide licensing and promotional tie-ins for television and movies. One such company, Sony, also manufactures, markets and sells popular playback equipment for many of these entertainment products.

Owning multiple companies enables conglomerates to use profits from some companies to cover the losses of others. For example, if a film division loses money, its losses may be covered by profits from record labels. A disadvantage to those record labels, however, is that the profits might better be used to nurture new artists and develop markets for broader genres of music.

Consolidation is occurring in other sectors that serve the entertainment business: media, such as newspaper conglomerates (News Corporation and Liberty Media); radio station conglomerates (Infinity Broadcasting and Clear Channel Entertainment) and concert promotion conglomerates (Clear Channel Entertainment and House of Blues). This makes it easier for entertainment conglomerates to efficiently and profitably market their products. Record companies can arrange tours for major artists with one concert promoter, instead of using dozens; they can hire one radio promotion company to service all the radio stations owned by a particular conglomerate.

The Federal Communications Commission is considering abandoning a regulation that separates the ownership of newspapers and other media holdings. This means that one company could own all the media-print, radio and television-in a particular city and it means that large conglomerates would be free to buy newspaper

ENTERTAINMENT CONGLOMERATES

Abundant information about the companies that are owned by entertainment conglomerates can be found on their Web sites. Business information and job opportunities can be found in the press, investor and corporate pages of those sites.

www.aoltimewarner.com

www.att.com

www.disney.com

www.emigroup.com

www.ge.com

www.sony.com

www.viacom.com

www.vivendiuniversal.com

companies, which could leave many cities without multiple news sources.

THE REGIONAL MUSIC INDUSTRY

Although the major entertainment conglomerates and their stars dominate media, there is another music industry, the value of which cannot be accurately determined. However, some music consultants say that its dollar value may equal that of the entertainment conglomerates.

Every city has a music economy that is comprised of many of the same elements as the major music industry, but serves regional music businesses, nonprofit organizations, niche music genres and artists that are beginning their careers.

Most cities and universities have resident dance companies, theaters, operas, symphony orchestras, chamber music groups, etc. Many private and public schools and universities provide music education and are committed to developing innovative cultural arts programs and artists' residencies.

Every city has live entertainment venues that hire local and regional musicians in every genre of music. They include nightclubs, dance halls, coffee houses, churches, etc. Many provide low-cost alternatives to the ticket prices charged by major acts and by cultural arts presenters.

This music industry also includes large institutions that hire musicians, vocalists and audio services: colleges and universities, religious institutions, the U.S. military and the Music Performance Trust Fund of the American Federation of Musicians.

Local musical instrument and audio product stores are largely dependent on amateur musicians as their main customers, but sales of instruments, sheet music and technological tools are increasing to professional musicians that have local and regional careers.

Many cities and towns have one or more independent recording labels—artists that put out their own recordings and labels that serve niche genres and are not allied to major labels. Local film, television and video game producers and advertising agencies also hire musicians.

Independent recording artists spend money to put out their recordings, which helps to support retail stores, recording and mastering studios, replicating facilities, fanzines, music schools and music business and audio technology schools, advertising agencies, graphic designers and photographers.

Some cities sponsor annual events that do not depend on the pop music scene for their talent, yet bring in considerable income. Austin, Texas, well-known for its pop music scene, is also host for South by Southwest, which brings nonmajor-label musicians and business people together from all over the country. In Elko, Nevada, an annual festival draws 30,000 people to hear cowboy bands, musicians and poets.

Some cities are known for their extraordinary opera, symphony orchestra or ballet companies. Miami, New Orleans and St. Louis are established centers for particular genres of music, such as Cuban jazz, Cajun and blues and bring in millions of tourists that spend money on local music performances and other entertainment events.

Some cities are entertainment meccas that employ thousands of musicians and auxiliary audio services. They include Los Angeles, Nashville, Memphis, New York, San Francisco, Las Vegas, Branson and New Orleans

Regional music businesses serve as training and proving grounds for musicians, performers, music businesses, audio professionals and new products. They provide jobs and revenue for city and state coffers.

Economic Impact Studies

Some Canadian music industry associations have initiated studies that show the importance of regional music. A study conducted in 1995 by the Saskatchewan Recording Industry Association revealed that their industry generated $87 million and employed over 3,000 people.

A 1998 study commissioned by the Manitoba Audio Recording Industry found that 81% of the money spent in the industry remained in the province—a total of $8.3 million-and created $4.6 million in labor income. Music generated from other sources, such as music festivals, added another $13 million to the local economy.

The economic impact of cultural arts presentations in many cities helps them bring in donations and grants from nonprofit foundations, business and private donors and state and government arts organizations.

Although figures are increasingly available about the annual sales generated by independent artists and labels in the United States, little information is available about the tremendous economic contribution they, and other popular entertainment businesses, make to regional economies.

Economic impact studies could help persuade potential sponsors to support tours, awards shows, special concerts, music business educational programs and the events of regional nonprofit organizations. For example, the Prairie Music Alliance in Saskatchewan, Canada, produces an annual weeklong music festival/music business conference. According to the Alliance, over $1 million is realized from attendees to the conference through hotel accommodations, food and beverage sales, shopping and other items. The ability to prove this helps the Alliance gain advertising support from local, regional and national sponsors. Similar studies could help many regionally based music businesses generate interest and support from banks, businesses and other local institutions.

FINANCIAL SUPPORT FOR MUSICIANS

In the United States, public and private funding for music education and for support of the cultural arts from nonprofit institutions and foundations is widely available. There is financial support to help classical musicians develop their careers and to tour, mostly from state and national arts grants and colleges and universities that have artist-in-residence programs. There is little financial support available for popular entertainment musicians and performers.

A major difference between the United States and Canada is the tremendous financial support available in Canada to musicians that are starting their careers in the popular music industries. The Foundation to Assist Canadian Talent on Records (FACTOR) provides over $12 million annually to help the independent recording industry grow and flourish. These funds assist Canadian recording artists and songwriters in having their recordings and videos produced and in touring international-ly, and they provide support for Canadian record labels, distributors, producers, engineers, direc-tors—those facets of the infrastructure that must flourish in order for the Canadian independent recording industry to progress in the international marketplace.

THE INTERNET'S EFFECT ON THE MUSIC INDUSTRY

The Internet has profoundly affected the market-ing and selling of entertainment products, chal-lenged the protection of intellectual property rights, provided new music licensing opportuni-ties and revenue sources and provided consumers with new options to easily access a wide spectrum of music. Email makes it fast and easy to send graphic, music, video and word files anywhere in the world.

Free file sharing opened a Pandora's box. The Internet became a vast public library where people can freely explore their musical interests and share their music collections with others. Consumer demand has challenged all music businesses to find methods to satisfy that demand without destroying the basic principle of copyright law: artists should be paid for their creative works.

Business has risen to that challenge by pro-viding a variety of subscription services: Internet jukeboxes, such as those provided by MusicMatch and Real Networks, enable consumers to choose what they listen to from vast music repositories for modest fees; Internet radio stations provide hundreds of musical genres; record label sites provide subscriptions for temporary and perma-nent downloads and streaming.

Perhaps the biggest challenge for major labels is how to continue to control marketing and influ-ence what consumers buy. Before the internet, most consumers learned about new music from major media radio, television and print resources, and labels could predict, with some accuracy, what consumers would buy.

The Internet is shifting the axis of control towards consumers.

Access to a wider range of music on the Internet will shift buying and listening habits in unpredictable ways. Perhaps many consumers will choose to listen only to selections from Internet jukeboxes, and their collections of recordings will be vestiges of the past.

CONCLUSION

New consumer demands for wider access to music and the ability of the Internet to satisfy that demand have provided springboards for innovation and evolution in the entertainment industry. The industry is in a state of flux, with the demise of some companies and the rise of others.

The dominance of popular entertainment mediums directly competes with cultural arts presentations, and, in some cases, threatens their survival. The Internet provides access to music for consumers and new revenue streams for some music businesses, while it has the potential to destroy others.

The next five years should bring as much change into the music business as did the last twenty. This makes it an exciting and rewarding time to be a part of the industry. Artists and business people must learn new ways of working together to strengthen the industry and develop audience support for music in all genres.

The Business of Music

* * *

THE LANGUAGE OF BUSINESS

BUSINESS NAMES

INTERVIEW HIGHLIGHT
Will Ackerman:
The Artist as Businessperson

RESOURCE HIGHLIGHT
The Small Business Administration

RESOURCES

The Language of Business

A business is any activity that provides skills, services or products to the public in exchange for money. The goal of business is to make a profit.

Businesses have rules and languages of their own. It is essential to know the vocabulary to understand the nature of the business relationships that exist in the music industry.

Successful business people build relationships and sell their skills, products and services. This is particularly true in the music industry. Record companies buy services from recording studios, manufacturers, wholesalers, etc. Few musicians sell their art directly without intermediaries to aid them, such as managers and talent agents. Retail stores need recorded products to sell. Club owners need to attract customers that will buy food and beverages. Businesses thrive when they find ways to increase their value to each other and accomplish common goals.

FINANCIAL STATEMENTS

Business people must accurately measure their financial operations. This is accomplished with financial statements that present the economic facts about a business at given points in time (monthly, annually). They include balance sheets (assets, liabilities and equities) and income statements (profit and loss).

Assets

Balance sheets reflect the assets and liabilities of businesses at particular points in time.

Assets are the resources owned by businesses that have economic benefit. They include—

- Cash on hand and in the bank

- Accounts receivable (monies owed to the business)

- Inventories (goods available for sale to customers)

- Fixed assets (depreciable assets)

- Intangible assets

Fixed assets are the tools of businesses: such as musical instruments, sound reinforcement equipment, computers, tape recorders, microphone stands, microphones, office equipment, recording studios, vehicles, land and buildings, etc.

Intangible assets are the values that businesses have built in their names, patents, copyrights, trademarks, good will (reputation in the marketplace), identity (brand) and their ability to invent new products or services. These are termed intangible because their value depends, to some extent, on public perception.

Generally, intangible assets are not reflected in a business' financial statements. However, monetary values are placed on intangible assets when they are sold, transferred or when business owners die. The combination of fixed and intangible assets helps to determine total value.

Liabilities

Liabilities are the obligations of business enterprises that must be satisfied through the disbursement of assets. They include—

- Accounts payable

- Taxes payable

- Loan (principle and interest)

Accounts payable are expenses incurred in the course of doing business, such as rent, phone, supplies, salaries and contracted services (recording studio time, graphic designer, advertising agency).

Most businesses depend on loans to help them succeed. Loans help purchase assets and finance business expansion. In the music business, some loans (advances) are made in anticipation of income and are commonly repaid from income earned, such as sales of records and revenues from publishing royalties. Record companies commonly pay artists advances to help them finance recordings. The companies recoup the advances from artists' earnings (royalties) that are payable when their recordings are sold.

Net Worth (Equity)

Net worth is the difference between the value of a business' assets and its liabilities. It is comprised of monies invested in the business by its owners and any profitability that the business retains.

When assets exceed liabilities, businesses have positive net worth. When liabilities exceed assets, businesses have negative net worth or deficit.

The summaries of assets and liabilities, as determined by company books of account, constitute balance sheets.

Businesses thrive when they find ways to increase their value to each other and accomplish common goals.

INCOME STATEMENTS

Income statements (profit and loss statements, P&L) measure the results of business operations. They measure revenues (income) earned versus expenses (monies paid out). When revenues exceed expenses, businesses are profitable.

Revenues (Income)

Revenues are monies earned in the course of doing business. They do not include monies invested in businesses by their owners (capital infusions).

Examples of income generators in the music business include—

- *Musicians:* performance, record royalties, teaching, recording studio performance, arranging

- *Composers:* royalties from public performances, licensing of music for use in films, recordings, video games

- *Recording studios:* recording studio time, expert services of in-house producers and arrangers, rental of equipment, mastering, editing

- *Record companies:* sales of recordings and other merchandise

- *Retail stores:* sales of CDs, videos, DVDs, books and magazines, blank tape

- *Talent agents:* commissions from sales of artists' performances to entertainment buyers

I CAN'T BE OVERDRAWN!
I STILL HAVE CHECKS IN MY CHECKBOOK!

Expenses

The monies that businesses spend in their day-to-day operations are considered business expenses. They do not include the personal expenses of business owners. Only business expenses are posted to income statements. Expenses do not include capital expenditures (see below).

Since business expenses are deductible when computing taxable income, the IRS provides the following criteria for defining business expense.

Expenses must be "ordinary and necessary." The word "ordinary" means expenses common to a particular business. For a guitarist, buying guitar strings would be considered an ordinary expense. The word "necessary" means those expenses that are "appropriate and helpful in developing and maintaining a trade or business."

Expenses must be "reasonable." A reasonable commission paid to a booking agent who helps a band get gigs is 10% to 20%. A commission of 50% would be considered unreasonable.

Common business expenses include rent, commissions, legal and accounting, communications, travel, supplies, salaries, repair maintenance, etc.

Capital Expenditures

Monies spent for long-lived assets (greater than one year) are called capital expenditures. Capital expenditures give rise to fixed assets (property, buildings and equipment). Long-lived assets are written off (depreciated) over their estimated, useful lives as expenses in income statements. They can include musical instruments, computers, furniture, buildings, manufacturing equipment, etc.) Land cannot be depreciated because it does not wear out.

Personal Expenses

Personal expenses are not business expenses and are not included in business financial statements. Here are some examples—

- A manager travels from St. Louis, Missouri to New York to visit record companies interested in his artists and stays an extra day to visit museums and visit friends. Only the expenses attributed to gaining the business goals are considered business expenses.

- A business uses one room in a house exclusively for business—rehearsing, recording, performing publicity services, writing magazine articles, teaching, etc. The business only can allocate a portion of the rent or mortgage as a business expense.

- The owner of a sound reinforcement company owns a van that is sometimes used to transport equipment to theaters and concert halls. Only the cost of the mileage used for business is a business expense.

BOOKKEEPING

Business' account books are maintained to accurately and clearly measure assets, liabilities, income and expenses. This information is needed to comply with tax laws and is invaluable to help businesses make timely, informed decisions that can make the difference between profit and loss.

The task of maintaining these records is called bookkeeping and a person who performs this function as a business or as a salaried employee of a company is called a bookkeeper. Examples of bookkeeping tasks include—

- Reconciliation of checkbooks (agreement of checkbook balance to the bank statement)

- Issuing salary checks to employees

- Paying social security and other taxes

- Recording cash receipts (revenues) and cash disbursements (expenses)

- Recording liabilities and assets

- Recording and paying payables (monies owed). Recording receivables (income due and collected)

The books of account of businesses are called general ledgers.

Certified Public Accountants (CPA) advise business owners about choosing business entities, tax planning, the financial consequences of borrowing and contractual decisions, retirement planning and general business questions, and they prepare taxes.

BUSINESS PLANS

According to the Small Business Administration, most small businesses take two years or more to show a profit. Many depend on loans and investments to fill the gap between start-up and profit.

Business plans help owners define their goals

BUSINESS FAILURES

According to the SBA, two out of five start-up businesses fail within the first five years. The reasons cited most frequently are—

- Poor management (lack of experience, education, sales ability or sheer incompetence)

- Poor planning

- Poor choice of business

- Unfavorable location

- Unplanned or uncontrolled growth

- Inadequate record keeping

- Excessive inventory or fixed assets

- Inadequate capital

and objectives in writing; outline strategies for achieving them; and figure out how much financing is needed. They outline future growth and anticipate change. Business plans are maps that show how businesses will get from idea to success. They show profitable businesses how to grow successfully. They help businesses maintain direction and ensure they will have enough money and energy to continue in their endeavors. Business plans force owners to plan ahead.

Business plans are critical elements in attracting lenders and investors. They include the operating plans for starting and running businesses and the sales plans that outline projected revenues to be collected and expenses to be paid. Investors look at business plans to determine how owners plan to use their investors' money and how long it will take before investments are repaid. They want to see well-grounded financial ideas. Investors understand that lack of planning and clarity on

OUTLINE OF A BUSINESS PLAN

I. PROJECT SUMMARY (EXECUTIVE SUMMARY)

A succinct, one-page overview that explains what the company's products or services will be (recording studio, record label, publicity company, expansion of a current business, etc.); the market segment that is being targeted; a description of current market conditions, including key competitors and challenges; projected financial goals; and the amount of investment that is needed.

II. ORGANIZATION, MANAGEMENT AND PEOPLE

What business is the enterprise in; how many people will initially run it; what is the business entity (sole proprietor, LLC, partnership, corporation); what are the skills and achievements of founders and managers.

III. OBJECTIVES AND PLAN OF ACTION

What does the business want to accomplish and by what means? Why do owners want to be in business? What are the business' major goals?

Sales plan.
Description of products and services and the benefits they will provide to customers. Description of what new/better/different advantages the business will offer in the marketplace. Pricing strategies.

Projected sales. Description of competitive products and services and how they will be surpassed.

IV. MARKETING OBJECTIVES AND STRATEGIES

Market size, market trends, how people will be persuaded to buy the products and services. Advertising and public relations plan.

V. PRODUCTION AND OPERATION

If selling products-how the products will be manufactured or where they will be purchased—including sources of suppliers, logistics, and facilities requirements.

If selling services-how the services will be delivered; what equipment and facilities are required.

VI. FINANCIAL DATA

If an existing business-financial statements for the past three years of operation. Monies needed for expansion; projected income statements for one, two and three years. How much capital will be needed for expansion and during operation?

If a new business-projections of what the business will earn in one, two and five years (projected cash flow) and what are the assumptions underlying these projections. How much capital will be needed at start-up and during operation?

How much financing is required and when.

strategic and financial goals are reasons that businesses fail and loans go unpaid. Business plans identify what the obstacles to success might be and how businesses will overcome them.

Before business owners invest their own money, they should ask themselves what is the risk of losing that money and how can it be best used to build successful businesses. Business plans are invaluable tools for answering those questions.

BUSINESS ENTITIES

The term business entities refers to types of business organizations. The most common forms of business entities are sole proprietorship, general partnership, limited liability company (LLC) and corporation. With the exception of a sole proprietorship, all business entities need written agreements that define the role of the owners and how the business is to be operated and managed.

For general and limited partnerships, the agreement is known as a partnership agreement; for LLCs, it is called an operating agreement; and for corporations, bylaws govern the relationship of the incorporators, boards of directors and officers.

Agreements clarify the following—

- Contributions of assets (money and property) to the venture

- Ownership of intellectual property (copyrights, trademarks, patents, etc.)

- Compensation of owners

- How critical business decisions are to be made (majority, unanimity, etc.)

- Retention of the name (who, if anyone, owns the business name)

- What happens when an owner dies

- What happens when an owner leaves the business

The choice of business entity and how agreements are to be drafted requires the counsel of attorneys and certified public accountants to ensure that they meet the legal requirements of state and federal statutes and the goals and priorities of the owners. It is easier and less expensive to properly plan a business from the beginning than try to resolve problems afterward. If people cannot discuss and agree on critical issues beforehand, they should not be in business together.

Although written agreements will not make a business that has soured run smoothly, they will help owners avoid legal entanglements when they disagree on critical issues or when one or more owners leave the business or the business is dissolved.

The following brief description of each entity provides basic terminology and operational and taxation features.

Businesses can change their legal entities from sole proprietorships to partnerships, LLCs or corporations. This is done to protect personal assets from claims of creditors or legal action; for tax-related purposes; or to allow for new investors; etc. Partnerships change their entities to LLCs or corporations to protect the partners' individual assets from losses and debts resulting from the actions of other partners.

Sole Proprietorship

A sole proprietorship is a business entity conducted by one person who is the sole owner. That person controls the checkbook, hires and fires employees, makes all the decisions about the focus of the business and keeps all the profits. He or she is personally responsible for business losses and the proprietor's personal assets are on the line should someone sue the business and win. It is the easiest business entity to start and operate.

The owners of sole proprietorships are not employees and do not pay themselves wages. The money proprietors take from their businesses is called draw.

A sole proprietorship is the only entity that needs to make a profit in any two of five consecutive years; otherwise the IRS considers it to be a hobby.

General Partnership

The association of two or more people for a business purpose constitutes a general partnership. General partners are jointly and severally (individually) liable for each other's acts, decisions and the debts the partners have incurred on behalf of the partnership. Each partner's assets are on the line if the partnership forfeits on a loan or gets sued. If one partner makes a bad decision, all partners are responsible for the consequences.

If one partner signs for a loan on behalf of the partnership for a piece of recording equipment, the other partners are responsible for making payments, whether or not this decision was made with the consent of the other partners. If the partner who signed the loan on behalf of the partnership walks out of the partnership, the other partners still have to pay back the loan.

Unless otherwise agreed to, the exit of one partner will usually mean the dissolution of the general partnership.

The operation of a general partnership should be governed by a written partnership agreement between its members that identifies the substantial elements of managing the business and addresses the issues outlined above.

Joint Venture

A joint venture is a partnership formed to accomplish a single business enterprise—such as recording a single CD or video—rather than to operate a continuous business.

Limited Partnership

A limited partnership enables investors to contribute capital to a partnership and incur only limited liability. Limited partners have no say in the running of the business. Therefore their risk is "limited" to the amount of their investments. The general partner(s) control the business and make financial decisions.

For example, a band could form a limited partnership to get investors to provide the capital to make a recording but the band does not want investors to make aesthetic decisions such as what songs should be included or business decisions about how much money to spend on recording and promotion.

BUSINESS PRINCIPLES

BUSINESSES ARE ABOUT RELATIONSHIPS BETWEEN PEOPLE. IN THE COURSE OF ANY MUSIC BUSINESS, THE OWNERS AND THEIR EMPLOYEES WILL DEVELOP REPUTATIONS FOR BEING EASY OR DIFFICULT TO WORK WITH; FOR DELIVERING WHAT IS PROMISED; FOR BEING ETHICAL OR NOT, AND SO ON.

BUSINESSES THAT INCORPORATE THE PRINCIPLES BELOW WILL HAVE A COMPETITIVE EDGE.

1. Commit to making the business succeed. Without 100% commitment, the motivation to overcome challenges will erode.

2. Work hard and provide leadership.

3. Develop personal relationships with the people your business works with: bankers, vendors, etc. Cultivate long-term relationships. Earn trust and good will.

4. Make it easy to for people to associate and do business with you.

   • Show up for gigs and appointments on time.

   • Keep promises you make.

   • Return phone calls in a timely manner.

   • Pay your bills on time. If you cannot, call people up and explain your situation.

   • Be kind to secretaries and receptionists.

   • Do not waste people's time. State what you want succinctly and politely.

   • Say thank you in person, with cards and by e-mail. Forgive easily.

   • When you make a mistake, apologize.

   • Cultivate positive attitudes.

5. Provide value added services to people you do business with. This could mean performing extra encores; providing free passes to concerts; providing 15 hours of free recording for every 1000 hours booked, etc.; or simply giving free advice when asked.

6. Treat your employees courteously; pay them a fair wage; be appreciative of their good work; and when you can afford it, reward them with bonuses and other benefits. They will repay you with loyalty and hard work. Training new employees costs time and money.

7. Listen to people of the businesses you work with. Find out what is important to them.

8. Do every job and gig as though it were for the kingpins of the music industry.

9. Keep track of your money. Negotiate prices and services. Keep debts to a minimum.

10. Cultivate a good reputation. Be principled in your dealings. Leadership in ethics and good conduct will be rewarded many times over in loyalty, in people speaking well of your business and dealing fairly and ethically with you.

11. Ask for and invite advice. Good advice is invaluable. Feedback is important, even when it is negative. Receive advice and criticism with enthusiasm and graciousness.

12. Give something back to the industry. Share information with others. Donate time or money to nonprofit organizations and other worthwhile causes. Count your blessings and help those that are less fortunate.

WHEN THERE ARE NO WRITTEN PARTNERSHIP AGREEMENTS

By Edward R. Hearn

MANY GENERAL PARTNERSHIPS DO NOT HAVE WRITTEN AGREEMENTS. IF THIS IS THE CASE, IT IS IMPORTANT FOR THE PARTNERS TO WORK OUT CRITICAL ISSUES AMONG THEMSELVES. A GOOD ISSUE ON WHICH TO FOCUS IS TO DETERMINE AT WHAT POINT THE BUSINESS SHOULD MAKE AN EFFORT TO HAVE A WRITTEN AGREEMENT.

LEGAL PRESUMPTIONS

If there is no written partnership agreement, state statutes generally presume that the following conditions apply—

- Each partner has an equal vote in the affairs of the partnership and a majority vote determines the decision of the partners.

- Each partner owns an equal share in the assets of the partnership, which include equipment purchased, the name, and income.

- Each partner shares equally in the profits and losses of the partnership.

- Each partner is responsible for the acts of all of the other partners performed in pursuing the partnership's business.

LEAVING MEMBERS

When there is no written agreement and a partner leaves the partnership, whether willingly or at the demand of the other partners, then the partnership terminates automatically. The business has a responsibility to pay all of the debts of the partnership and, if necessary, sell the partnership's assets to do so. If thereafter, the remaining members of the partnership wish to continue as a business, they must form a new partnership and start over again. If the businesses' creditors cooperate, the business may be able to avoid having to liquidate the former businesses' assets so long as the remaining partners continue to pay the creditors. The remaining partners will need to work out with the departing partners how they will continue to make payments owed or to receive payments due to satisfy partnership obligations.

If the partnership does not want to deal with dissolution and liquidation under these circumstances they need a written partnership agreement.

Limited partnership agreements *must* be spelled out in a manner that satisfies federal securities and exchange law requirements.

Limited Liability Company (LLC)

An LLC is a legal entity that is created for the purpose of conducting a business. It is established by compliance with state statutes. This entity is separate from its owners, who are legally referred to as members, and provides them limited liability regarding the actions of the LLC. If the entity is sued, the members' personal assets are protected and generally cannot be touched by legal or financial actions against them. This means that the owners are protected from personal loss from any business claims or lawsuits that arise from the LLC's debts, transactions and activities.

In an LLC, the name of the entity is the property of the LLC and not any individual members. The formation of an LLC under a given state's statute formally reserves that name for the entity and protects that name in the state the LLC was formed.

A person may create a single-member LLC instead of a sole proprietorship and be provided with the same liability protection as a multimember LLC.

An LLC provides the greatest flexibility with regard to operation and taxation (see below). It is often the entity of choice for small businesses, particularly for business startups. Many recording studios, bands and small recording labels use LLCs as their form of entity.

Organizational documents describe how an LLC will be managed. LLCs with multiple members can be managed by the members (member-managed) or by a manager (manager-managed). This is an important decision because in a member-managed LLC, one member can sign contracts that are negotiated on behalf of the LLC without permission of the others. In a manager-managed LLC, the manager can sign contracts on behalf of the LLC without the consent of other members. Generally, performing and recording groups that set up their businesses as LLCs are manager-managed.

The operation of an LLC is governed by its operating agreement, which identifies the substantial elements of managing the business. The agreement helps members avoid legal entanglements during the operation of the LLC and during its dissolution. By statute, signatures of all LLC members are required on the operating agreement.

The operating agreement sets forth which business decisions require unanimous consent of the members and which can be made by majority consent, how profit is to be shared, how exiting and new members are to be accommodated and how new members are admitted.

Here are the areas that should be addressed in an operating agreement:

- *Contribution of assets:* Members will contribute money, property and equipment during formation and operation of an LLC. Although no law specifies that members have to make equal or simultaneous contributions, the operating agreement must be clear about what each member will contribute in cash, property (such as recording equipment) and time, and what happens if contributions become unequal. All contributed assets are assigned the cost the member paid for them, even if they are used or have appreciated in value.

  The LLC takes title to the business assets; individual members do not own the assets. They own an interest in the business entity. If property is acquired by the LCC with financing, the LLC owes the debt.

- *Profits:* The operating agreement states how profits are shared. In an LLC, profits need not be shared in proportion to the ownership interest of its members. The rationale that underlies the stated division of profits does not have to be spelled out in the operating agreement.

- *Losses:* The operating agreement can provide for a disproportionate allocation of losses.

- *Name:* In cases where the LLC's name may have continuing value upon dissolution of the LLC, the operating agreement must discuss who has the right to the name. It could state that none of the members can use the name if the LLC should completely disband, or that any one of the members could buy the name from the others upon dissolution. The agreement should state how the financial value of its name would be determined and how that the value would be established.

- *Decisions:* Although its organizational documents specify whether an LLC is a member-managed or manager-managed, its operating agreement must distinguish between key business decisions—such as which recording and publishing contracts to pursue; when the business is to expand or sold; when major asset purchases are to be made)—and day-to-day operational decisions—such as which songs to record; which to send to producers; what staff to hire; and what office equipment to purchase. Specificity is important to avoid disputes and legal problems among LLC members during its operation.

  The number of votes needed to make key business decisions should be spelled out in the operating agreement. Each member can have one vote, or the votes can be weighted according to each member's capital contribution (money and assets contributed to making the LLC work) or on some other basis.

- *Leaving members:* The operating agreement should discuss the terms of how members can exit the LLC. The rights that leaving members have to tangible assets and intellectual property created during their involvement with LLC and which assets can be removed from the LLC, at what price and terms, must be spelled out.

  Withdrawal of one member does not constitute automatic cessation of the LLC. However, the conditions of withdrawal should be made a part of the operating agreement, particularly as regards continuing loan guarantees, existing contractual obligations, and so on.

- *Death of a member:* The operating agreement should discuss whether the LLC will continue to operate upon the death of a member, and if so, how.

- *New members:* The operating agreement should establish the terms under which new members can enter the LLC. In many states, unanimity is required for a new member to be admitted.

Corporation

A corporation is a legal entity that is created for the purpose of conducting a business. It is established by compliance with state statutes. A corporation is separate from its owners and therefore provides them limitation of liability. The owners are called shareholders. The personal assets of the shareholders are protected from any business claims or lawsuits that arise from the corporation's debts, business transactions and other activities.

Corporations differ from LLCs in the following ways—

- Continuity of operation is uninterrupted by the death of an owner.

- Ownership interests (as reflected by ownership in the corporation's stocks) are freely transferable (can be bought, sold, given away, listed on national stock exchanges).

BREAD AND ROSES

Bread & Roses volunteer performer James Jenkins thrills seniors at the Tamalpais Convalescent facility in Marin County, California with his classical violin playing.

Founded in 1974 by performer Mimi Fariña, Bread & Roses is a nonprofit corporation that brings free, live performances to people isolated in San Francisco Bay Area institutions.

Over 500 shows are produced yearly for a total audience of 19,000 in convalescent homes, hospitals, AIDS facilities, homeless and senior centers, psychiatric, rehabilitation and correctional facilities and centers for abused and neglected children. Over 1,200 performing

Bread & Roses is a nonprofit corporation that brings free, live performances to people isolated in San Francisco Bay Area institutions.

artists, from amateurs to professionals, donate their time and talents on an annual basis.

Bread & Roses receives no government funds, charges no fees for services and relies on individual contributions and foundation grants.

www.breadandroses.org

www.breadandroses.org

Nonprofit (not-for-profit) corporations use their profits to further charitable, religious, scientific, social, literary or educational purposes.

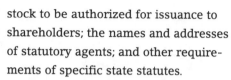

- They have boards of directors.

- Shareholders have voting rights that are in proportion to their ownership interest (amount of stock held). A holder of 51% of the stock controls the operation of the corporation.

- Corporations can elect to operate as Subchapter S or Subchapter C corporations, a choice that has legal, business and tax ramifications that must be discussed with an attorney and CPA (see *Taxation* below).

Corporations cease to exist when they are legally liquidated under state statutes. At that time, assets are distributed to the shareholders in exchange for their shares. The name of the corporation dies a statutory death upon liquidation and is then available to a newly formed entity.

Filing a certificate of incorporation with the appropriate state office creates a corporation. The incorporators are those persons that initially form the corporation. Since the corporation is not an individual (or group of individuals) and is intangible, no one individual or individuals can be served with legal documents. For that reason, the corporation will appoint a person called a statutory agent for service of official documents (for example, a lawsuit).

The certificates of incorporation include the names of the businesses; physical addresses; names and addresses of incorporators; initial purposes for which they were formed; the amount and types of

stock to be authorized for issuance to shareholders; the names and addresses of statutory agents; and other requirements of specific state statutes.

Shares of stock are initially allocated among owners in proportion to their investments (money, property and other assets turned over to the corporation). Sometimes blocks of shares are made available for future sale to the public. Shareholders own percentage stakes, have voting privileges and are invited to annual shareholder meetings.

Corporations can be owned by up to 35 shareholders (closely held) or they can have many shareholders and be publicly traded. Closely held corporations do not have to disclose financial, organizational and other information to the public. The majority shareholders control corporate decision making.

Publicly traded companies must make financial and organizational information available to their stockholders and abide by rules established by the Securities and Exchange Commission. Because corporate managers are accountable to shareholders of publicly traded corporations, minority shareholders can influence management decisions.

The incorporators elect boards of directors. In small corporations, they are generally the same people as the incorporators. In larger corporations, they are often people of influence. Boards of directors are ultimately responsible for making key business decisions and their main responsibility is to return the greatest profit to shareholders, at whose direction they serve. The incorporators draw up corporations' by-laws. In most states, they can be held personally responsible for acts of corporations that are particularly heinous (fraud, deceit, nondisclosure of critical financial information, etc.) that affect companies financial positions and reputations.

The purpose of bylaws is to outline the

corporations' operation; discuss the powers and duties of boards and officers; and define the differences between them.

Boards of directors hire officers that are responsible for the operation of the corporation, consistent with the provisions of the bylaws.

Nonprofit Corporation

For profit corporations exist to advance the interests and increase the income of shareholders. Nonprofit (not-for-profit) corporations use their profits to further charitable, religious, scientific, social, literary or educational purposes. Nonprofit corporations do not issue stock and their profits cannot benefit their officers and board members.

The IRS grants nonprofit status. But the terms nonprofit or not-for-profit are misnomers. As long as a nonprofit corporation operates for legally recognized nonprofit purposes, it may have more revenues than expenditures without owing income taxes, as long as the operations are in furtherance of its purposes, as recognized by the IRS.

A major advantage of nonprofit corporations is that they can receive grants and contributions from other business entities, government agencies and individuals. Donations to nonprofit corporations can be deducted on individual and business tax returns.

Other advantages for nonprofits include lower rates on bulk mailings and free radio and television public service announcements.

TAXATION

The type of business entity chosen determines which tax filings are required and how taxes are to be paid. General and limited partnerships, most LLCs and Subchapter S corporations are known as flow-through entities: the liability for taxes flows from the entity to the individual owner. This means that taxes are paid by individuals and not the entity itself.

Sole proprietors report taxable income on their individual tax returns (Form 1040) and accompanying schedules.

Partnerships annually file Form 1065, which allocates the amounts of income, loss, deductions and credits to the individual partners. The partners then report these shares on their individual income tax returns (Form 1040).

The Internal Revenue Code allows LLC members to choose whether the entity will be taxed as a partnership, Subchapter C or Subchapter S corporation. If the members are to be taxed as a partnership, the LLC files Form 1065, which allocates the amount of income, loss, deductions and credits to the individual members. If the members elect to be taxed as a Subchapter C corporation, the LLC files form 1120, and the entity pays its own income tax. If the members elect to be taxed as a Subchapter S corporation, the LLC files Form 1120 S, which allocates the income, loss, deductions and credits to the members. The members report that share on their individual income tax returns (Form 1040).

Subchapter C corporations pay income tax on taxable income (profits) and file Form 1120. They have tax benefits that are not available to Subchapter S corporations, such as the deductibility of health insurance premiums. The working shareholders are paid salaries, which they report on their individual tax returns (Form 1040).

Subchapter S corporations file form 1120 S and report each shareholder's proportion of corporate income, loss and credit. Those amounts are then reported on the individuals' tax returns (Form 1040). Subchapter S shareholders are paid reasonable salaries and may withdraw excess profits in the form of dividends. These are reported on their individual tax returns (Form 1040).

Annual tax filings are required for nonprofit corporations, although no taxes are payable so long as they fulfill the requirements of their tax-exempt status. Contributions by individuals and

Although written agreements will not make a business that has soured run smoothly, they will help owners avoid legal entanglements when they disagree on critical issues or when one or more owners leave the business or the business is dissolved.

businesses to legally recognized nonprofits are deductible against taxable income of the contributors, subject to IRS limitations.

Sole Proprietors

Sole proprietors report their taxable income (profit or loss) on Schedule C of Form 1040. Profitable proprietorships pay income tax and self-employment tax. The latter can exceed the income tax. In 2002, the amount of the self-employment tax is 15.3% of 92.35% of the net profits that are generated.

The self-employment tax is the means by which sole proprietors pay into the social security system. When individuals are employed by an entity, one half of their social security tax is withheld from their wages and the business pays the other half.

Tax Planning

Tax planning begins with the choice of entity. The financial implications that underlie each business entity are extremely complex and should be discussed with an attorney and CPA prior to formation.

CPAs can help businesses with tax planning and advise taxpayers about any legitimate savings that are available. Businesses should keep accurate books to assist in making informed decisions and to help anticipate tax liability. CPAs assist in tax planning during the business year, *not* at the end of the businesses' fiscal year, when taxes are due.

CONCLUSION

The music industry is about the exchange of money, skills and services between people and businesses. It is made up of individual businesses that talk the same language and have the same goal: to make a profit. The choices of which entity to use and how to manage and operate the business are guided by the advice and counsel of attorneys and CPAs.

Business Names

The name of a business is an important asset. Choosing a name is one of the first tasks that business owners have. Names are chosen for their ease of memorability and implied associations with the type and style of business that is being conducted. This choice is so important that some businesses hire people that are experts in naming businesses.

Names must be original to the business they are being used for, and, for the fullest protection, be unused by any other businesses, regardless of type. This avoids being sued for infringing on someone else's name. Care should also be taken not to use a name that is similar to one being used by another business since it could sue for trading on its reputation.

RESEARCHING A NAME'S ORIGINALITY

New business owners must research desired names to ensure originality. Good sources to check are music industry trade directories, such as the *Billboard International Talent and Touring Directory, Recording Industry Sourcebook, PhonoLog* and *The Trademark Register.*

Names can also be researched by inquiries to the Internet Network Information Center (InterNIC) *(http://rs.internic.net)* and the Domain Registry *(http://www.domainregistry.com).* But, not all businesses have Internet Web sites.

Professional search bureaus and some attorneys specialize in researching the originality of business names. They also check to see whether or not names have been registered as federal or state trademarks or service marks.

Businesses cannot copyright names, only ensure beyond some reasonable doubt that they are original.

Businesses can, however, register their logos and the distinctive lettering for their business names with the U.S. Patent and Trademark Office. Trademarks are registered for businesses that sell products, such as CDs, videos, coffee mugs, posters. Service marks are registered for businesses that primarily sell services, such as recording studios, composers, performing groups, etc. Obtaining federal registration takes approximately one year.

Business owners can reserve names in advance of opening their businesses by filing "Intent to Use" trademark and service mark forms. For further information on trademarks, contact the United States Patent and Trademark Office (listed in resource highlights at the end of this segment).

Sole proprietorships and general partnerships must file fictitious name certificates, which establish the names of businesses in particular counties and prevent other businesses in the area from using the same names. Corporations and

LLC's file start-up certificates, which contain their names, with their states, thus preventing others from using them.

Business names (domain names) can be registered with the Internet Network Information Center (InterNIC) *(http://rs.internic.net)* and the Domain Registry *(http://www.domainregistry.com)*. Registrations are renewed annually. If registrations lapse, the names become eligible for registration by others. Domain names do not have to be the same as business names, but many businesses try to have them either be the same, or find a convenient short-form domain name that is similar.

ESTABLISHING RIGHTS TO A BUSINESS NAME

According to law, rights to a name for a business or organization belong to the first user in a given territory. Proof that a business had first use of a name is established by using it—on checks, letterheads, business cards, invoices, recording covers, labels and advertising—and by showing invoices, receipts and purchase orders from other businesses that have purchased its products and services.

Registering names with state and federal agencies, or reserving them for future Web sites and applying for trademarks and service marks do not establish use. They do, however, place names in searchable databases where other businesses can locate them and where new businesses can be made aware that the names are in use.

By establishing use, businesses are entitled to full protection of the law for their names. A business will not lose it rights to their name even if another business that is bigger or more famous uses it later. The business will, however, have to sue the offending business to defend its rights to use the name.

If a business' name becomes well-known and another business starts using it, the newer business can be required to stop and choose a new

name—or it may be able to buy use of the name from the original business, in which case the original user will have to choose a new one.

Businesses must hire lawyers to protect their rights when they discover that another business is using their name or to defend them against claims of infringement by other businesses.

OWNERSHIP OF THE NAME

Many people assume that the person who thought up the business name will own it if he or she leaves the business or when the business dissolves. But who owns the name is governed by the statutes that regulate the formation of the business entity and the written documents that are legally required for its operation.

Sole proprietors, however, do own the names of their businesses.

The ownership of names in general partnerships is reflected in the partnership agreements. Since names are assets, agreements specify how they are to be valued when partnerships are dissolved or when partners leave.

LLCs and corporations own the names of the businesses. When members of an LLC or incorporators exit businesses, the names still belong to the businesses. When LLCs dissolve, however, theirs names can belong to individual members if that is so stated in their operating agreements.

Upon the dissolution of corporations, new business entities can claim their names.

BRANDING

The term "branding" means strongly imprinting on the public the name, purpose and philosophy of businesses and their products. This is accomplished by giving names distinctive lettering styles and by promoting symbols (logos) and tag lines that indicate the philosophies and purposes of the businesses.

Will Ackerman:
The Artist as Businessperson

WILL ACKERMAN is that rare artist who combines business and art as though they were simply different facets of the same gem.

During the mid-seventies, his mastery of the steel-string guitar and unusual compositions in open tunings had friends imploring him to make a record. He collected $5 from each of them, recorded *The Search for The Turtle's Naval* and gave copies to the contributors. One friend sent records to 10 radio stations, eight of which started playing the record. This set up demand in the record stores, which Ackerman satisfied by going store-to-store with armloads of records.

That modest beginning birthed Windham Hill Records. Will and his wife Anne Robinson nurtured their independent instrumental acoustic music label into a multimillion-dollar business. Among the artists signed were pianists George Winston, Phillip Aaberg, Tuck and Patti, Shadowfax and Liz Story and guitarists Alex de Grassi and Michael Hedges.

In 1982, Windham Hill Records made deal with A&M Records to distribute their label; and in 1985, Ackerman resigned as CEO and served as chairman of Windham Hill and Head of A&R, until the company was sold to BMG in May 1992.

Ackerman kept composing and recording his own music and released eleven albums on Windham Hill, including *Hearing Voices*, in the fall of 2001.

PHOTO: JOHN COOPER

* * * * * * * *

Rapaport: Do you make a separation about doing business and doing art?

Ackerman: I remember the very moment of liberation when I made that separation for myself. I was talking to Gil Batemen, a record distributor in Denver, Colorado, who liked *Turtle's Naval*, my first record. He asked, "So what's next on your label?" I said rather incredulously, "You mean you'll distribute anything I release?" And he said, "Yeah, we want to distribute your label." In inadvertently creating a record label, I had now only to sell an entity separate from me personally. That took the artist selling his own art out of the equation and made it into a less vulnerable experience for me.

Rapaport: Is there room for the new entrepreneur, a person with a good idea, to break into the business today?

Ackerman: To me business is what it was-having an inspiring idea then putting together a network of people that can facilitate it. Some of the structures are now more Kafkaesque, but the essence of what I enjoy doing is still there; the inspiration and the solution. As long as people have inspirations and inventive ways of implementing them there will be room in one venue or another to be heard.

When I went to Jordan recently to perform for the queen, I met pianist Zade Dirani and knew I wanted to work with him. I got involved producing a music video for EMI Arabia that we shot in the Siq, a remarkable canyon leading to Petra, that most beautiful and mystical Nabatean city that was carved into sandstone. Concept to conclusion took four days: I had the idea around noon of one day; wrote the story board by noon the next; and spent the next two days shooting and editing. It meant making the arrangements with the record company to mobilize a film crew and directing a shoot in the desert. But it also meant finding a piano to be delivered to the Siq and finding some Bedouin boys that could round up some camels in under an hour. As I said, that's business—finding the means to achieve an idea or dream and involving people that can help facilitate it.

Rapaport: How do you make core decisions about what you want to do?

Ackerman: I honestly don't make core decisions about what I'm doing for business reasons. I don't think of myself as a businessman first. I think of myself as an artist-for my own music and for someone else's. I start out with the germ of an idea, which is art, and invent methods of realizing that dream, which, to me, is business. It may become about the business but it's not where the process starts out. For me it's about passion. I have to be connected emotionally to an idea; money alone doesn't give me enough fuel. I quit Stanford in my senior year with just a few units to go for graduation simply because I discovered I loved the smell of cut lumber on building sites and went to work for a building contractor.

Rapaport: What happens when an idea fails? I'm thinking specifically of poet/songwriter Frank Tedesso with whom you created a beautiful record.

Ackerman: The only master I wanted to leave with when I left Polygram was Frank's. That was a very pure recording, the one I was proudest of. Even though it was a dismal financial failure, it was utterly true to what I wanted to do.

And yes, you do get to a point when you have tremendous success that you think you can fall off a log and be successful, no matter what choices you make. So there was a feeling of disappointment when some of them were not successful. I couldn't help thinking, "Gee, have I lost my touch? Maybe I'm not the genius I thought I was." There's always self-questioning.

Rapaport: What are your business ethics?

Ackerman: I don't separate business from personal ethics. It's terribly important to me to be trusted and to have the trust of those I work with.

One of the people that was important to me when I was growing up was a Chinese immigrant who changed his name to Frank Locke and opened up one of the earliest convenience stores in Palo Alto. I can remember being in college and going in there one day flat broke and saying to him, "Frank, I'm kind of short right now, can I pay you next Tuesday." His visage darkened and he started banging the cash register. I thought I had stepped over some line. He started yelling. I couldn't understand him. Then he began pulling twenties out of the cash register and handing them to me. He said, in his mixed English, "I give you money, you want," meaning, "Hey, I know you. I trust you. I see you are a little down on your luck right now." I ended up working for him, and then we became friends. He taught me how to use chopsticks at his house. His daughter Linda named her first child Will.

Later, when I quit college and opened up a construction business, I got stiffed by one of my customers, and was left owing the owner of a lumber store $1200 for materials. When I told the owner what happened, he ended up marking down the price of materials. He not only minimized my suffering by sharing in that loss, he made it clear that he did not want his profit if I didn't have mine. And he did not give me a time frame for repayment. "Look, I trust you. Don't worry." That meant a lot to me.

I bought that same ethic of trust with me to Windham Hill. In the early days of Windham Hill, there weren't any contracts. Everything was done on a handshake. Everyone was paid on time. And I think we were the only record company that voluntarily increased record royalties when we started making money.

ACKERMAN'S RECORDING STUDIO IN VERMONT.

What was important was to provide our artists with the freedom to manifest their creativity and relationships based on trust. It made me so happy that Liz [Story], Michael [Hedges], Alex [de Grassi] and other artists could make a living at what they loved to do best.

I also have great faith in people's ability to change for the better. There was a talented man I used to work with who was involved in our early productions and lost himself to drugs. But sometime in the late '80s, the phone rang and it was he. "Hey, I just wanted you to know that I've been clean for years. I've got a family now and my own excavation business in Hawaii. I wanted to call and tell you how proud I am of all that you've accomplished." He wasn't looking for anything. And then I said, "I didn't know where you'd gone, but we set up an escrow account for your producer's royalties." He said, So is there actually any money in there?" I said, "I don't know, I'll go look." When I told him it was around $170,000, he went crazy. "Wow, I can buy a house." That made me so happy.

I don't hold grudges. That's part of accepting that people can change. I can have an argument with someone and forget about it.

Some business owners thrive on antagonism. I don't. I'm a wonderful manager for people who are self-starting and can run with my ideas and what I'm trying to do. I'm not a great teacher because I can't break down what I do into coherent steps. But I can be a mentor and teach by example. On the other hand, I am very hard to work for if the person is in need of very specific direction. Anne [Robinson] always said I hired people and she hired job descriptions. I hired someone I found to be intelligent and creative and had faith they could somehow find their way. I was not always right by any means. Frankly, Anne's method became more successful as the company became larger and in need of corporate management.

I am a firm believer in being faithful to vendors and employees. RTI, our record presser, started with us and stayed with us until we went with CDs. Virginia Andrew, who was my right hand in Mill Valley, is still with me seventeen years later even though I now live in Vermont and she lives in Maine.

Rapaport: What conditions artists against doing business, or even adapting to such business realities as getting a lawyer to review a contract?

Ackerman: I must say, there are few places that I feel more impatient with human nature than the notion of the artist as child, the perception that artists are rebels and therefore have the license to mess up. I don't know who created the image that artists need to be irresponsible, incompetent, arrested adolescents. It gives artists a bad name. Where did the notion that the artist is a flake come from? It makes me nuts.

The very fact that the artist is someone who isn't going along with the herd means they have a greater responsibility than others to be disciplined. The freedom sought is at a price and that price is to create structures that still work in society, even if you have to do it with duct tape and baling wire.

Rapaport: To what to you attribute the success of Windham Hill?

Ackerman: I was lucky to be at the right place at the right time. My instincts were right on, but we also made a lot of decisions that transcended luck. Thinking back I conclude, however idealistic it may sound, that Windham Hill succeeded because it offered a real alternative at the time and did so with obvious pride and care. We created a loyalty that simply could not be bought.

Rapaport: What is different today?

Ackerman: I'm completely over trying to create enormous financial success. These days, it's about doing what I want to do, creating some peace in my life. That doesn't mean there are no new challenges. Nor am I any less ambitious for my new projects than for anything else I've ever done. But what's different is that I'm more present. Not so distracted. I'm fully there. I was usually scattered before, not able to find a peaceful center from which to gain real strength.

Rapaport: What are some of your new projects?

Ackerman: I'm working on an autobiography, which will include a lot regarding my history with Windham Hill. I always heard about the agony of writing and assumed it was largely self-serving melodrama on the part of writers. I no longer think so. It is as demanding of both sides of the brain as anything I've attempted creatively and leaves me exhausted in mind and body beyond anything I've ever experienced.

Rapaport: Sounds like life is great.

Ackerman: Life is great.

www.WilliamAckerman.com

The Small Business Administration

America's 25 million small businesses employ more than 50 percent of the private work force, generate more than half of the nation's gross domestic product (GDP) and are the principal source of new jobs in the U.S. economy.

The U.S. Small Business Administration (SBA), established in 1953 by Congress, provides financial, technical and management assistance to help Americans start, run and grow their businesses. It is the nation's largest financial backer of small businesses, with a portfolio of business loans, loan guarantees and disaster loans worth more than $45 billion. Last year, the SBA offered management and technical assistance to more than one million small business owners and provided 17,000 loans and financing to start-up businesses. It is actively seeking to increase small business ownership by women, minorities and veterans, as well as stimulate business start-ups and growth in inner cities, rural areas and low and moderate income areas.

The SBA also plays a major role in the government's disaster relief efforts by making low-interest recovery loans to both homeowners and businesses.

The SBA Web site provides a great deal of information for start-up businesses. They offer free interactive online classes such as, "The Business Plan," "Building Your Business," and "How to Raise Capital for a Small Business." They offer classes in Web commerce, including "Basics of the Internet," "Growing Your Business on the Web," "Basics of E-Commerce" and "Building Your Business with Web Marketing."

RESOURCES

Bread & Roses
233 Tamalpais Drive, Suite 100
Corte Madera, CA 94525-1415
(415) 945-7120
www.breadandroses.org

Service Core of Retired Executives (SCORE)
409 3rd Street SW
Washington, DC 20024
(800) 634-0245
www.score.org

U.S. Small Business Administration (SBA)
409 3rd Street SW
Washington, DC 20416
(202) 205-6770
www.sba.gov

United States Patent and Trademark Office
2021 Jefferson Davis Highway
Arlington, VA 22202
(800) 786-9199 or (703) 308-4357
www.uspto.gov

NOTES

Creative Rights

* * *

PROTECTING CREATIVE RIGHTS

CHALLENGES TO COPYRIGHTS

INTERVIEW HIGHLIGHT
Pete and Pat Luboff: Songwriters,
Publishers and Songwriting Educators

RESOURCE HIGHLIGHT
The Nashville Songwriter's
Association International

RESOURCES

Protecting Creative Rights

Original musical works can produce more income than performing and recording. They can be recorded by other artists and thus earn mechanical royalties on each recording sold and public performance royalties from their being played on radio and television. They can be used in films, television programs, video games and training videos. They can earn money by being issued as sheet music. Fortunes have been reaped from songs and compositions that became popular and were recorded time and again by numerous artists in many countries.

Original songs are important assets. To protect them, prevent unauthorized use and have them earn money, composers must first understand the basics of intellectual property rights (copyrights).

COPYRIGHTS: MUSICAL WORKS

The major goal of the U.S Copyright Act, which went into effect on January 1, 1978, is to help composers protect their creative rights with regard to the use of original works of authorship. The Act has been amended several times since then to accommodate new technologies and clarify or extend principles.

The Copyright Act grants composers five specific rights regarding their compositions (bundle of rights)—

- The right to reproduce the song and make copies. Composers can record their songs on cassettes, CDs, lyric sheets, etc. by using their own equipment or by hiring a manufacturer.

- The right to distribute copies. Once composers have reproduced copies, they have the right to distribute them to businesses and to the public. However, once one copy is placed for sale, it is considered published. Performing the work in public, such as at a club or concert, does not constitute publication.

- The right to perform the song in public.

- The right to make derivative works. This refers to using the original song to make new versions—arrangements, adaptations, abridgments and additions of new materials. Derivative works can be registered with the U.S. Copyright Office and get individual copyright protection.

- The right to display musical works, such as printed sheet music and lyric sheets.

These copyrights belong to composers and songwriters, whether or not they choose to register them with the U.S. Copyright Office. They belong to them from the date of creation, provided that they fix them in a tangible medium of expression—works which can be seen or auditorily perceived either directly or with the aid of a machine or device—such as sheet music, cassettes, CDs, film, videotape, computer, etc. The date of creation should be written or spoken on the medium.

Titles and ideas for songs and particular genres of music are not copyrightable. What is protected is the *expression* of composers' ideas.

Duration

Copyrights have a limited life.

Original compositions that were written before January 1, 1978 are protected for a total of 75 years from the end of the year the copyright was first secured: 28 years from the date on which copyright was secured; and an additional 47 years if the copyright was renewed in the 28th year. Copyright begins either on the date a work was published and contained the proper notice of copyright or on the date of registration, if the work was registered in unpublished form.

A 1992 amendment to the Copyright Act provided for automatic renewals of copyright for works secured between January 1, 1964 and December 31, 1977.

An amendment to the Copyright Act passed on October 27, 1998, extended the duration of copyrights that were still in effect on that date for an additional 20 years of protection, thus providing a renewal term of 67 years and a total term of protection of 95 years.

Original compositions that were created or published after January 1, 1978 automatically belong to creators for their lifetimes plus 70 years. If compositions are created by two or more persons, the rights last for 70 years after the last surviving author's death.

Original compositions created before January 1, 1978, but not published or registered by that date are given the same duration as works created on or after January 1, 1978.

For works made for hire and for anonymous and pseudonymous works (unless the author's identity is revealed in Copyright Office records), the duration of copyright is 95 years from publication or 120 years from creation, whichever is shorter.

Once the copyright term expires, compositions are in the public domain.

Transfer

Composers can transfer one or more of their copyrights to other persons or other businesses, so long as there is a written contract that states the nature of the transfer and is signed by the owner(s) of the copyrights (or someone who is the owner's authorized agent). The transfer gives new owners the rights to license the use of the copyrights to others.

Transfers are not the same as licenses. Copyright owners can authorize the use of one or more of their copyrights through licenses (the subject of Segment 4, Music Licensing) and can sue anyone that uses their creations to make money without a license to do so.

The Copyright Office does not furnish contract forms for transfers. These contracts are generally drawn up by attorneys.

Transfers should be recorded with the U.S. Copyright Office to establish the new record of ownership and to make it easy for others to research ownership.

A copyright may also be bequeathed by will or pass as personal property by the applicable laws of intestate succession.

Copyright Registration: Musical Works

Creative rights belong to composers as soon as they create their works and fix them in tangible mediums of expression. But, the only way to establish proof of authorship, the identities of songs (what they sound like) and positive proof of dates of creation is to register them with the U.S. Copyright Office. Registration establishes a public

SONGWRITERS NEED TO TRAIN THEIR EARS TO CRITICALLY LISTEN TO THEIR OWN MUSIC AND THAT OF OTHERS. IT IS IMPORTANT FOR THEM TO KNOW WHY SONGS THAT ARE WRITTEN FOR TOP 40 RADIO, MUSICAL THEATER AND FILM HAVE DIFFERENT REQUIREMENTS. IT IS IMPORTANT FOR THEM TO KNOW THE MANY TECHNIQUES TO ACHIEVE DYNAMICS AND IMPACT IN A SONG AND WHY AN ARTISTIC CHOICE THAT WOULD WORK IN ONE SITUATION MAY NOT IN ANOTHER. KNOWLEDGE SERVES THEIR INSPIRATION, THEIR CRAFT AND THEIR BUSINESS.

— JOHN BRAHENY, AUTHOR
The Craft and Business of Songwriting

record of these claims and helps potential users get information about copyright owners. Copyright registration is mandatory for works of U.S. origin, before anyone can file a complaint in court that his or her rights have been violated. Registration will establish prima facie evidence of the validity of the copyright, if made within 5 years of publication. In effect, the U.S. Copyright Office is an objective third party about claims that are made in copyright registrations.

Some composers try to establish proof and time of authorship by sending copies of their songs to themselves by registered mail and not opening the letters. They believe the postmark on the letter is evidence the song was original as of that date. Variations of this include the stamping of lead sheets by notaries public or placing songs

in a safety deposit box. Most attorneys consider these methods (poor man's copyright or common-law copyright) very risky. Although they satisfy the requirement of fixing the song in a tangible medium, proof of authorship and date of creation and identity can only be legally established with copyright registration.

Composers should place proper copyright notice on anything they reproduce, such as lyric sheets, demos and recordings. Using the notice serves to inform people that the work is original to the composer and in what year. It helps people that want to license these rights locate the owners.

The notice must include the symbol ©, or the word "Copyright," or the abbreviation "Copr.," the year of first publication and the name of the owner of the copyright; for example, "© 2002 J. Smith." If the copyright owner is a publishing company, the notice could read, "Copyright 2002 J. Smith Publishing Company."

Composers do not have to first register their songs with the Copyright Office to put the copyright notice on their works. Amendments to the Copyright Act, passed in 1989, specify that artists do not automatically forfeit their rights and lose royalties owed to them if they omit the notice. However, it is very important to register compositions to establish proof or authorship, identities of songs and positive proof of dates of creation before licensing compositions or pursuing infringement suits.

Form PA, Application for Copyright Registration for a Musical Recording, is used to register published and unpublished musical works, including those that have lyrics; dramatic works that have accompanying music; pantomimes and choreographic works; and other audiovisual works, such as movies and television shows. (Other forms are used for copyrighting works of visual art, sculptures, books, etc.)

Composers can use Form PA to register copyrights of one song or a collection of songs. The collections are given titles and lists of songs must be provided. The copyright claimant for all the songs in the collection must be the same. As of 1996, composers that cowrite songs may only copyright a collection in which all songs are written with the same cowriter. (Previously, composers could protect collections with several of their cowriters as long they were writers on each of the songs.)

Composers can register songs from a collection separately as the need arises without destroying the integrity of the copyrighted collection. The remaining songs are still protected.

The current cost for each song or collection of songs that is registered on Form PA is $30. Songs are protected as soon as the Copyright Office receives them, although it can take as long as eight months for the sender to receive copyright certificates. Form PA should be sent certified mail so that there is an official record of the date it was sent.

The registration form must be accompanied by reproductions of the work in a "tangible medium of expression." This means they must be reproduced on paper (musical notation and lyrics together) or as a phonorecord (cassette tape, album, CD, videocassette, DVD etc.).

Joint Works

Songs that are composed by more than one person are called joint works. All authors co-own the entire work. The copyright form asks that all the authors that created the joint work be identified. Information on how earnings are to be divided is not requested.

Joint owners can divide their song ownership in whatever proportion they want. In the absence of an agreement, they share income equally, even if it is clear that their contributions are not equal. Thus, two songwriters own the song fifty-fifty; three songwriters, one-third each; etc. (See article "Collaborator/Songwriter Agreements" in Segment 3, Publishing.) One common method to divide ownership is that the lyrics are worth 50% and the music 50%. For example, if two people

write the music and one person writes the lyrics, they can agree to divide the ownership 25% each for the two music writers and the lyricist retains the remaining 50%. However, if there is no written agreement, each owns 33.3% of the song.

Derivative Works

Derivative works are new versions of songs that have already been registered, works that have been published and works in the public domain. This includes musical arrangements, adaptations, translations, dramatizations, abridgements and compilations. Here are some examples of derivative works—

- The copyright holder adds new instrumentation to the tracks of previously released sound recordings

- Songs (belonging to the composer) that have new musical arrangements

- Manipulation of samples

- Songs in English translated into foreign languages

- Music and lyrics, with lyrics based on words from a work in the public domain or when permission has been granted by the copyright holder

- Musical arrangement based on a work in the public domain

Only owners of copyrights have the right to create, or to give permission for someone else to create, derivative versions of their work.

Works in the Public Domain

When the copyright term has expired, the material is in the public domain. It no longer belongs to copyright owners. Public domain music is not protected by copyright and anyone is free to use it in any way they choose without permission.

However, a song that is in the public domain

✍ Application Form PA ✍

Detach and read these instructions before completing this form.
Make sure all applicable spaces have been filled in before you return this form.

When to Use This Form: Use Form PA for registration of published or unpublished works of the performing arts. This class includes works prepared for the purpose of being "performed" directly before an audience or indirectly "by means of any device or process." Works of the performing arts include: (1) musical works, including any accompanying words; (2) dramatic works, including any accompanying music; (3) pantomimes and choreographic works; and (4) motion pictures and other audiovisual works.

Deposit to Accompany Application: An application for copyright registration must be accompanied by a deposit consisting of copies or phonorecords representing the entire work for which registration is made. The following are the general deposit requirements as set forth in the statute:

Unpublished Work: Deposit one complete copy (or phonorecord).

Published Work: Deposit two complete copies (or one phonorecord) of the best edition.

Work First Published Outside the United States: Deposit one complete copy (or phonorecord) of the first foreign edition.

Contribution to a Collective Work: Deposit one complete copy (or phonorecord) of the best edition of the collective work.

Motion Pictures: Deposit *both* of the following: (1) a separate written description of the contents of the motion picture; and (2) for a published work, one complete copy of the best edition of the motion picture; or, for an unpublished work, one complete copy of the motion picture or identifying material. Identifying material may be either an audiorecording of the entire soundtrack or one frame enlargement or similar visual print from each 10-minute segment.

The Copyright Notice: Before March 1, 1989, the use of copyright notice was mandatory on all published works, and any work first published before that date should have carried a notice. For works first published on and after March 1, 1989, use of the copyright notice is optional. For more information about copyright notice, see Circular 3, "Copyright Notice."

For Further Information: To speak to an information specialist, call (202) 707-3000 (TTY: (202) 707-6737). Recorded information is available 24 hours a day. Order forms and other publications from the address in space 9 or call the Forms and Publications Hotline at (202) 707-9100. Most circulars (but not forms) are available via fax. Call (202) 707-2600 from a touchtone phone. Access and download circulars, forms, and other information from the Copyright Office Website at www.loc.gov/copyright.

Please type or print using black ink. The form is used to produce the certificate.

1 SPACE 1: Title

Title of This Work: Every work submitted for copyright registration must be given a title to identify that particular work. If the copies or phonorecords of the work bear a title (or an identifying phrase that could serve as a title), transcribe that wording *completely* and *exactly* on the application. Indexing of the registration and future identification of the work will depend on the information you give here. If the work you are registering is an entire "collective work" (such as a collection of plays or songs), give the overall title of the collection. If you are registering one or more individual contributions to a collective work, give the title of each contribution, followed by the title of the collection. For an unpublished collection, you may give the titles of the individual works after the collection title.

Previous or Alternative Titles: Complete this space if there are any additional titles for the work under which someone searching for the registration might be likely to look, or under which a document pertaining to the work might be recorded.

Nature of This Work: Briefly describe the general nature or character of the work being registered for copyright. Examples: "Music"; "Song Lyrics"; "Words and Music"; "Drama"; "Musical Play"; "Choreography"; "Pantomime"; "Motion Picture"; "Audiovisual Work."

2 SPACE 2: Author(s)

General Instructions: After reading these instructions, decide who are the "authors" of this work for copyright purposes. Then, unless the work is a "collective work," give the requested information about every "author" who contributed any appreciable amount of copyrightable matter to this version of the work. If you need further space, request additional Continuation Sheets. In the case of a collective work such as a songbook or a collection of plays, give information about the author of the collective work as a whole.

Name of Author: The fullest form of the author's name should be given. Unless the work was "made for hire," the individual who actually created the work is its "author." In the case of a work made for hire, the statute provides that "the employer or other person for whom the work was prepared is considered the author."

What is a "Work Made for Hire"? A "work made for hire" is defined as: (1) "a work prepared by an employee within the scope of his or her employment"; or (2) "a work specially ordered or commissioned for use as a contribution to a collective work, as a part of a motion picture or other audiovisual work, as a translation, as a supplementary work, as a compilation, as an instructional text, as a test, as answer material for a test, or as an atlas, if the parties expressly agree in a written instrument signed by them that the work shall be considered a work made for hire." If you have checked "Yes" to indicate that the work was "made for hire," you must give the full legal name of the employer (or other person for whom the work was prepared). You may also include the name of the employee along with the name of the employer (for example: "Elster Music Co., employer for hire of John Ferguson").

"Anonymous" or "Pseudonymous" Work: An author's contribution to a work is "anonymous" if that author is not identified on the copies or phonorecords of the work. An author's contribution to a work is "pseudonymous" if that author is identified on the copies or phonorecords under a fictitious name. If the work is "anonymous" you may: (1) leave the line blank; or (2) state "anonymous" on the line; or (3) reveal the author's identity. If the work is "pseudonymous" you may: (1) leave the line blank; or (2) give the pseudonym and identify it as such (example: "Huntley Haverstock, pseudonym"); or (3) reveal the author's name, making clear which is the real name and which is the pseudonym (for example: "Judith Barton, whose pseudonym is Madeline Elster"). However, the citizenship or domicile of the author **must** be given in all cases.

Dates of Birth and Death: If the author is dead, the statute requires that the year of death be included in the application unless the work is anonymous or pseudonymous. The author's birth date is optional, but is useful as a form of identification. Leave this space blank if the author's contribution was a "work made for hire."

Author's Nationality or Domicile: Give the country of which the author is a citizen, or the country in which the author is domiciled. Nationality or domicile **must** be given in all cases.

Nature of Authorship: Give a brief general statement of the nature of this particular author's contribution to the work. Examples: "Words"; "Coauthor of Music"; "Words and Music"; "Arrangement"; "Coauthor of Book and Lyrics"; "Dramatization"; "Screen Play"; "Compilation and English Translation"; "Editorial Revisions."

3 SPACE 3: Creation and Publication

General Instructions: Do not confuse "creation" with "publication." Every application for copyright registration must state "the year in which creation of the work was completed." Give the date and nation of first publication only if the work has been published.

Creation: Under the statute, a work is "created" when it is fixed in a copy or phonorecord for the first time. Where a work has been prepared over a period of time, the part of the work existing in fixed form on a particular date constitutes the created work on that date. The date you give here should be the year in which the author completed the particular version for which registration is now being sought, even if other versions exist or if further changes or additions are planned.

Publication: The statute defines "publication" as "the distribution of copies or phonorecords of a work to the public by sale or other transfer of ownership, or by rental, lease, or lending"; a work is also "published" if there has been an "offering to distribute copies or phonorecords to a group of persons for purposes of further distribution, public performance, or public display." Give the full date (month, day, year) when, and the country where, publication first occurred. If first publication took place simultaneously in the United States and other countries, it is sufficient to state "U.S.A."

4 SPACE 4: Claimant(s)

Name(s) and Address(es) of Copyright Claimant(s): Give the name(s) and address(es) of the copyright claimant(s) in this work even if the claimant is the same as the author. Copyright in a work belongs initially to the author of the work (including, in the case of a work made for hire, the employer or other person for whom the work was prepared). The copyright claimant is either the author of the work or a person or organization to whom the copyright initially belonging to the author has been transferred.

Transfer: The statute provides that, if the copyright claimant is not the author, the application for registration must contain "a brief statement of how the claimant obtained ownership of the copyright." If any copyright claimant named in space 4 is not an author named in space 2, give a brief statement explaining how the claimant(s) obtained ownership of the copyright. Examples: "By written contract"; "Transfer of all rights by author"; "Assignment"; "By will." Do not attach transfer documents or other attachments or riders.

5 SPACE 5: Previous Registration

General Instructions: The questions in space 5 are intended to show whether an earlier registration has been made for this work and, if so, whether there is any basis for a new registration. As a general rule, only one basic copyright registration can be made for the same version of a particular work.

Same Version: If this version is substantially the same as the work covered by a previous registration, a second registration is not generally possible unless: (1) the work has been registered in unpublished form and a second registration is now being sought to cover this first published edition; or (2) someone other than the author is identified as copyright claimant in the earlier registration, and the author is now seeking registration in his or her own name. If either of these two exceptions applies, check the appropriate box and give the earlier registration number and date. Otherwise, do not submit Form PA; instead, write the Copyright Office for informa-

tion about supplementary registration or recordation of transfers of copyright ownership.

Changed Version: If the work has been changed and you are now seeking registration to cover the additions or revisions, check the last box in space 5, give the earlier registration number and date, and complete both parts of space 6 in accordance with the instructions below.

Previous Registration Number and Date: If more than one previous registration has been made for the work, give the number and date of the latest registration.

6 SPACE 6: Derivative Work or Compilation

General Instructions: Complete space 6 if this work is a "changed version," "compilation," or "derivative work," and if it incorporates one or more earlier works that have already been published or registered for copyright or that have fallen into the public domain. A "compilation" is defined as "a work formed by the collection and assembling of preexisting materials or of data that are selected, coordinated, or arranged in such a way that the resulting work as a whole constitutes an original work of authorship." A "derivative work" is "a work based on one or more preexisting works." Examples of derivative works include musical arrangements, dramatizations, translations, abridgments, condensations, motion picture versions, or "any other form in which a work may be recast, transformed, or adapted." Derivative works also include works "consisting of editorial revisions, annotations, or other modifications" if these changes, as a whole, represent an original work of authorship.

Preexisting Material (space 6a): Complete this space **and** space 6b for derivative works. In this space identify the preexisting work that has been recast, transformed, or adapted. For example, the preexisting material might be: "French version of Hugo's 'Le Roi s'amuse'." Do not complete this space for compilations.

Material Added to This Work (space 6b): Give a brief, general statement of the **additional** new material covered by the copyright claim for which registration is sought. In the case of a derivative work, identify this new material. Examples: "Arrangement for piano and orchestra"; "Dramatization for television"; "New film version"; "Revisions throughout; Act III completely new." If the work is a compilation, give a brief, general statement describing both the material that has been compiled **and** the compilation itself. Example: "Compilation of 19th Century Military Songs."

7,8,9 SPACE 7, 8, 9: Fee, Correspondence, Certification, Return Address

Deposit Account: If you maintain a Deposit Account in the Copyright Office, identify it in space 7a. Otherwise, leave the space blank and send the fee of $30 (effective through June 30, 2002) with your application and deposit.

Correspondence (space 7b): This space should contain the name, address, area code, telephone number, fax number, and email address (if available) of the person to be consulted if correspondence about this application becomes necessary.

Certification (space 8): The application cannot be accepted unless it bears the date and the **handwritten signature** of the author or other copyright claimant, or of the owner of exclusive right(s), or of the duly authorized agent of the author, claimant, or owner of exclusive right(s).

Address for Return of Certificate (space 9): The address box must be completed legibly since the certificate will be returned in a window envelope.

MORE INFORMATION

How to Register a Recorded Work: If the musical or dramatic work that you are registering has been recorded (as a tape, disk, or cassette), you may choose either copyright application Form PA (Performing Arts) or Form SR (Sound Recordings), depending on the purpose of the registration.

Form PA should be used to register the underlying musical composition or dramatic work. Form SR has been developed specifically to register a "sound recording" as defined by the Copyright Act—a work resulting from the "fixation of a series of sounds," separate and distinct from the underlying musical or dramatic work. Form SR should be used when the copyright claim is limited to the sound recording itself. (In one instance, Form SR may also be used to file for a copyright registration for both kinds of works—see (4) below.) Therefore:

(1) **File Form PA** if you are seeking to register the musical or dramatic work, not the "sound recording," even though what you deposit for copyright purposes may be in the form of a phonorecord.

(2) **File Form PA** if you are seeking to register the audio portion of an audiovisual work, such as a motion picture soundtrack; these are considered integral parts of the audiovisual work.

(3) **File Form SR** if you are seeking to register the "sound recording" itself, that is, the work that results from the fixation of a series of musical, spoken, or other sounds, but not the underlying musical or dramatic work.

(4) **File Form SR** if you are the copyright claimant for both the underlying musical or dramatic work and the sound recording, *and* you prefer to register both on the same form.

(5) **File both forms PA and SR** if the copyright claimant for the underlying work and sound recording differ, or you prefer to have separate registration for them.

"Copies" and "Phonorecords": To register for copyright, you are required to deposit "copies" or "phonorecords." These are defined as follows:

Musical compositions may be embodied (fixed) in "copies," objects from which a work can be read or visually perceived, directly or with the aid of a machine or device, such as manuscripts, books, sheet music, film, and videotape. They may also be fixed in "phonorecords," objects embodying fixations of sounds, such as tapes and phonograph disks, commonly known as phonograph records. For example, a song (the work to be registered) can be reproduced in sheet music ("copies") or phonograph records ("phonorecords"), or both.

FORM PA
For a Work of the Performing Arts
UNITED STATES COPYRIGHT OFFICE

REGISTRATION NUMBER

_____

PA _____ PAU

EFFECTIVE DATE OF REGISTRATION

_____

Month _____ Day _____ Year

DO NOT WRITE ABOVE THIS LINE. IF YOU NEED MORE SPACE, USE A SEPARATE CONTINUATION SHEET.

1

TITLE OF THIS WORK▼

PREVIOUS OR ALTERNATIVE TITLES▼

NATURE OF THIS WORK▼ See instructions

2

a

NAME OF AUTHOR▼

DATES OF BIRTH AND DEATH
Year Born ▼   Year Died ▼

Was this contribution to the work a "work made for hire"?
☐ Yes
☐ No

AUTHOR'S NATIONALITY OR DOMICILE
Name of Country
OR { Citizen of ▶ _____
Domiciled in▶ _____

WAS THIS AUTHOR'S CONTRIBUTION TO THE WORK
Anonymous?   ☐ Yes ☐ No
Pseudonymous?   ☐ Yes ☐ No
If the answer to either of these questions is "Yes," see detailed instructions.

NATURE OF AUTHORSHIP Briefly describe nature of material created by this author in which copyright is claimed. ▼

NOTE

Under the law, the "author" of a "work made for hire" is generally the employer, not the employee (see instructions). For any part of this work that was "made for hire" check "Yes" in the space provided, give the employer (or other person for whom the work was prepared) as "Author" of that part, and leave the space for dates of birth and death blank.

b

NAME OF AUTHOR▼

DATES OF BIRTH AND DEATH
Year Born ▼   Year Died ▼

Was this contribution to the work a "work made for hire"?
☐ Yes
☐ No

AUTHOR'S NATIONALITY OR DOMICILE
Name of Country
OR { Citizen of ▶ _____
Domiciled in▶ _____

WAS THIS AUTHOR'S CONTRIBUTION TO THE WORK
Anonymous?   ☐ Yes ☐ No
Pseudonymous?   ☐ Yes ☐ No
If the answer to either of these questions is "Yes," see detailed instructions.

NATURE OF AUTHORSHIP Briefly describe nature of material created by this author in which copyright is claimed. ▼

c

NAME OF AUTHOR▼

DATES OF BIRTH AND DEATH
Year Born ▼   Year Died ▼

Was this contribution to the work a "work made for hire"?
☐ Yes
☐ No

AUTHOR'S NATIONALITY OR DOMICILE
Name of Country
OR { Citizen of ▶ _____
Domiciled in▶ _____

WAS THIS AUTHOR'S CONTRIBUTION TO THE WORK
Anonymous?   ☐ Yes ☐ No
Pseudonymous?   ☐ Yes ☐ No
If the answer to either of these questions is "Yes," see detailed instructions.

NATURE OF AUTHORSHIP Briefly describe nature of material created by this author in which copyright is claimed. ▼

3

a YEAR IN WHICH CREATION OF THIS WORK WAS COMPLETED This information must be given ◀Year in all cases.

b DATE AND NATION OF FIRST PUBLICATION OF THIS PARTICULAR WORK
Complete this information ONLY if this work has been published.
Month▶ _____ Day▶ _____ Year▶ _____ ◀ Nation

4

COPYRIGHT CLAIMANT(S)Name and address must be given even if the claimant is the same as the author given in space 2. ▼

TRANSFERIf the claimant(s) named here in space 4 is (are) different from the author(s) named in space 2, give a brief statement of how the claimant(s) obtained ownership of the copyright. ▼

See instructions before completing this space.

DO NOT WRITE HERE
OFFICE USE ONLY

APPLICATION RECEIVED

ONE DEPOSIT RECEIVED

TWO DEPOSITS RECEIVED

FUNDS RECEIVED

MORE ON BACK ▶ • Complete all applicable spaces (numbers 5-9) on the reverse side of this page.
• See detailed instructions.   • Sign the form at line 8.

DO NOT WRITE HERE

Page 1 of _____ pages

FORM PA

FOR COPYRIGHT OFFICE USE ONLY

DO NOT WRITE ABOVE THIS LINE. IF YOU NEED MORE SPACE, USE A SEPARATE CONTINUATION SHEET.

PREVIOUS REGISTRATION Has registration for this work, or for an earlier version of this work, already been made in the Copyright Office?

□ Yes □ No If your answer is "Yes," why is another registration being sought? (Check appropriate box.) ▼ If your answer is "no," go to space 7.

a. □ This is the first published edition of a work previously registered in unpublished form.

b. □ This is the first application submitted by this author as copyright claimant.

c. □ This is a changed version of the work, as shown by space 6 on this application.

If your answer is "Yes," give: **Previous Registration Number▼**   **Year of Registration▼**

5

DERIVATIVE WORK OR COMPILATION Complete both space 6a and 6b for a derivative work; complete only 6b for a compilation.
Preexisting Material Identify any preexisting work or works that this work is based on or incorporates. ▼

Material Added to This Work Give a brief, general statement of the material that has been added to this work and in which copyright is claimed. ▼

a

6

b

See instructions before completing this space.

DEPOSIT ACCOUNT If the registration fee is to be charged to a Deposit Account established in the Copyright Office, give name and number of Account.
Name▼   **Account Number▼**

a

7

CORRESPONDENCE Give name and address to which correspondence about this application should be sent.   Name/Address/Apt/City/State/ZIP ▼

b

Area code and daytime telephone number ▶ (   )   Fax number ▶ (   )

Email ▶

CERTIFICATION* I, the undersigned, hereby certify that I am the

Check only one ▶ {
□ author
□ other copyright claimant
□ owner of exclusive right(s)
□ authorized agent of _____
Name of author or other copyright claimant, or owner of exclusive right(s) ▲
}

8

of the work identified in this application and that the statements made by me in this application are correct to the best of my knowledge.

Typed or printed name and date▼ If this application gives a date of publication in space 3, do not sign and submit it before that date.

_____   ▶ Date _____

Handwritten signature (X) ▼

X _____

Certificate will be mailed in window envelope to this address:

Name ▼

Number/Street/Apt ▼

City/State/ZIP ▼

9

YOU MUST:
• Complete all necessary spaces
• Sign your application in space 8
SEND ALL 3 ELEMENTS IN THE SAME PACKAGE:
1. Application form
2. Nonrefundable filing fee in check or money order payable to *Register of Copyrights*
3. Deposit material
MAIL TO:
Library of Congress
Copyright Office
101 Independence Avenue, S.E.
Washington, D.C. 20559-6000

As of July 1, 1999, the filing fee for Form PA is $30.

How much music from someone else's song or music samples can be used without violating copyrights? Virtually none.

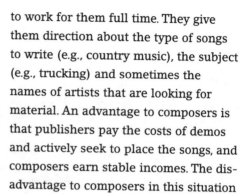

in the United States may still be protected by international copyright. This means that an artist who wants to publish a public domain song worldwide must make sure that it is not protected by copyright in another country.

When composers add new material to public domain songs, such as new arrangements, lyrics or melodies, they are creating a derivative work. The new material that has been added can be copyrighted (but not the material that is in the public domain). Registration of copyright for new material enables composers to receive income from recording and performance royalties.

Artists that want to record only original melodies or lyrics that are in the public domain, and not add copyrighted material, should request a clearance check from the U.S. Copyright Office. There is an hourly fee. They have to supply the original title and either a recording or lead sheet of the version they want to use. Circular 22, "How to Investigate the Copyright Status of a Work" provides more complete information.

The Copyright Office will check versions sent against any other derivative copyrights have been issued for titles in the public domain.

Works Made for Hire

Composers can be hired to write songs, either as full or part-time employees of companies or as independent contractors. Under the Copyright Act, these songs are considered "specially ordered or commissioned works."

Some publishing companies hire songwriters

to work for them full time. They give them direction about the type of songs to write (e.g., country music), the subject (e.g., trucking) and sometimes the names of artists that are looking for material. An advantage to composers is that publishers pay the costs of demos and actively seek to place the songs, and composers earn stable incomes. The disadvantage to composers in this situation is that they are not the copyright owners of their work. In a work-for-hire agreement, the employers that hire songwriters become the authors of the songs and own the copyrights.

Producers of films and television shows and video games also hire composers under work-for-hire agreements to score projects.

When employers hire composers as independent contractors to write one or several songs, there must be written agreements between them that state that those songs are "works made for hire."

Fair Use

Although businesses that want to use songwriters' works must seek permission from the copyright holders, there are many circumstances where songs can be legally performed without violating copyrights. The concept, termed "fair use," dates back to the 19th century. It originated for purposes of allowing the use of copyrighted works without permission for criticism, comment, news reporting, teaching, scholarship and research. The specific fair uses that the U.S. Copyright Act provides are—

- Performance or display of a song by a non-profit educational institution or a religious institution. But *not* the making of a tape of several songs from various albums to be sold as "educational material," without permission of copyright holders.

- Performance of a song without "any direct or indirect purpose of commercial advantage" if there is no direct or indirect admission charge and proceeds are used for educational, religious or charitable purposes.

Basically the rule of thumb for fair use is a one-time use for charitable, educational or religious purposes without commercial exploitation.

How much music from someone else's song or music samples can be used without violating copyrights? Virtually none. There is no specific number of words, lines, music samples or musical notes that may safely be taken without permission.

Only copyright owners can grant permission to someone else to use some or all of a portion of their works. Acknowledging the source of the copyrighted material is not a substitute. This includes reprinting portions of lyrics in books or magazines.

In the lawsuits against Napster and My.MP3.com, lawyers for the defendants claimed that users that accessed databases, which contained music they already owned and file-sharing (downloading other composers' works from the Internet) constituted fair use. The courts disagreed. (See article "Challenges to Copyrights" in this segment.)

COPYRIGHTS: SOUND RECORDINGS

Legally speaking, recordings are entities in themselves, apart from the songs contained on them, and copyrights for the recordings must be registered. Sound recordings are works that are comprised of a series of recorded sounds that are physically embodied on phonorecords, such as cassettes, vinyl records, DVDs and CDs.

The U.S. Copyright Act grants recording companies similar rights to their creations as it does to composers. The companies are officially referred to as "authors" and their works as "sound recordings." According to the law, when record companies issue new releases, they involve two distinct "works:" the "musical works" that were recorded (e.g. original songs), and the "sound

THE DIFFERENCE BETWEEN COPYRIGHTS, PATENTS AND TRADEMARKS

Artistic works, such as songs, paintings, novels and software are protected by copyright. The symbol © is used to indicate the copyright holders. The symbol ℗ is used to indicate the copyright holder of a sound recording.

Inventions, such as computers, machines and medicines are protected by patents. The symbol ® is used to indicate that an invention has been patented.

Trademarks are words or symbols used in association with products or services to distinguish those goods and services in the marketplace and establish their brands. Trademarks include special lettering, labels and logos. Although no one can copyright the title of a song or software or the name for a business, they can trademark a name for a product or service, as well as the "look" of that name or title. The symbol ™ is used to indicate that name or the look of a word or symbol is trademarked.

Patents and trademarks are administered by The United States Patent and Trademark Office.

recording." The material objects record companies sell are the physical reproductions of the musical work and the sound recording (CDs, DVDs, cassettes, vinyl records, etc.).

The Act grants recording companies the following rights—

- The right to duplicate the actual sounds fixed in the sound recordings.

- To duplicate and distribute sound

recordings that contain new arrangements or versions of the copyrighted work.

- To sell (distribute) sound recordings to the public.

One reason to distinguish between musical works and sound recordings is to provide owners of sound recordings with the ability to sue people that illegally duplicate and sell their recordings.

Another reason is that the income that can be earned by the owners of musical works (composers and publishers) is different from the income that can be earned from the owners of sound recordings (record companies).

Record companies make money by selling sound recordings. They pay composers and publishers royalties that are based on the number of recordings delivered and paid for; and they pay different types of royalties that are also based on the number of recordings delivered and paid for.

In 1995, Congress passed the Digital Performance Right in Sound Recordings Act (DPRSA), which amends the U.S. Copyright Act. The DPRSA provides the owners of copyrights in sound recordings (e.g., recording labels) and the artists that perform on them the right to be paid public performance royalties for digital audio transmissions. Further information is found in Segment 4, Music Licensing.

Laws now provide the owners of copyrights in sound recordings (recording labels) the right to be paid public performance royalties in limited circumstances (discussed in Segment 4, Music Licensing).

Record companies secure their rights by printing the correct copyright notice on the labels they affix to their recordings and packaging. These notices include the symbol π, the year of first publication of the sound recording and the name of the owner of the copyright.

Copyright Registration

Record companies protect their rights by registering their recordings with the Register of Copyrights in Washington, D.C. They use form SR, Application for Copyright Registration for a Sound Recording. Circulars 56 and 56a provide instructions and additional information. The forms and circulars are free.

Copyrights are secured in the name of the "copyright claimants," or "authors," generally, the recording company.

Form SR can also be used to copyright songs, if the names of the copyright claimants for all the songs on the recording are the same. In this case, a correct notice would be "© ℗ 1979 J. Smith Music." Usually, the copyright claimants for recordings are record companies while the copyright claimants for the songs are composers and publishing companies.

Recording companies must send two copies of their recordings, form SR and $30 (current price) to the Register of Copyrights, within three months of release.

COPYRIGHTS FOR U.S. COMPOSERS IN FOREIGN COUNTRIES

Copyright protection for U.S. composers can be granted under the laws of individual countries. It

ⓒ Application Form SR ⓒ

Detach and read these instructions before completing this form.
Make sure all applicable spaces have been filled in before you return this form.

BASIC INFORMATION

When to Use This Form: Use Form SR for registration of published or unpublished sound recordings. It should be used when the copyright claim is limited to the sound recording itself, and it may also be used where the same copyright claimant is seeking simultaneous registration of the underlying musical, dramatic, or literary work embodied in the phonorecord.

With one exception, "sound recordings" are works that result from the fixation of a series of musical, spoken, or other sounds. The exception is for the audio portions of audiovisual works, such as a motion picture soundtrack or an audio cassette accompanying a filmstrip. These are considered a part of the audiovisual work as a whole.

Deposit to Accompany Application An application for copyright registration must be accompanied by a deposit consisting of phonorecords representing the entire work for which registration is to be made.

Unpublished Work: Deposit one complete phonorecord.

Published Work: Deposit two complete phonorecords of the best edition, together with "any printed or other visually perceptible material" published with the phonorecords.

Work First Published Outside the United States: Deposit one complete phonorecord of the first foreign edition.

Contribution to a Collective Work: Deposit one complete phonorecord of the best edition of the collective work.

The Copyright Notice: Before March 1, 1989, the use of copyright notice was mandatory on all published works, and any work first published before that date should have carried a notice. For works first published on and after March 1, 1989, use of the copyright notice is optional. For more information about copyright notice, see Circular 3, "Copyright Notices."

For Further Information: To speak to an information specialist, call (202) 707-3000 (TTY: (202) 707-6737). Recorded information is available 24 hours a day. Order forms and other publications from Library of Congress, Copyright Office, 101 Independence Avenue, S.E., Washington, D.C. 20559-6000 or call the Forms and Publications Hotline at (202) 707-9100. Most circulars (but not forms) are available via fax. Call (202) 707-2600 from a touchtone phone. Access and download circulars, forms, and other information from the Copyright Office Website at www.loc.gov/copyright.

LINE-BY-LINE INSTRUCTIONS

Please type or print neatly using black ink. The form is used to produce the certificate.

1 SPACE 1: Title

Title of This Work: Every work submitted for copyright registration must be given a title to identify that particular work. If the phonorecords or any accompanying printed material bears a title (or an identifying phrase that could serve as a title), transcribe that wording completely and exactly on the application. Indexing of the registration and future identification of the work may depend on the information you give here.

Previous, Alternative, or Contents Titles: Complete this space if there are any previous or alternative titles for the work under which someone searching for the registration might be likely to look, or under which a document pertaining to the work might be recorded. You may also give the individual contents titles, if any, in this space or you may use a Continuation Sheet. Circle the term that describes the titles given.

2 SPACE 2: Author(s)

General Instructions: After reading these instructions, decide who are the "authors" of this work for copyright purposes. Then, unless the work is a "collective work," give the requested information about every "author" who contributed any appreciable amount of copyrightable matter to this version of the work. If you need further space, request additional Continuation Sheets. In the case of a collective work such as a collection of previously published or registered sound recordings, give information about the author of the collective work as a whole. If you are submitting this Form SR to cover the recorded musical, dramatic, or literary work as well as the sound recording itself, it is important for space 2 to include full information about the various authors of all of the material covered by the copyright claim, making clear the nature of each author's contribution.

Name of Author: The fullest form of the author's name should be given. Unless the work was "made for hire," the individual who actually created the work is its "author." In the case of a work made for hire, the statute provides that "the employer or other person for whom the work was prepared is considered the author."

What is a "Work Made for Hire"? A "work made for hire" is defined as: (1) "a work prepared by an employee within the scope of his or her employment"; or (2)

"a work specially ordered or commissioned for use as a contribution to a collective work, as a part of a motion picture or other audiovisual work, as a translation, as a supplementary work, as a compilation, as an instructional text, as a test, as answer material for a test, or as an atlas, if the parties expressly agree in a written instrument signed by them that the work shall be considered a work made for hire." If you have checked "Yes" to indicate that the work was "made for hire," you must give the full legal name of the employer (or other person for whom the work was prepared). You may also include the name of the employee along with the name of the employer (for example: "Elster Record Co., employer for hire of John Ferguson").

"Anonymous" or "Pseudonymous" Work: An author's contribution to a work is "anonymous" if that author is not identified on the copies or phonorecords of the work. An author's contribution to a work is "pseudonymous" if that author is identified on the copies or phonorecords under a fictitious name. If the work is "anonymous" you may: (1) leave the line blank; or (2) state "anonymous" on the line; or (3) reveal the author's identity. If the work is "pseudonymous" you may: (1) leave the line blank; or (2) give the pseudonym and identify it as such (for example: "Huntley Haverstock, pseudonym"); or (3) reveal the author's name, making clear which is the real name and which is the pseudonym (for example: "Judith Barton, whose pseudonym is Madeline Elster"). However, the citizenship or domicile of the author must be given in all cases.

Dates of Birth and Death: If the author is dead, the statute requires that the year of death be included in the application unless the work is anonymous or pseudonymous. The author's birth date is optional, but is useful as a form of identification. Leave this space blank if the author's contribution was a "work made for hire."

Author's Nationality or Domicile: Give the country in which the author is a citizen, or the country in which the author is domiciled. Nationality or domicile must be given in all cases.

Nature of Authorship: Sound recording authorship is the performance, sound production, or both, that is fixed in the recording deposited for registration. Describe this authorship in space 2 as "sound recording." If the claim also covers the underlying work(s), include the appropriate authorship terms for each author, for example, "words," "music," "arrangement of music," or "text."

Generally, for the claim to cover both the sound recording and the underlying work(s), every author should have contributed to both the sound recording and the underlying work(s). If the claim includes artwork or photographs, include the appropriate term in the statement of authorship.

3 SPACE 3: Creation and Publication

General Instructions: Do not confuse "creation" with "publication." Every application for copyright registration must state "the year in which creation of the work was completed." Give the date and nation of first publication only if the work has been published.

Creation: Under the statute, a work is "created" when it is fixed in a copy or phonorecord for the first time. Where a work has been prepared over a period of time, the part of the work existing in fixed form on a particular date constitutes the created work on that date. The date you give here should be the year in which the author completed the particular version for which registration is now being sought, even if other versions exist or if further changes or additions are planned.

Publication: The statute defines "publication" as "the distribution of copies or phonorecords of a work to the public by sale or other transfer of ownership, or by rental, lease, or lending"; a work is also "published" if there has been an "offering to distribute copies or phonorecords to a group of persons for purposes of further distribution, public performance, or public display." Give the full date (month, date, year) when, and the country where, publication first occurred. If first publication took place simultaneously in the United States and other countries, it is sufficient to state "U.S.A."

4 SPACE 4: Claimant(s)

Name(s) and Address(es) of Copyright Claimant(s): Give the name(s) and address(es) of the copyright claimant(s) in the work even if the claimant is the same as the author. Copyright in a work belongs initially to the author of the work (including, in the case of a work made for hire, the employer or other person for whom the work was prepared). The copyright claimant is either the author of the work or a person or organization to whom the copyright initially belonging to the author has been transferred.

Transfer: The statute provides that, if the copyright claimant is not the author, the application for registration must contain "a brief statement of how the claimant obtained ownership of the copyright." If any copyright claimant named in space 4a is not an author named in space 2, give a brief statement explaining how the claimant(s) obtained ownership of the copyright. Examples: "By written contract"; "Transfer of all rights by author"; "Assignment"; "By will." Do not attach transfer documents or other attachments or riders.

5 SPACE 5: Previous Registration

General Instructions: The questions in space 5 are intended to show whether an earlier registration has been made for this work and, if so, whether there is any basis for a new registration. As a rule, only one basic copyright registration can be made for the same version of a particular work.

Same Version: If this version is substantially the same as the work covered by a previous registration, a second registration is not generally possible unless: (1) the work has been registered in unpublished form and a second registration is now being sought to cover this first published edition; or (2) someone other than the author is identified as copyright claimant in the earlier registration and the author is now seeking registration in his or her own name. If either of these two exceptions applies, check the appropriate box and give the earlier registration number and date. Otherwise, do not submit Form SR. Instead, write the Copyright Office for information about supplementary registration or recordation of transfers of copyright ownership.

Changed Version: If the work has been changed and you are now seeking registration to cover the additions or revisions, check the last box in space 5, give the earlier registration number and date, and complete both parts of space 6 in accordance with the instructions below.

Previous Registration Number and Date: If more than one previous registration has been made for the work, give the number and date of the latest registration.

6 SPACE 6: Derivative Work or Compilation

General Instructions: Complete space 6 if this work is a "changed version," "compilation," or "derivative work," and if it incorporates one or more earlier works that have already been published or registered for copyright, or that have fallen into the public domain, or sound recordings that were fixed before February 15, 1972. A "compilation" is defined as "a work formed by the collection and assembling of preexisting materials or of data that are selected, coordinated, or arranged in such a way that the resulting work as a whole constitutes an original work of authorship." A "derivative work" is "a work based on one or more preexisting works." Examples of derivative works include recordings reissued with substantial editorial revisions or abridgments of the recorded sounds, and recordings republished with new recorded material, or "any other form in which a work may be recast, transformed, or adapted." Derivative works also include works "consisting of editorial revisions, annotations, or other modifications" if these changes, as a whole, represent an original work of authorship.

Preexisting Material (space 6a): Complete this space and space 6b for derivative works. In this space identify the preexisting work that has been recast, transformed, or adapted. The preexisting work may be material that has been previously published, previously registered, or that is in the public domain. For example, the preexisting material might be: "1970 recording by Sperryville Symphony of Bach Double Concerto."

Material Added to This Work (space 6b): Give a brief, general statement of the **additional** new material covered by the copyright claim for which registration is sought. In the case of a derivative work, identify this new material. Examples: "Recorded performances on bands 1 and 3"; "Remixed sounds from original multitrack sound sources"; "New words, arrangement, and additional sounds." If the work is a compilation, give a brief, general statement describing both the material that has been compiled and the compilation itself. Example: "Compilation of 1938 Recordings by various swing bands."

7, 8, 9 SPACE 7,8,9: Fee, Correspondence, Certification, Return Address

Deposit Account: If you maintain a Deposit Account in the Copyright Office, identify it in space 7a. Otherwise, leave the space blank and send the filing fee of $30 (effective through June 30, 2002) with your application and deposit. (See space 8 on form.)

Correspondence (space 7b): This space should contain the name, address, area code, telephone number, fax number, and email address (if available) of the person to be consulted if correspondence about this application becomes necessary.

Certification (space 8): This application cannot be accepted unless it bears the date and the **handwritten signature** of the author or other copyright claimant, or of the owner of exclusive right(s), or of the duly authorized agent of the author, claimant, or owner of exclusive right(s).

Address for Return of Certificate (space 9): The address box must be completed legibly since the certificate will be returned in a window envelope.

MORE INFORMATION

"Works": "Works" are the basic subject matter of copyright; they are what authors create and copyright protects. The statute draws a sharp distinction between the "work" and "any material object in which the work is embodied."

"Copies" and "Phonorecords": These are the two types of material objects in which "works" are embodied. In general, **copies** are objects from which a work can be read or visually perceived, directly or with the aid of a machine or device, such as manuscripts, books, sheet music, film, and videotape. **Phonorecords** are objects embodying fixations of sounds, such as audio tapes and phonograph disks. For example, a song (the "work") can be reproduced in sheet music ("copies") or phonograph disks ("phonorecords"), or both.

"Sound Recordings": These are "works," not "copies" or "phonorecords." "Sound recordings" are "works that result from the fixation of a series of musical, spoken, or other sounds, but not including the sounds accompanying a motion picture or other audiovisual work." Example: When a record company issues a new release, the release will typically involve two distinct "works": the "musical work" that has been recorded, and the "sound recording" as a separate work in itself. The material objects that the record company sends out are "phonorecords": physical reproductions of both the "musical work" and the "sound recording."

Should You File More Than One Application?

If your work consists of a recorded musical, dramatic, or literary work and if both that "work" and the sound recording as a separate "work" are eligible for registration, the application form you should file depends on the following:

File Only Form SR if: The copyright claimant is the same for both the musical, dramatic, or literary work and for the sound recording, and you are seeking a single registration to cover both of these "works."

File Only Form PA (or Form TX) if: You are seeking to register only the musical, dramatic, or literary work, not the sound recording. Form PA is appropriate for works of the performing arts; Form TX is for nondramatic literary works.

Separate Applications Should Be Filed on Form PA (or Form TX) and on Form SR if: (1) The copyright claimant for the musical, dramatic, or literary work is different from the copyright claimant for the sound recording; or (2) You prefer to have separate registrations for the musical, dramatic, or literary work and for the sound recording.

Fees are effective through June 30, 2002.
After that date, check the Copyright Office
Website at www.loc.gov/copyright or call
(202) 707-3000 for current fee information.

FORM SR
For a Sound Recording
UNITED STATES COPYRIGHT OFFICE

REGISTRATION NUMBER

_____

SR _____ SRU _____

EFFECTIVE DATE OF REGISTRATION

_____

Month   Day   Year

DO NOT WRITE ABOVE THIS LINE. IF YOU NEED MORE SPACE, USE A SEPARATE CONTINUATION SHEET.

1
TITLE OF THIS WORK▼

PREVIOUS, ALTERNATIVE, OR CONTENTS TITLES (CIRCLE ONE)

2

a

NAME OF AUTHOR▼

DATES OF BIRTH AND DEATH
Year Born ▼   Year Died ▼

Was this contribution to the work a "work made for hire"?
☐ Yes
☐ No

AUTHOR'S NATIONALITY OR DOMICILE
Name of Country
OR { Citizen of ▶ _____
     Domiciled in ▶ _____

WAS THIS AUTHOR'S CONTRIBUTION TO THE WORK
Anonymous?   ☐ Yes ☐ No
Pseudonymous?   ☐ Yes ☐ No

If the answer to either of these questions is "Yes," see detailed instructions.

NATURE OF AUTHORSHIP Briefly describe nature of material created by this author in which copyright is claimed. ▼

NOTE

Under the law, the "author" of a "work made for hire" is generally the employer, not the employee (see instructions). For any part of this work that was "made for hire," check "Yes" in the space provided, give the employer (or other person for whom the work was prepared) as "Author" of that part, and leave the space for dates of birth and death blank.

b

NAME OF AUTHOR▼

DATES OF BIRTH AND DEATH
Year Born ▼   Year Died ▼

Was this contribution to the work a "work made for hire"?
☐ Yes
☐ No

AUTHOR'S NATIONALITY OR DOMICILE
Name of Country
OR { Citizen of ▶ _____
     Domiciled in ▶ _____

WAS THIS AUTHOR'S CONTRIBUTION TO THE WORK
Anonymous?   ☐ Yes ☐ No
Pseudonymous?   ☐ Yes ☐ No

If the answer to either of these questions is "Yes," see detailed instructions.

NATURE OF AUTHORSHIP Briefly describe nature of material created by this author in which copyright is claimed. ▼

c

NAME OF AUTHOR▼

DATES OF BIRTH AND DEATH
Year Born ▼   Year Died ▼

Was this contribution to the work a "work made for hire"?
☐ Yes
☐ No

AUTHOR'S NATIONALITY OR DOMICILE
Name of Country
OR { Citizen of ▶ _____
     Domiciled in ▶ _____

WAS THIS AUTHOR'S CONTRIBUTION TO THE WORK
Anonymous?   ☐ Yes ☐ No
Pseudonymous?   ☐ Yes ☐ No

If the answer to either of these questions is "Yes," see detailed instructions.

NATURE OF AUTHORSHIP Briefly describe nature of material created by this author in which copyright is claimed. ▼

3

a **YEAR IN WHICH CREATION OF THIS WORK WAS COMPLETED**
_____ Year ◀ This information must be given in all cases.

b **DATE AND NATION OF FIRST PUBLICATION OF THIS PARTICULAR WORK**
Complete this information ONLY if this work has been published.
Month ▶ _____ Day ▶ _____ Year ▶ _____ ◀ Nation

4

a **COPYRIGHT CLAIMANT(S)** Name and address must be given even if the claimant is the same as the author given in space 2. ▼

b **TRANSFER** If the claimant(s) named here in space 4 is (are) different from the author(s) named in space 2, give a brief statement of how the claimant(s) obtained ownership of the copyright. ▼

See instructions before completing this space.

APPLICATION RECEIVED

ONE DEPOSIT RECEIVED

TWO DEPOSITS RECEIVED

FUNDS RECEIVED

DO NOT WRITE HERE OFFICE USE ONLY

MORE ON BACK ▶ • Complete all applicable spaces (numbers 5-9) on the reverse side of this page.
• See detailed instructions.   • Sign the form at line 8.

DO NOT WRITE HERE

Page 1 of _____ pages

EXAMINED BY

CHECKED BY

CORRESPONDENCE
❑ Yes

FORM SR

FOR
COPYRIGHT
OFFICE
USE
ONLY

DO NOT WRITE ABOVE THIS LINE. IF YOU NEED MORE SPACE, USE A SEPARATE CONTINUATION SHEET.

PREVIOUS REGISTRATION Has registration for this work, or for an earlier version of this work, already been made in the Copyright Office?

❑ Yes ❑ No If your answer is "Yes," why is another registration being sought? (Check appropriate box) ▼

a. ❑ **This work was previously registered in unpublished form and now has been published for the first time.**

b. ❑ **This is the first application submitted by this author as copyright claimant.**

c. ❑ **This is a changed version of the work, as shown by space 6 on this application.**

If your answer is "Yes," give: Previous Registration Number ▼   Year of Registration ▼

5

DERIVATIVE WORK OR COMPILATION
Preexisting Material Identify any preexisting work or works that this work is based on or incorporates. ▼

a

Material Added to This Work Give a brief, general statement of the material that has been added to this work and in which copyright is claimed. ▼

b

6

See instructions
before completing
this space.

DEPOSIT ACCOUNT If the registration fee is to be charged to a Deposit Account established in the Copyright Office, give name and number of Account.
Name ▼   Account Number ▼

a

CORRESPONDENCE Give name and address to which correspondence about this application should be sent.   Name/Address/Apt/City/State/ZIP ▼

b

Area code and daytime telephone number ▶   Fax number ▶
Email ▶

7

CERTIFICATION* I, the undersigned, hereby certify that I am the

Check only one ▼

❑ author   ❑ owner of exclusive right(s)
❑ other copyright claimant ❑ authorized agent of
                    Name of author or other copyright claimant, or owner of exclusive right(s) ▲

of the work identified in this application and that the statements made by me in this application are correct to the best of my knowledge.

Typed or printed name and date ▼ If this application gives a date of publication in space 3, do not sign and submit it before that date.

                                                                              Date

          Handwritten signature (x) ▼
     X
     _

8

Certificate
will be
mailed in
window
envelope
to this
address

Name ▼

Number/Street/Apt ▼

City/State/ZIP ▼

YOU MUST:
• Complete all necessary spaces
• Sign your application in space 8
SEND ALL 3 ELEMENTS
IN THE SAME PACKAGE:
1. Application form
2. Nonrefundable filing fee in check or money
   order payable to Register of Copyrights
3. Deposit material
MAIL TO:
Library of Congress
Copyright Office
101 Independence Avenue, S.E.
Washington, D.C. 20559-6000

As of
July 1, 1999,
the filing fee
for Form SR
is $30.

9

*17 U.S.C. § 506(e): Any person who knowingly makes a false representation of a material fact in the application for copyright registration provided for by section 409, or in any written statement filed in connection with the application, shall be fined not more than $2,500.
June 1999—50,000
WEB REV: June 1999   ♻ PRINTED ON RECYCLED PAPER   ☆U.S. GOVERNMENT PRINTING OFFICE: 1999-454-879/48

is automatically granted in every country that has entered into a copyright treaty with the United States.

Each country's laws differ, however, as to the categories of works, rights and duration, infringement, compulsory licensing and performance rights.

Infringement suits must be filed in the courts of infringing countries, not in U.S. courts.

COPYRIGHT INFRINGEMENT

When composers' copyrights are violated, copyright infringement (a federal crime) has occurred and the people that infringed are subject to civil and criminal penalties. Infringement occurs when recordings of published songs are made, whether for commercial or noncommercial use, without payment of a mechanical license. In 2001, the courts ruled that swapping music files via Napster, Inc. infringed on the copyrights of reproduction and distribution. (See article, "Challenges to Copyright" in this segment.)

Copyright owners must establish three things to prove infringement—

- That they are owners of the songs, proved by having registered the songs with the U.S. Copyright Office.

- That the infringing songs (or the sound recordings) are "substantially similar to the original songs" (or the sound recordings). This phrase has no precise definition. Juries have to decide whether the songs are so similar they can be easily mistaken for one another. Musicologists are called to testify whether or not the construction of the melodies, rhythms, harmonies and words are substantially the same.

- That infringers had access to the music. This means that composers or their publishers must prove a reasonable possibility that the infringer heard the song or saw it in print after the date of registration. If the

PRINCIPLE SOURCES OF INFORMATION ON INTERNATIONAL COPYRIGHT CONVENTIONS, TREATIES AND AGREEMENTS

General Agreement on Tariffs and Trade (GATT) Accord on Trade-Related Aspects of Intellectual Property Rights (TRIPS). Information on GATT and the TRIPS agreement may be found on *www.WTO.org.*

Berne Convention for the Protection of Literary and Artistic Works. Berne agreements are administered by the World Intellectual Property Organization (WIPO). *www.wipo.org*

Universal Copyright Convention (UCC), administered by the United Nations Educational, Scientific and Cultural Organization (UNESCO). *www.unesco.org/culture/laws/copyright.*

World Trade Organization. *www.wto.org*

song had substantial airplay on radio and MTV and became a major hit, juries could say that there was a reasonable possibility that infringers heard it. But, if the song was only played at a few clubs, composers or their publishers would have to prove that the alleged infringers were present. Publishers usually return unsolicited material unopened to avoid allowing composers to sue for infringement and prove "access" by providing proof that they had sent unpublished demos.

Infringement lawsuits are very expensive and time consuming and are not worth pursuing unless substantial sums of money are likely to be

EVEN A BEATLE HAS INFRINGED

George Harrison, one of the members of the Beatles music group, was found to have infringed the song "He's So Fine," recorded in 1962 by the Chiffons, with his 1970 hit, "My Sweet Lord."

On 1963, the Chiffons' song "He's So Fine" was No. 1 on the Billboard charts in the United States and, for seven weeks, was one of the top hits in England. From these facts the court inferred Harrison had access and had subconsciously recreated "He's So Fine" by writing "My Sweet Lord," which constituted an infringement.

recovered. If infringement can be proved, composers and publishers are eligible to receive statutory damages and recover legal fees.

Contributory Infringement and Vicarious Liability

Contributory infringement is found when a person has knowledge of an infringing activity and induces, causes or materially contributes to the infringing conduct of another. For example, a Web site operator may be liable for contributory infringement by knowingly linking to music files without the copyright owners permission.

Vicarious liability is found when an entity or person has the right and ability to control the activities of the direct infringer and receives a financial benefit from the infringing activities. For example, a Web site that retransmits infringing music files and provides direct access to them may have a right and ability to control the activities of the direct infringer. Receiving revenue from banner ads or e-commerce on the site can be evidence of a financial benefit.

Contributory infringement and vicarious liability were cited in the rulings against Napster.

PIRACY

Bootlegging, counterfeiting and pirate recording are major industry problems. According to the International Intellectual Property Alliance (IIPA), a coalition of seven trade associations that represent U.S. copyright-based industries, losses due to piracy of U.S. copyrighted materials around the world are $20-$22 billion annually.

Despite some spectacular lawsuits, efforts to curb this problem have been largely ineffectual, because policing infringement is difficult and expensive.

Piracy is the illegal duplication and distribution of sound recordings for commercial gain.

- Pirate recordings are the selling of unauthorized duplications of the sound of published recordings, mixed tapes and compilation CDs that feature one or more artists.

- Counterfeit recordings are unauthorized recordings of the sound *as well as* the duplication of original artwork, label, trademark and packaging.

- Bootleg recordings are made from the illegal copying of live concerts and broad casts of live concerts on television and radio.

- Online piracy is the unauthorized uploading of copyrighted sound recordings and making them available to the public or downloading sound recordings from Internet sites, even if they are not resold. This concept is still being tested in the courts.

The U.S. Congress has passed laws that clarify piracy and infringement issues; and the RIAA has an active antipiracy program.

Digital Audio Recording Technology (DART) Act

Digital Audio Tape (DAT) recorders make it easy for consumers to copy CDs, vinyl and cassette recordings onto a digital tape medium. The Digital Audio Recording Technology (DART) Act clarified that doing so does not constitute infringement and does not violate the fair use doctrine when consumers do so for noncommercial purposes. However, the Act predates the uploading of digital files to the Internet via computers and does not cover the legality of this aspect.

To mollify copyright holders that felt copying was infringement, the DART Act created a small percentage royalty to be paid on recording media (DAT tape) by manufacturers and importers of DAT recorders and blank tape. The royalties are paid to the Licensing Division of the Copyright Office and are distributed by the Copyright Arbitration Royalty Panel (CARP) to copyright holders according to the following percentages:

Record companies	38.41%
Featured artists	25.60%
Songwriters	16.66%
Music publishers	16.66%
Musicians	1.75%
Background vocalists	0.92%

The Act requires manufacturers of digital audio equipment to install copy prevention systems that permit copies to be made from original recordings, but not from copies made from them, to prevent illegal duplication.

No Electronic Theft Act

The 1997 No Electronic Theft Act imposes criminal penalties against anyone that intentionally distributes copies of phonorecords and software over the Internet for "commercial advantage or

The ease of distribution of intellectual property via the Internet combined with the availability of inexpensive and accessible reproduction technologies makes it difficult to adequately protect artists' rights, ensure that they are fairly paid when their art is used for commercial purposes and pursue infringers.

provide financial gain." Additionally, the Act amended the definition of "commercial advantage or private financial gain" to include the receipt (or expectation of receipt) of anything of value, including receipt of other copyrighted works, such as MP3 files.

Digital Millennium Copyright Act (DMCA)

The 1998 DMCA makes it a crime to circumvent antipiracy measures that are built into commercial software and CDs. Many record companies are now encoding CDs in a manner that prevents their being copied when placed in the CD drives of computers as a method to circumvent free peer-to-peer file sharing services. (The licensing provisions of the DMCA are covered in Segment 4, Music Licensing.)

Worldwide public opinion is not in favor of the antipiracy measures of this Act. Adobe Systems dropped a lawsuit that involved the distribution of software product that circumvented copyright protection measures after a loud public outcry. Colleges and universities feel that the DMCA hinders fair use copying of materials for educational purposes.

If music and other creative properties continue to be freely available—from piracy or file sharing—what incentives do composers and record companies have to spend money on recording and marketing?

Code-breaking programs are available virtually as fast copy prevention systems are installed. The programmers are anonymous, which makes them very difficult to find and to prosecute.

RIAA Antipiracy Program

The RIAA pursues record pirates and prosecutes copyright infringers. The RIAA was a major party in the lawsuits against Napster.

The RIAA has also filed lawsuits against several CD manufacturers, accusing them of being parties to illegal replication. According to the RIAA, those manufacturers knew their clients were infringers. A precedent setting case was between Americ Disk, a large California replicator and the RIAA for illegal replication of copyrighted material. Americ Disc had to pay the RIAA $13 million.

IRMA Antipiracy Compliance Program

The International Recording Media Association (IRMA), a nonprofit organization composed of CD replicators worldwide, has an Antipiracy Compliance Program that was adopted in 1999. The program established a set of business practices and standards to help prevent unauthorized manufacture and distribution of copyrighted materials. The program applies to CD, VCD, DVD-Audio and DVD-Video products and software.

It requires replicators to verify the ownership of copyrighted works and the authority for customers to place orders according to specific guidelines.

Manufacturers that participate in the IRMA program require each customer (person, jobber, record company or other business) to provide the paperwork that shows that it is either the rightful owner of, or has licensed or otherwise possesses legally enforceable rights, to use the copyrighted materials contained on the CDs and other products that will be manufactured. Without that paperwork, manufacturers refuse to replicate the products. Copies of copyright registrations and mechanical licenses satisfy those requirements.

Here are some of the components of the IRMA program—

- Incorporate a source code into the production of all digital audio and video glass masters. These are transferred to digital products, such as CDs and DVDs, and to pirated products, thus enabling enforcement officials with a means to track down pirates.

- Require brokers and sales representatives to provide identification regarding their clients, which includes phone numbers and street addresses (no post office boxes).

- Obtain and maintain proof of intellectual property rights and trademark authorization.

- Quarantine for disposition, all product and materials, including masters, which do not comply with IRMA guidelines.

- Review artwork for copyright information.

According to IRMA, some of the red flags that might lead to identifying pirates are—

- Customers that present compilation CDs, which contain the work of top artists that are signed to major record companies

- Customers that want to pay in cash or refuse to provide an address or phone number

- Customers that want to place small orders, which involve major artists on a rush turnaround basis or request orders without printing

- Customers that ask for false or misleading information to be printed

- Customers that request replication, but give no instructions for printing and no orders for packaging

CONCLUSION

The protection of intellectual property rights is a worldwide issue for all artists and businesses that profit from them. The ease of distribution of intellectual property via the Internet combined with the availability of inexpensive and accessible reproduction technologies makes it difficult to adequately protect artists' rights, ensure that they are fairly paid when their art is used for commercial purposes and pursue infringers. Piracy is increasing, despite increased enforcement, new laws and lawsuits that attempt to curb them

Lawsuits against file-sharing Web sites continue. As soon as one site is shut down, others arise.

Record companies are encrypting CDs, DVDs and other digital products so that they cannot be uploaded to computers, a controversial move that is not appreciated by consumers and many businesses that sell devices that enable people to upload, store and listen to music they have purchased.

Legislation designed to further protect intellectual property rights is being introduced in the Senate. A bill introduced to the United States Senate in March 2002, asks representatives of digital media device manufacturers, consumer groups and copyright owners to reach agreement on security system standards and encoding rules for use in digital media devices (Consumer Broadband and Digital Television Promotion Act—S2048). Any agreements about security standards will be incorporated as amendments to the Copyright Act.

If music and other creative properties continue to be freely available—from piracy or file sharing—what incentives do composers and record companies have to spend money on recording and marketing? How will composers and other artists profit from their art? How can intellectual property be protected?

Participation by all stakeholders—consumers, music businesses, technology providers and artists—is critical to ensure that business and consumer needs are balanced with protection of artists' creative properties and their intellectual property rights.

Challenges to Copyrights

In 1987, the Moving Picture Experts Group, an organization that sets international standards for digital formats for audio and video, developed a standard digital file format for the storage of audio recordings called MPEG-3, abbreviated as MP3. MP3 files are created through a process called ripping, which enables computer users to copy CDs onto their computer's hard drive and compress the audio information into MP3 format. This allows rapid transmission of digital audio files from one computer to another via the file transfer protocols of electronic mail software.

This format is used to send music files from one computer to another. Many artists use the MP3 format to send their music to musicians and producers in other cities; publishers send files to record, video and film producers that are looking for material; and so on.

In 1999, the ability to compress music into even smaller digital files and make them available via the Internet resulted in a number of companies that offered consumers free, innovative music services.

Napster provided a centralized directory for uploaded music to be stored, indexed, accessed and swapped. Other companies allowed consumers to swap files without going through any centralized directory (Gnutella, FastTrack, etc.). They all used a process called peer-to-peer (P2P) file sharing. Still other companies provided users

Consumers object strongly to having their tastes and listening habits dictated to by the marketing needs of major conglomerates.

with the ability to conveniently access digital files of their own music, sequence the songs and play them on a variety of MP3 (MyMP3.com and Doug and Jimmy's Farm Club).

File sharing was an instantaneous success with consumers and a failure with major copyright holders—record companies, publishers and artists— that responded by filing lawsuits against them.

For copyright holders, file sharing is theft of intellectual property. Free downloads mean no payments to copyright holders. (A major tenet of copyright law is that the copyright owners control the rights of reproduction and distribution and earn money by licensing their works for compensation.)

Record companies feared that consumers would buy fewer recordings. When The Recording Industry Association of America (RIAA) and Canadian Recording Industry Association (CRIA) reported sales for 1999 and 2000, statistics showed that fewer recordings were sold than in the previous year. Both organizations attributed the cause of fewer sales to the use of file-sharing technologies and not to other possible causes, such as consumers spending leisure dollars on other entertainment products, recession economics or releases of mediocre recordings.

NAPSTER

Napster's free file-sharing service resonated so strongly with consumers that, when the legal system clamped down, it had more than 40 million registered users.

As soon as Napster began offering their service, nine record companies—A&M, MCA, Island, Motown, Geffen and Interscope (subsidiaries of Universal), Sony Music Entertainment, Atlantic (subsidiary of Warner Music Group), and Capitol Records (subsidiary of EMI Group)—filed a copyright infringement lawsuit in the Northern California District Court. A similar (but separate) lawsuit was filed in the same federal court by the National Music Publishers Association (NMPA) on behalf of major publishing companies.

In October 2000, Napster formed a strategic alliance with Bertelsmann AG to develop a membership-based service that would legally compensate artists and record labels. (BMG Entertainment, Bertelsmann's record company, was not among the record companies that sued Napster.) According to industry sources, Bertelsmann loaned Napster about $50 million dollars and received rights to take a controlling interest in the company. Bertelsmann gained access to valuable marketing information about the music that Napster subscribers were downloading and its list of subscribers.

On July 26, 2000, Judge Marilyn Hall Patel issued a preliminary injunction and ordered a halt to the trading of music files on Napster. Napster's lawyers persuaded the 9th Circuit U.S. Court of Appeals to stay the court order until a hearing was held.

"ANI WANTS TO CONTROL HER OWN ART AND NAPSTER TAKES AWAY THAT FREEDOM. There are some songs available on NAPSTER that Ani never recorded. [Ani allows fans to record her concerts.] And that gets to the core of this issue. It was Ani's choice not to record those songs. Maybe they weren't working for her. Maybe she wants to change them before recording them. What is important is that she decides as an artist what to perform and what to record and how to make her work available to her audience. NAPSTER takes away those choices. She wasn't even asked if she wanted that music spread to a larger audience. What's at stake here is the artist's right to choose what an audience hears and in what form."

— SCOT FISHER, MANAGER, ANI DI FRANCO *(Righteous Babe Records)*

At an October 2000 hearing, Judge Patel ruled that Napster's users were engaged in the wholesale reproduction and distribution of copyrighted works, which constituted direct infringement. According to Patel, users that upload files for others to copy violate distribution rights. Users that download files containing copyrighted music violate reproduction rights.

Napster's attorneys unsuccessfully argued that users were engaged in the fair use of copyrighted materials. After examining the fair use issue, the court determined that Napster users engaged in commercial use of the copyrighted materials largely because "a host user sending a file cannot be said to engage in a personal use when distributing that file to an anonymous requester" and "Napster users get for free something they would ordinarily have to buy." The court also said that, "Direct economic benefit is not required to demonstrate a commercial use. Rather, repeated and exploitative copying of copyrighted works,

"It's going to be my first protest song, as soon as I can figure out some words that rhyme with 'Napster,' 'Bertelsmann,' and 'service charge.'"

even if the copies are not offered for sale, may constitute a commercial use."

Under fair use doctrine, copying is limited to circumstances that do not materially impair the marketability of the copied work. Judge Patel found that the use of the Napster service reduced audio CD sales among college students and raised "barriers to plaintiffs' entry into the market for the digital downloading of music. . . Having digital downloads available for free on the Napster system necessarily harms the copyright holders' attempts to charge for the same downloads."

Judge Patel also ruled that Napster was a contributory infringer because it "knowingly encourages and assists the infringement of plaintiffs' copyrights." The judge said Napster was potentially liable for vicarious infringement for failing to patrol its system and preclude access to infringing files.

Napster attorneys unsuccessfully contended that it was protected under the statutes of the Audio Home Recording Act, contending that MP3 file exchanges are types of "noncommercial use." (The Act reads in part: "No action may be brought under this title alleging infringement of copyright based on the manufacture, importation, or distri-

bution of a digital audio recording device, a digital audio recording medium, an analog recording device, or an analog recording medium, or based on the noncommercial use by a consumer of such a device or medium for making digital musical recordings or analog musical recordings.")

The court rejected Napster's arguments, stating that the Audio Home Recording Act was irrelevant because plaintiffs did not bring claims under the Act and that it did not cover the downloading of MP3 files. "There are simply no grounds in either the plain language of the definition or in the legislative history for interpreting the term 'digital musical recording' to include songs fixed on computer hard drives."

Judge Patel's decision was appealed and upheld by the 9 th Circuit Court of Appeals in San Francisco in February 2001.

In July 2001 Napster was disabled, pending changes that would make it a legal service.

Napster attorney David Boies commented, "The recording industry is attempting, in this case, to try to maintain control over music distribution. By repeatedly refusing Napster's offers of a reasonable license and opposing a compulsory license, they have demonstrated that they are not seeking to be appropriately compensated, but rather to kill or control a technology they view as competition."

In the late Fall of 2001, Napster filed charges in federal court alleging that the major labels have sought to impose anti-competitive licensing terms with Napster and other online rivals, while creating joint venture subscription services among themselves.

In September 2001, Napster agreed to pay $26 million to music publishers and composers, but the NMPA, individual publishers and the federal court must still approve the settlement. According to the terms of the deal, the owners of music publishing rights will receive one-third and record labels will get two-thirds. Napster also said it would pay an advance of $10 million against future licensing fees. The agreement includes terms under which songwriters and music publishers will license their music to Napster.

In January 2002, Napster launched a free beta test version that offered the content of independent labels to a selected group of subscribers to the old Napster. The version did not contain content from major labels for downloading, an issue contested by Napster.

In February 2002, Judge Patel ordered a scrutiny into Napster's antitrust allegations.

In April 2002, Bertelsmann offered to acquire Napster outright.

In May 2002, Napster accepted a buy-out from Bertelsmann.

MUSIC SUBSCRIPTION SERVICES PROBED FOR POTENTIAL VIOLATIONS OF ANTITRUST LAWS

In October 2001, the U.S. Justice Department began an investigation into whether paid music subscription services that were to be launched by the major record company conglomerates in December 2001 (PressPlay and MusicNet) were attempts to restrain trade and competition and whether their owners (the major record company conglomerates) colluded to influence price and terms of use, thereby violating antitrust laws.

Among the questions being asked by the Justice Department are these—

- Why are the only music services that are partially or wholly-owned by major labels the only ones to receive licenses that enable them to provide major label content for limited or permanent downloading?

- Are major conglomerates trying to freeze out independent services that want to offer limited or permanent downloads, even if they agree to pay licensing fees for doing so?

- Why was Napster refused major label content for their new service?

LAWSUITS AGAINST OTHER FREE FILE-SHARING SERVICES

Copyright infringement lawsuits are pending against Grokster, Music City and KaZaA. All are licensees of FastTrack, a P2P system that is owned by an Amsterdam, Netherlands company called Consumer Empowerment, whose technology and service is similar to Napster's.

In March 2002, a Dutch appeals court overturned a lower-court ruling that found KaZaA was liable for copyright infringement. The court said, "Insofar as any infringing use is being made. . . these acts are committed by its users, not by KaZaA." The case was filed by a Dutch music copyright organization. The case against Fast Track and its licensees will be tried in the United States in October 2002.

As of May 2002, no lawsuits had been filed against iMesh, Audiogalaxy and Gnutella, other free, popular P2P file-sharing services.

MP3.COM

In late 1999, MP3.com began offering a free locker service called My.MP3.com. This service enabled users to access music that they owned from a centralized database via any computer. To avoid having users spend time uploading their music collections or duplicating uploads already in the system, the owners of MP3.com purchased some 80,000 CDs and uploaded them to their database.

Each user had a password-protected account. To access music in the database, users verified that they owned the CDs by inserting them into their computers' CD players and clicking on "Beam-It." If the music was not in the database, the file would be uploaded and stored. Because accounts were password protected, users could not access the files of others. MP3.com was a personal virtual jukebox.

On January 21, 2000, The Recording Industry Association of America (RIAA) filed an infringement lawsuit on behalf of all the major labels — Universal Music Group, Sony Music Group, BMG Entertainment, Warner Music Group and EMI Group—in the U.S. District Court in New York.

In April 2000, the judge ruled against MP3.com, finding that it had intentionally violated copyright holders rights by copying CDs into their database without permission, instead of licensing their use. The judge did not settle the issue of damages and left the door open for record companies to make out-of-court settlements.

During the summer of 2000, all the record companies, except Universal, settled for fees that amounted to more than $160 million dollars. The record companies agreed to nonexclusively license the use of their music on MP3.com. They also negotiated a prospective license, which calls for a payment of a one-time per track fee of ten cents for each recorded version of each song added to the My.MP3.com database and a payment of one-quarter cent each time the song is streamed to a customer.

In November 2000, MP3.com settled with Universal and agreed to pay it approximately $53.4 million. MP3.com also agreed to sell Universal warrants for the right to buy up to 3 million shares of MP3.com stock. At the time this deal was made, those shares were valued at approximately $4 each.

Although the record companies say they will share some of their settlement fees with artists, the exact amount and how it will be allocated to individual artists has not been disclosed.

In August 2001, Vivendi Universal bought MP3.com for about $372 million in cash and stock.

Today, consumers can access My.MP3.com (*www.mp3.com*) and the locker service is still free. What changed? Ownership—and the agreements by record companies to license their music to My.MP3.com, to satisfy the licensing tenets of copyright laws.

In August 2001, fifty small publishers filed a suit against MP3.com in federal court in California for copyright violations. This time the use of MP3 technology was attacked. In their complaints, the publishers alleged that MyMP3.com was liable for direct infringement because they converted songs to the MP3 format and that conversion constituted a new and unauthorized use.

The case is expected to be decided in May 2002.

DOUG AND JIMMY'S FARM CLUB

In 1999, Universal Records copied thousands of recordings from their catalogs to a database and launched a beta test of Doug and Jimmy's Farm Club (*www.farmclub.com*), a site that streamed music to subscribers for free.

In December 2000, several major songwriters and publishers filed an infringement lawsuit in a New York Federal Court against Universal Records, alleging that the record company failed to license the use of the copyrighted music embodied in these sound recordings before reproducing them on their database. Universal's prior legal victory was cited as a precedent.

According to Universal's attorneys, the record company did not need to seek the permission of the song's copyright owners because its existing licenses to manufacture and distribute recordings permitted them to make digital copies for use on the site's servers.

The judge rejected Universal Records' argument and determined that this was a new use and that songwriters and publishers must be compensated for uses of their works. A summary judgment, in favor of the songwriters, was issued.

CONCLUSION

According to Webnoize, an online music service that specializes in digital entertainment issues, consumers downloaded approximately 1.5 billion music files a month on file-sharing sites in 2001. Although lawsuits continue to be filed against these sites, major recording conglomerates are taking a new tack to prevent illegal copying of copyrighted materials. They are asking that copy protection systems be built into computers and other digital devices (MP3 players and Palm Pilots), software, operating systems and Web browsers. And they have found some friends in

Congress, where at least one bill was proposed in early 2001 that would make it a civil offense to make or sell digital technologies that do not contain some kind of security protection system. Many computer giants, including Microsoft, Intel, Adobe Systems and IBM, disagree with this. And so do consumers.

Many consumers feel that free music file-sharing sites are the equivalent of large public libraries that provide them with the means to access music that is not available on major music media networks. Free file sharing gives them opportunities to be disc jockeys and share the music of artists that is out of print, listen to new artists that cannot get media exposure and sequence strings of songs by subject, mood, etc.

How many consumers will pay for file-sharing subscription services that enable them to download content is unpredictable.

Consumers object strongly to having their tastes and listening habits dictated to by the marketing needs of major conglomerates. The public's overwhelmingly negative response to the legal shut down of Napster and continued use of free file-sharing Web sites can be interpreted as a backlash at monopolistic control of the marketing and distribution of music. Whether, or how, this will change industry practices, is not known.

Pete and Pat Luboff:
Songwriters, Publishers and Songwriting Educators

PETE AND PAT LUBOFF are a songwriting team. They own their publishing company, Pea Pod Music. They have published songs that have been covered by other artists including Bobby Womack, Calvin Richardson, Snoop Dogg and Patti LaBelle. Their song, "Hometown, USA", was the featured song in the John Travolta movie, *The Experts*.

The Luboffs have been teaching songwriting workshops since 1979 for songwriting associations, colleges and music and songwriting expos nationwide. An interesting part of their workshops is the collaboration segments in which all participants spend several hours writing a song together. Pete conducted workshops in Los Angeles for 19 years at the National Academy of Songwriters (NAS), an organization that has become part of the Songwriters Guild of America, and taught advanced songwriting for 13 years at the University of California Los Angeles (UCLA).

In 1986 the Luboffs received the NAS's "Excellence in Education" award.

After moving to Nashville in 2001, Pat and Pete started conducting Monday night workshops at the Music School on Music Row.

They have written two books: *12 Steps to Building Better Songs* (self-published) and *88 Songwriting Wrongs and How to Right Them,* published by Writer's Digest Books.

They created the *Grammy Pulse* magazine for

PHOTO: KATE RETTINO

the National Academy of Recording Arts and Sciences (NARAS, the Grammy organization); the *L.A. Record* for the Los Angeles Chapter of NARAS and the newsletter for the California Copyright Conference. Both have served as board members for the National Academy of Songwriters; Pete as vice chairman and Pat as president. Pete was a governor of the Los Angeles Chapter of NARAS for many years, including stints as vice president, secretary and National Trustee.

They screen songs for TAXI, an organization that has helped hundreds of songwriters place their songs with artists and film and TV producers. (An interview with Michael Laskow, TAXI's founder, can be found in the Segment 3, Publishing.)

* * * * * * *

Rapaport: It seems to be that you have been on a dual track as artists and businesspeople ever since you started your careers. Was this difficult for you?

Luboffs: There was resistance to the business part in the beginning. We let our egos get in the way and any rejection was devastating. If you take people's opinions and critiques personally, then the business is colder than dry ice, colder than cold. You could have a great song and lose confidence in it after one person gives a negative opinion.

Now we know that you just need to find the right audience for the song. Not all songs are universally liked. And if you are playing a song at a showcase and people start talking in the middle of it, it still doesn't mean it's not a great song. It could mean that you haven't found the right audience—or that the song needs more work.

When you go to pitch a song to professional listeners with your heart in your hand, and you are thinking they can make or break you, they can sense that. They don't want to know you if you have that kind of attitude. They have to feel free to critique your song and to say "no" without you making them uncomfortable. That's part of having a professional attitude and getting your ego out of the way. The ego screws up the situation and makes you defensive.

When we were younger, we were like every songwriter and band. We wanted to find someone to do the business for us. We pitched our songs to publishers and had some songs signed, but they never got any cuts for us. Then we got lucky and pitched a song directly to an artist who recorded it. From then on we took care of business ourselves. Once we let go of the resistance to business and got down to being working songwriters, it became a pleasure.

But business isn't just about pitching songs. It's about collecting the money. There are so many reasons that money due doesn't get to you, even from respectable organizations. If you don't take responsibility, no one else will. A lot of songwriters think it is a pain in the butt to make sure they're getting paid, that they get a good contract, keep records and do the bookkeeping. And they're right! But there's no getting around it. If you're counting on songwriting to make a living, then business goes side-by-side with creativity.

The one piece of business we do not do is negotiate our own deals. Once someone wants one of our songs, we let our lawyer make the deal. We've learned from personal experience this cold fact: as soon as money starts coming in, everything changes. You'd be shocked at the things people will do. If you don't have an iron-clad contract, it will be a bloody mess. Our lawyer saved us from many misunderstandings. In any situation where the uses of songs are negotiated, you need to remember that you do have control over what you sign. We learned early on that whatever we signed needed to be something we approved of and understood completely. It is worth any investment you make to have a really good lawyer negotiate your deal.

Rapaport: What was the first song that got recorded by someone else and how did it happen?

Luboffs: That would be the song "Body Language"

You need to remember that you do have control over what you sign. We learned early on that whatever we signed needed to be something we approved of and understood completely.

by Patti LaBelle. Here's how it happened. We were living in Los Angeles and writing a tip sheet for *Songwriter Magazine*—collecting information about which producers were about to go into the studio, which publishers were looking for songs, etc. One of the tips we got (and passed on in the magazine) was that Philadelphia International (a record company) was looking for songs for Patti. So we sent in our song just like everyone else.

Now here's the funny part. They actually recorded the song and put it on the album before calling to tell us. They asked for the publishing. At that point we knew we could say no, because they had already recorded the song and put it on the album. We said, "We'll have to consult with our lawyer." We didn't have to give up anything.

Rapaport: Do you write songs with the marketplace in mind?

Luboffs: We stay aware of the marketplace by listening to the radio and watching Country Music Television (CMT). But we do not write with specific artists in mind. We concentrate on the message we want to deliver. We're dedicated to writing uplifting songs and messages we want to hear. We believe that we teach what we want to learn and that each song is a lesson in what the writer has learned about survival. We use our knowledge of the market-

place to make (hopefully) appropriate pitches.

Rapaport: What was it about Nashville that drew you there?

Luboffs: We came for three weeks the first time. Some friends had arranged for us to showcase our songs at one or two clubs. We came on a Monday and by Wednesday our minds were blown. We knew instantly we wanted to move here.

The songwriting culture and community is at the highest level here. In those first days, we heard breathtaking songs you'd never hear on the radio, wouldn't hear unless you were in that room at the time. Almost everywhere we went, we were offered opportunities to play. Writers encourage and support each other at every level of writing here. It is palpable. They show you such immediate respect for what you are doing; every club you play is a nurturing zone; everywhere you go you get the feeling that none of this is about competition, its about encouraging and inspiring each other. So we found ourselves weeping and laughing and stopped in our tracks by the quality of the songs we were hearing and the genuine friendliness of everyone. We felt very welcomed. The message that came across loud and clear is that everybody can do what they want to do, everybody can write about what they think is important, and what's important is to write from the heart. It's a songwriting love fest here. We just jumped right into it and are swimming like dolphins.

Rapaport: What about getting songs placed? Is it easier there?

Luboffs: getting songs placed is always a "Camel through the eye of a needle" proposition, but it does feel easier to get heard here. One of the well-known facts about Nashville is that if you personally walk in the door and drop off a tape or a CD, it will be listened to. Often when a producer or publisher is looking for songs for a project, they leave a box outside of their building or on the steps that's marked for that project. Songwriters just leave their CDs there. We'll go up and down Music Row, going in and out of offices, handing out CDs. Some have rickety backdoor steps, some have fancy reception areas, but in every place you can hand in the CD and know it will get listened to. It's so much fun. It's an adventure. With the current shrinking of the industry, fewer people have more work to do at many of the companies, so you probably won't meet people one-on-one until they hear something that excites them.

We also have a lot of opportunities to meet artists and producers and publishers at professional member gatherings held by The Nashville Songwriters Association International (NSAI), at club showcases and parties. You quickly get to know most all the people who are connected in this business, the system they operate under and how you can fit in.

Inspired by the high level of writing in Nashville and the feeling of mutual support among songwriters here, we're writing great songs. We're being listened to. And we're getting great turndowns. At least if someone calls and says they're "passing" [rejecting] on a song, you know it was heard! Our friend Randy Sharp, who wrote "You Will" and "Then What," among other hits, just told us that all of his hits were turned down many times for years before they were covered. So we're just stacking up the turndowns that could turn into hits.
www.writesongs.com

The Nashville Songwriters Association International

In the United States and Canada, there are many nonprofit songwriters associations dedicated to protecting the rights of songwriters and educating aspiring and professional songwriters in all genres of music. Most provide critiques of members' songs by professionals and educational workshops in the art and business of songwriting.

The largest is the Nashville Songwriters Association International (NSAI), founded in 1967, with more than 5000 members. According to their mission statement, NSAI, "consists of a body of creative minds, including songwriters from all genres of music, professional and amateur, who are committed to protecting the rights and future of the profession of songwriting, and to educate, elevate, and celebrate the songwriter and to act as a unifying force within the music community and the community at large." Their slogan is, "It all begins with a song."

NSAI memberships are divided into four categories:

- *Professional membership—$100 annually.* For songwriters whose primary source of income is derived from songwriting or who are generally recognized as professional songwriters by the professional songwriting community.

- *Active membership—$100 annually.* For songwriters who have at least one song contractually assigned to a music publisher.

- *Associate membership—$100 annually.* For unpublished songwriters or persons that wish to support songwriters.

- *Students—$80 annually.* For full-time college students (12 or more credit hours) or students of an accredited senior high school.

In addition to numerous monthly workshops held in Nashville, NSAI presents over 100 regional workshops in other states, called "Music Row To [name of city/state]" and online workshops.

TinPan South, NSAI's annual songwriting festival, features a day packed with songwriter symposiums and performances by aspiring and professional songwriters. An annual Song Camp, NSAI's three-day songwriting fest, provides an opportunity for songwriters to hone their craft under the guidance of successful, professional songwriting mentors.

NSAI educates members online about legislative and other issues of importance. For example, in 2001, NSAI took 20 Nashville-based songwriters to meet with legislators on the Judiciary and Commerce committees, which have jurisdiction over copyright matters. They protested a bill sponsored by Internet companies that asked for a compulsory license that would have allowed them, for a small payment, to use copyrighted music forever, without the copyright holders sharing in the profits. Their advocacy helped kill the bill.

RESOURCES

SONGWRITER ASSOCIATIONS. THE BEST LIST, BY STATE, OF ASSOCIATIONS THROUGHOUT THE UNITED STATES IS FOUND ON *www.songwriter-suniverse.com/songwriterassociations.html.* THEY REGULARLY UPDATE THEIR LIST.

Canadian Country Music Association (CCMA)
3800 Steeles Avenue West, Suite 127
Woodbridge, Ontario L4L 4G9 Canada
(905) 850-1144
www.ccma.org

Canadian Music Week (CMW)
5399 Eglinton Avenue West, Suite 301
Toronto, Ontario
Canada M9C 5K6
(414) 695-9236
www.cmw.net

Copyright Arbitration Royalty Panel (CARP)
PO Box 70977
Southwest Station
Washington, DC 20024
(202) 707-8380
www.loc.gov/copyright/carp

Country Music Association (CMA)
1 Music Circle South
Nashville, TN 37203
(615) 244-2840
www.countrymusic.org

International Intellectual Property Alliance
(IIPA)
1747 Pennsylvania Avenue NW, Suite 825
Washington, DC 20006-4604
(202) 833-4198
www.iipa.com

International Recording Media Association
(IRMA)
182 Nassau Street, Suite 204
Princeton, NJ 08542-7005
(609) 279-1700
www.recordingmedia.org

Nashville Songwriters Association
International (NSAI)
1701 West End Avenue, 3rd Floor
Nashville, TN 37203
(800) 321-6008 or (615) 256-3354
www.nashvillesongwriters.com

Pea Pod Music
2605 Barclay Drive
Nashville, TN 37206-1507
(615) 277-8195
www.writesongs.com

Recording Industry Association of America
(RIAA)
1330 Connecticut Avenue NW, Suite 300
Washington, DC 20036
(202) 775-0101
www.riaa.org

Society of Composers and Lyricists (SCL)
400 South Beverly Drive, Suite 214
Beverly Hills, CA 90212
(301) 281-2812
www.filmscore.org

Songwriters Association of Canada
31 Madison Avenue, Suite 202
Toronto, Ontario
Canada M5R 2S2
(416) 961-1588
www.songwriters.ca

The Songwriter's Guild of America (SGA)
1222 16th Avenue South, Suite 25
Nashville, TN 37212
(615) 269-7664
www.songwriters.org
   SGA-Hollywood
   6430 Sunset Boulevard, Suite 705
   Hollywood, CA 90028
   (323) 462-1108

   SGA-New York
   1560 Broadway, Suite 1306
   New York, NY 10036
   (212) 768-7902

Songwriter Universe
11684 Ventura Boulevard, Suite 975
Studio City, CA 91604
www.songwriteruniverse.com

United States Copyright Office
Register of Copyrights
Library Of Congress
101 Independence Avenue SE
Washington, DC 20559
(202) 707-3000
www.loc.gov/copyright

United States Patent and
Trademark Office
2021 Jefferson Davis Highway
Arlington, VA 22202
(800) 786-9199 or (703) 308-4357
www.uspto.gov

World Intellectual Property Organization
   (WIPO)
2 United Nations Plaza, Suite 2525
New York, NY 10017
(212) 963-6813
www.wipo.org

World Trade Organization (WIPO)
Centre Wiliam Rappard
Rue de Lausanne 154
CH-1211 Geneva 21, Switzerland
+41 22 739 51 11
www.wto.org

Publishing

* * *

THE BUSINESS OF PUBLISHERS

COLLABORATOR/SONGWRITER AGREEMENTS

INTERVIEW HIGHLIGHT
Michael Eames:
Publisher and Musician

RESOURCE HIGHLIGHT
The Songwriters Guild of America

RESOURCES

The Business of Publishers

Publishing companies help composers exploit their talents by selling and licensing uses of their music in recordings, videos, video games, films, advertising, sheet music and songbooks.

Although some composers have been successful in exploiting their talents themselves, most depend on publishing companies to accomplish this for them. Persuading major publishers to represent composers that do not have major label recording deals is difficult. Even after composers make publishing deals, it is difficult to get publishers to familiarize themselves with their music and actively push their songs over those of more established writers.

Today, publishing companies that are subsidiaries of large entertainment conglomerates dominate the music industry. All have print music divisions. They have long-standing relationships with decision makers, such as record and film producers; they own the rights to the entire catalogues of composers in virtually every genre of music, many of them exceptionally famous; and have the deep pockets that are necessary to pursue infringements on behalf of their clients.

The large entertainment conglomerates have purchased the catalogues of many composers and music publishers. The Beatles catalogue was bought by Michael Jackson, and subsequently Jackson and his properties were acquired by Sony Music Entertainment, Inc. Acquisitions such as these provide two major revenue streams: income from previously manufactured products (e.g., Beatles recordings, etc.) and the exploitation of new revenue sources.

These conglomerates own record, film, video and video game companies (content providers); manufacturing and distribution companies; media providers (TV stations, magazines and books); and Internet content providers. They have the means to control the exploitation of their properties. Conglomerate publishers provide their record companies with music for their artists; conglomerate magazines advertise the recordings and feature the artists editorially; conglomerate TV stations feature the artists; and conglomerate internet subsidiaries place that music on their paid subscription services. The income from all those revenue streams stays within the same conglomerate.

Publishers that are not allied to conglomerates must specialize in particular genres of music or license to particular mediums, such as film. Some are attached to independent labels or are composer owned and operated.

LEGAL REQUIREMENTS

There are no state and federal certifications or licenses required for publishing companies. Publishers must choose a business entity and abide by state statutes governing it. Publishers must abide by the worldwide laws and agreements that govern the intellectual property rights of composers.

HOW PUBLISHERS MAKE MONEY

Publishing companies make money by selling licenses for the use of composers copyrights in commercial ventures. Profits are generated every time music is used in commercial products and played in public performances. The type of use governs the type of license that will be issued and the amount of money it can potentially earn. Licenses are the subject of Segment 4, Music Licensing.

Publishing companies can be exceptionally profitable because they sell services, not products that require production, manufacturing and marketing. There is little cost to publishers other than the salaries paid to their employees. A successful song can generate thousands of revenue streams worldwide.

According to the National Music Publishers Association's (NMPA) *Tenth Annual Income Survey* for the year 1999, U.S. publishers collected $6.57 billion in royalty payments worldwide, which is an increase of 2% over the music revenues of 1998. (The NMPA is a nonprofit trade organization; over 900 U.S. publishing companies are members. See Resource Highlight in Segment 4, Music Licensing.)

U.S. publishers enter into licensing copyrights worldwide (subpublishing). The revenues from foreign sources are extremely lucrative. Only 28% of the total U.S. publishing revenues are derived from sales in the United States. Other large contributors are Japan (14%), Germany (12%), France (9%) and the United Kingdom (9%).

The main sources of publishing revenues are these—

- Performance-based income (revenues collected from performance rights societies worldwide)

- Reproduction-based income (revenues collected for mechanical and synchronization licenses worldwide)

- Print income (royalties collected on sales of sheet music and rentals of videos/DVDs worldwide)

- Investment income (dividends on investments, lawsuit settlements, etc.)

According to the NMPA's survey, revenues for U.S. publishers from sources within the United States during 1999 accounted for $1,816.32 million: $752.29 million in performance-based income; $742.16 million in reproduction-based income; $301 million in print income; and $19.36 million in investment income; and $1.51 million in miscellaneous income.

Of the $752.29 million dollars in performance-based income, satellite broadcasts accounted for $305.54 million and $260.96 million was collected from radio and television broadcasts.

No figures are available at this time for revenues that derived from webcasting and other Internet services.

Division of Revenues

By music industry custom, not law, revenues that are derived from mechanical, print and synchronization licenses or royalties are shared equally between writers and publishers. Monies are collected by the publishing companies and distributed to the writers. Percentages of publishing income can, under certain publishing contracts, be shared between writers and publishers. By music industry custom, not law, writers' revenues are shared only with cowriters.

Publishing companies share income that is derived from print income (sheet music and songbooks) fifty-fifty with writers.

Publishing companies receive the publishers' share of performance rights income; writers are sent their share directly from the performance

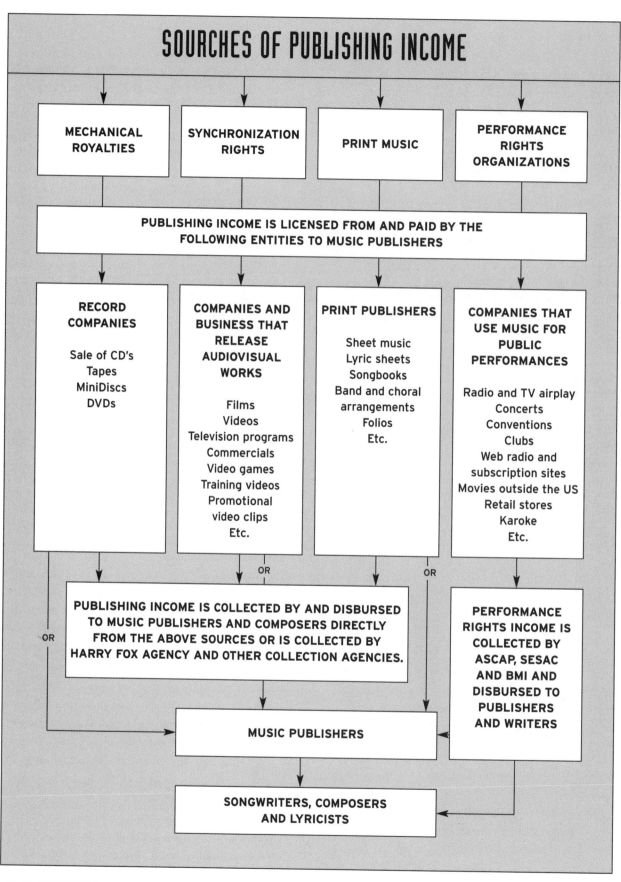

SOURCES OF PUBLISHING INCOME

| MECHANICAL ROYALTIES | SYNCHRONIZATION RIGHTS | PRINT MUSIC | PERFORMANCE RIGHTS ORGANIZATIONS |

PUBLISHING INCOME IS LICENSED FROM AND PAID BY THE FOLLOWING ENTITIES TO MUSIC PUBLISHERS

RECORD COMPANIES

Sale of CD's
Tapes
MiniDiscs
DVDs

COMPANIES AND BUSINESS THAT RELEASE AUDIOVISUAL WORKS

Films
Videos
Television programs
Commercials
Video games
Training videos
Promotional
video clips
Etc.

PRINT PUBLISHERS

Sheet music
Lyric sheets
Songbooks
Band and choral
arrangements
Folios
Etc.

COMPANIES THAT USE MUSIC FOR PUBLIC PERFORMANCES

Radio and TV airplay
Concerts
Conventions
Clubs
Web radio and
subscription sites
Movies outside the US
Retail stores
Karoke
Etc.

OR

OR

PUBLISHING INCOME IS COLLECTED BY AND DISBURSED TO MUSIC PUBLISHERS AND COMPOSERS DIRECTLY FROM THE ABOVE SOURCES OR IS COLLECTED BY HARRY FOX AGENCY AND OTHER COLLECTION AGENCIES.

PERFORMANCE RIGHTS INCOME IS COLLECTED BY ASCAP, SESAC AND BMI AND DISBURSED TO PUBLISHERS AND WRITERS

OR

MUSIC PUBLISHERS

SONGWRITERS, COMPOSERS AND LYRICISTS

rights society, regardless of the type of publishing contract they hold.

The reason that publishing revenues are not higher is the sales of pirated product worldwide. According to the NMPA, the U.S. music industry loses up to $300 million annually in the Ukraine alone.

Through organizations like the NMPA, publishers lobby for new legislation that will increase their revenue sources and licensing fees in the United States, actively work with global world property rights organizations for treaties and other agreements that are protective of U.S. composers' rights; and pursue infringers, through organizations such as the World Intellectual Property Organization (WIPO).

PRINCIPLE JOB RESPONSIBILITIES

Publishers must acquire talent, sell songs and issue licenses, pursue infringers, develop new revenue from sources such as webcasting, streaming and Internet subscription-based services, lobby for laws and regulations that will be favorable to publishers and composers and administer their composers' accounts.

Talent Acquisition
Publishers acquire talent by signing new composers and by buying the catalogues of established talent.

Publishers that are allied with entertainment conglomerates like to sign composers as soon as they make recording deals with major labels. If their recordings become hits, the revenues from licensing, performance and print royalties will be high. Composers like to hold back until they know if they do have hits, because they will have the leverage to negotiate more favorable contract terms with the publishers.

The risk of signing new talent is low because so little expense is involved. A record company that signs new talent will make a considerable investment in recording and marketing that will result in publishing income, even if the recording does not become a hit. If it does become a hit, the publishing company can sit back and collect recording and performing income or it can actively exploit new sources, such as selling songs to other artists to record.

Publishing companies that are not yet allied with conglomerates must actively seek talented composers because if they succeed, their catalogues will become valuable assets.

Valuation of Publishing Catalogues
Before catalogues of composers are acquired, they must be valued. This involves examining how much money they have earned and making projections about their potential earnings.

The first goal is to arrive at the net publisher's income per artist: income less payments to third parties, such as writers' royalties and costs for publishing administration (such as Harry Fox). The income from the last three to five years is calculated. Any income that was derived from a special one-time event, such as the release of a greatest hits recording, is deducted. Once the net publisher's income has been determined for all artists, the average income is calculated for the period.

Then some multiple will be used, for example 8 times the average, to arrive at a sales figure. This figure is always a hotly negotiated item. The basis of the multiple is a combination of tangible and intangible factors. Tangible factors include whether the catalogues were actively exploited and whether collection of all monies due has been aggressive, including audits where necessary. Intangible factors include the value of new songs that composers' might write and record; the potential value of aggressively exploiting new licenses; and the increases to stock prices that may occur because of the increase of a company's net worth due to the combined value of the tangible and intangible assets that were acquired.

One of the most important functions that songwriter associations and music conferences provide is feedback from songwriting and publishing professionals.

Selling Songs

The art of selling songs for uses of composers' music in records, film and television, etc., depends on matching the music to the need. Publishers cultivate relationships with record producers, film and video music supervisors and advertising executives. They understand their tastes in music, know project budgets and can project income. They know the music in their companies' catalogues and the talents of their composers. They match talented lyricists with composers and have them cowrite songs for particular needs.

Publishing companies that are subsidiaries of large entertainment conglomerates have easy access to the decision makers in their record, movie, game and video subsidiaries than their competitors, which provides them with a distinct advantage in selling songs.

Publishers that are not allied with major conglomerates must build relationships with decision makers in nonconglomerate record, film and video companies, low-budget advertising agencies and others that present opportunities the larger publishers often ignore. They must also build relationships with film and television music supervisors at companies owned by conglomerates, because independent publishers can often supply music that fits supervisors' tight budgets, as is often the case with nonprime time sit-coms and pilot projects.

Administration

Publishers conduct title searches, register copyrights and renewals, negotiate and register

transfers; issue mechanical and synch licenses; and collect and allocate revenues. They negotiate contracts with composers and foreign subpublishers; seek mergers and acquisitions; and pursue infringements.

Many publishing companies contract with the Harry Fox Agency (HFA) to process requests for mechanical licenses and collect and distribute mechanical and synch royalties. The HFA typically deducts 3-5% of that income for their services. (See Resource Highlight: NMPA and The Harry Fox Agency in Segment 4, Music Licensing). Canadian publishers use the services of the Canadian Mechanical Rights Reproduction Agency (CMRAA). The HFA processes over 200,000 licenses a year.

CONTRACTS BETWEEN COMPOSERS AND PUBLISHERS

Publishing contracts between composers and publishers are complex. The more famous the composers and the more prestigious their attorneys, the more leverage they have in negotiating favorable terms. Composers whose music has been often listed on pop charts are more sought after than composers that have released records on major labels that have sold less than 100,000 copies. Although publishers seek to acquire new talent and opportunities to build their catalogues, new composers and their managers must ask how much priority are potential publishers will give to exploiting their music.

Given the complexity of these contracts and their long-term implications on composers' careers, composers should use the services of attorneys that specialize in music publishing to negotiate on their behalf.

Types of Contracts

There are four main types of contracts between publishers and composers: single-song agreements, exclusive term songwriter agreements, copublishing agreements and administration agreements. There are no standard agreements: legal representatives for publishers and composers try to negotiate terms that are in the best interests of their clients. The Songwriters Guild of America (see Resource Highlight later in this segment) has a sample contract to help songwriters understand what clauses will most benefit them.

Single-song agreements: Composers transfer ownership of one or more of their copyrights to publishing companies for specified terms, such as one to seven years or for the life of the copyright, during which time the companies will seek to exploit the copyrights. The owners of copyright are the only ones that can license their use.

These contracts contain clauses that enable composers to sign similar agreements for other songs they have written with other publishers.

Publishers seek single-song agreements when they hear songs they feel would be recorded by other artists or are suitable for a particular film or television show or that fill particular needs.

Exclusive term songwriter agreements: Publishing companies sign composers for specified amounts of time, generally one to seven years, or for the life of the composers' copyright. The word exclusive is used because during the term of these contracts, composers may only write songs for the publishing companies and the copyrights are owned by the publishing companies. In return, composers receive advances and weekly salaries, which will be recouped from the composers' first earnings from the writers' shares of publishing income. These are not work-for-hire contracts (unless there is specific language to that effect). The copyrights are usually transferred back to the composers when the term of the contract has expired.

Composers make exclusive term agreements because that assures them of stable incomes, which enable them to compose full-time, and they believe that their publishers will introduce their work to record producers and film and video music supervisors that they could not access themselves. Publishers may also have particular recording artists that are excellent matches or collaborators for their composers.

Copublishing agreements: Composers share copyright ownership with their publishing companies and share percentages of publishing revenue. Copublishing contracts are generally reserved for composers that have proven their value in the marketplace.

Administration agreements: Publishers accept administration duties. They issue and keep track of mechanical licenses and foreign sublicenses, register compositions with performance rights organizations and collect and disburse publishing income. Fees range from 7% to 25% of the publishing income, depending on the scope of services. Composers retain ownership of their copyrights.

Publishers that have administration agreements may, because of their industry contacts, be able to place a song in a television or film. At that point, they may ask to share some of the publishing income because they helped place the song. A contract that specifies the terms of that agreement will then be made.

Areas of Negotiation

Here are important areas for negotiation in publishing contracts—

- *Copyright ownership:* In single-song and exclusive term contracts, copyrights are generally transferred to publishing companies for the term of the contract in order to provide them with the rights to license the works in all mediums. Care must be taken in the latter contract to avoid any language that makes the composers' services works for hire. The contracts should specify that copyrights are transferred back to composers after contracts have expired.

Copyrights in copublishing deals are generally co-owned by the composer and publisher.

Copyrights in administration agreements are owned by the composers, who are acting as their own publishers.

- *Term:* Contracts can be for specified periods of time, such as one to seven years, or be tied to the life of a record deal (if the publisher and record company are owned by the same conglomerate).

- *Advances and royalty payments:* In single-song and exclusive term contracts, advances to composers to be recouped from royalty payments are made based on their leverage and on the negotiating skills of their attorneys. They can be one-time advances or monthly advances. The composers receive 100% of the writers' shares. In copublishing contracts, composers assign percentage shares of publishing revenue to publishing companies, generally 25%. This means that when publishing companies receive $10,000 in licensing income, they send 50% of the writers' share ($5000) and 25% of the publisher's share ($2500)—a total of $7500 to the composers.

- *Administration expenses:* Publishers must be clear about how administrations expenses will be dealt with. These include fees for copyright registrations, fees to Harry Fox Agency and fees expended for the collection of monies from foreign sublicenses. Some contracts state that publishing companies will subtract a percentage, generally 10%, of gross income from the writers and composers share and apply it to administration expenses. Some specify that the 10% will only be subtracted from the publishers' share; others will subtract the 10% from the writers' share. Others

state that only the actual expenses will be deducted from gross income from writers' and publishers' shares or from only the writers' or only the publishers' share.

- *Cancellation and reversion:* Composers' attorneys should seek terms under which they can cancel their publishing agreements and have their copyrights revert to them. They should specify the conditions under which their copyrights will be returned, for example, if their music has had not had charted hits within two years or has not been placed in feature films within three years. Generally, reversion clauses specify that all monies advanced to composers must be recouped before reversions are final.

- *Alteration of music:* When composers transfer copyright ownership to publishers, their attorneys will try to limit the right of the publishers to alter music or to make derivative works without the composers' consents. If publishers do make derivative works, new copyrights will be filed and the publishers may be able to participate in the writers' share of any new licenses issued for the derivative work because, in effect, they become collaborative composers.

- *Consent for certain uses:* Composers' attorneys should ask that publishers get their written consents if their music is to be used for religious, moral or political purposes or in advertising.

- *Assignment of contracts:* Generally, publishing contracts remain in force when publishing companies sell their companies or merge with other companies. Attorneys may try to limit this right by providing composers with options to buy back their rights.

COMPOSERS CAN FORM THEIR OWN PUBLISHING COMPANIES

Many composers own their own publishing companies and exploit their works themselves. They file copyrights and collect performance royalties as writers and publishers. They make written agreements with cocomposers about how earnings are to be shared. (See the article, Collaborator/Songwriter Agreements, later in this segment.) They sell songs and issue use licenses.

The first step is to determine whether their talents warrant making the business of publishing worth pursuing. Composers need objective, professional critiques of their writing capabilities. One of the most important functions that songwriter associations and music conferences provide is feedback from songwriting and publishing professionals.

Composers that publish themselves must develop professional relationships with people that will license their songs—performers; record, film and video producers; advertising agency executives, etc. Music conferences, workshops, songwriters associations are the places that composers can make those business contacts.

Some composers also perform and make and sell their own recordings. They prove their worth in the marketplace by establishing fan bases and getting reviews and airplay. Their CDs are the primary means for introducing their music to business professionals.

Composers that do not perform and do not live close to major music centers, such as New York, Los Angeles, Nashville and Montreal, have a more difficult time introducing their music to industry professionals. Because they do not perform, they do not gather fan bases; without performances, radio stations are reluctant to grant airplay; and publishers and producers do not open unsolicited material.

When composers do have access to music industry professionals, they must be good salespeople and have the ability to know when their music does and does not fit particular needs. Composers have to pick out songs they might feel are appropriate and sell them. Yes, songs more or less sell themselves, *if* they get heard, but composers have to present the songs to key decision-makers and make sure they are heard.

The important steps in forming publishing companies are to—

- Ensure that the name of the company is original

- Choose a business entity and obtain the licenses that are required by state statutes

- Join a performance rights organization as writers *and* publishers

SONGSHARKS AND QUESTIONABLE PRACTICES

Some companies advertise in popular songwriting and music magazines that they will help composers publish their songs or send the songs to publishing companies. Some are legitimate companies; others are songsharks that gobble money for no benefit to composers. Composers must learn the difference by researching reputations, references and successes. Most attorneys and songwriter associations can distinguish between legitimate and illegitimate companies and advise composers whether they will be wasting their talents, time and money in pursuing them.

Songsharks urge composers to send them copies of the songs (cassettes, lead sheets, etc). Then they ask for fees to record demos and to pay for mailing costs to send them to record and film producers. They do not offer to meet with the composers and the composers have no say about how their music is recorded. If these companies make 500 CDs, sell 5 CDs to friends, and mail the rest out via bulk mail to record and film producers, they have fulfilled their obligations and cannot be cited for fraud. They have "published"

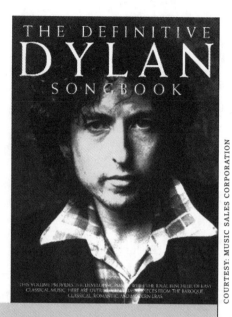

ONE OF PRINT MUSIC PUBLISHER MUSIC SALES' STRONGEST SELLERS IN 2001 WAS THE 850-PAGE *The Definitive Dylan Songbook.* THAT SAME YEAR DYLAN CAME OUT WITH HIS ALBUM *Love & Theft* AND SUPPORTED IT WITH LIVE PERFORMANCES. THIS STIMULATED PEOPLE TO LEARN MORE ABOUT THE ARTIST AND HIS SONGS.

the composers' songs because they have made them available for sale to the general public and fulfilled their promise to mail them to record and film producers. Composers are not told that the people that receive these demos send them back unopened.

Some producers risk their own money to record promising talents and present them to record companies in the hope of making deals for themselves and their artists. They sign artists contingent on receiving some share of the revenues their compositions bring in (a piece of the publishing).

Sometimes producers enhance, arrange or rework composers' songs and ask composers to file new copyright registrations for the derivative works and name the producers as coauthors.

Whether producers are entitled to share in publishing revenues in these cases is controversial.

On one hand, producers risk time and capital on composers' behalfs and want to be compensated for that risk. Depending on the degree of enhancement, they may be entitled to coauthorship. On the other hand, if the demos are turned down, composers have given away pieces of their copyrights for no gain and may find themselves at disadvantages when they make future recording deals. Composers must seek the advice of their attorneys before making such deals.

PRINT MUSIC PUBLISHERS

The publishing of sheet music is an extremely lucrative business, which accounts for approximately $300 million annually. These publishers are referred to as print music publishers to distinguish them from music and book publishers.

There are three primary markets: pop music (current popular music in all categories), church music and serious music (classical, jazz).

Pop sheet music is an integral part of musical instrument stores. They also carry instruction books for vocalists and individual instruments.

The primary buyers of serious music are educational institutions, symphony, ballet and opera orchestras, choral groups, chamber music groups, musical theater groups and the U.S. military. These buyers generally will buy directly from music publishers.

A great deal of serious music is in the public domain. This means that no use licenses are required from music publishers. However, if arrangements for particular pieces of music have been copyrighted by music publishers, use licenses must be acquired from them by the print music publisher and royalties must be paid for each copy sold and paid for.

Music that is not in the public domain must be licensed for print use from audio publishing companies. Print music publishers generally pay music publishers companies a percentage of the retail price (12%-25% royalty) of each copy that has been sold and paid for and the monies disbursed to composers according to the contracts they have signed.

Several nonprofit organizations serve the print music industry, including the Music Publishers Association (MPA), the Church Music Publishers Association (CMPA) and the Retail Print Music Dealers Association (RPMDA). These are listed in the Resources section at the end of this segment.

CONCLUSION

Revenues that are earned by publishers depend on the talent they acquire and the competence with which they pursue exploitation and protect their copyrights and the diligence with which they pursue collections. They must have good contacts with industry professionals and keep abreast of musical and technological changes to ensure that their composers are paid for the use of their work in new mediums. Many publishers are members of the National Music Publishers Association (NMPA), which works with the Copyright Office and the Copyright Arbitration Royalty Panels to protect publishers' and composers' rights and to lobby on their behalf when new laws are proposed.

Collaborator/Songwriter Agreements

MARK HALLORAN AND EDWARD R. HEARN

]f you cowrite a song with someone, both of you own the song as "joint owners" in what the copyright law calls a "joint work." This is irrespective of whether one of you writes the music and the other the lyrics, or you both write music and lyrics. Both of you have an "undivided" ownership in the song (i.e., you each own 50% of the whole song). There is not a separate copyright in the music and lyrics. There is one copyright in both.

The essence of cowriting is writing together to create a single song, regardless of who contributes what. This does not mean that you have to work together, or that your creative contribution be equal in quality or quantity. You also do not need to have an express "collaboration agreement," although it is a good idea, given the myriad issues that can arise.

One of the most famous cowriting teams is Bernie Taupin and Elton John. Bernie, on his own, first writes the lyrics. John, on his own, then writes the music. Since both Bernie and Elton intend that their work be a united whole, the result is a joint work, which they co-own fifty-fifty.

PERCENTAGE OWNERSHIP

As joint owners you and your cowriter can divide your song ownership in whatever proportion you want. In the absence of an agreement you share equally, even if it is clear that your contributions are not equal. Thus, if there are two songwriters, you own the song fifty-fifty; three songwriters, one-third each; etc. Dividing the ownership ratably is also the most common way to divide ownership in a written collaboration agreement.

One common benchmark in dividing ownership is that the lyrics are worth 50% and the music 50%. For example, if two people write the music and one person writes the lyrics, they may agree to divide the ownership 25% each for the two music writers, with the lyricist retaining the remaining 50%. However, if there is no such agreement, each would own 33.3% of the song.

GRANT OF RIGHTS

Now that we have determined who owns the song, who controls it? It is crucial to the exploitation of the song that there be a central place to license the work and collect money.

Coadministration of Licenses

It is usually more convenient for one music publisher to collect and divide all the income. Licensing can become complicated when a licensee has to seek the approval of, and document permission from, multiple publishers. However, many cowriters prefer that there be separate administration among the various publishing companies. This has its advantages. You have control over to whom licenses are granted, how much is charged, how the money is collected and what costs are incurred.

As joint owner (in the United States), you may exploit the song yourself and also grant nonexclusive licenses. Still, you must account to your cowriters for the money that is generated from the nonexclusive licenses.

A license is permission to use a work. It is not a transfer of copyright ownership, which requires the permission of all songwriters (although you could transfer just your share to another without affecting the ownership interests of the other cowriters/co-owners) (see discussion below).

- *Public performances:* Public performances agreements must be entered into with ASCAP, BMI or SESAC. Typically, they are done in the name of the songwriter's publishing company. If cowriters want to use one company, they may use that company and divide the publisher's share of the income. Or, each of the separate publishing companies may enter into a performance agreement for its share with ASCAP, BMI or SESAC with each collecting its respective percentage of the publisher's share of the public performance income. Writers should join ASCAP, BMI or SESAC to collect their portion of the songwriters' shares of the public performance income.

- *Mechanical licenses:* Mechanical licenses are nonexclusive, any cowriter can grant them, but must account to and pay the other cowriters, or instruct the licensed party that the cowriter's shares be paid directly to them.

- *Print rights:* These agreements are usually exclusive, and all cowriters must agree in writing.

- *Subpublishing rights:* Foreign subpublishing

deals are usually exclusive, and all cowriters must agree in writing. Additionally, most foreign jurisdictions require that all co-owners agree to licensing, so the subpublishers are going to want to have all cowriters sign. If agreement cannot be reached on a shared subpublisher, you can, however, still make arrangements with one to represent just your interest share in the songs' copyrights.

DIVISION OF INCOME

A writer is also entitled to the same ratable share of income, absent an agreement to the contrary.

PURSUIT OF INFRINGEMENT

One obligation that cowriters have together is to protect the copyright. This includes pursuing infringers. Can you sue even if a co-owner does not want to sue? The answer appears to be yes, at least with respect to your interest in the copyright. However, the court may require that you bring in the cowriter(s) as a coplaintiff, so it is best that you decide to sue together.

What if you have to sue a co-owner, for example, for failure to account to and pay you? You may, but you do not have to, bring in all the other co-owners in order to sue.

COPYRIGHT DURATION

The basic rule is that the copyright of a song written after January 1, 1976 lasts for the life of the author plus 70 years. In the case of a joint work, the copyright lasts for the life of the last surviving author plus 70 years.

COPYRIGHT TRANSFERS

Each collaborator, independently of the other collaborators, has the right to transfer his or her copyright ownership to another party. That transfer may be for the full copyright share of the collaborator to a publisher, or a partial copyright transfer to a copublisher. A collaborator may also grant all administration and supervision rights of that collaborator's share to a third party as the publishing administrator, while still retaining ownership of the copyright.

If one collaborator transfers his or her copyright interests to a third party, but the second collaborator does not do the same, then the third party would co-own the copyright with the other collaborator. At the same time, the second collaborator has the option to transfer his or her copyright interest, in the whole or in part, or just the administration rights, to the same new owner as did the first collaborator, or to a different party.

Unless either collaborator has granted to the other collaborator the administration rights in the copyright for the song, the new co-owner will have to share decision-making and the publisher's income share with the collaborator that did not transfer his or her interests. The accounting can become cumbersome if income sharing and accounting procedures are not coordinated.

DIFFERENT PERFORMING RIGHTS SOCIETY AFFILIATIONS

It is also possible for each coauthor to belong to a different performing rights society, namely ASCAP, BMI or SESAC. If that is the case, then a share of the performance income collection would be allocated to each collaborator's affiliated performing rights society. For example, if the song is performed as a part of a soundtrack to a television program, then, with the performance rights for that song being divided between two different performing rights groups, the performance fee also would be so divided. Each performing rights group would receive its allocated share and distribute it to the collaborator affiliated with it. It is quite possible that one collaborator, being paid by

a different performing rights society, would not receive the same amount of writer and publisher performance income as the other, since each of the performing rights societies uses a different reporting mechanism.

SONGWRITERS AS MEMBERS OF DIFFERENT BANDS

In the event one of the collaborating songwriters is a member of a band and the other is not, the collaborator who is a member of the band will have the authority to allow the band to rehearse and perform the collaborated song in live concerts and to record the song for release on phonorecords. While, technically, it is best to have both writers approve and issue a combined use license, i.e., a mechanical license to reproduce the song on phonorecords, each has the authority to do so, but must account to the collaborator who is not a band member for their share of writer and publisher income. Most record labels will want to get both coauthors and copublishers to provide written authorization for the initial reproduction of that song on phonorecords. After the first release of the phonorecords, a compulsory mechanical license procedure may apply to any future recordings of that song, whether by that same or any other band.

CONTROLLED COMPOSITION CLAUSE

Of particular significance is the situation where one of the coauthors is a band member (while the other is not) and has a recording agreement with a record label that requires the writer/band member to agree to a controlled composition clause in the recording agreement. This clause authorizes the record company to pay a reduced mechanical royalty, usually 75% of the prevailing statutory mechanical rate, as the royalty fee for the right to reproduce the song on phonorecords that are sold to the public.

Generally, the recording artist/collaborating writer will be required by the record company to represent that he or she has obtained permission from the collaborating writer who is not the band member and not a signatory to the recording agreement to issue a mechanical license for the reduced rate. But often, the recording artist/collaborating writer cannot guarantee that, and most likely will not be able to provide the record label with written authorization from the collaborator accepting a reduced mechanical royalty rate. In those situations, the record company will have to pay the collaborating writer who is not a member of the band nor a signatory to the recording agreement that cowriter's share of mechanicals, both as writer and copublisher, at full statutory rate, while paying the collaborator, who is a signatory, the reduced rate. It is also possible that the rate for the recording artist/collaborating writer will be reduced even further, given the need to pay the unsigned collaborator the higher amount, which will reduce the amount available to pay the recording artist/collaborating writer.

By way of illustration, assume that the maximum pool of mechanical royalties for all of the songs on the recording artist's album is 60¢ (75% of 80¢), as distinct from the current statutory rate of 8¢ per song, which would earn 80¢ if ten songs are on the album. The payout to the collaborating coauthor who is not a signatory to the recording agreement will reduce the overall pool available for mechanical royalties, causing the amount payable to the collaborator/band member to be even less than the 75% fractional statutory rate. For example, if that nonsignatory collaborating coauthor has contributed half of the material on four different songs, he/she will get full statutory for his/her share of those songs, .5 x 8¢ x 4 = 16¢, which will be deducted from the maximum pool of 60¢, leaving 44¢ to be allocated to the signatory collaborating songwriters for the other six songs that were fully written by them and for the other four coauthored by them with the nonsignatory collaborator. This is effectively 7.66¢ for each full song and 3.83¢ for each of the four collaborated songs.

COACCOUNTING

Any income that either collaborating writer receives from the commercial exploitation of the song, whether it is from their own use or from use by an authorized third party, must be accounted for and apportioned to the other collaborating songwriter. Such payments should be made in a timely manner, for example, no less than 30 days after receipt. Also, statements that accompany the payments to the first collaborator should be copied and forwarded with the payment to the other collaborator.

FUTURE GENERATIONS

The rights of each deceased coauthor will pass on to the benefit of the heir(s) and descendant(s) of that coauthor, either by way of a will (testate) or without a will (intestate). If there is no will, the distribution will be governed by state statutes, usually to surviving spouses and children, on a first priority basis, before other relatives. It then would be the heir or the executor of the estate of the deceased who will have the authority to grant and make decisions with respect to the use of a collaborated composition. By the same token, the surviving collaborator will have the authority to continue to exploit the song while having a reporting and payment sharing obligation to the deceased's descendants or executor. The estate of the deceased collaborator can exploit the song too, and must account to the surviving coauthor.

Michael Eames:
Publisher and Musician

MICHAEL EAMES is President of PEN Music Group, Inc., a full-service music publishing company he cofounded in 1994 with Pat Hoyman. The company presents songwriters and composers with an alternative to the multinational music publishing companies.

PEN Music Group administers the publishing catalogues of such artists as Dave Mason, Oleta Adams, Devo and its cofounder Mark Mothersbaugh, The Captain and Tennille, Dan Bern, E.G. Daily, Michael Ruff and Gypsy Soul; writer/producers such as Mark Nubar, John Scott, Jeeve, and Matt and Paul Sherrod; and existing catalogues such as Westbury Music Consultants, Ltd./Fairwood Music, Ltd. (of London) and Conway Music Group. The company places around 20 songs per month in film and TV projects. PEN songs are found on records by artists, such as Macy Gray, O-Town, Brooke Allison, A.J. Croce, Basement Jaxx and Lina, among numerous others.

Prior to PEN, Michael oversaw the international activities and film and television department of Don Williams Music Group where he was responsible for the song catalogues of Jimi Hendrix, Chicago, Roy Orbison and numerous others.

Michael has an undergraduate degree from Cornell University in Music and Business Management and has also completed the film scoring certificate program at UCLA Extension. He is a trained composer, songwriter and keyboardist.

PHOTO: ??????

* * * * * * *

Rapaport: You came to LA with the $5000 you got from selling your piano. What was your dream?

Eames: My dream was to become a film and television composer and to pay my way in the interim by playing piano at recording sessions. Essentially, I cannot say I had it mapped out in my mind any more than that. I was a good piano player at Cornell, but I jumped into a very big pond full of a lot of great fish that could play circles around me. It was a very healthy reality check to see how many great people were here.

Rapaport: What were the next lessons you learned?

Eames: I was lucky to land a job working with Brian Wilson of the Beach Boys as an office and studio assistant. In many respects, success is not directly related to talent but to the opportunities people develop and who they know. This is a business built on relationships.

Second, it gave me a good look at how competitive and how little known the music publishing field was. There was very little written information on publishing and music supervision and not a whole lot of seminars. Essentially, you learned on the job.

Finally, I learned that even if a song only has a modicum of success that it can earn its composers a lot of money. They can make money from all over the world while they sleep.

Rapaport: What was the advantage of working for small companies and not going to work for one of the larger ones?

Eames: At a big company, I would have probably learned to wear only one hat. In the companies I worked for, we had to do everything: place songs on recordings and in films; write foreign subpublishing agreements; collect royalties, etc. Don Williams was especially great: anything I wanted to learn he would teach me or let me dive in. I excel in those environments.

Rapaport: What advantage does a small publisher like yours have over the large ones?

Eames: Even though there are wonderful people that work at the large companies, they have millions and millions of songs to look after. There are only so many songs that they can actively take care of and that means some artists are just going to get lost.

These days, the only reason it would make sense for a songwriter or composer to get involved in a large company was (1) if they are offering a ridiculous amount of money that would be stupid to turn down (2) you are such a hot commodity, there is some chance they might pay you the attention you need and deserve. Otherwise your music gets put into a filing cabinet and the only way to get it out of there is to basically schmooze people there to pay attention or to put very tight termination clauses into your contract.

These days, the major motivation for multinational companies to become involved in publishing deals is to gain market share. The more properties you own, the larger the market share. At the end of the year, the people responsible for helping increase it keep their jobs, even if the companies never recoup the money they put out. Bragging rights are more important than delivering what is implied in the contracts: exploiting the works.

A small company like ours cannot afford to outlay money that is not going to come back to us and cannot afford to disappoint our songwriters. If they do not make money from our efforts, we do not make money. At the end of the day, what counts is our reputation for delivering what we promised. Period.

Rapaport: Why did you start your own company?

Eames: Well, once I felt I had learned most everything, the next logical step seemed to be to hang out my own shingle and see what would happen. I knew I did not want to be restricted

In many respects, success is not directly related to talent but to the opportunities people develop and who they know. This is a business built on relationships.

to just one aspect of the business, as I most likely would have at a larger company

And I took the long-term view. Hey, I want to do this for the rest of my life. And the only way to do that is to take responsibility for the successes and the failures and reap the rewards when I succeed.

Rapaport: Why failures? Most entrepreneurs only think about success?

Eames: Failure is a part of life and it is a real part of the music business. You cannot secure every film or record you go after. You meet up with a lot of noes in this business.

Failure is also taking responsibility for mistakes and learning from them rather than letting yourself be defeated by them.

One thing that I had heard from friends at large companies is how politics are played out in a corporate environment. Since everyone is basically out to protect their jobs, if something does go wrong, the first thing that happens is they look at whom they can blame. I pretty much knew that I did not have the patience to deal with that.

In my business, if I make a mistake, I will immediately own up to it. And you know what, our clients appreciate it.

I also looked at the worst case scenario: if I fail at this business, I will have met so many people along the way that I would have increased my chances at finding a really good gig ten-fold.

Rapaport: So what niche did you go for? What did you see as being the opportunity?

Eames: We started the hardest way, doing administration deals with song-writers and composers that owned their own publishing and not giving them any advance. The pitch we offered was this: "We know you own your own publishing and we do not want a piece of that. But we would like to dedicate some resources to help generate some income for you that does not currently exist. When we do, we would like some percentage of that deal. That is a win-win for both of us. That means if we place a song in a film, we only make money on that deal. And of course, this puts the pressure on us to deliver."

Rapaport: What was your first success?

Eames: Through the Don Williams job, I met Francis Pettican, who owned his own music publishing company in London. There was an instant connection. When he learned I would be going out on my own, he said, "Let me know when you do that; maybe we can do some business together." Two weeks after I started PEN, he called and said, "We do not have anyone in the United States looking after us and we have not been particularly happy with Harry Fox." I said, "Send me a few titles and we will see what we can do."

The first thing I did was to get a printout from Harry Fox of the licenses they had issued for the titles Pettican gave us. And the first thing I noticed was that HFA had forgotten to issue a mechanical license for one of the titles. So I checked further and found that there was $12,000 sitting to be claimed just from that one title. And that was in the first week. So, of course, Francis was happy. The next thing that happened was that he asked us to administer Oleta Adams work in the

United States. I was thrilled because I had been a huge fan of hers for years!

Rapaport: What are the principles of business that you operate with?

Eames: First, I am only going to be honest and straightforward about everything. In the corporate world, it takes time and energy to attempt to not necessarily lie, but to protect your butt. There is a lot of time and energy wasted doing that and I do not have time or patience. In all of our dealings, I am going to be direct and honest about what I have done and not done. That is how I have developed rapport and trust among our clients.

Second, we are doing business fair and straightforward. I have never been audited by any of my clients, but I look forward to it because there will be no money to find. We pay out all of the money as it is earned.

Third, as clichéd as this sounds, I am a very hard and dedicated worker. I have been doing this for almost eight years now and I work 70 to 80 hours a week. And the work is beginning to pay off. I know that if I do not work, I do not make money. Ownership of a business is equity, but to get the equity you have to work.

Fourth, we pay attention to all our writers, we have a diverse pool of income. We do not want to count on only one writer to be our bread and butter.

Finally, I try to create a place for employees to work in that I would like-a place where people believe in what they do, have fun and share a common goal.

www.penmusic.com

The Songwriters Guild of America

The nonprofit Songwriters Guild of America (SGA) provides songwriters with information, education and programs to further their careers in the music industry. It is an advocate for the promotion of fair contracts with publishing companies.

SGA services include—

- A songwriting contract that sets forth favorable royalty rates for licensed uses and reversion clauses for songwriters

- Review of publishing/songwriter contracts

- Royalty collection plan

- Audits of publishing companies

- Catalog administration

- Financial evaluation of catalogs

- Group life and medical insurance

- Educational programs

Songwriting workshops and songwriting critique sessions are regularly held in New York, Nashville and Los Angeles

Newsletters keep members up to date on songwriting workshops and relevant lawsuits and legislation.

The SGA's nonprofit educational foundation offers university scholarship grants.

Annual dues are as follows—

- *Associate member* (nonpubished songwriter)—$70

- *Regular member* (published songwriter)—$85 to $450 depending on the amount of royalties collected by the Guild from your publishers during the prior year.

- *Estate members* (estates and heirs of deceased songwriters)—$70 to $400 depending on the amount of royalties collected from publishers during the prior year.

The National Academy of Songwriters (NAS) became part of the SGA in 1999.

RESOURCES

Association of Independent Music Publishers
(AIMP)
120 East 56th Street
New York, NY 10022
(212) 758-6157
www.aimp.org
AIMP
P.O. Box 1561
Burbank, CA 91507-1561
(818) 842-6257

Church Music Publishers Association (CMPA)
PO Box 158992
Nashville, TN 37215
(615) 791-0273
www.cmpamusic.org

The Harry Fox Agency, Inc. (HFA)
711 3rd Avenue
New York, NY 10017
(212) 370-5330
www.harryfox.com

International Publishers Association (IPA)
Av. Sarriá 130-132
08017 Barcelona, Spain
+ 34 93 252 3701
www. ipa-uie.org

Music Publishers' Association (MPA)
PMB 246
1562 First Avenue
New York, NY 10028
(212) 327-4044
www.mpa.org

Music Sales Corporation
257 Park Avenue South
New York, NY 10010
(212) 254-2100
www.musicsales.com

National Music Publishers Association (NMPA)
475 Park Avenue South
New York, NY 10016-6901
(646) 742-1651
www.nmpa.org

Retail Print Music Dealers Association
(RPMDA)
13140 Coit Road Suite 320, LB 120
Dallas, TX 75240-5737
(972) 233-9107
www.printmusic.org

The Songwriter's Guild of America (SGA)
1222 16th Avenue South, Suite 25
Nashville, TN 37212
(615) 269-7664
www.songwriters.org

TAXI
5010 North Parkway Calabasas, Suite 200
Calabasas, CA 91302
(800) 458-2111
www.taxi.com

NOTES

Music Licensing

* * *

LICENSING MUSIC

SAMPLING
by Gregory T. Victoroff

INTERVIEW HIGHLIGHT
Michael Laskow: Founder, TAXI

RESOURCE HIGHLIGHTS
The National Music Publishers
Association
The Harry Fox Agency
The Future of Music Coalition

RESOURCES

Licensing Music

Copyright laws protect composers against the unauthorized alteration and use of their works without permission and lay the foundation for paying copyright holders for the use of their music in commercial applications. The U.S. Copyright Act also provides the means to control the use and compensation of compositions in different mediums through the issuance of licenses.

Use licenses are issued by composers and publishers (they can be the same entity) to users. The division of the monies between composers and publishers received from these licenses is governed by contracts. (The business of publishers is discussed in Segment 3, Publishing.)

Licenses must be issued by composers and publishers each time their music is—

- Recorded, reproduced and sold via cassettes, vinyl records, CDs, DVDs, minidisks, etc. (mechanical licenses)

- Recorded and sold as permanent downloads from the Internet (mechanical licenses)

- Played publicly on radio, television, internet or other media (performance rights licenses)

- Used as segues in radio and television shows (mechanical license)

- Used in film, video, TV and video games (synch licenses)

- Used in advertising commercials (synch licenses)

- Sold as sheet music (sheet music licenses)

The use of a song in one medium, such as a CD, does not automatically confer the use on another CD, such as a compilation CD, or another use, such as a film. Licenses are issued for each use, which results in multiple sources of publishing income.

RESEARCHING SONG OWNERSHIP

Companies and individuals that do not know the names of the composers or publishers of material they wish to use must research song ownership. The first place to look for song ownership is on the covers, sleeves and discs of recordings, which will reveal the composer's name and often, the publishing company and performing rights society they are affiliated with.

If that copyright information is absent, songs can be researched on the Harry Fox Agency's (HFA) online database *www.songfile.com*. The HFA is the world's largest information source, clearinghouse and monitoring service for licensing musical copyrights.

WHAT A RECORDED SONG EARNS AT THE STATUTORY MECHANICAL RATE

EARNINGS BELOW ARE BASED ON ONE SONG, FIVE MINUTES OR SHORTER IN LENGTH.

Amount sold	2002-2003	2004-2005	2006-2007
1000.00	$80.00	$85.00	$90.10
10,000.00	$800.00	$850.00	$900.10
100,000.00	$8,000.00	$8,500.00	$9,001.00
1,000,000.00	$80,000.00	$85,000.00	$90,010.00

Searchers can make phone inquiries about whether a song is listed with ASCAP, BMI or SESAC. They do not have online databases.

The U.S. Copyright Office has a research service. It also maintains an online database of all songs catalogued after January 1, 1978 (*http://www.loc.gov/copyright/search/cohm.html*). For songs catalogued before then, researchers can go to the Library of Congress in Washington, D.C. and search the card catalogues. When the copyright office makes the search, the fee is $65 an hour.

COMPULSORY MECHANICAL LICENSES

According to provisions of the Act, once compositions are published (sold to the public), publishers must issue compulsory mechanical licenses to record companies for their use on recordings sold in the United States.

The right to reproduce (record) songs for the first time belongs to composers. They can exercise that right in one of two ways: they can record the songs themselves, as is done by many singer songwriters, or they can transfer that copyright to someone else via a written contract. In either case, publishing companies will issue mechanical licenses to record companies for use of the songs.

Anyone that replicates music in quantity and makes it available to the public is considered to be a record company—major, independent and artist-owned record labels, churches, schools, community groups, nonprofit organizations, Internet-only businesses, etc. A record company could be JOE SMITH songwriter who makes and sells his own recordings; or JOE SMITH MOTORCYCLE BUSINESS that manufactures 25,000 CDs of favorite motorcycle songs to sell to its mailing list of business customers; or an individual who wants to manufacture 50 CDS that contain some of their favorite dance music to distribute to their friends at Christmas.

According to the U.S. Copyright Act, record companies must—

- File a notice of intention with publishers before recordings are distributed

- Pay composers the statutory rate set by the U.S. Copyright Act or a negotiated rate for the use of the song, or a portion of the song, for each recording sold and paid for

- Not change the melody and words (unless permission has been granted in writing by the copyright holder)

- Make regular accountings of all records sold and paid for

Separate payments, termed record royalties, are paid by record companies to the performers of recordings. (See Segment 8, Record Companies.)

Statutory Rate

From January 1, 2002 to December 31, 2003, the statutory rate is 8.0 cents per song or 1.55 cents per minute, whichever amount is larger, per record sold.

From January 1, 2004 to December 31, 2005, the rate will be 8.5 cents per song or 1.65 cents per minute, whichever amount is larger.

From January 1, 2006 to December 31, 2007, the rate will be 9.1 cents per songs or 1.75 cents per minute, whichever amount it larger.

Controlled Composition Rates

Recording companies can negotiate lower statutory rates than the law specifies with composers and publishers, typically 75% of the minimum statutory rate, and limit the number of songs on recordings that will receive mechanical royalties. The recording contract clause that governs this negotiation is called a "Controlled Composition Clause." The negotiation of this type of clause can become quite complex when the songs are written by several collaborators, only some of whom are actually involved in recording. (See "Songwriter/Collaborator Agreements," Segment 3, Publishing).

Share of Mechanical License Income

Income from mechanical licenses is divided between publishing companies and songwriters according to the contracts they have signed. The songwriters and the publishers can be the same entity. (See Segment 3, Publishing.)

When singer/songwriters and record companies are the same, as in the case of musicians that have made and sold their own recordings, no mechanical royalties are paid. However singer/songwriters can exploit the use of their songs in other ways, such as selling them to other artists to record.

EXAMPLE OF A CONTROLLED COMPOSITION CLAUSE

(1) You grant to Label and its Licensees and their designees an irrevocable license, under copyright, to reproduce each Controlled Composition on Phonograph Records of Master Recordings made under this Agreement, other than Audiovisual Records and to distribute them in the United States and Canada.

(2) For that license, Label will pay Mechanical Royalties, on the basis of Net Sales, at the following rate: The rate equal to seventy-five percent (75%) of the minimum compulsory license rate applicable to the use of Compositions on phonorecords under the United States copyright law on the date of initial release of the Master Recording concerned.

(3) The total Mechanical Royalty for all Compositions on any Album, including Controlled Compositions will be limited to ten times the amount which would be payable.

Once a song is published, the songwriter has exercised one of their copyrights—the right to reproduce their work for the first time. Then other artists can record the song as long as the record companies fulfill the requirements of the U.S. Copyright Act and obtain compulsory mechanical licenses from the publishers and pay for use. Publishers and composers cannot refuse to grant compulsory mechanical licenses even if they dislike the performers or the record companies.

COMPULSORY MECHANICAL LICENSE

MECHANICAL LICENSE AGREEMENT

Date: _____

Composition Title: _____

Composer(s): _____

Gentlepersons: _____

We own or control the mechanical recording rights in the copyrighted musical composition referred to above (hereinafter referred to as the "Composition"). You have advised us that you wish to use the Composition pursuant to the terms of the Compulsory License provisions of the United States Copyright Act (Title 17) relating to the making and distribution of phonorecords. We accede to such use, upon conditions specified below.

1. You shall pay royalties and shall render detailed accounting statements quarterly, within forty-five (45) days after each March 31, June 30, September 30, and December 31 for the calendar quarter year just concluded, whether or not royalties are due and payable for such period, for phonorecords made and distributed.

2. You shall pay us at the following rate for each part embodying the Composition manufactured by you, distributed and not returned (except for promotional copies distributed without charge to radio and television stations):
   _____ for a "single" recording;
   _____ for a "CD" or "cassette" recording.

3. This license is limited solely to the recorded performance of the Composition on the phonorecord, which is identified as follows:
   Record #: _____
   Artist: _____
   Label: _____
   This license shall not supersede or in any way affect any prior agreements now in effect with respect to recordings of the Composition.

4. In the event that you fail to account to us and pay royalties as herein provided, we may give you written notice that, unless the default is remedied within thirty (30) days from the date of such notice, this compulsory license will be automatically terminated. Such termination shall render either the making or the distribution, or both, of all phonorecords for which royalties have not been paid, actionable as acts of infringement under, and fully subject to the remedies provided by the Copyright Act.

5. You need not serve or file the notice of intention to obtain a compulsory license required by the Copyright Act.

6. This license is specifically limited to the use of the Composition, and the sale of the recording within the United States of America, unless we grant you written permission to the contrary.

7. On the label affixed to each part manufactured by you, you will include the title of the Composition, our name as Publisher, the name of the performing rights society with which we are affiliated (_____) and the last names of the composer and lyricist.

8. You will not use or authorize the use of the title of the Composition in any manner whatsoever on the label, cover, sleeve, jacket or box in which the recording is sold, except in a list of musical compositions contained thereon and then only in print of size, type and prominence no greater than that used for the other musical compositions contained thereon.

Very truly yours,

By: _____
(Record Company)
We acknowledge the receipt of a copy hereof and the accuracy of the terms contained herein:

By: _____
(Publisher)

*Courtesy: The Musician's Business and Legal Guide.
Reprinted with permission from the publisher.*

MECHANICAL LICENSE FOR SAMPLING

Sampling is the collecting of any aural event in any format for further incorporation into a song. It is commonly defined as the digital acquisition of an aural event—usually of short duration—that will be manipulated before final use. This could be a portion of keyboard phrasing, the sound of a horn trio, a vocal, a rhythm pattern or three words from a lyric.

When sounds are taken from existing recordings and used as part of new ones, users must obtain mechanical licenses from the publishing companies, even if they are of very short duration. The rates are negotiable. If they wish to change these samples in any way, they must obtain permission of the publishers, and these changes will be considered derivative works. Users must also negotiate licenses with record companies, since they own the copyrights to the sound recording. (See the article "Sampling" in this segment.)

MECHANICAL LICENSES FOR DIGITAL PHONORECORD DELIVERIES (DPDS)

According to the 1995 Digital Performance Right in Sound Recordings Act (DPRSA), a mechanical license must be issued by composers and publishers for digitally delivered and commercially distributed songs and recordings (digital phonorecord deliveries or DPDs) over the Internet.

Permanent (general) DPDs are available from artist sites, major and independent labels, Internet record stores, music subscription services and some record store kiosks. Essentially, customers purchase selections of songs and are provided with CDs that contain the selections they buy or download to computer hard drives.

The permanent downloads are encoded in such a way that if the user makes and sells commercial copies, they can be traced back to the particular subscription service, although not necessarily the individual user that made the copies.

Promotional downloads that are offered by record companies are not permanent and no mechanical royalties are owed.

The mechanical royalty rate for permanent DPDs published before December 31, 2000 is the same as for phonorecords. A new rate was to be established by end of 2001 by the CARP; to date none has. The reason is that the DPRSA did not adequately define the term incidental DPDs (digital phonorecord deliveries where the reproduction or distribution of a phonorecord is incidental to the transmission) to cover all music that is streamed. For example, if customers subscribe to streaming services that enable them to choose the music they want to listen to at specific times and for a limited number of times (limited downloads), does that constitute incidental DPDs?

On-demand streams are digital transmissions of sound recordings delivered by streaming technology, such as Real Audio, which can be listened to whenever convenient, but not downloaded to a computer's hard drive. Limited (conditional) downloads can be downloaded to a computer's hard drive for a limited period, listened to whenever convenient, but not transferred to other devices, such as burning them onto CDs or downloading them to MP3 devices. Limited downloads can be downloaded to a computer's hard drive, but only for a limited period and cannot be transferred to other devices.

On October 5, 2001, the Recording Industry Association of America (RIAA), the Harry Fox Agency (HFA) and the National Music Publisher's Association (NMPA) agreed that, mechanical licenses for on-demand streams and limited downloads will be issued to companies that offer them to customers for recurring fees (subscription services), however they are defined. (The U.S. Copyright Act authorizes voluntary negotiations for determining mechanical royalty rates.)

FOR IMMEDIATE RELEASE
November 27, 2001
Contact: Carey Ramos
NMPA/HFA
212-373-3240
cramos@paulweiss.com

MUSIC PUBLISHERS SUPPORT LANDMARK ACCORD WITH RECORD INDUSTRY FOR LAUNCH OF INTERNET SUBSCRIPTION SERVICES

NEW YORK – November 27, 2001 – The National Music Publishers' Association (NMPA) and The Harry Fox Agency (HFA) announced today that their recent agreement with the Recording Industry Association of America (RIAA) to provide licenses for use of copyrighted musical works for Internet music subscription services has received overwhelming support from the more than 27,000 music publishers represented by HFA.

As a result, HFA is poised to issue licenses for hundreds of thousands of musical works for delivery over the Internet. Under the agreement, the licensing process has been streamlined, allowing for "bulk" licensing of musical works. As a result, Internet music services will be able to obtain licenses immediately so that they may offer their subscribers the most diverse repertoire of music ever licensed for the Internet.

HFA is committed to making licenses available to music services not covered by the RIAA agreement on substantially the same terms as those licenses are available to RIAA members under the agreement. On November 14, 2001, NMPA, HFA, and one such service – Listen.com, based in San Francisco – announced that they had reached agreement on the licensing of musical works for Rhapsody, Listen.com's digital music subscription service.

"We are gratified that the agreement we made with RIAA has received such broad support in the industry," said Edward P. Murphy, President and CEO of NMPA. "Making licenses available to legitimate services is a critical part of making our publishers' broad repertoire of music available to consumers over the Internet. This marks an important step for music publishers and songwriters in making their works available through licensed Internet outlets, and in providing consumers a legitimate alternative to the rampant piracy of musical works that has plagued the Internet."

"HFA is here to assist record and Internet companies that want to license music for online use," said Gary Churgin, President and CEO of HFA. "Our electronic licensing capabilities allow us to clear hundreds of thousands of titles at a time so an online service can launch with everything from hip hop to show tunes."

Courtesy: National Music Publishers Association

There are no practical means for copyright owners individually to license performance rights to every public user and find users that have not been issued licenses. Performance rights organizations meet that need.

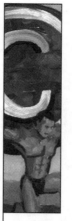

The agreement did not specify what the rates for these licenses should be. The rates will be established by negotiations between RIAA, the HFA and NMPA or by the CARP. The RIAA agreed to pay the HFA a nonrefundable advance of $1 million to be distributed to composers and publishers once rates are established.

Although no dates were specified for establishing royalty rates, the agreement did establish that further advances would be paid to the HFA if no rates were established within two years (October 5, 2003).

Music Subscription Services

In December 2001, a number of companies launched music subscription services. For monthly fees, users are provided with on-demand streams and limited downloads of a specified number of tracks (songs). Some services allow users to download a limited number of tracks of month that can be burned onto CDs (permanent downloads). Some sites offer only streaming.

Pressplay is a joint venture between Sony Music Entertainment and Vivendi Universal. The music content is licensed from record companies owned by Sony Music and Universal Music Group, from the EMI Group and several independent record companies, such as Navarre and Rounder. Their premier service allows a limited amount of permanent downloads per month. These can be burned onto CDs. The songs are digitally fingerprinted so that bootlegs can be traced back to the Pressplay (though not the individual user that may have initiated the bootleg.)

MusicNet, a joint venture between RealNetworks, AOL Time Warner, Bertelsmann AG and the EMI Group, is a technology and content platform, that is distributed to companies that have large consumer bases, such as AOL Time Warner. MusicNet licenses content from EMI Group, Warner Brothers, BMG, Zomba and other record companies. It offers only conditional (limited) downloads that exist for discrete periods on subscribers' computers. These downloads cannot be burned onto CDs or otherwise transferred.

Other subscription services include PluS from MP3.com, Rhapsody and MusicMatch.com.

Many record companies now encode CDs in a manner that prevents their being copied when placed in the CD drives of computers. This prevents peer-to-peer file sharing.

FOREIGN SUBLICENSES

U.S. record companies sublicense recordings and compositions to publishers in foreign countries. Each song made available for sale in each country requires a mechanical license. Most publishers have affiliations with foreign publishers.

Mechanical royalties for foreign sublicenses are computed on a percentage of the wholesale price of the recordings, typically 6% to 8%.

LICENSES FOR PUBLIC PERFORMANCES OF MUSICAL COMPOSITIONS

One of the rights granted to composers by the U.S. Copyright Act is the right to perform their songs publicly. Copyright owners (composers and publishers) must license that right to users that play their music in public mediums. These include radio and television stations; jukeboxes, concerts and nightclubs; background music in supermarkets, elevators, malls, shopping centers, health clubs, etc.; cable, satellite, Internet-only radio stations and Internet digital transmission services; commercial AM/FM and noncommercial stations that rebroadcast on the Internet.

There are no practical means for copyright owners individually to license performance rights to every public user and find users that have not been issued licenses. Performance rights organizations meet that need.

Performance Rights Organizations

In the United States, the American Society of Composers, Authors & Publishers (ASCAP), Broadcast Music, Inc. (BMI), and SESAC (formerly Society of European Stage Authors and Composers, Inc.) are organizations that grant performance rights on behalf of composers and publishers. The Society of Composers, Authors and Music Publishers of Canada (SOCAN) is the performance rights organization of Canada.

These organizations collect annual fees from users and distribute them to their members. In return, users receive "blanket licenses" that allow them to play the music of their choice.

The performance rights revenue that can be earned for a hit song can exceed any other royalty source. A hit song that reaches the top of the Billboard radio chart might earn composers and publishers more than $500,000 in domestic performance rights income, but only $160,000 in mechanical royalties for sales of two million copies at the full 2002-2003 statutory rate.

The organizations only have the right to license nondramatic works for public performances (small rights). Dramatic works (grand rights) are reserved compositions that are integral to musical theater, ballet, operas, etc. Dramatic works are licensed directly from the composers or their talent agents.

By joining these organizations, composers technically license their performance rights to them and give them permission to license these rights to users. Placement of the organizations' names on recording and other audio and audiovisual products gives notice that users have permission to publicly perform those composers' songs.

Once composers and publishers join, they must ensure that all of their licensed songs are registered with the performance rights organizations. Otherwise, the organization has no way of knowing what song belongs to whom or where payments should go. This is especially important for foreign performance rights societies, where a great deal of money is held in escrow because the composers and publishers have not been identified.

Only U.S. motion picture theaters are exempt from being issued public performance licenses. Although films contain music that is publicly performed, theater owners won this exemption in an antitrust case. However, performance rights organizations distribute performance royalties on behalf of songwriters and publishers when films that contain their music are aired on television and cable programs.

Licensing Fees

ASCAP, BMI and SESAC collect approximately $800,000,000 annually in licensing fees from users, most of it from radio and television broadcasters. The fees vary according to how many people are reached by a particular medium. Network television stations are charged far higher license fees than radio stations and nightclubs because they reach wider audiences.

Nightclubs can pay as little a few hundred dollars a year in fees; television networks pay millions.

Licensing fees have now been established for uses on the Internet. These are based on the value of the Web sites, as measured by the amount of revenue the site generates from advertising and merchandising sales or by the amount of traffic, and by whether the site is interactive. (On interactive sites, users select specific pieces of music to listen to or download.)

Foreign Performance Rights

Performance rights organizations license rights to foreign performance rights organizations through reciprocal agreements. They collect performance right royalties of U.S. composers and publishers and send them to the appropriate organization for distribution to its members.

Public Performance Royalties for Owners of Copyrights in Sound Recordings

For many years, featured artists and record companies lobbied for payment of public performance royalties, arguing that their performance and interpretation of the songs were equal in importance to their creation. Record companies argued that their copyrights in sound recordings gave them rights to required mechanical use licenses but not performance royalties. The U.S. is the only country that does not do so.

In 1995, Congress passed the Digital Performance Right in Sound Recordings Act (DPRSA), which amends the U.S. Copyright Act. The DPRSA provides the owners of copyrights in sound recordings (e.g., record labels) and the artists that perform on them the right to be paid public performance royalties for the streaming of sound recordings via satellite, cable and webcasting. With the exception of webcasting, the licensing fees and terms were decided by negotiation between the RIAA (acting on behalf of member record labels and their artists) and the performance rights organizations.

FCC-licensed commercial and noncommercial stations that simultaneously transmit their programs over the Internet (webcasters) could not come to an agreement with the performance rights organizations about what the licensing fees for webcasting should be. In February 2002, the CARP stepped in and recommended that com-

mercial terrestrial broadcasters pay the recording industry $0.14 each time they play a song over the Internet. In June 2002, the Librarian of Congress rejected the CARP rate and ruled that both commercial terrestrial broadcasters and webcasters pay $0.07. Small webcasters were displeased because they felt that rates would dwarf total revenues. The RIAA, representing the major recording labels, felt the rate was too low. Noncommercial broadcasters will pay $0.02 for simultaneous Internet transmissions of AM and FM broadcasts.

The CARP named the RIAA as the distributing agency for the DPRSA fees. The name of the RIAA's collection organization is SoundExchange. The DPRSA licensing fees will be distributed according to the following percentages:

Recording labels	50%
Artists	45%
Background singers	2.5%
Session players	2.5%

Artists, session players and background singers will be paid directly by the performance rights organization. (During negotiations, the RIAA asked that fees to artists be paid to the record companies, but the Future of Music Coalition negotiated with the RIAA and got them to agree to pay artists directly.)

The fees are distributed according to the information supplied by satellite, cable, and Internet radio service providers about the music they provide.

This new law opens up the potential for performance royalties to be paid to artists and record labels for all broadcasts. The United States is one of the only countries that does not already do so.

License Fee Allocation

The methods used by the performing rights organizations for distributing licensing fees to composers and publishers are extremely complex. The underpinning philosophy is this: The greater the number of people that hear a particular performance of a song, the more the money that song earns.

For example, ASCAP assigns credits to a particular performance. The amount of the credit is valued (weighted) according to a number of factors for each medium (e.g., radio, TV, etc.). These factors include—

- Time of day

- Audience reach (how many people hear the song)

- Frequency (how many times the song is played by any one user)

For radio, an additional factor is the total amount of times a song is played on all licensed radio stations per quarter.

For television, additional factors are the type of use of a song on a particular show—background, theme, live performance, jingle, etc.—duration and the type of show.

Generally, a song that is featured on a prime-time major network television show will receive more credits than one that is featured on one large-market radio station because a greater number of people will hear it.

How Public Performances are Monitored

ASCAP, BMI and SESAC have different, complex methods for monitoring radio station airplay. Generally, they depend on a combination of some of the following: listening surveys of selected commercial and noncommercial stations, by the societies or independent services, such as Broadcast Data Systems; and airplay logs compiled by stations and sent to the organizations. This information is collated and used to make assumptions about what similar stations are playing all over the country (statistical sampling). Not all stations are surveyed.

BROADCAST DATA SYSTEMS (BDS)

Broadcast Data Systems monitors airplay of more than 1100 radio stations in the United States, Canada and Puerto Rico and music video channels, such as MTV, M2, VH1, BET, CMT and Great American Country. Computers track performances by "listening" to radio stations, 24 hours a day, 7 days a week. The information is used by performance rights societies to track airplay and by magazines such as Billboard that chart performances.

Music radio coverage includes Adult Alternative, Adult Contemporary (AC), Christian AC, Country, Latin, Modern Rock, Oldies, Rock, R&B and Top 40. Subformats used for Billboard and Monitor Magazines include, Mainstream Top 40, Rhythmic Top 40, Crossover Top 40, Adult Top 40, Modern Adult, R&B Adult, Rap, Active Rock, Heritage Rock, Latin Pop, Latin Regional Mexican and Latin Tropical.

Surveys can miss songs that attract airplay on radio stations in small towns, or even on major stations in a state. Generally, songs must at least be minor national hits (played on many radio stations throughout the country) before they are picked up. That is why composers and publishers that have charted hits get the greatest share of the broadcast fees collected by SESAC, ASCAP and BMI.

Because many network television shows are shown across the country at the same time, the performance rights organizations can accurately track the music that is featured on shows and commercials. Statistical surveys and cue sheets (playlists) supplied by the stations are used to

Most composers join the organization that is responsive to their initial questions and makes them feel most comfortable.

track the use of music in local television and cable programs.

Subscription and Internet radio service providers send in cue sheets to the performance rights organizations.

Cue sheets and logs are used by television and radio stations to list the music used, timing in seconds, and identify the artists, writers and publishers and their performance rights affiliations. Television stations also list the music's use (theme, background, etc.). Cue sheets are sent to the performance rights organizations and to publishers to enable them to check whether they have registered the songs with the organizations. Publishers should routinely register the names of published songs with performance rights organizations.

How Performance Rights Fees are Distributed to Composers and Publishers

After performance rights organizations deduct administration costs (up to 20%), the fees are distributed equally between composers (writers) and publishers. Even if writers have assigned shares of their publishing to other publishers, they still receive all of the writers' share and whatever percentage of the publisher's share that has been agreed to by contract. Writers do not split their fees with publishers. Their performance rights income is, however, shared with collaborators, according to their agreed-on percentages.

Joining a Performance Rights Organization

Composers cannot join more than one U.S. performance rights organization in the same year or for the same songs, and they cannot join until they know they will be publishing their songs on records, sheet music, film, TV shows, etc. *Both* the writers (composers) of the songs and the publishing company that owns their copyrights must join ASCAP or SESAC to receive writers' and publishers' share of royalties. If only writers (composers) join BMI, BMI will pay the writer both the writers' and the publisher's, because it is assumed they are the same entities.

Although composers can join ASCAP, BMI or SESAC after their recordings are published, most join before, so they can include their affiliation on their recordings' covers and labels.

ASCAP charges annual dues of $10 for composers and $50 for publishers. Composers that have not published any songs may join ASCAP temporarily as associate members, provided they have had at least one work written and registered with the Copyright Office. Annual dues are not charged. BMI charges no fees or dues for composers, but imposes a one-time processing fee of $100 on publishers. SESAC charges no fees or dues.

The question of which organization is the most beneficial to join has been widely debated. Most composers join the organization that is responsive to their initial questions and makes them feel most comfortable. Sometimes, these organizations give advances as incentives for composers to join or to switch their affiliations.

SYNCHRONIZATION LICENSES

The integration of music in audiovisual works, such as films, television programs, video games and advertising is referred to as synchronization (timed to the picture). Producers that want to use music in audiovisual mediums must obtain synchronization (synch) licenses from publishers and composers, unless they have commissioned the music under a work-for-hire agreement.

The various mediums that require synchronization licenses include—

- Films
- Television shows
- Radio dramas
- Commercials
- Video games
- Commercial advertising
- Promotional music video clips
- Noncommercial (training) videos

Additionally, mechanical licenses must be obtained if the music is to be reproduced and sold in formats such as CDs, cassettes, vinyl records, DVDs, video games and CD-Roms.

Synch License Fees

The U.S. Copyright Act does not provide guidelines for the amount of synch license fees users. These fees must be negotiated between the users and the publishers. The fees depend on a variety of factors. These include (but are not limited to)—

- Type of project (feature film, training video, video game) and projected distribution
- Importance (name recognition/brand) of the producer and actors or sponsoring company
- Importance (name value) of the composer
- If the work is newly commissioned or already exists
- Projected public exposure
- Importance of the music in the context of the medium (title theme, background theme, segue, etc.)
- Duration of the music

- Duration of the license
- Negotiating power of each entity
- Project budget
- Potential for other uses (such as a soundtrack)

Synch license fees are as low as $250 for a few seconds of use of a relatively unknown composer's song in a training video or cable television documentary or as high or higher as $25,000 for a song by a well-known singer/songwriter that is used in a major film.

Income from synch licenses are divided between publishing companies and composers according to the contracts they have with each other.

Individual synch licenses must be sought for each medium that a song will be used in, such as network television, pay (subscription) television, cable television, public broadcasting television, home video, promo series.

Sometimes, blanket licenses are negotiated for all mediums.

Music Sources

Music that requires synch licenses can be purchased from many sources. New music can be commissioned directly from composers. It can be purchased from publishers of preexisting recordings and from owners of collections of music sample libraries.

Rights Clearance

The copyrights of published works can be owned by any number of collaborators and publishers. Synch and mechanical licenses must be obtained from each. Otherwise, copyright infringement may occur and producers, broadcasters and distributors can be held liable. Finding composers and their publishers and obtaining the appropriate licenses from them is termed "clearing the rights."

Because of the enormous amount of music used in television shows, films, commercials, etc., clearing the rights is an expensive, complex and lengthy process. Some film and television studios have full-time staff to clear rights and negotiate synch licenses. Others use the services of the Harry Fox Agency or other music clearing houses.

SHEET MUSIC LICENSES

Use licenses must be obtained for including copyrighted songs in songbooks, sheet music, arrangements for bands, choral groups and orchestras and reprints of lyrics in books or magazines. Users that produce and sell sheet music are called "print music publishers" to distinguish them from music publishing companies that license the use of music in audio mediums.

Print publishers generally pay music publishers a percentage of the retail price (12% to 25%) of each copy that is sold and paid for.

Income from sheet music licenses is divided between publishing companies and composers according to their contracts.

CONCLUSION

The U.S. Copyright Act lays the foundation for paying copyright holders for the use of their music in commercial applications through the issuance of use licenses. Hundreds of use licenses can be issued for one song and earnings can be millions of dollars for hits.

The wide availability of music over the Internet via free file sharing has raised important issues about how composers' and publishers' rights can continue to be protected and fair payment received for use.

Sampling

GREGORY T. VICTOROFF, ESQ.

At its best, sampling benefits society by creating valuable new contributions to modern music literature. At its worst, sampling is vandalism and stealing; chopping up and ripping off songs and recordings by other artists without permission or payment and fraudulently passing off the joint work as the work of a single artist, without giving credit to the sampled work or the unwilling collaborators. The practice is not new. In the 19th century, Rachmaninoff, Brahams, and Liszt "borrowed" material from contemporary Niccolo Paganini's Caprice for use in their own compositions.

With the advent of digital technology, MP3, Napster, more refined MIDI programs, affordable off-the-shelf samplers and widespread use of personal computers, sampling sounds and manipulating them has become relatively easy. As a result, sampling has opened a Pandora's box of old and new sound combinations, and with that, the necessity for new interpretations of the issues of copyright infringement, privacy rights, and unfair competition.

COPYRIGHT INFRINGEMENT

One of the many rights included in copyright is the right to copy a copyrighted work. Unauthorized sampling violates this right by copying a portion of a copyrighted work for a new recording.

The music publisher, by itself or together with the songwriter, usually owns the copyright in the song. The recording company usually owns the copyright in the sound recording. In December 1999, Congress amended section 101 of the Copyright Act to include sound recordings among the nine (now ten) categories of works that may be owned by an employer or commission party as works made for hire. These copyright owners are most directly affected by sampling and have the right to sue unauthorized samplers in federal court for copyright infringement.

Breaches of Contract

Copyright infringement from illegal sampling may breach warranty provisions in recording contracts. Provisions called "Warranties," "Representations" and "Indemnifications" are almost always found in contracts between musicians and record companies; musicians and producers; producers and record companies; music publishers and record companies; songwriters and music publishers; record companies and distributors; and between distributors and record stores. According to these clauses, the person who provides the product (e.g., the songs, recordings, publishing rights, records, tapes, CDs) promises the person buying or licensing the product (the record company, Web site or record store) that the recordings do not infringe anyone's copyrights or other rights.

If a lawsuit for illegal sampling is filed, it could result in lawsuits for "breach of warranty" between each person that sells the illegally sampled product. Claims apply from person to person along the record-making and marketing chain, creating a duty to indemnify each other person along the chain. Unless expressly disclaimed, the same chain of written and implied indemnities apply to transmissions of digital sound recordings using the Internet. Final legal responsibility may lie with the recording artist. The indemnification rights that exist between each person or company in the process trigger one another like a chain reaction. This can result in hundreds of thousands of dollars in liability to the sampling artist.

Indemnification provisions require the record distributor to pay the retailer's damages and attorneys' fees, the record company is required to pay the distributor's fees and damages, the producer pays the record company's fees and damages and the artist may be technically liable for everyone's attorneys' fees and damages.

Unsatisfactory Masters

Another potential problem for musicians that sample is that most recording contracts give the record company the right to reject unsatisfactory masters. Masters that infringe copyrights of other sound recordings or musical compositions can be so rejected.

Artists are required to obtain copyright licenses ("clearances") from the owners of sampled material or deliver substitute masters, which do not contain samples, to satisfy contract obligations to record companies.

Failure to comply with a record company's master delivery requirements could result in the artist having to repay recording fund advances and possibly defending legal claims for breach of contract.

Fair Use Defense

The defense of fair use permits reasonable unauthorized copying from a copyrighted work, when the copying does not substantially impair present or potential value of the original work, and in some way advances the public benefit.

One rationale for the so-called fair use defense to copyright infringement is that only a small portion of the copyright work is copied. For many years there was a popular myth among musicians and producers that up to eight bars of a song was fair use and could be copied without constituting copyright infringement. This is not true. The rules determining which uses are fair uses, and not copyright infringement are not clear or simple. Many different economic and artistic factors go into determining whether or not a given use will be a productive and fair use. All of the circumstances of each case must be considered. The fair use standard for sound recordings is, however, generally stricter than for fair uses of musical compositions.

The reason for this difference is that U.S. copyright law only protects the expression of ideas, not the idea itself. Since there are a limited number of musical notes, copyright law treats single notes like ideas, and does not protect them. For this reason, it is safe to say that borrowing one note from a song will usually be a fair use of the copyright in the song, and not an actionable infringement. Borrowing more than one note, however, could be trouble. Lawsuits have involved copying as few as four notes from "I Love New York" and three words from "I Got Rhythm."

By selecting and arranging several notes in a particular sequence, composers create copyrightable musical compositions, or songs. Songs are the expression of the composer's creativity and are protected by copyright.

But different fair use standards apply to sound recordings. Since there is virtually an unlimited number of sounds that can be recorded, sound recordings are, by definition, comprised of pure, copyrightable expression.

For musicians, engineers and producers, the practical effect of the two different fair use standards is that sampling a small portion of a musical composition may sometimes be fair use because copying a small portion may borrow uncopyrightable single notes like uncopyrightable ideas. But sampling even a fraction of a second of a sound recording is copying of pure, copyrightable expression and is more likely to be an unfair use, constituting copyright infringement.

One way some producers and engineers that sample attempt to reduce the chances of a successful copyright infringement lawsuit is by electronically processing ("camouflaging") portions of the sampled sounds beyond the point of their being easily recognizable. Filtering, synthesizing, or distorting recorded sounds can help conceal the sampled material while still retaining the essence of an instrumental lick or vocal phrase embodied in a few seconds of sound. Adding newly created sounds to the underlying sampling further dilutes the material. This is an attempt to change the sampled materials so that even though material was illegally copied, there is no substantial similarity, thus avoiding a suit for copyright infringement.

UNFAIR COMPETITION

State and federal unfair competition laws apply when the record buying public is misled as to the source or true origin of recordings that contain sampled material.

The Lanham Act is a federal law that punishes deceptive trade practices that mislead consumers about what they are buying or who made the product.

If a consumer is confused by hearing sampled vocal tracks of James Brown, or sampled guitar licks by Eddie Van Halen, and mistakenly buys a record only to discover that he or she has bought a recording by a different artist, the consumer has been deceived by the sampling. Such confusion and deception is a form of unfair competition, which can give rise to legal claims for Lanham Act

violations that can be brought in state or federal court, or unfair competition claims that may be brought in state court. All of the previous warnings about the costs of litigation apply here as well.

RIGHTS OF PRIVACY VIOLATIONS

When sampled material incorporates a person's voice, statutory, and common-law rights of privacy ("rights of publicity") may be violated. In California, Civil Code section 3344 establishes civil liability for the unauthorized commercial use of any living person's voice. Such a use would include sampling.

Although current federal moral rights legislation does not protect sound recordings or voices, such protection may be available in the future. Meanwhile, many state laws make unauthorized sampling of voices a violation of state right-of-publicity laws. Further, if the sampled voice was originally recorded without the vocalist's permission, sampling such an unauthorized recording may violate other state privacy laws as well.

FEDERAL ANTIBOOTLEGGING STATUTES

Effective December 8, 1994 the adoption of the Uruguay Round Agreements Act by the U.S. Congress amended U.S. law by adding both civil and criminal penalties for the unauthorized recording or videotaping of live musical performances.

Any person who recorded or sampled in the past, or records or samples in the future, any part of any live musical performance without the performer's consent, can now be sued under the new federal law for the same statutory damages, actual damages and attorneys' fees that are available in a traditional copyright infringement suit.

Previously, unauthorized recording of live performances was prohibited only under certain state laws.

Federal copyright law (17 U.S.C. §1101 et seq.) can now be used to prosecute so-called bootleggers

LANDMARK LAWSUITS

In one of the most publicized sampling cases, the publisher of songwriter Gilbert O'Sullivan's song "Alone Again (Naturally)" successfully sued rap artist Biz Markie, Warner Brothers Records, and others for sampling three words and a small portion of music from O'Sullivan's song without permission for Markie's rap tune "Alone Again."

A lawsuit involving the unauthorized use of drumbeats sought strict enforcement of copyright laws against sampling. Tuff City Records sued Sony Music and Def Jam Records claiming that two singles by rap artist L. L. Cool J ("Around the Way Girl" and "Six Minutes of Pleasure") contained drum track samples from "Impeach the Presidents," a 1973 song by the Honeydrippers and that another Def Jam Record, "Give the People" included vocal samples from the same Honeydrippers song.

The case is important because the common practice of sampling drumbeats is often overlooked as a minor use, too insignificant to bother clearing. This lawsuit reinforces the rule that any sampling of a sound recording may lead to a lawsuit for copyright infringement. Courts have also found a particular harmony or the repetition of the word "uh-oh" in a distinctive rhythm sufficiently original to be protectable by copyright.

A lawsuit testing the limits of the fair use defense was brought by the Ireland-based rock group U2. The band, its recording company, Island Records, and music publisher Warner-Chappell Music sued the group Negativland for sampling a part of the U2 song, "I Still Haven't Found What I'm Looking For" without the group's permission. While attorneys for U2 claimed that the sampling was consumer fraud, Negativland maintained that the use was parody, satire, and cultural criticism, and was therefore protected under the fair use doctrine. The case was settled out of court. Negativland agreed to recall the single and return copies to Island Records for destruction.

Jarvis v. A&M Records was a lawsuit over the taking of eight words ("Ooh ooh ooh ooh...move...free your body") and a keyboard line. The sampling party argued that the amount of material taken was too insignificant to constitute copyright infringement. The federal district court in New Jersey disagreed and refused to dismiss the suit, ruling that even similarity of fragmented portions of the song could constitute infringement if the portions taken were qualitatively important.

that secretly record or sample live musical performances, or copy such illegal recordings by including sampled portions in new recordings. This strict new law also prohibits selling or even transporting bootlegged recordings.

Remarkably, the law is retroactive, protecting even pre-1994 recordings if they are currently being sold or distributed, and has no statute of limitations, so that arguably suit can be brought against bootleggers and sellers of bootlegged recordings 10, 20, even 100 years after the unauthorized recording was made, if the unauthorized recordings are sold or distributed after the effective date of the Act. Unlike copyrights, which usually only last for the life of the author plus 50 years, the new federal musical performance rights are perpetual, lasting forever. Moreover, the defense of fair use may not apply to such unauthorized recordings because the fair use defense in section 107 of the Copyright Act was not incorporated into the statute.

Of even greater concern are newly enacted criminal penalties (18 U.S.C. §2319A) of forfeiture, seizure, destruction, and up to ten years imprionment for knowingly, for profit, making or distributing copies of illegally recorded performances, transmitting an illegally recorded performance, or distributing, selling, renting, or even transporting illegally recorded performances, even if the performance occurred outside the United States!

The serious implications of this new law for outlaw samplers are obvious. Sampling any part of a live performance, or any part of an unauthorized recording of a live musical performance triggers a minefield of federal civil and criminal penalties. Great care should be taken to avoid using such bootlegged recordings in any way.

NO ELECTRONIC THEFT ACT

Both civil and criminal liability may result from sampling preexisting recordings or compositions

For many years there was a popular myth among musicians and producers that up to eight bars of a song was fair use and could be copied without constituting copyright infringement. This is not true.

acquired from unauthorized MP3-type files in electronic or digital form using the global computer network, commonly referred to as the Internet. In late 1999, Jeffrey Gerard Levy, a 22-year-old University of Oregon student was sentenced to two years probation after pleading guilty to illegally distributing copyrighted materials including MP3 files, movie clips, and software. As the first person convicted under the No Electronic Theft (NET) Act, Levy could have been sentenced to three years in prison and fined up to $250,000.

PENALTIES

Attorneys are always expensive. Entertainment attorneys usually charge $200 to $400 per hour. Those that are experienced in federal court copyright litigation often charge even more. Court costs and one side's attorneys' fees in a copyright trial average about $350,000. If you lose the trial you will have to pay the judgment against you, which could be as high as $100,000 for a single willful infringement (higher if there are substantial profits involved). An appeal of a judgment against you involves still more attorneys' fees and sometimes requires the posting of a bond.

In some cases a copyright infringer may have to pay the winning party's attorneys' fees.

Sampling has opened a Pandora's box of old and new sound combinations, and with that, the necessity for new interpretations of the issues of copyright infringement, privacy rights, and unfair competition

Copyright law also authorizes injunctions against the sale of CDs, tapes, and records containing illegally sampled material, seizure and destruction of infringing matter, and other criminal penalties.

In short, defending a copyright infringement lawsuit is a substantial expense and a risky proposition, exposing one to the possibility of hundreds of thousands of dollars in legal fees and costs.

Even if a particular sampling does not constitute copyright infringement, and is a fair use, it must still avoid violation of state and federal unfair competition laws.

COPYRIGHT CLEARANCES

Obtaining advance "permission," "copyright licenses" or "clearances" from owners of both the musical composition and the sound recording you want to sample is the best way to avoid the problems and expenses that can result from illegal sampling.

Many factors affect whether and when musicians should request and pay for clearances for samples. Although copyright laws and general music industry practices do not give rise to a lawsuit in every sampling situation, the enormous expenses of any sampling dispute should be avoided whenever possible.

In many cases, it is wise to clear samples early in the recording process even if, eventually, they are not used, because when the record is finished and the sample must be cleared, the artist will have little leverage in negotiating clearance fees.

In some cities, special music clearance firms routinely request, negotiate, prepare, and process clearances for sampled materials for a fee. They know reasonable rates for clearances and will prepare valid copyright licenses for less cost to the requesting party than will most music attorneys.

Sample Use Agreements

The Master Sample Use License Agreement and Mechanical License are short-form examples of licenses to incorporate or sample portions of a recording of a musical composition. Permission to sample the musical composition is granted by the music publisher(s) in the Mechanical License; permission to sample the recording of the musical composition is granted by the record company in the Master Sample Use License Agreement.

Fees for using the master and the musical composition are expressed as a one-time flat fee or buyout, and perpetual, worldwide rights are granted. As discussed above, such extensive rights may not always be granted. Limits on the term, territory or number of units that may be sold, co-ownership and coadministration of the recording and co-ownership of the musical composition embodying the sampled material, or statutory compulsory license fees on every copy sold, may be required by certain record companies and music publishers.

Clearance Costs: Royalties

The cost of clearances is a major consideration in deciding whether to sample. Generally, record companies will not pay an artist more than the full statutory mechanical license fee for permission to sell recordings of the artist's composition. In 2000, the statutory rate was 7.55¢ per unit, for up to five minutes of a recording. However, most record companies and others typically negotiate mechanical license fees of only 50% to 75% of the statutory rate to record an entire composition. Out of that mechanical license fee, the sampling artist must pay the owners of any sampled material. If the clearance fees for the sampled material are too high, none of the mechanical license fee will be left for the sampling artist, and the sampled cut may end up costing the artist more than is earned by the entire composition.

Sampling royalty rates for musical compositions can range from 10% to 25% of the statutory rate. Sampling royalty rates for sound recordings range from .5¢ to 3¢ per unit sold.

Clearance costs double or triple when more than one sampled track is included in a recording. Imagine, for example, a composition containing Phil Collins' snare drum sound, Jimi Hendrix's guitar sound, Phil Lesh's bass, and Little Richard's voice. In this case, combined sampling clearance fees would make the multitrack recording impossibly expensive.

Sampling clearance practices vary widely throughout the music industry. Fees are affected by both the quantity of material being sampled (a second or less is a "minor use," five seconds is a "major use") and the quality of the sampled material (i.e., a highly recognizable lyric sung by a famous artist would be more expensive than an anonymous bass drum track). Certain artists demand exorbitant fees to discourage sampling. On the other hand, some music publishers offer compositions in their catalogs and actively encourage sampling. Prices are affected by the popularity and prestige of the sampling artist and the uniqueness and value of the sampled sounds.

Clearance Costs: Buyouts and Co-Ownership
A percentage of the mechanical license fee (royalty) is one type of clearance fee. Another, is a one-time flat-fee payment (buyout) for the use of sampled material. Buyout fees range from $250 to $10,000, depending on the demands of the copyright owners. Up to $50,000 may be charged for a major use of a famous artist's performance or song. An upper limit on the number of units embodying the sampled material that may be sold may be imposed by some licensors, requiring additional payment at a higher royalty rate or an entirely new license if the maximum is exceeded.

More frequently, music publishers and record companies demand to be co-owners of the new composition as a condition of granting permission to sample. The option of assigning a share of the publishing (i.e., the copyright) in the song containing the sampled material to a publisher or record company may be helpful to the sampling artist, particularly when a buyout of all rights is not possible. Assigning a portion of the copyright in lieu of a cash advance may be less of a financial burden on an artist, enabling a song to be released where the cost or unavailability of a license would otherwise preclude the record from being distributed legally. If you license the sample for a percentage of the statutory rate, and you later want to license your song with the sample in it for a film, the film producer must obtain separate permission from the publisher who has granted the license. That publisher must always be consulted in new licensing situations. On the other hand, if you negotiate a buyout, you are free from any continuing obligation to the publisher. Similarly, if you negotiate income participation, which is to sell a percentage of your song in return for permission to sample, the publisher becomes a part owner of your song, and may or may not have approval rights in future licensing of the new work depending on the administration terms in the sampling license. Percentage of income participation ranges from 5% for a minimal use within the song to as much as 75% if the sample has been utilized throughout the song and is an integral part of the work.

MASTER SAMPLE USE LICENSE AGREEMENT

In consideration of either (the sum of $ _____ which covers ____ % of the copyright) or (granting ____ % of the copyright and publishing right [and coadministration rights]) for the rights and license herein granted thereto, _____ (Record Company), hereinafter referred to as "Licensor," hereby grants to _____ (sampling Artist and/or recording company), hereinafter referred to as "Licensee," the nonexclusive, limited right, license, privilege and authority, but not the obligation, to use a portion of the Master Recording, defined below (hereinafter referred to as the "Master"), as embodied in the tape approved by Licensor, with no greater usage of the Master than is contained in the approved tape (the "Usage"), in the manufacture, distribution, and sale of any phonorecord (as that term is defined in Section 101 of the Copyright Act) entitled "_____ " ("Album"), performed by _____ ("Artist") embodying the recording _____ ("Master") as performed by _____ "Sample Artist"), and produced by _____ ("Producer"). Licensor additionally grants to Licensee the right to exploit, advertise, publicize, and promote such Master, as embodied in the phonorecord, in all media, markets, and formats now known or hereafter devised.

1. The term of this agreement ("Term") will begin on the date hereof and shall continue in perpetuity.

2. The territory covered by this agreement is _____.

3. It is expressly understood and agreed that any compensation to be paid herein to Licensor is wholly contingent upon the embodiment of the Master within the phonorecord and that nothing herein shall obligate or require Licensee to commit to such usage. However, such compensation shall in no way be reduced by a lesser use of the Recording than the Usage provided for herein.

4. Licensor warrants only that it has the legal right to grant the aforesaid master recording use rights subject to the terms, conditions, limitations, restrictions, and reservations herein contained, and that this license is given and accepted without any other warranty or recourse. In the event said warranty is breached, Licensor's total liability shall not exceed the lesser of the actual damages incurred by Licensee or the total consideration paid hereunder to Licensor.

5. Licensor reserves unto itself all rights and uses of every kind and nature whatsoever in and to the Master other than the limited rights specifically licensed hereunder, including the sole right to exercise and to authorize others to exercise such rights at any and all times and places without limitation.

6. This license is binding upon and shall inure to the benefit of the respective successors and assigns of the parties hereto.

7. This contract is entered into in the State of California and its validity, construction, interpretation, and legal effect shall be governed by the laws of the State of California applicable to contracts entered into and performed entirely therein.

8. This agreement contains the entire understanding of the parties relating to the subject matter herein contained.

IN WITNESS WHEREOF, the parties have caused the foregoing to be executed as of this _____ day of _____ , 200___.

AGREED TO AND ACCEPTED:

_____

LICENSOR (Company Name)_____

By (Signature)_____

LICENSEE (Company Name)_____

By (Signature)_____

Name and Title (an authorized signatory)

_____

Federal I.D./SS#_____

Name and Title (an authorized signatory)

_____

Federal I.D./SS#_____

MECHANICAL LICENSE

In consideration of the sum of $ _____ which covers _____ % of the copyright and full payment for the rights and license herein granted thereto, _____ ("Licensor") hereby grants to _____ ("Licensee") the nonexclusive right, license, privilege, and authority to use, in whole or in part, the copyrighted musical composition known as _____ written by _____ and _____ (hereinafter referred to as the "Composition"):

1. In the recording, making, and distribution of phonorecords (as that term is defined in Section 101 of the Copyright Act) to be made and distributed throughout the world in accordance with the provisions of Section 115 of the Copyright Act of the United States of America of October 19, 1976, as amended (the "Act"), except it is agreed that: (1) Licensee need not serve or file the notices required under the Act; (2) consideration for such license shall be in the form of a one-time flat-fee buyout; (3) Licensee shall have the unlimited right to utilize the Composition, or any portion thereof, as embodied in the phonorecord, in any and all media now known or hereafter devised for the purpose of promoting the sale of the phonorecord which is the subject of this agreement; and (4) this license shall be worldwide.

2. This license permits the use of the Composition or any portion thereof, in the particular recordings made in connection with the sound recording _____ ("Album") by _____ ("Artist"), and permits the use of such recording in any phonorecord in which the recording may be embodied in whatever form now known or hereafter devised. This license includes the privilege of making a musical arrangement of the Composition to the extent necessary to conform it to the style or manner of interpretation of the performance involved.

3. Licensor warrants and represents that it has the right to enter into this agreement and to grant to Licensee all of the rights granted herein, and that the exercise by Licensee of any and all of the rights granted to Licensee in this agreement will not violate or infringe upon any common-law or statutory rights of any person, firm, or corporation including, without limitation, contractual rights, copyrights, and rights of privacy.

4. This license is binding upon and shall inure to the benefit of the respective successors, assigns, and sublicensees of the parties hereto.

5. This agreement sets forth the entire understanding of the parties with respect to the subject matter hereof, and may not be modified or amended except by written agreement executed by the parties.

6. This license may not be terminated for any reason, is entered into in the State of California, and its validity, construction, interpretation, and legal effect shall be governed by the laws of the State of California applicable to contracts entered into and performed entirely therein.

IN WITNESS WHEREOF, the parties have entered into this license agreement as of this _____ day of _____ , 200__.

AGREED TO AND ACCEPTED:

_____

LICENSOR (Company Name)_____

By (Signature)_____

LICENSEE (Company Name)_____

By (Signature)_____

Name and Title (an authorized signatory)

_____

Federal I.D./SS#_____

Name and Title (an authorized signatory)

_____

Federal I.D./SS#_____

Special thanks to Suzy Vaughan, Esq. and Ron McGowan for their generous assistance in the preparation of these agreements.

AMERICAN FEDERATION OF MUSICIANS PAYMENTS

Under certain circumstances, the American Federation of Musicians (AFM) collects fees for its member musicians when a record company uses a sample of a preexisting recording in a new recording. When a portion of a recording containing the performance of an AFM member, who is a "nonroyalty artist," (i.e., a musician who plays on the recording but does not receive record royalties), not a self-contained royalty group or symphonic musician, is sampled under the following AFM definition, the company owning the recording that is being sampled makes a one time lump sum payment of $400 for the first sample (regardless of how many times it is used in the new recording) and a one-time lump sum payment of $250 for each additional sample from the same recording, plus 2% of the gross revenue received by the company in excess of $25,000, less the lump sum payments that have already been made. These payments are made to the Phonograph Record Manufacturers' Special Payments Fund, which are then distributed to the musician members. The AFM's definition of sampling is "a recording encoded into a digital sampler, computer, digital hard drive storage unit or other device for subsequent playback on a digital synthesizer or other play-back device for use in another song (but not a remix or reedit of the new song)." Note that the definition includes not only samples embodied in traditional tapes and CDs, but also includes samples embodied on synthesizers, samplers, and other playback devices.

SOUNDTRACK SAMPLING

Occasionally, artists sample things other than music, such as audio bytes from feature films, television shows, or news footage. In these cases, permission must be obtained from the owner of the footage. Fees range from $1000 to $8000 per minute for buyouts, which must be negotiated directly with the representative for the actor whose voice is being sampled. The minimum fee for such use is the Screen Actors Guild's full day rate, which is currently $617. Private licensing agents such as CMG in Indianapolis, Indiana may charge far more for permission to sample the voice of someone of the caliber of Elvis or Marilyn Monroe. If a film or television program is used, payments may also be due to the writers' and directors' guilds and to the American Federation of Musicians.

CONCLUSION

Throughout history, every new development in music has been greeted with suspicion by the music establishment of the day. Polyphony (playing harmonies) was considered demonic in medieval times, and was punishable by burning at the stake. As modern musicians explore innovative chord progressions, syncopated rhythms, and new electronic instruments, we all learn more about the musical landscape around us. Only time will tell whether samplers will be viewed as musical innovators or plagiarists.

Michael Laskow:
Founder, TAXI

TAXI helps songwriters, artists, bands and composers place their music in records, films, television and advertising commercials. It does so by acting as a channel between the musicians and the businesses that are looking for material. Companies provide TAXI with descriptions of the types of music they are looking for. TAXI informs its membership. The musicians that feel they can meet those needs send their songs to TAXI, where they are screened by A&R professionals. The best material is sent on to the companies that requested it, and those submissions are treated as solicited (requested) material.

If a company wants a song or artist that is submitted, they call the composer directly and make a deal. TAXI does not take percentages of deals and does not get involved in negotiating contracts.

TAXI has helped placed many songs for their members, the primary reason it has become so successful. In 1997, TAXI forwarded "Buy Me A Rose" by member songwriters Erik Hickenlooper and Jim Funk to Kenny Rogers. It became a number one country hit. TAXI also sent "Kiss Me" by Sixpence None The Richer to TV show *Dawson's Creek,* which helped propel the song to hit status. Interscope and MCA have signed artist deals with acts they found through TAXI.

TAXI aggressively pursues the film and television market. Their new Dispatch service enables them to put out calls to member songwriters and

PHOTO: MICHAEL LASKO

deliver quality material to music supervisors within 48 hours.

TAXI's A&R people send detailed critiques to its members, whether or not their songs were submitted to any particular company. This fills one of the biggest needs that writers and artists have: feedback from professionals about their songwriting.

TAXI's income is dependent on annual membership fees. A one-year membership is $299.95; a two-year membership is $499.95; and a three-year membership is $599.95. There is a $5.00 per song submission fee.

Other member benefits include a musician referral services and free passes for members and their guests to TAXI's annual Road Rally convention, which holds workshops and seminars by industry professionals from major label recording, television, publishing and advertising companies and provides many opportunities for attendees to network.

* * * * * * *

Rapaport: How did you get the idea for starting TAXI?

Laskow: I had been working for almost two years as the general manager for one of the largest postproduction facilities in the United States. Their primary business was TV commercials and music videos. I was in charge of East and West Coast operations, had homes on both coasts, had a company BMW and earned a six-figure salary. During the time I worked there, I substantially increased their business and reputation. One day, I walked in and asked the owner for a raise. When he said no, I quit, handed him back the keys to the car, walked into my office, put my feet on the desk and asked myself what I was going to do next.

A little voice went off inside me that said, "You know, what I miss most is working with unsigned talent, going into the studio with them for the first time with fire in their bellies and creating music." The next thing that happened was that I had a clear vision of creating a network that helped unsigned composers get their music into the hands of producers, publishers and music supervisors in records, film and television.

I walked out of the office that day with that vision and went for it.

Rapaport: What was your first step?

Laskow: I called up half a dozen music industry friends that were potential investors and invited them over for a Monday night football game. At half time, I turned off the TV and said, "I have an idea and I want to run it by you."

They began by telling me how crazy the idea was: "The last thing this industry wants is a bunch of unsolicited tapes by amateurs." I said, "What if you tell me what you want and I hire some of our peers and we prescreen the songs?" They could not find a flaw in that plan, but they wanted to mull it over more before they decided to ante up the money.

Then I called Michael Lederer, one of my oldest and dearest friends who was not in the music business. He asked for a business plan. I took a week to draw one up, flew to Dallas and presented it to him. That wonderful, brave soul gave me $75,000 and made me promise that even before the company was profitable that we would donate money to good causes.

Even after I started the business, lots of people told me it would not succeed. There was still a good old boy's network in the business that only took songs from people they knew. Writers and artists were skeptical at first because so many of them had been ripped off by songsharks and were gun-shy.

I knew that if TAXI was going to succeed, I would have to take the highest road possible.

Rapaport: What does taking the high road mean?

Laskow: I grew up in a family-owned clothing business in a farm town in Illinois and my grandfather always told me, "If a farmer wants a red flannel shirt and we do not have it, walk him across the street to a competitor that does, and you will make a client for life."

TAXI needed to deliver more than it promised to our members and treat them equally, not play favorites. We would never make a claim what we could not live up to. We hired the best A&R people that we could and treated them well.

We set standards for customer service that few businesses can match.

We also have the industry side of the coin

to deal with, meaning that the material we send them has to be extremely good, or they won't continue to use us as a resource.

Rapaport: How did you think of the name?

Laskow: I woke up with it about two days after I walked off my job. I shook my wife awake. "Honey, I've got it, I am calling it Taxi because it takes you from where you are to where you want to be." I wrote the name on a napkin and went back to sleep.

Rapaport: How long did it take for TAXI to make a profit?

Laskow: During our first year, TAXI grossed $59,000 dollars and we used all of it for expenses. We lived off $22,000 savings. My wife was going to graduate school, so there was no income from her. We literally lived on rice and black and red beans for lunch and dinner. We went from a 3-bedroom place to a 1-bedroom apartment that was also our office. I was juggling groceries and rent on a monthly basis. I racked up 20 grand on two gold cards.

I worked 18 hours a day, to the point where I did not think I had emotional and physical strength to continue. I can remember plenty of times being up at one in the morning with my face buried in my hands and tears running through my fingers. I would look at my wife sleeping and think, "If you only knew how close were are to living in a cardboard box." It was not until the end of the second year that I knew TAXI was going to succeed.

Rapaport: What got you through those two years?

Laskow: What kept me from quitting was that I was too embarrassed to fail in front of my wife, my kids and my investor. And after the first year, I felt I could not let members down. How could I take their money if I believed the company was on shaky ground?

The Independent A&R Vehicle

TAXI's LOGO HELPS MAKE SONGWRITERS AND COMPOSERS REMEMBER THE NAME AND SERVICE.

Rapaport: How do you pick your A&R staff?

Laskow: All our screeners have been directly involved in creating or selecting hits, such as former radio station program directors, publishers, A&R people, music supervisors at film and television studios, or they are hit songwriters. Each of them has specialties in particular genres and understands the needs of the market.

Our A&R are also people that understand what it means to mentor songwriters and give them the kind of feedback that enables them to improve.

Rapaport: What makes film and television music supervisors look to TAXI members for music?

Laskow: There are four major reasons. First, because many of our songwriters are not signed to major publishers and record companies, they can afford to offer their music at a reasonable cost. They are thrilled to get the exposure and credits for their portfolios and will not command the numbers that a platinum artist will. Second, most film and television shows do not need to have all the music written by name composers. The music supervisors can afford to take risks on unknown

My grandfather always told me, "If a farmer wants a red flannel shirt and we do not have it, walk him across the street to a competitor that does, and you will make a client for life."

writers and their companies are happy to save money. Third, TAXI consistently provides higher quality music than is available from many of the production music libraries at a fraction of the cost. Finally, we have a phenomenally fast turnaround time. A music supervisor can call us today and, within 48 hours, we will send a variety of quality music to choose from.

Rapaport: What is your philosophy with regard to your employees?

Laskow: I have to thank some of my past employers for my success with employees who work here today. I learned so much about what not to do with people who work for you. I would cringe when my former bosses would yell at and berate their employees and did not give a damn about the emotional climate in their businesses. So many of them did not care about their employees' families or struggles at home.

I try to treat people the way I would like to be treated. I take it very personally when someone on my staff is suffering financially. Running this company has made me a more mature, ethical and caring person. There have been years where I have had people on the staff that have made more money than I did, but it has been well worth it. The feelings you get when you make it possible for an employee to buy their first home or send their kid to college are unforgettable. Some of the best profits are the emotional kind.

Rapaport: Have you kept your promise to give donations?

Laskow: Yes. We really enjoy donating to charities, but sometimes we will help a family or person directly. For example, we heard about a single dad who was a police officer killed in the line of duty at during a shootout at LAX. We put out the word to members that we would match whatever they donated. Members gave $7000; we matched it and put it into a fund for that kid's college education. That was five years ago and the fund is growing. We initiated an annual scholarship that will be given away to a deserving student at Musician's Institute. We feel really good about helping people in our community. We feel like we have been really fortunate and that it is our responsibility to give something back.

The National Music Publishers' Association

The National Music Publishers Association (NMPA) is a nonprofit trade organization of over 900 U.S. publishing companies. Its primary goal is to protect members' creative rights and ensure that they are paid for the use of their work in all mediums. They are the lobbying arm for the U.S. publishing industry and most of their funding derives from the HFA.

Some of their recent accomplishments include—

- Successful litigation against MP3.com, Scour and Universal Music Group for not licensing copyrighted music for use on the Internet

- Successful litigation against Napster for copyright infringement

- Agreement with Streamways.com for streaming on-demand music

- Landmark agreements with RIAA and Listen.com for the issuance of licenses for limited downloads and limited streaming from paid-for-subscription services. Approval by the U.S. Copyright Office is expected

Any U.S. publishing company can join NMPA. Dues are $100 per calendar year.

The Harry Fox Agency

The Harry Fox Agency, a wholly owned subsidiary of NMPA, is the world's largest information source, clearinghouse and monitoring service for licensing musical copyrights.

The HFA acts as licensing agent for more than 27,000 U.S. publishers in connection with the issuance of mechanical licenses that cover the majority of musical compositions contained in U.S. records, tapes, compact discs, and imported phonorecords. The HFA also collects and distributes royalties for licenses that it issues and performs audits to ensure the accuracy of licensees' accountings. Through reciprocal representation agreements with similar collecting societies throughout the world, the HFA provides these services to its publisher principals on a global basis. In addition, the HFA often licenses on a worldwide basis on behalf of its publisher principals, for use in films, commercials, television programs and other types of audiovisual media.

The HFA maintains an online database of over 2 million songs (Songfile) that they license (*www.songfile.com*).

Both the NMPA and the HFA play an active role throughout the world in protecting copyright interests of the U.S. music publishing industry.

www.nmpa.org

The Future of Music Coalition

The Future of Music Coalition (FMC) is a nonprofit organization comprised of members of the music, technology, public policy and intellectual property law communities. The FMC seeks to educate the media, policymakers and the public about music/technology issues and create solutions to some pressing industry issues. The FMC identifies and promotes innovative business models to help independent musicians benefit from new technologies. It works to organize musicians from the independent music community to speak out on issues that impact the value of their labor. It offers alternatives regarding intellectual property rights and music issues that affect the interests of the independent music community, which may differ from those proposed by organizations, such as the RIAA, which largely represent the interest of entertainment conglomerates.

In 2001, the FMC filed a formal protest with the U.S. Copyright Office against the RIAA's proposal to collect and distribute webcasting royalties (SoundExchange) because they are largely funded by and work for the interests of, the large entertainment conglomerates. The FMC felt that many independent musicians, record companies, composers and publishers would not be fairly represented nor receive any royalties. It advocated that an impartial and accountable organization be set up to guard the value of all artists' webcasting royalties.

The FMC was successful in persuading the U.S. Copyright Arbitration Panel to pay monies directly to artists without regard to unrecouped royalties.

The FMC also protested the webcasting fees proposed by the CARP in early 2002.

FMA activities include—

- Public discussion of music/technology issues through its annual "Future of Music" conference and speaking tours at college campuses and participation at other music conferences, such as The New Orleans Music Conference.

- Submission of testimony to legislative committees on music/technology issues.

- Lobbying of music organizations, such as the RIAA

- Operation of an informational Web site that includes articles, research, reports, newsletters, etc.

www.futureofmusic.org

RESOURCES

American Society of Composers, Authors, and
Publishers (ASCAP)
One Lincoln Plaza
New York, NY 10023
(212) 621-6000
www.ascap.com

ASCAP-Los Angeles
7920 Sunset Boulevard, Suite 300
Los Angeles, CA 90028
(323) 883-1000

ASCAP-Nashville
2 Music Square West
Nashville, TN 37203
(615) 742-5000

Broadcast Data Systems (BDS)
1 North Lexington Avenue
White Plains, NY 10601
914-684-5600
www.bdsonline.com

Broadcast Music Incorporated (BMI)
320 West 57th Street
New York, NY 10019
(212) 586-2000
www.bmi.com

BMI-Los Angeles
8730 Sunset Boulevard
Hollywood, CA 90069-2211
(310) 659-9109

BMI-Nashville
10 Music Square East
Nashville, TN 37203-4399
(615) 401-2000

Canadian Mechanical Rights Reproduction
Agency (CMRAA)
56 Wellesley Street, West, Suite 320
Toronto, Ontario Canada M5S 2S3
(416) 469-3186
www.cmraa.ca

Copyright Arbitration Royalty Panel (CARP)
PO Box 70977
Southwest Station
Washington, DC 20024
(202) 707-8380
www.loc.gov/copyright/carp

Future of Music Coalition (FMC)
601 13th Street NW, Suite 900 South
Washington, DC 20005
(202) 783-5588
www.futureofmusic.org

The Harry Fox Agency, Inc. (HFA)
711 3rd Avenue
New York, NY 10017
(212) 370-5330
www.harryfox.com

National Music Publishers Association (NMPA)
475 Park Avenue South
New York, NY 10016-6901
(646) 742-1651
www.nmpa.org

PEN Music Group, Inc.
1608 North Las Palmas Avenue
Los Angeles, CA 90028-6112
Ph: 323.993.6542
www.penmusic.com

RESOURCES CONTINUED

Recording Industry Association of America
   (RIAA)
1330 Connecticut Avenue NW, Suite 300
Washington, DC 20036
(202) 775-0101
www.riaa.org

SESAC, Inc.
55 Music Square East
Nashville, TN 37203
(615) 320-0055
www.sesac.com

SESAC-New York
421 West 54th Street
New York, NY 10019
(212) 586-3450

SESAC-Santa Monica
501 Santa Monica Boulevard, Suite 450
Santa Monica, CA 90401-2430
(310) 393-9671

Society of Composers, Authors and Music
Publishers of Canada (SOCAN)
41 Valleybrook Drive
Don Mills, Ontario
Canada M3B 2S6
(416) 445-8700
www.socan.ca

TAXI
5010 North Parkway Calabasas, Suite 200
Calabasas, CA 91302
(800) 458-2111
www.taxi.com

Attorneys and
Artists' Managers

* * *

THE BUSINESS OF ATTORNEYS

THE BUSINESS OF ARTISTS' MANAGERS

INTERVIEW HIGHLIGHT
Stan Hertzman:
Umbrella Management

RESOURCE HIGHLIGHT
The Electronic Music Defense and
Education Fund

RESOURCES

The Business of Attorneys

Every music business will need the services of one or more attorneys. Some attorneys that specialize in the music business build expertise in particular areas, such as publishing, recording and intellectual property rights (copyrights, trademarks, service marks and patents). Others are well-versed in all aspects of business law, including business entity set-up, fair trade, antitrust, libel, slander and taxation.

Most of the prominent music attorneys are located in New York, Los Angeles, Nashville and Toronto.

LEGAL REQUIREMENTS

Attorneys generally have a four-year college degree and a three- to four-year law degree (JD). They must pass a state bar exam in order to practice law. Some states also provide certifications for some areas of legal specialization: criminal law, workers' compensation, taxation, patent law and family law. There is no certification for entertainment law.

Attorneys have a legal and ethical duty to avoid conflicts of interest. Attorneys may not represent two clients that have adversarial interests. Neither can a law firm have two attorneys representing clients that have conflicting interests.

Here are two examples of conflicts—

- An attorney has performed services for Record company X for a number of years. The attorney also helped Jazz Trio Y draft their partnership agreements. The trio wants the attorney to get them a record deal with record company X.

- Attorney X's law firm is on retainer for a large talent agency. Another member of the firm represents a musical group that wants to sue the talent agency.

Attorneys must declare potential conflicts of interest to their clients and bow out or obtain written consents from the adverse parties that will be represented.

HOW ATTORNEYS MAKE MONEY

Law is a well-paid profession. The more famous and in demand the attorneys and the more money that they make or save for their clients, the more clients will have to pay for their services. Here are common ways attorneys charge for services—

- *Hourly fee agreement:* $100 to $400 an hour, or more

- *Annual retainer:* guaranteed number of hours at an hourly fee

- *Percentage of income* generated by contracts (2% to 10%, or more)

- *Percentage of court settlements* (30% to 50%)

- *When directly employed,* salaries plus such benefits as annual bonuses and stock ownership

Attorneys are reimbursed for expenses incurred on behalf of their clients, such as phone, photocopies, travel, court costs, and so on. Most attorneys require a retainer (an advance for fees and expenses that will be incurred).

Most attorneys require contracts or letters of agreement that spell out the scope of work and their fees or percentage arrangements.

Attorneys can be in business for themselves, with small rosters of clients and work from offices in their homes. They can be sole proprietors, members in small and large LLCs or founders, directors or stockholders in corporations. They can be salaried employees of large music business entities or nonprofit trade associations, such as the Recording Industry Association of America (RIAA).

PRINCIPLE JOB RESPONSIBILITIES

Attorneys consult with clients about business strategies and decisions, negotiate and draft contracts, settle disputes and misunderstandings that occur during the life of a contract, represent clients in court and advise them how to comply with the local, state and federal laws and ordinances that apply to their businesses.

Some attorneys find record deals for their clients. They have developed relationships with record company executives and know what the companies are looking for and how deals are structured and valued. Many of their clients have deals with these companies.

EXAMPLES OF CONTRACTS THAT LAWYERS NEGOTIATE AND DRAFT ON BEHALF OF THEIR CLIENTS–

- Setup of partnerships, corporations and other business entities

- Investor agreements

- Sale, merger and acquisition agreements

- Licensing agreements

- Recording agreements

- Distribution agreements

- Publishing agreements

- Production agreements

- Merchandising agreements

- Talent agency agreements

- Manufacturing agreements

A lesser-known aspect of their jobs is to draft new laws on behalf of their clients and lobby state and federal legislators for their adoption. These include some of the new copyright protection laws pending in Congress (see Segment 2, Creative Rights).

Many music industry lawyers volunteer services to nonprofit associations. They provide free legal advice, hold seminars and workshops and write for legal publications. Some associations, such as the American Civil Liberties Union (ACLU), are noted for defending constitutional rights, such as freedom of speech and assembly. Others, such as Recording Industry Association of America (RIAA), serve the particular interests of their members.

Contract Negotiation

Businesses make agreements between people and businesses about their mutual goals and the

A MODEL MEDIATION PROGRAM

According to Alma Robinson, the California Lawyers for the Arts (CLA) Executive Director, "What distinguishes our mediation program from others is that our program is not just a lawyer-driven process. Artists are an integral part of our mediations because they bring a lot of hard-core experience and caring. Almost always, an artist and lawyer team up: the artist brainstorms one range of possibilities to help people feel through their situation; the attorney another. They help clients repair their relationships and walk away with dignity."

money and services they will exchange. These agreements form the bases of contracts. Lawyers that draft, negotiate and administer contracts are termed transactional lawyers.

In the music business, contracts can be for relatively simple transactions, such as purchasing time from a recording or video production studio; hiring a graphic designer or photographer; buying a specified amount of products; and the leasing of office equipment or vehicles. Or they can be for complex transactions, that have many long-term consequences, such as the setup of a music business entity; agreements between performers and record companies and composers and publishing companies; and acquisition agreements between record companies or record stores.

Litigation

Legal disputes and criminal prosecutions are legion in the industry and generate millions of dollars for attorneys. Lawyers that argue cases in the courts are called litigators.

Some recent music industry disputes and prosecutions that required litigation are—

- Crackdown on rave concert promoters, discussed later in this segment.

- Record companies and publishers against Napster (copyright infringement), discussed in Segment 2, Creative Rights.

- Artist Courtney Love against Vivendi Universal discussed in Segment 8, Record Companies.

- The Black Promoters Association against 11 US Booking Agencies and 29 top concert promoters, discussed in Segment 6, Talent Agents.

ALTERNATIVE DISPUTE RESOLUTION

Alternative dispute resolution can be used instead of going to court when disagreements occur. It is extremely cost-effective, legal and court fees are minimized, the atmosphere is less formal, and it takes less time to conclude than court processes.

There are two main procedures: arbitration and mediation.

Arbitration

In arbitration, a dispute between two parties is submitted to an arbitrator for a decision.

In binding arbitration, each party agrees, in advance, to accept the arbitrator's decision and presents their evidence and point of view. In non-binding arbitration (advisory litigation), the arbitrator's decision is not final, but their opinion provides the parties with guidance and can be accepted.

Many music industry contracts mandate that binding arbitration be used as the first (and sometimes only) method for settling grievances or resolving contractual disagreements; and some court rules mandate that certain disputes be submitted to arbitration, rather than be settled by a jury.

Arbitration may also be voluntary. Here, two

parties will ask an arbitrator to settle a dispute in advance of or during a court case to minimize expense, delay or adverse publicity.

A major benefit of arbitration is that no legal precedents are established and the terms of the settlement can be kept secret. Agreements are not made part of any public record.

Mediation

In mediation, the disputing parties sit down with a trained, neutral third party (mediator) and work out a solution in a nonadversarial and cooperative environment. The mediator does not decide in favor of either party: they resolve their own differences. Mediation is generally informal, with few rules, procedures or legal precedents that must be followed. If the parties cannot work out an agreement, they can pursue arbitration and litigation.

Mediators specialize in particular areas, such as disputes between club owners and musicians. They are trained in mediation techniques. Mediators may or may not be attorneys. This depends on state laws and the types of mediation they provide (divorce, contractual disputes, etc.).

Service Providers

Although most arbitrators and many mediators are attorneys, business people that have been trained in dispute resolution techniques can be very successful, particularly if they are experts in particular business areas. These techniques can be learned from a number of institutions that offer continuing education courses for professionals and from several nonprofit organizations that specialize in providing alternative dispute resolution services.

According to the American Arbitration Association (AAA), qualifications for inclusion in the AAA's national roster of arbitrators and mediators include a minimum of 10 years of senior-level business or professional experience or legal practice, the ability to evaluate and apply legal, business or trade principles and completion of a training program under the guidelines of their

NONPROFIT LEGAL ASSOCIATIONS FOR THE ARTIST

Many states have nonprofit legal associations that provides a wide range of affordable legal and other services to arts organizations and artists of all disciplines. They have panels of attorneys that will meet with members for moderate fees for consultations on arts-related business problems, including copyright, contract review, business entity setup and tenant disputes.

These associations offer lawyer referral services, arbitration and mediation services, legal workshops and seminars and libraries of art related books and materials and information about grants for artists.

Three Web sites that list volunteer legal associations by state are—

- *www.libertynet.org/pvla/vlas.htm*

- *www.starvingartistslaw.com*

- *http://arts.endow.gov/artforms/ Manage/VLA2.html*

Commercial Arbitration Development Program.

Many nonprofit legal associations provide arbitration and mediation services.

CONCLUSION

Attorneys are the power brokers of the music industry and they are valuable team members in every music business. Many specialize in particular aspects of the music business and know key executives in record companies, concert promotion companies, etc., on a first name basis.

The Business of Artists' Managers

Managers run artists' businesses. They create and administer strategic plans that advance artists' careers, public recognition, profit and business stability in ways that are congruent with the artists' goals. Managers must be knowledgeable about every aspect of the music business and the contracts that govern them. They must have the ability to inspire, build and maintain relationships with people and businesses to ensure their artists become successful. Managers must understand the markets that their artists serve; the nature of the people that are likely to buy their products and services; the distribution and promotional networks that serve their artists' genres; the competition their artists face; and their fans, whose allegiance and loyalty must be won.

Artist management is a long-term job. Generally, the careers of artists do not skyrocket immediately; few performers become overnight sensations. It may take up to two years to find and negotiate a recording deal; another year to record, manufacture and tour when the recording is released. It takes time before the fruits of any particular strategy are realized.

LEGAL REQUIREMENTS

There are no state and federal certifications or licenses required for artist managers.

However, New York and California statutes expressly forbid managers without talent agency licenses to get jobs for artists. Because many talent agents are not willing to sign artists until they have proven themselves in the marketplace, many managers do find performance jobs for their artists early in their careers, at some peril. This is because artists can later us this as an excuse to drop their managers or, worse, sue them.

When managers procure work for artists that are members of music unions, such as the American Federation of Musicians (AFM), they must ensure that their artists abide by the AFM contract agreements that specify wage and performance requirements.

HOW ARTISTS' MANAGERS MAKE MONEY

Artists' managers operate two businesses: one on behalf of their artists and the other on behalf of themselves. They are dependent on each other. When artists make money, managers make money.

Managers typically make 15% to 25% of their artists' gross earnings from their artistic activities, such as recording, performing and composing. From these earnings, managers try to run profitable businessed for themselves or maintain a specified percentage of profitability when they work for management organizations. Managers are reimbursed for expenses that are incurred when performing their jobs for artists, in addition to their percentages from artists' earnings.

Managers can be in business for themselves, be part of a partnership, LLC or corporation. They may manage one or more artists. They may specialize in one genre of music, or in many.

PRINCIPAL JOB RESPONSIBILITIES

Managers understand that talent is only one component of success.

Two other major components are—

- The artists' willingness to commit themselves to long-term careers

- Competent teams of professionals and businesses that will work on their behalf.

Managers must provide the leadership and motivation to help build stable psychological bases around their artists and assemble the teams that will advance their careers. The primary teams include attorneys, certified public accountants, talent agents, record labels and publishing companies. Secondary teams include publicists and business managers. Other team members are used to bolster and enhance artists' aesthetic talents. These include other musicians, sound reinforcement professionals, record producers and choreographers.

Managers' Relationships with Artists
The most important relationships that managers have are with their artists. Managers are the chief executive officers: the front persons for all their artists' business dealings; the strategists; the salespersons; the savvy money persons; the problem solvers; and the contract finders and administrators.

Managers are artists' trusted friends. They provide important emotional support and must be able to discuss aesthetic and personal problems with compassion and objectivity. These may

> **ONE OF THE REAL PROBLEMS IN THE RAP GENRE IS THAT THE ARTISTS DON'T HAVE REAL MANAGEMENT.** The artist's cousin, mother, friend, the kid down the street, acts as manager. It is very difficult to get artists past the mentality of using the people that they grew up with and trust to be their managers. To meet this challenge, Rap Coalition decided to try and train them. People are hired to work for $300-500 a week so they can learn hands-on. They do things like fill out paperwork for a tour; go out with a band on tour, etc. Black Rob, Wu Tang's manager, came through our program.
>
> — WENDY DAY
> *Founder, Rap Coalition*

include chronic lateness at concerts, interviews and other appointments; drug and alcohol problems; personality conflicts with other artists; emotional heartaches; and personal debts. Just keeping a pop band or classical chamber music trio together, through the pressures of touring and recording, is enormously challenging.

Setting Goals and Priorities
The first task that managers have is to find out what their artists' expectations and goals are, to assess where their artists' careers stand and prioritize what needs to be done. They must reconcile differences between aesthetic and business needs. For example, an artist may want a bigger sound system and their manager knows the money should be spent on promotional materials. A band may want their manager to pursue a major label recording deal, but the manager knows that the band must perform more, increase its fan base and put out a record on an independent label.

Once managers have prioritized short- and long-term goals and the tasks that will achieve them, they must draw up business plans and set out to fulfill them.

SETTING GOALS

THESE ARE GOALS THAT COULD BE SET FOR A TALENTED SINGER/SONGWRITER THAT HAS ALREADY RELEASED A CD OF THEIR OWN MUSIC AND SOLD 2500 COPIES.

FIRST-YEAR GOALS

- Start a fan list and fan club

- Create a first-rate press kit and Web site to provide information to business people and fans

- Sign the artist with a talent agency

- Hire a guitarist and bass player to tour with the artist

- Direct the talent agency to procure at least 8 college concerts a month, at no less than $1500 a performance

- Find an investor for a second CD

- Record, manufacture and sell 5000 CDs

- Make a deal with an independent distributor

- Earn the artist a gross income of $75,000

SECOND-YEAR GOALS

- Procure a major label deal for the artist

- Have the artist take four months off to record

- Make a video

- Hire a full-time publicist

- Persuade a publishing company to sign the artist

- Have the talent agent procure at least 8 college concerts and 5 nightclub gigs per month, at no less than $2000 a performance

- Have the talent agent book the artist into two major festivals

- Earn the artist a gross income of $125,000

THIRD-YEAR GOALS

- Have record release parties in New York and Los Angeles

- Promote the new record with a three-month, four-concert-a-week tour, earning no less than $2500 a performance, as the opening act for an American superstar act

- Air a video of the artist's hit song on MTV

- Hire a full-time publicist

- Earn the artist a gross income of $250,000.

Managing the Finances

Managers are the chief financial officers for the artists. They must ensure that their artists' businesses are profitable and financially stable. They are fiduciaries for their artists—persons that are entrusted with money—whether or not this relationship is specified in the management contract. Fiduciaries have legal responsibilities and artists can claim damages for any breach.

Managers are responsible for receiving

THE CRUSADER RABBIT STEALTH BAND AT THE
OAKLAND AUDITORIUM ARENA: BILL KREUTZMANN,
MICKEY HART, ROB BARRACO, BOB WEIR, JOHN MOLO,
PHIL LESH AND WARREN HAYNES.

income, allocating expenses, writing checks, researching insurance and filing tax returns. They hire staff and contract with other businesses for services and they are accountable for the efficiency and honesty with which these services are performed. Managers hire the services of bookkeepers to provide profit and loss statements and certified public accountants to prepare tax returns. They are responsible for finding out what the implications are of contractual decisions regarding the profitability of their artists' businesses.

They must be able to raise money by arranging credit lines with banks or finding investors. They must reserve some of the artists' income for when the artists have slow periods (they will). Some managers hire specialized business managers to advise their clients with regard to investments and tax planning to help them maximize their after-tax earnings and increase their assets.

Hiring and Firing

Managers also hire musicians, producers, road managers and sound reinforcement specialists. A major aspect of managers' jobs is keeping employees happy, involved, interested and working hard throughout arduous tours, hassles, emotional upheavals and disappointments. They must be knowledgeable about labor laws and employment practices.

They will contract with other businesses and vendors to perform such services as recording, mastering, graphic design, manufacturing, printing, etc., and send out requests for bids and negotiate prices and services.

Image Making

Making artists memorable to the public involves the art of image making. To differentiate their artists in the marketplace, managers must have

Managers need strong personalities, commitment, leadership, will power, self-confidence, self-discipline, courage, initiative, patience and above all, a sense of humor.

easily recognizable messages and images created for them artists (branding). Managers contract with public relations firms and advertising agencies to create consistent graphic and visual statements. This includes how a performer dresses on and off stage; backdrops and light shows to accompany the artists' performances, and so on.

The business of image making and promotion is the subject of Segment 9, Marketing and Selling Records.

Getting and Administering Contracts

Managers sell the talents of their artists and the products those talents produce. They must convince other businesses to help exploit their clients' talents—talent agents, record companies, public relations firms, publishers, and so on. This is not an indiscriminate task: managers must be assured that the chosen entities will satisfy their strategic plans for their artists and the images they want to create. They must weed out bad offers and, with the help of attorneys, secure contracts and negotiate them on behalf of their artists.

One of the hardest parts of the job is getting contracts to go well once they have been signed. Managers must maintain the goodwill that existed when contracts were signed and keep all the parties working hard and enthusiastically. Contracts are only a first step. Unexpected problems can surface after contracts have been signed.

Sometimes, an artist's first album does not turn out as well as was hoped and the record company becomes reluctant to put the artist on tour, as contractually promised. The record company may suggest that the artist wait to tour until after the second album is released. The manner in which managers handle these types of problems with record companies will affect the future of their artists' recording careers.

Learning to successfully, continuously and consistently administer contracts is one of the major challenges facing managers and one of the greatest challenges in maintaining a good working relationship with artists.

Managers' Relationships with Attorneys

Managers and attorneys work together to set up appropriate business entities; protect artists' intellectual property rights; help them avoid lawsuits and criminal acts; and negotiate and administer contracts. Attorneys explain the options to managers; but mangers make the decisions and sign the documents.

Managers should find attorneys that are artist advocates and have reputations for knowledge and effectiveness. Attorneys are the first team members to be sought by managers because of the key roles they play in setting up artists' businesses. Managers may hire more than one attorney: one that specializes in setting up business entities and another to negotiate recording deals.

Managers' Relationships with Talent Agents

Managers need talent agents that are willing and capable of booking work for their clients. They understand that agents must invest in new talent in order to build their own business and increase their profitability. Both know that new acts, given the right exposure, can become profitable clients.

When researching agents, managers try to ascertain their reputations and competency to make sure that agents have solid relationships with club owners, concert promoters, other agents (for packaging), managers and record companies. Managers want to be assured that agents will—

- Find profitable employment for their clients

- Secure employment that is financially or promotionally good for the client

- Accurately represent the drawing power of the acts

- Communicate well

- Be honest and ethical

Managers must be able to communicate the following information about their artists to talent agents—

- *History and performing and drawing power*

- *Sales history of recordings*

- *Promotional success* (airplay, reviews, articles, videos)

- *Musicianship and stage performance*

- *Team support:* manager, road manager, publicist, record company, etc.

- *Stability:* Acts that have been together for a year or more show a commitment to staying together. Agents do not want to invest time and money setting up good showcases or packaging artists as opening acts and then have them break up or quit performing.

- *Accountability:* Do artists show up on time for gigs and sound checks, work hard and put on good performances.

Once talent agents are selected, managers work with them to implement the managers' goals and priorities (See Segment 6, Talent Agents.)

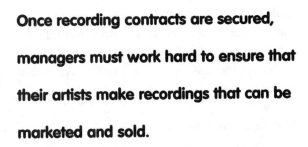

Once recording contracts are secured, managers must work hard to ensure that their artists make recordings that can be marketed and sold.

Managers' Relationships with Record Companies

Recordings reach more people than performances. They provide diversified revenue bases and increase the potential to advance artists' careers by increasing their opportunities to sell original songs and find lucrative performing opportunities. Recordings are the main medium for showcasing artists' talents.

Managers must be knowledgeable about which companies are appropriate at particular stages of their artists' careers and what those recording companies are looking for. They must decide if their artists' interests will be best served by signing with independent labels and be able to justify this strategy to their artists.

They must plan strategic sales campaigns to attract the record companies of choice and get them to sign their artists.

Once recording contracts are secured, managers must work hard to ensure that their artists make recordings that can be marketed and sold. This includes selecting good producers and engineers; helping artists successfully navigate the pressures of recording; and talk with key marketing and promotion people at the record companies so that they will be enthusiastic when their artists' recordings are finished; and ensuring that promotional and marketing materials are top notch.

Managers must work with record companies to plan marketing and promotional campaigns and coordinate touring, advertising, public relations and record promotion (airplay). Their major challenge is to ensure that record companies give their artists' work marketing priority over others they are simultaneously releasing.

Marketing and selling records is the subject of Segment 9.

Managers' Relationships with Publishing Companies

Managers must keep publishers interested in their clients' compositions. Composers' songs can bring in more publishing revenue than that derived from sales of recordings and concert performance fees. Finding publishers that will actively exploit composers' talents is another major challenge facing artists' managers. (Licensing is discussed in Segment 4, Music Licensing. Publishing is discussed in Segment 3, Publishing.

CONTRACTS BETWEEN ARTISTS AND MANAGERS

Contracts between artists and managers can be controversial because of the vagueness with which they define managers' duties and accountability to their artists. Artists should have their own attorneys when they negotiate contracts with managers to ensure that they are afforded as much protection as possible.

Often these contracts only outline managers' roles as advisors and counselors to artists and do not describe the actual services that managers will perform.

A typical clause reads—

"Manager agrees during the term thereof, to advise, counsel and assist Artist in connection with the matters relating to Artist's career in all branches of the entertainment industry, including, but not limited to—

- *Selection of literary, artistic and musical material*

- *Matters pertaining to publicity, promotion, public relations and advertising*

- *Adoption of proper formats for the presentation of Artist's artistic talents in determination of the proper style, mood, setting, business and characterization in keeping with Artist's talents*

- *Selection of talent to embellish Artist's presentation*

- *Selection of agreements and contracts for Artist's services*

- *Selection, supervision and coordination of those persons, firms and corporations that render services to or on behalf of the Artist, such as accountants, attorneys, publicists, talent agents and record companies."*

Nothing in this clause says that managers must perform these services, only counsel, advise and assist. Nothing holds the managers accountable for making bad contracts and choosing the wrong agents and attorneys.

Artists' attorneys should eliminate this vagueness by negotiating terms that provide performance benchmarks for managers and bases for artists to break their contracts. Here are a few examples—

- The manager must secure a recording contract with a major label by the end of the two years from the signing of the contract

- The manager must ensure that the artist is earning a gross income of $250,000 at the end of contractual year three.

Management contracts confer blanket powers of attorney to managers, which makes them fiduciaries. This authorizes them to sign and approve any contract or document without artists' knowledge or consent; to receive the artists' gross income; set up bank accounts for which artists may or may not be signatories; and to deduct expenses that the managers incur.

CODE OF ETHICS: THE NATIONAL CONFERENCE OF PERSONAL MANAGERS (NCOPM)

PERSONAL MANAGERS THAT EXHIBIT PROFESSIONAL EXPERIENCE, CONDUCT AND ETHICS HAVE BEEN ELECTED TO MEMBERSHIP IN THE NATIONAL CONFERENCE OF PERSONAL MANAGERS, AN ASSOCIATION COMMITTED TO THE ADVANCEMENT OF PERSONAL MANAGERS AND THEIR CLIENTS. THEY ASK THEIR MEMBERS TO ADHERE TO THEIR CODE OF ETHICS.

For the privilege of membership in the National Conference of Personal Managers, a personal manager agrees to—

- Have as a primary occupation the management of entertainers, performing artists and creative personalities

- Always deal honestly and fairly with clients

- Not derive personal gains at the expense of clients

- Treat relationships with clients in a confidential manner

- Not encourage or induce an artist to breach an existing personal management contract; not represent an artist while the artist is under a valid contract to another member in good standing of the National Conference of Personal Managers, except by written agreement with all parties concerned (and, in the event an agreement cannot be reached, the matter must be taken to the NCOPM Arbitration Committee before any other action is taken)

- Be proud of the personal management profession and the National Conference of Personal Managers and not publicly or privately disparage a fellow member of the National Conference of Personal Managers. In the event of a difference of opinion between any members, refer such matter to the appropriate committee for arbitration

- To the extent that it does not conflict with the best interest of clients, exchange information wherever possible and advisable with other members of the National Conference of Personal Managers.

Courtesy NCOPM. Used with permission

Here are some examples of how attorneys can limit the power-of-attorney clause for their artist clients—

- Limit the amount that managers can spend without written approvals

- Have artists approve three-month budget projections

- Ensure that the artists be offered major contracts that managers negotiate

- Provide artists with the means to independently audit managers' books

- Provide clauses that clearly specify the managers' fiduciary responsibilities

Limitations on the financial power of managers are necessary because there have been cases where managers' allocations of expenses provided little net wage to artists and cases where managers inflated their expenses.

Typical expenses that managers incur for which they are entitled to reimbursement—

- Travel incurred on behalf of the artist

- Office

- Employees

If managers work with more than one artist, expenses are allocated appropriately among them.

If artists sign management contracts with large firms, their attorneys may specify key-person clauses that determine who will be responsible to the artist.

Attorneys should clarify what happens to managers' earnings once contracts with their artists expire, including for how long they are entitled to receive income from the recording and publishing contracts they negotiated.

ARTISTS AS MANAGERS

Many artists and bands begin their careers by being their own managers: they book clubs; send out promotion; make and sell their own recordings; and hire attorneys and other personnel. They do this because, at the early stages of their careers, experienced managers are not usually available.

Some artists find they are competent at business. Even so, most will cede this job and to a professional manager when they can.

Many music businesses—such as talent agents and major label recording companies—do not like doing business directly with artists and prefer to work with professional managers. They feel that artists should use their time rehearsing, performing and composing and let professionals manage their businesses. They feel that artists too often cannot put their egos aside to understand the business needs and expectations of the people and businesses they work with.

CONCLUSION

Managers must understand all aspects of the music business and be familiar with the contracts that govern them.

They must be comfortable in dealing with artists, road managers, concert promoters, record company presidents, secretaries, recording studio owners, graphic designers, attorneys, and so forth. They must be excellent communicators, negotiators and mediators.

They must be willing to make decisions from a wide variety of choices and take responsibility for the success or failure of those decisions.

They must work long and improbable hours and cope with failure and rejection. It is not easy to take responsibility for artists' careers. Managers need strong personalities, commitment, leadership, will power, self-confidence, self-discipline, courage, initiative, patience and above all, a sense of humor.

Crackdown on Rave Concerts

Federal, state and local police are carrying out a systematic, nationwide crackdown on electronic music dance concerts (raves) in their war against drugs. The electronic music industry is largely made up of local concert promoters, dance clubs and independent record labels that have no affiliations to major labels.

The crackdown includes police harassment of concert promoters and venue managers.

According to a promotional video distributed by The Drug Enforcement Administration (DEA), "Raves are just a venue for drug purchases. They are analogous to crackhouses, in which you go buy the drugs and go out the back door. Although there's music being played, and the people at the raves are saying, 'I come here for the music,' drugs are predominant in these rave clubs." The narrator of the video is Donnie Marshall, DEA Administrator.

The tactics are effective. In New York City, one of the largest rave nightclubs has shut its doors. Club Twilo was closed in May 2001, after a three-year legal battle, when the State Supreme Court Appellate Division ruled that the city did not have to renew its cabaret license. A month later, Peter Gatien, the owner of the Limelight and the Tunnel clubs shut down after the State Liquor Authority revoked his clubs' liquor licenses. When Gatien filed for bankruptcy, the judge ruled that he needed his liquor license back in order to pay credi-

tors. He recently sold the Limelight to the owner of The Roxie, a dance club.

USE OF THE CRACKHOUSE LAW

In January and June of 2001, federal indictments were handed down by grand juries against the owners of major venues in Louisiana and Florida. These allege that the club owners were operating crackhouses.

The federal case against the owners of the State Palace Theater in New Orleans, Louisiana was settled with a plea bargain agreement in May 2001. The historic movie theater at the edge of the French Quarter hosted many types of concerts, including rock and blues. The owners had neither the heart nor the financial muscle to fight a very long legal battle. The American Civil Liberties Union (ACLU) helped the defendants with legal strategy while the Electronic Music Defense and Education Fund (EMDEF) assisted in paying a portion of the $210,000 costs incurred.

The owners pled guilty to one count of operating a crackhouse and agreed to pay a $100,000 fine. None will go to prison. A condition of the agreement was a ban on the use of glow sticks, pacifiers, masks, chill rooms and other items at the theater.

The ACLU challenged the ban and, in early 2002, prevailed. In his ruling, U.S. District Judge G.

THE CRACKHOUSE LAW

The 1986 crackhouse law prohibits any individual from engaging in the following acts: "Manage or control any building, room or enclosure, either as an owner, lessee, agent, employee or mortgagee, and knowingly and intentionally rent, lease or make available for use, with or without compensation, the building, room or enclosure for the purpose of unlawfully manufacturing, storing, distributing or using a controlled substance." 21 U.S.C. § 856(a)(2).

It has been invoked to hold venue owners and concert promoters responsible for the behavior of their guests. The government's view is that the owners knowingly and intentionally make their venues available for the use and sale of the illegal drugs (club drugs) commonly associated with rave dances: ecstasy, ketamine, GHB, LSD, etc.

"The use of the law is discriminatory," said Adam Burns, former rave promoter and co-owner of Offworld Music, a record label that specializes in electronic music. "Why are law officials targeting only promoters of rave concerts? Why aren't they going to sports events and rock concerts, where drug use is equally prevalent?"

Thomas Porteous said that while there is a "legitimate government interest in curtailing illegal drug use, the government cannot ban inherently legal objects that are used in expressive communication because a few people use the same legal item to enhance the effects of an illegal substance." He also noted that, "There is no conclusive evidence that eliminating the banned items has reduced the amount of ecstasy use at raves."

According to Will Patterson, spokesperson and fundraiser for the EMDEF, "This is a good example of why the federal government is very successful in many of these cases. They target people that have active lives and cannot afford to take two or more years to fight these cases. The government can just sit back and wear them down."

In June 2001 a federal indictment that involved the anticrackhouse law was served against the owners of Club La Vela in Panama City, one of Florida's largest and most successful nightclubs. The indictment included a criminal forfeiture motion, which would have allowed the federal government to seize the club and the personal assets of the owners, valued at over $15,000,000.

According to Patterson, "The club was targeted because it featured electronic music. While there is no consensus on what defines a rave, only the broadest definition of a rave would include Club La Vela. Several law enforcement experts agreed that the club was not holding rave parties."

Unlike the owners of the State Palace theater, Club la Vela owners are prominent, angry and wealthy and battled the case into a jury trial.

On November 27, 2001, after less than two hours of deliberation, jurors returned a verdict of "not guilty" on all charges for the defendants. Although they were accused of violating federal narcotics laws, no drugs were ever found on them or inside their club. As evidence that the owners knew that patrons were using drugs at the club, trial prosecutors showed the jury BlowPops, gum and glow sticks, items seized in a April 27th raid on the club and a picture downloaded from Club La Vela's Web site of a man giving a massage to another man. The owners will be reimbursed for reasonable legal fees, which amounted to over three million dollars.

Even so, attorneys general in other states are applying the same strategy. In San Antonio, Texas, promoters cancelled a small rave concert after Texas Alcoholic Beverage Commission (TABC)

FREE
ECSTASY

WWW.ILLEGALSUBSTANCE.COM

ILLEGAL SUBSTANCE IS THE NAME OF AN ELECTRO-HIP HOP TRIO ON INDEPENDENT RECORDING LABEL OFFWORLD MUSIC. *Free Ecstasy* IS THE NAME OF THE TRIO'S FOUR SONG EP.

agents and local San Antonio vice squad detectives threatened the venue's management with arrest for violating the crackhouse laws. The officers also threatened to have the venue's liquor and occupancy licenses revoked.

The American Civil Liberties Union vigorously opposes the use of the crackhouse law against rave promoters on the constitutional ground that it is a violation of the First Amendment rights of free speech and right to assemble. Music is a form of free speech, and attempts to ban any form of free expression should be fought. In a motion filed to dismiss the case against the State Theater, the ACLU wrote "Here, the government has singled out a particular form of music concert based on its content, threatening to pursue any electronic music concert where drugs are present and actually prosecuting these defendants because they hosted concerts where some members of the audience allegedly used drugs. This effort to

silence music amounts to an unconstitutional restriction on speech. Moreover, the government runs afoul of the guarantee of equal protection under the law when it decides to selectively target its prosecution on the basis of providing electronic music, while ignoring the many other kinds of concerts and public events where drugs are equally present. In the end, the mere act of providing music to the public cannot be a crime."

OTHER LEGAL TACTICS

Two ecstasy prevention laws are now pending in Congress. Both drafts encourage [Community] "ordinances restricting rave clubs," and, "seizing lands under nuisance abatement laws to make new restrictions on an establishment's use."

A third bill provides sentences of entertainment

ISSUES RAISED BY THE CRACKDOWN ON RAVE CONCERTS

- Do crackdown tactics profile only one segment of the industry?

- What tactics are effective in reducing drug use at electronic music concerts?

- Does the crackdown contribute to stereotyping of the electronic music genre and its fans?

- Are these tactics discriminatory?

- Does the crackdown stifle musical expression?

- What steps should be taken to provide safe environments at concerts?

promoters to up to 9 years in federal prison if it is proved that they that "knew or reasonably ought to have known" that illegal drugs will be sold or consumed at an event.

Local ordinances against rave concerts and their promoters have already been passed. In May 2001 Chicago, Illinois made it a crime for landlords to knowingly rent buildings for rave parties. The passage of the ordinance was justified by city and law enforcement officials that equated rave concerts with dangerous drug use. Charlotte, North Carolina passed an ordinance that requires that applications for rave dance permits must be submitted on forms prescribed by the chief of police, which are then submitted to the Charlotte-Mecklenburg Police Department Vice and Narcotics Bureau. The ordinance also requires that juveniles (under 18) be prohibited from attending dances where adults will be present and vice versa (ostensibly to protect kids from predatory sex crimes and drugs) and sets curfews (no rave dances after 11 pm on weekdays and 12 am on weekends).

A new bill pending in the California Assembly in 2002 would require that local law enforcement be notified before any agency issues a permit for any dance event that could be attended by more than 1,000 persons and that promoters present evidence "hat the promoter is sufficiently knowledgeable about illegal drugs and drug paraphernalia."

CONCLUSION

While the State Palace Theater in New Orleans continues to allow rave dances, many dances at other venues have been cancelled. The crackdown seems to be succeeding. "There is no doubt that the heat is on right now," one promoter told me (he asked that his name not be used). He also said that promoters that did not put a priority on providing safe environments at their concerts should take responsibility for creating the monster that threatens to sabotage the entire industry and culture.

Many rave promoters and others connected to the electronic music industry feel it is entirely possible to have a safe show. According to Raymond Roker, publisher and founder of *URB Magazine*, "In England, promoters have learned to manage their events by taking a zero-tolerance attitude towards the small percentage of people that are acting irresponsibly and bringing down the party. At these events, drug use and drug sales are not tolerated. To try and impose a drug friendly culture in the middle of mainstream America and expect authorities to look the other way is just plain stupid. Promoters and fans need to understand the gravity of what they are trying to do and find a way to manage the events so safe environments prevail."

Stan Hertzman: Umbrella Artist Management

Sᴛᴀɴ Hᴇʀᴛᴢᴍᴀɴ, owner of Umbrella Artist Management, Cincinnati, Ohio, has managed an array of bands and artists for 22 years, including guitarist Adrian Belew, The Greenhornes, The Bears, The Raisins, Ellen Tanner, THEM, The Blue Birds and Mike Reid.

Hertzman is honest, intelligent, energetic and hard working. He has an impressive network of business contacts and a rare perspective on the follies and magic of the business. But after his long career in the music business, Herztman let go of being a personal manager and formed 2, 4, 7 Virtual Management, a management consultant firm. He consults with artists on an hourly basis, pursues (shops) recording and publishing deals for bands and artists and administers publishing contracts.

* * * * * * * *

Rapaport: What were some of the factors that went into your decision to step out of long-term management?

Hertzman: At 57, I'm no longer interested in being on the long-term career bus with artists. I no longer manage Adrian Belew, although I still administer some of his business interests. I still work with the Greenhornes' music.

I no longer want to deal with the social, economic, religious, psychological and reli-

gious ramifications of a band. That's the reality of being a full-time manager. It is a younger person's game. But I am interested in helping bands evaluate their businesses and help them make career plans. I will give them specific advice based on my experience and knowledge of how the business works. If they take it fine; if they do not, that is also fine.

Rapaport: How did you get to be a manager?

Hertzman: During the mid-sixties, I was a guitarist/singer/keyboardist in a mid-West band that got to be vastly popular. We were constantly offered more work than we could play. There were other good bands in the area that could do these gigs. So I started a booking agency.

This came about after I met with all the agents in Cincinnati, asking them what they could do for my band. What I found was a lot

CD COVER FOR ADRIAN BELEW ALBUM.

of old line companies that did really know how to book rock cover bands. And what I got out of those meetings was that in terms of being in the agency business at the level of club gigs, its pretty moronic. You have a roster of 20-30 bands; you call up a bar; you establish a track record for giving them what they want; and you collect the money.

When I was 22, I was smart enough to know that although I was a good singer and a decent player, but more than anything, I realized that I was the best business go-getter. And once I started an agency, I realized that by playing in a band and booking, there was conflict of interest that was constantly challenged by some of the bands: "Of course you keep the best jobs for yourselves." Once I recognized that it hampered representing other bands effectively, I gave up being a musician and started being a booking agent.

During that time I also realized that I did not want to be a dentist and switched majors in college from organic chemistry to business management and marketing and took a lot of psychology electives.

From 1968 to 1973, the agency built up a tremendous business. We had a huge roster of bands, 4 secretaries and 5 agents. Our bands did a lot of showcasing for NACA and we were booking some of the biggest mid-West clubs. Then one day, a friend of mind said to me: "You're not going to get anywhere booking 40 bands. Pick a few bands and manage them." I thought about that and said to myself: "He's probably right: every year you're just going to get variations of the same *movie*—showcase bands at NACA, have some club close that weren't supposed to; have a band breaks up at some inopportune time, etc.

Rapaport: What were your first bands?

Hertzman: In 1974, I heard a song "Black Betty" on a tape from a band called Starstruck. And I signed them on the basis of that song and made it a huge regional hit. It went on to become a top 15 hit after a little editing and name change of the band to RAM JAM. My second band, The LeBlanc-Carr Band had a hit with a song called "Falling." So I knew I had an ear for hit songs. But both bands failed because they broke up. And that's how I learned that to make money as a manager, you need to have bands that are committed to staying together.

In 1976, Belew called me and asked me to manage his band "Sweetheart." I said no way did I want Sweetheart. The band wasn't going anywhere. But I persuaded him to sign to management with the thought of shopping his music. I knew from the get go that he was a great talent (I had worked with him before, including getting him the gig in Sweetheart) and I also knew that he had a tendency to turn in his work with less than he was capable of most all the time and be permanently incomplete with stuff; not just quite getting something done.

Just after he signed to a management deal, Zappa saw him playing in Sweetheart and out of nowhere called him for an audition. I had little to do with that, but it is part of the serendipity that this business is known for.

Rapaport: Didn't Zappa reject him first time around?

Hertzman: True. It was a good lesson that not every attempt at a step forward succeeds. Belew knew he failed the audition, even before Zappa told him. But the next day, he got up his nerve and asked Zappa if he could try again. See, he knew he could do it. The second time he blew Zappa away and was offered the gig on the spot.

That's a good parable about how this business tests musicians. I tell my bands, "If I can put you out of this business by rejecting you, you should go home. This is too barbed and callous a business for you to bounce around in feeling sorry for yourself. You have to use your rejections to reach back and find your strengths." Artists have to develop the fiber to say, 'Damn the torpedoes.' Adrian had that quality. He had the strength that allowed him to look at another way to approach Zappa's rejection. I look for those qualities of resilience and confidence in the artists that I represent.

Rapaport: What is the job of a manager?

Hertzman: When I first started managing, I was always looking for accountability and reasoning to make success happen. It was Larry Lighter, my New York City attorney of more than 20 years, who said, "Stanley, this business does not have that accountability." He was right.

I take an agrarian approach to management: it is important to plant the seeds for the future and tend your gardens every day. You can plan for success; you can have good strategies, but over the years I have learned that timing and actual success are not always in your control. Sometimes your least favorite record is the most successful and vice versa.

To be a manager means that I have to understand how the dynamics of booking and record releases play into an artists' career; how to make good deals for publishing, merchandising or endorsements. I have to know about all the areas in which my bands do business in and what are considered fair terms.

Second, it is essential to understand where the industry is moving and be prepared to deal with very fast moving changes. I read the trade bulletins weekly—*Billboard and College Music Journal*—and I make an extra effort to stay on top of what is going on through networking because I don't live in a music center.

Third, and perhaps most important, you have to try to find people you can work with all the year around because this is primarily a relationship business.

Rapaport: Is accountability important?

Hertzman: One of my goals as a business was to build a reputation for accountability. You cannot breach a management contract or a recording contract by playing sick. You cannot go back on your word. And by doing so, you build moral accountability as well. You teach the bands that if they do something immoral, it will likely impair their earnings and make actions subject to lawsuits and damage claims. But not all managers and record companies act with that kind of accountability. There is no regulation over this field. You can come out of jail and be a manager. Or have an MBA. And there is a disgusting range of people to deal with—from the honest and competent to the fraudulent and incompetent.

Rapaport: What are a manager's responsibility with regard to the bands?

Hertzman: I have to be a psychologist, friend, businessperson and ally. I have to know how to problem solve and motivate. Artists expect a lot. They often have little humility and strong egos; and that can be a hindrance. Many of them have said to me, "All I want to do is write and do my music." But they still have to

I tell my bands, "If I can put you out of this business by rejecting you, you should go home. This is too barbed and callous a business for you to bounce around in feeling sorry for yourself. You have to use your rejections to reach back and find your strengths."

understand my part, so we can, together, move ahead. They have to understand that this is a highly competitive business. I tell them, "There are a thousand bands that want your band's gig every day, a thousand bands that want to be dead center. This is a business about bands displacing bands. For your band to get another step ahead, you have to bypass or displace someone. And you have to work extra hard to do it."

Rapaport: What is your commitment with regards to the artists you manage?

Hertzman: My commitment to my artists does not have anything to with their initial level of success. It has to do with my belief in them. A manager's alignment must always be with the artist, not the record company that signs them or the agency that books them. You are representing your artists to others and you have to make their interests your priority on a daily basis. It is not that these relationships have to be adversarial. It is just that, at the end of the day, your loyalty is with your artist.

You have to know and respect what other businesses that you are working with want, but you also have to give them alternatives, and let them know how their choices fit in within a long view of their careers. Some deals and some gigs may seem very attractive in the short term, yet be completely wrong in the context of career building.

Rapaport: What was it about the Greenhorns that led you to sign them?

Hertzman: The Greenhorns are part of the new wave of bands—what you might call the antigloss, antiestablishment, mod-garage bands that kids like so much today. I instantly liked the raw energy of their R&B lyrics; their strong vocals. I liked their youth, the great enthusiasm with which they perform. I liked the fact that they are flexible—they will play anywhere, go anywhere, play in weird places, sleep in their trucks. Their audiences love them.

When I first saw them they were at a preproduction level, maybe not even there. They were rough and disorganized. But that raw substance had many of the elements that a successful band needs. I saw that I could help put structure in them, help the business tighten up around them and let the music move forward.

Rapaport: How do you work with a band when you first sign them?

Hertzman: First you have to figure out where the artist' career is at that particular moment in time and get to understand the different personalities and dynamics of the band. You have to assess what you have to work with, where the improvements have to be, what talent needs to be nurtured. You have to figure out how to create a bigger than life thing about the band. There has to be some star quality, some element that is charismatic and unique. Only then can you figure out a good starting place for them to begin to make real progress It usually takes a couple of month to distil a vision of where their career might go as they grow and get better.

Rapaport: Do you teach bands about money?

Hertzman: Teaching artists to manage money is tough. At the beginning of their careers there's never enough and the bands get into debt. They can go on accumulating debt for years. Suddenly there is a change; their careers crank over; and they begin to taste success. Then the illusion is that there is money on the table. The reality is that there is debt on the table. Musicians have a hard time with that. Its not that they want to ignore the accumulated debt, but when the gains come in, they want the gains. Often, the artists will ask, "How much money did we get?" Rarely will they say how much do I owe?"

It is very difficult to get musicians to be aware and responsible about their finances. I try to be conscientious. Give them financial statements. Have them sign off on debts. But there is a fine line. Over time a manager has to help the bands to become adults with their money. The way I work with the bands is that they handle the money at early stages and then, once they are more liquid, our office maintains their account. I advise and counsel them, but I don't do the finances.

Rapaport: What is involved in working with someone like Adrian Belew when they begin to be successful?

Hertzman: Adrian Belew is a very complex, creative, intelligent person, with very high sights on what he wants to do. That gives us both a range of goals to strive for. And he is very diverse. For instance, at one point, Adrian was working on his new solo album; wanted to support his album "Salad Days," by touring; was working on a new album by "The Bears," as well as a new album by King Crimson; and was contemplating an offer to produce the Jaguars from Mexico for BMG. There are choices to be made here. Not everything can happen. In addition, there are always lot of other smaller events to mix into the equation such as interviews and promotional appearances.

But sometimes all the choices are quantitative as far as the money or career enhancement goes and you're just helping the artist choose between equivalent events. I look for the opportunities to make something special, something really productive happen.

Rapaport: How has the business changed?

Hertzman: In the seventies, a band's career depended on a manager helping a band find a major label deal. Everything was based on signing a group and getting them a hit song. It used to be a feat to get a record out, because the costs were so high. Even for demos, bands tended to wait until their songs and their arrangements were really tight.

Today, any band can have a CD. Many bands record virtually as soon as they start rehearsing the songs they are writing, before they are really ready to even know whether they want to make a career of the business or can stay together as a band.

And many have all the accoutrements of being top bands—the look, the good Web sites, records with classy covers. But when you look beyond the packaging, you find that the music is ordinary and that their careers are at a standstill.

There is a lot of premature music being recorded. One of the downsides to the indie business is that the amount of work artists take on, in the long run, depletes their creative energy. It puts test marketing on bands that are not really good at it, so that they become engaged in a competition of incompetence. This is where the indie scene breaks down for me. It gluts the field with a lot of mediocre music. In the old days, you had to make a demo attractive enough for someone else to put up the money and time to do it. The glut of music makes it more difficult to find the winners. It's like the lottery: the more tickets that are sold, the less anyone's chances for winning.

My marketing professor in college once said, "You can eliminate the middle man, but you cannot eliminate his function." There is this general feeling that if you manage yourself you can eliminate that need. There is some truth in this as long as you are moving slowly or want to give yourself the illusion of being busy. But often, if you are your own manager, record label, publicist and booking agent—well, there goes the music. It is counterproductive and subjective.

By counterproductive, I mean the artist's main function is creative and management's is business. In short time, the artist will find himself spending lots of time doing things they are not particularly proficient in doing and losing valuable creative time. At the same time, the artist fails to calculate the cost of this approach. I submit that this is where the initial competitive edge gets lost and relative field positions change in this most competitive industry.

At the same time, major labels expect a band to have its own recordings. "Show me how your record is doing," they say. They won't sign a band until it shows record sales and has a local hit. That is what is necessary to even be considered to get into that part of the race. And because the field is very congested, it makes it much more difficult to find the stand-out music, the band or artist that is going to emerge from that heap and be the new superstar.

But at some point a band has to be willing to put together a team of professionals and get out of self-management. They need to recognize what expertise they do not have and hire people they can trust.

Rapaport: Has consolidation been good for the health of the music industry?

Hertzman: Only conglomerates have the deep pockets to make success happen on the level that it happens. They are the only ones that can develop star power. And that is what fills arenas and keeps people buying instruments. The two or three major artists that drive the industry inspire tens of thousands of bands. Elvis inspired a generation of musicians and so did Hendrix and the Beatles. At the end of the day, people want stars and conglomerates are in the business of making stars happen. The fewer the people in control, the less the risks and the better the chances of someone coming in number one. And yes, some talent will be left behind. That is the nature of the business. It is a dream stealer and it is not always fair.

I think that the business is worse off because of the conglomerates. The industry can stuff you pretty good. The fact is, if you are not on a major label, you are entirely insignificant. You're not in the business as I know it.

Today, the major labels face a wake up call. They did not effectively understand what drove the popularity of Napster and ignored the fact that Napster or music sharing has been going on since the 50s (of course, in balance with the technology of those days). These are symptoms of an industry in tailspin. The basis of promotion, and the major underpinning of the music industry, is this well established maxim: interest in music sells music. Providing free music has never replaced ownership of valuable music. Find great music, package it well, don't feel compelled to "fill" albums, price music reasonably and the public will want to have it and will pay for it. Don't misunderstand me, I'm against piracy (which will always go on), but it is getting music to those who share it effectively—what I've always know as promotion—that drives this industry. So far, this is something the majors have not figured out effectively for 21st Century realities.

www.247virtualmanagement.com

The Electronic Music Defense and Education Fund

The Electronic Music Defense and Education Fund (EMDEF) is a nonprofit organization that was formed to defend the professionals and fans of electronic music that have been targeted in the growing "War on Club Drugs." It is an example of effective activism in the music industry.

The organization has raised over $100,000 to assist electronic music professionals that have been targeted by law enforcement officials and to find a more legitimate approach to fighting illegal drug use. It also serves as an advocate for the electronic dance music industry and provides an independent voice on behalf of industry professionals.

"The government has chosen to target the rave promoter in its war against drugs," said Will Patterson, EMDEF spokesperson. "If the government wishes to win the war against so-called club drugs, this is a major misdirection of resources. Drug dealers, not promoters of music events, should be the targets."

The EMDEF Web site *(www.emdef.org)* provides updates on the legal status of major lawsuits and legislative bills; links to the full text of those lawsuits and bills; a library of newspaper and magazine articles that highlight rave incidents nationwide; and an incident report form, which enables people to report profiling and harassment cases. The organization also sends out a newsletter every few weeks to update sub-

scribers on the progress of pending cases, EMDEF fundraising efforts and notices of educational panels at music and music business events.

EMDEF is a project of the Lindesmith Center—Drug Policy Foundation.

RESOURCES

American Arbitration Association
335 Madison Avenue
New York, NY 10017-4605
(212) 716-5800
www.adr.org

American Bar Association
750 North Lake Shore Drive
Chicago, IL 60611
(312) 988-5000
www.abanet.org

American Civil Liberties Union (ACLU)
125 Broad Street
New York, NY 10004
(212) 344-3005
www.aclu.org

RESOURCES CONTINUED

California Lawyers for the Arts (CALA)
Fort Mason Center
Building C, Room 255
San Francisco, CA 94123
(415) 775-7200
www.calawyersforthearts.org

Electronic Music Defense and Education Fund
  (EMDEF)
c/o The Lindesmith Center
4455 Connecticut Avenue NW
Washington DC 20008
(310) 450-9036
www.emdef.org

The Lindesmith Center - Drug Policy Foundation
4455 Connecticut Avenue NW
Washington DC 20008
(202) 537-5005
www.drugpolicy.org

Music Managers Forum (MMF)
PO Box 444, Village Station
New York, NY 10014-0444
(212) 213-8787
www.mmf-us.org

National Conference of Personal Managers
c/o National President
Gerard W. Purcell
46-19 220th Place
Bayside, NY 11361
(718) 224-3616
www.ncopm.com

North American Performing Arts Managers and
  Agents (NAPAMA)
459 Columbus Avenue #133
New York City, NY 10024
(888) 745-8759
www.napama.org

Talent Agents

* * *

THE BUSINESS OF TALENT AGENTS

**BLACK PROMOTERS SUE
TALENT AGENCIES AND
CONCERT PROMOTERS**

INTERVIEW HIGHLIGHT
Edna Landau: IMG Artists

RESOURCE HIGHLIGHT
The National Association for
Campus Activities

RESOURCES

The Business of Talent Agents

Talent agents (booking agents) get jobs for musicians, performers and vocalists in clubs, concerts, festivals, churches, etc. More than 10,000 talent agents are registered in the United States and Canada.

There are full-service (general service) agencies, such as International Creative Management, Creative Arts Agency and William Morris. They represent actors, writers, record and movie producers, composers, directors, etc., and can package talent for movies and television specials. They find corporate sponsors for special events and tours. There are also one-person and limited-service agencies that specialize in booking acts for particular venues or genres of music.

LEGAL REQUIREMENTS

Talent agents are legally considered to be employment agencies and must be licensed in the states in which they do business. State laws regulate their commissions, the lengths of their contracts and otherwise restrict the scope of their businesses. For example, talent agents may get performers jobs in nightclubs, but not as computer programmers.

Talent agents sign agreements (signatory agreements) with music-related unions, such as the AFM and AFTRA and agree to abide by their rules. Generally, these are—

- Work only with artists that are members of the unions

- Work with artists for terms specified by the unions

- Procure work for artists for no less than the minimum wage specified by the unions

Some talent agencies also perform management functions. California and New York statutes expressly forbid managers without talent agency licenses to get jobs for artists, but there is no proscription against talent agents managing artists.

HOW TALENT AGENTS MAKE MONEY

Agents typically make 10% to 20% of their artists' gross earnings from performances—that is the income artists receive before any expenses are deducted. Agents deduct the expenses they incurred in getting the performance from the payments due their artists. These expenses include telephone, travel, mailings, and so on. Talent agents do not get a percentage of the income earned by artists from publishing and recording.

PRINCIPLE JOB RESPONSIBILITIES

Talent agents act between the buyers of entertainment and artists or their managers. To be profitable, they must establish networks of buyers; have rosters of clients that can satisfy those buyers' needs; and know how to package new artists with established acts to make them successful business properties. Though talent agents are paid by artists, they must remain responsible to buyers and make all parties feel that they have been given a fair deal. Talent agents are under pressure to ensure profits for three businesses: themselves, their clients and the buyers of talent.

Relationship Between Talent Agents and Artist Managers

Once artists are signed with talent agencies, the agents must learn from the artists' managers what their overall strategic plans are for the acts and where and when dates should be booked. They work closely together to select which offers to accept. When acts have record contracts, the agents, record companies and managers work together to arrange tours that coincide with record releases and other promotional activities. All of the team members work together towards common ends. Managers must immediately communicate to the agents any changes in personnel, recording plans, dates of record releases, and so on.

Here are some of the things managers and acts need to spell out so that talent agents can find appropriate gigs and negotiate acceptable contracts—

- *Money:* What are the least acceptable amounts artists are willing to play for? What are the artists' attitudes about doing benefits.

- *Travel:* How far artists are willing to travel for one-night performances. Whether they are willing to go on the road. For how long they are willing to tour.

For talent agents and buyers of entertainment, draw defines how many people will come to an event on a particular day at a particular time for a particular price. Events can have draw and so can artists.

- *The characteristics of each acts' ideal audience.*

- *Packaging:* The kinds of acts clients would like (or not like) to be packaged with.

- *The acts' plans for recording and releasing albums.*

- *Types of performances:* Clubs, concerts, dances, etc. Lengths of performances.

- *Sound reinforcement and lighting requirements and sound check needs.*

- *Special contract needs (performance contract riders):* As acts become more successful, they want to specify conditions, such as numbers of free tickets and backstage passes; billing and stage security; the method of accounting for box office receipts; and the amenities they want in their dressing rooms.

These requirements are set forth in the performance contracts, but managers must ensure that the talent agent understands them and that they are feasible within the context of buyers' needs to have profitable events.

Talent agents must have adequate promotional materials to present to potential buyers, as part of their sales efforts. These are generally provided

2002 YOUNG CONCERT ARTIST INTERNATIONAL

ALL YCA PHOTOS: CHRISTIAN STEINER

The winners of the 2002 Young Concert Artist International auditions, sponsored by Young Concert Artists, Inc. The auditions are unique in that there are no rankings and any number of winners, or none, can be selected. The sole criteria are musicianship, virtuosity, communicative power and readiness for a concert career. The organization provides comprehensive and ongoing support and opportunities to the winners, including the booking of concert engagements, publicity, promotional materials and career guidance at no cost to the artists, until they are signed by commercial management (usually three to five years).

Young Concert Artists is supported by contributions from foundations, corporations and private donors.

nicholas kendall
vassily primakov
anton belov
naoko takada

by the acts' managers. Agents need press kits that contain biographies, performance and recording histories, articles and reviews, samples of recordings and videos, etc. Managers should send copies of new articles and reviews to talent agents as soon as possible and inform them about radio and television stations that are playing their acts' music or are interviewing them.

Relationship Between Talent Agents and Concert Promoters

Talent agents succeed by establishing long-term relationships with buyers of talent (concert promoters and arts presenters). They must understand their buyers' business needs; the types of audiences their venues draw; the competition they face; and the types of artists they are looking for.

Talent agents must understand the businesses of concert promotion, nightclub operation, and so on. They must negotiate the terms of contracts according to the specifications that manager have provided, but be mindful of buyers' needs to make profits. They must understand the expenses that buyers of talent incur in the course of putting on performances, including the costs of the demands that artists want in their contracts.

They must understand how to represent artists in terms of buyers' business needs. Sometimes, buyers of entertainment do not know exactly what they are looking for. They only know that they want good acts that will make them money. Buyers know that most managers and artists are going to tell them that the artists are fantastic. Agents are expected to be more objective: they can discuss artists' drawing power in particular cities, their reliability and their ability to meet buyers' needs.

Talent agents usually field any complaints from buyers about artists, such as lateness, poor stage manners, rudeness to buyers, etc., and mediate contractual misunderstandings. Chronic problems, such as lateness or misconduct must be discussed with artists' managers.

When performances are booked, talent agents have to ensure that buyers have adequate promotional materials to help advertise the shows.

Understanding Draw

In Western movies, "draw" means pull out your six-shooter. But in the music business, it has a different meaning. For talent agents and buyers of entertainment, draw defines how many people will come to an event on a particular day at a particular time for a particular price. Events can have draw and so can artists.

How is potential draw ascertained? The agents and buyers will look at artists' performing histories and try to ascertain how many people attended past performances. They analyze such variables as the sizes of acts' mailing lists; the recognition of acts' names (branding); CD sales; airplay and reviews; competing acts that will be performing at different venues at the same time; and competing leisure activities (movies, sports, festivals, etc.). The results of that research helps talent agents and buyers determine what to pay acts, what to charge customers, what dates to book, the size of auditoriums to be hired, and so on.

Talent agents represent artists' draw as accurately as possible to potential buyers because they understand that draw is critical to whether an act will make or lose money for the buyer.

TALENT AGENCY CONTRACTS

Contracts between talent agents and their clients are among the most straightforward and simple in the industry. They state what the duties of the agents are; what commission will be taken from the jobs they book; whether they have exclusivity for a type of venue or region; and termination clauses that specify how the contracts can be broken.

Talent agency contracts specify that the duties of agents are to obtain and negotiate offers for performance engagements; promote and utilize artists' names and talents with respect to the engagements; counsel artists on career direction; and maintain office and staff necessary to perform these tasks. The contracts also specify that artists are to communicate any offers of work to their agents.

These contracts generally include clauses that specify the circumstances under which a client can terminate the contract. Talent agencies that have agreements with music-related unions are required to supply a termination clause in every contract. Here is an example of an AFM mandated termination clause—

- *If the client is unemployed for four consecutive weeks at any time during the term hereof.*

- *If the client does not obtain employment for at least twenty cumulative weeks of engagements to be performed during each of the first and second six month periods during the term hereof.*

- *If the client does not obtain employment for at least 40 cumulative weeks of engagements to be performed during each subsequent year of the term hereof.*

When talent agencies have large rosters, clients may try to negotiate key man clauses that specify which agent they will work with. This helps ensure that clients are not continually shuffled among agents or assigned to rookie agents. Artists may also specify that if their agents change employment to other talent agencies the artists will have the option of going with them.

CAN ACTS BE THEIR OWN TALENT AGENTS?

Many artists act as their own booking agents at the onset of their careers until they have enough drawing power or are earning enough money to attract a talent agent to work with them.

CONCLUSION

Talent agents are important members of the team that helps artists profit from their talents. Good agents are superb negotiators and communicators. They are honest and exercise good judgment and follow through on their commitments.

Black Promoters Sue Booking Agencies and Concert Promoters

In 1999, The Black Promoters Association of America (BPA) filed a $700 million lawsuit in the Federal District Court of Southern New York against 11 major booking agencies and 30 top concert promoters. The defendants included William Morris, Creative Artists Agency, Monterey Peninsula Artists, SFX Entertainment (now Clear Channel Entertainment) and Bill Graham Enterprises.

The lawsuit suit alleges that a group of white-owned and controlled talent agencies violated black promoters' civil rights and broke antitrust laws. According to the complaint, "Because of an all-white concert promotion fraternity, black concert promoters were systematically excluded from the promotion of concerts given by white performers." No black promoter has been able to contract to promote a contemporary music concert given by a white artist, or even been given the opportunity to bid on such promotion. In addition, black promoters were regularly excluded from the promotion of concerts given by top-drawing black performers. The suit also charges that the agents and promoters maintained an illegal conspiracy to boycott the plaintiffs on the basis of race.

Although many black promoters promoted many black artists before they were signed to major talent agencies, such as Maxwell, The Commodores, Prince (before he changed his name), Toni Braxton and Erykah Badu, talent agencies did not give them the opportunities to bid when those acts (and others) appeared in their regions.

According to Leonard Rowe, President of the BPA, "We were excluded from promoting most concerts given by superstar black performers, which suggests they betrayed their own people and business communities." Black-owned businesses such as limousine and catering services that would routinely profit from concerts promoted by black promoters were adversely affected also.

According to the lawyers for the Black Promoters Association, the booking agencies were "able to maintain ultimate control over the concert-promotion market and guarantee promotion of all acts, including the less successful ones, by assuring promoters that they would always be given the opportunity, to the exclusion of others, of promoting the booking agents' top acts in promoters' assigned territories, at highly profitable rates."

An important ally for the BPA is Rev. Joseph Lowery, cofounder with Martin Luther King, Jr., of the Southern Christian Leadership Conference. He helped ensure that the case was well-publicized. He organized demonstrations in front of some of the talent agencies and at the 2000 GRAMMIES. "These agencies have systematically excluded black promoters from handling concerts with any white artists as well as black artists who

No black promoter has been able to contract to promote a contemporary music concert given by a white artist, or even been given the opportunity to bid on such promotion.

become superstars," he said. "This is one of the last bastions of segregation in the entertainment industry and it severely restricts economic opportunities for black entrepreneurs."

A victory for the Black Promoters Association occurred in July 2000 when New York Southern District Judge Robert P. Patterson Jr. refused to dismiss the case because he found sufficient merit on both the antitrust and civil-rights violations.

Although a few small agencies have settled (APA and Variety), the case has been stalled. The defendants have an array of over 70 lawyers and delaying tactics are stock-in-trade.

In May 2002, Clear Channel Entertainment settled with the Black Promoters Association for an undisclosed figure.

According to Bob Donnelly, a music law attorney, settlement for the rest of the defendants may not occur until Fall 2002 or 2003. "The defendants' lawyers would be crazy to allow the case to go to jury," said Donnelly. "Since the beginning of this case, we cannot find one instance where one black promoter has been allowed to promote one white artist in any one venue. This isn't a matter of 6% or 13%; the black promoters are not even getting pittances. White promoters are given all the black acts that have signed with large talent agencies. Nor have the talent agencies shown any desire to change their ways since the lawsuit was filed. What the black promoters want is a chance to bid and a fair and just system for how promoters for concerts are determined…Black music is the soul of the music business. Unfortunately we are a business that was first built on discrimination, with people like Pat Boone covering Little Richard songs because white media didn't want race music played on the air waves and black artists receiving considerably lower royalties than their white counterparts. Now that we've have erased so much of that discriminatory bias, it's time to remove the last vestiges."

Edna Landau:
IMG Artists

ITZHAK PERLMAN AND EDNA LANDAU

Edna Landau is the director of IMG (International Management Group) Artists in North America. The company represents prestigious classical artists and up-and-coming new artists in addition to dance and world music attractions. IMG works on all aspects of their careers, managing, booking and recording. Ms.

Landau manages several artists and conductors, including pianists Evgeny Kissin, violinist Itzhak Perlman and conductor Franz Welser-Möst (Music Director of the Cleveland Orchestra).

* * * * * * * *

Rapaport: How do you find the time to administer and manage?

Landau: We take a layered approach at IMG. Although each artist has a main contact, there are five to seven others that share responsibilities. If artists only had one person that knew what was going on, we would be in deep trouble.

For example, I'm the main contact for Itzhak Perlman. I do the booking of the top orchestras and the most important concert series. I help coordinate two other people that do orchestral booking; three that do nonorchestral booking (colleges and universities) and one person that coordinates public relations and makes travel arrangements. Perlman has always supervised his own recordings and works directly with his lawyer on contractual arrangements. When there is a new recording, we work extremely closely with the record company to ensure that Perlman plays some of the repertoire that is featured on the recording and in that way help publicize it.

Rapaport: Are you a musician?

Landau: I studied piano from the age of 5. I received my B.A in music from City University of New York with a major in Music and minor in Education and an M.A. in musicology from the same university. I also had an interest in conducting and took some courses at the Juilliard School of Music.

Rapaport: What was your first job?

Landau: My first job was teaching theory and history at New York's High School of Music and Art. They asked me to also teach voice, which I had never done. I took voice lessons, stayed a few steps ahead of my students and ended up loving it. I taught there for five years, a difficult period in New York's history because of the turmoil on university campuses, including City College, where the High School of Music and Art was located. Few kids could keep their mind on their work during those troubled times and I found that I did not want to force them to learn curriculum they did not want to learn.

Rapaport: What happened next?

Landau: I answered an ad in *The New York Times* from Young Concert Artists for the job of assistant to the director and got it. I worked there for five years and got the bug for booking. At one of the major booking conferences, I met Charles Hamlen, a former schoolteacher who had recently started his own agency. We liked each other immediately and Hamlen Management soon became Hamlen-Landau Management. We built a great reputation, even though we were booking artists that few arts presenters had heard of. We were going to competitions to look for talent and developed relationships with heads of conservatories so that they would call us about their best students. That is how we found violinist Joshua Bell when he was 14.

But, we knew that to become a major force in the business, we needed a big fish, a big star and an infusion of money to travel and entertain and nurture relationships with presenters.

We sat down with a wonderful accountant that worked for the Small Business Administration and he helped us write a business plan and put together a private stock offering. Our goal was to raise $210,000. Then we started taking it around to potential investors. We raised $60,000. Not enough. But we kept pounding away. One of the persons that we eventually made an appointment with was James Wolfensohn, Chairman of Carnegie Hall. While we were there, he said, "Look, you have an excellent reputation and IMG has put out feelers about wanting to get into the classical business. Would you be interested?"

At that time, he told us that IMG was a huge multinational company that represented

NINETEEN-YEAR-OLD CHINESE PIANIST LANG LANG. "HIS ELECTRIFYING MAGNETISM AND TALENT ARE MARRIED; HE CAPTIVATES YOUNG AND OLD. HE IS DEFINITELY TOMORROW," EDNA LANDAU SAID.

many of the world's leading athletes. When we expressed interest, Wolfensohn picked up the phone and called Mark McCormack, IMG's founder, and said, "I have something to talk to you about." We met Mr. McCormack in the summer of 1983 and shortly thereafter Hamlen-Landau was subsumed into IMG and the company entered the classical music business. We were a nucleus of expertise.

It was so incredible to us that a company like that would be interested in us solely because we loved what we did and had a good reputation. We found Mr. McCormack to be an incredible visionary who had a feel for where things were going to go. We all knew that with a large company backing the idea that it would be easier to build a wonderful roster of artists and perhaps even get television shows and sponsorship opportunities for them.

Rapaport: Who was the first major artist that you signed?

Landau: Itzhak Perlman. The formation of the classical division, IMG Artists, virtually coincided with the death of Perlman's manager at International Creative Management (ICM). He was looking for a change. He knew about Charles and me, but would not have come to us as Hamlen-Landau because we weren't major players. To be the manager of Perlman, you have to be wining and dining with the major arts presenters and symphony orchestras directors. But Perlman knew that with a larger company behind us, he would likely get the wider visibility, level of service and range of opportunities that he was seeking.

Rapaport: What are some of the new challenges that face classical music?

Landau: We need to attract more young people by making concerts more user-friendly and educating them about what they are hearing. We can learn much from the entertainment industry about how to effectively link artists' performances more closely with the release of recordings and even movies that feature their work. A good example of this is the Academy Award-winning soundtrack for "The Red Violin," composed by John Corigliano and fea-

We need to attract more young people by making concerts more user-friendly and educating them about what they are hearing.

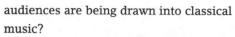

turing violinist Joshua Bell. The composer wrote a separate work derived from the score, "The Red Violin: Suite for Violin and Orchestra," which was performed by Mr. Bell with leading orchestras in major venues such as Carnegie Hall at the height of the film's popularity. This helped to attract new audiences to John Corigliano's music and Joshua Bell's artistry.

Rapaport: What is the difference between art and entertainment?

Landau: That is a tough question. I think there is a traditional line, but it is getting blurred. I would like to think that on some level, great music from the cultural side should be entertaining. At the very least it should capture your imagination and keep you involved. But perhaps the difference is that certain kinds of entertainment do not presuppose knowledge about what you are hearing. Entertainment's ability to please as spectacle matters more. And perhaps the standards of performance that artists strive for in the classical world may be less critical to the audience's enjoyment. Certainly, it is much harder to walk into a classical concert if you have absolutely no background and enjoy it. We ask ourselves all the time, what will make people that go to a large stadium to hear the three tenors [Carreras, Domingo and Pavarotti] also buy tickets for the Metropolitan opera?

Rapaport: What are some of the new ways that audiences are being drawn into classical music?

Landau: Artists and conductors are becoming more involved with their audiences. Sometimes, they talk to them before they begin to play a piece or give pre-concert lectures; sometimes, artists go out and give workshops in the schools and in the community. One of our artists, Jeffrey Kahane, a pianist we signed who was a Van Cliburn competition winner, later became a conductor and now works with the Santa Rosa Symphony Orchestra in California. He wanted to introduce a new contemporary oratorio called "A Child of Our Time" by Michael Tippett that had a theme of oppression and injustice. Kahane helped organize a year-long extracurricular arts program for area high school students that centered around the work. Students made photographs, paintings, sculpture and other art and it was featured in the lobby of the concert hall during performances. It was the cultural event of the year. It helped break down perceptions that classical music was some sort of snobby and inaccessible art form. If people are going to choose to spend time coming to classical music performances, they need to feel a connection with the artists. If they feel the artists are elitist, they will not come back. Today, artists have to do more than just sit down and play a piece. Playing like an angel and not having some kind of charisma, just doesn't fly with younger audiences that have grown up in a much more visual world and are used to seeing entertainers that know how to connect. So it is important for educators, arts presenters and symphony directors to encourage artists and conductors to creatively engage their audiences and communicate with them.

Rapaport: What are your principles of doing business?

Landau: Maintaining the highest quality, in terms of artists we take on, how we treat them, the people that hire them and the people that we hire to work on their behalf. And having impeccable honesty.

We are fortunate to maintain the wonderful level of reputation that we had when we were Hamlen-Landau. I am fairly humble as a person, but I am not humble about reputation. We enjoy the best reputation in this business. We are known for our honesty, our good judgment and for always going the extra mile. I can remember hearing one of our receptionists begin to tell a caller that we did not represent someone they wanted to know about. I asked her to put the caller on hold and told her to say that we would find out the contact and phone number and call them back immediately. I told her, "They will not forget the courtesy and who knows they might end up coming back to do business with us someday."

I like to hire people that know what I do not and let them fly. We did not have a dance division or vocal division. Now we do. We have grown through the strength of people that complement each other's skills.

All the people that work here have excellent taste, know their field thoroughly, are imaginative and give their highest level of work.

We are sticklers for having all our materials look good and be accurate; and for being completely prepared when we talk to presenters.

When we talk with our artists on the phone, we make them feel that there is nothing else going on, that we are 100% concentrated on them. We do not interrupt our conversations with them. This is terribly important.

We do not piggyback artists: we do not pressure presenters by saying, "If you don't book X, we will not give you Y." We do not try to push artists into situations that are not right for them because we want a commission. Our reputation is built on signing artists of good quality and making good matches.

www.imgartists.com

The National Association for Campus Activities

The NACA is the largest collegiate organization for campus activities. It offers programs and services for student leadership development as well as entertainment programming. The cornerstone of their activities is a "Cooperative Buying" program that enables talent buyers in schools with geographic proximity to share travel and other logistical costs for performers.

Nearly 1200 schools are members of NACA, including two- and four-year public and private colleges, major universities and community, junior and technical colleges.

The goal of the organization is to help members create better programs for their schools, teach concert buying skills and keep talent buyers up-to-date with the latest in the campus activities marketplace.

The NACA presents an annual national convention and 11 regional conferences that offer exhibit opportunities, talent showcases and cooperative buying programs. The audition process begins with the artists submitting their videos, promotional materials and submission fees. The NACA screening committees select the talent that will be showcased at the convention and conferences. The showcases are seen by school concert buyers, talent agents and others that offer programs, products or services to the college market.

The NACA publishes a variety of publications, including Campus Activities Programming, Programming on the Road and a Membership Directory and Buyer's Guide and Supplement.

www.NACA.org

RESOURCES

Agency for the Performing Arts (APA)
888 Seventh Avenue
New York, NY 10106
(212) 582-1500
No URL

American Symphony Orchestra League (ASOL)
33 West 60th Street
New York, NY 10023-7905
(212) 262-5161 phone
www.symphony.org

Association of Performing Arts Presenters (APAP)
1112 16th Street NW, Suite 400
Washington, DC 20036
(202) 833-2787
www.artspresenters.org

Association for the Promotion of Campus
    Activities (APCA)
1131 South Fork Drive
Sevierville, TN 37862
(800) 681-5031
www.apca.com

Black Promoters Association of America
5825 Glenridge Drive, Bldg. 2, Suite 214
Atlanta, GA 30328
(404) 303-7700
No URL

Canadian Arts Presenting Association
    (CAPACOA)
17 York Street, Suite 200
Ottawa, Ontario
Canada K1N 9J6
(613) 562-3515
www.capacoa.ca

Canadian Conference of the Arts
189 Laurier Avenue East
Ottawa, Ontario
Canada K1N 6P1
(613) 238-2631
www.culturenet.ca/cca

Creative Artists Agency (CAA)
9830 Wilshire Boulevard
Beverly Hills, CA 90212
(310) 288-4545
www.caa.com

Fischoff Chamber Music Association
PO Box 1303
South Bend, IND 46624-1303
(219) 237-237-4871
www.fishoff.org

Folk Alliance
North American Folk Music and Dance Alliance
1001 Connecticut Avenue NW, Suite 501
Washington, DC 20036
(202) 835-3655
www.folk.org

House of Blues Entertainment, Inc.
6255 Sunset Boulevard
Hollywood, CA 90028
(323) 769-4600
www.hob.com

IMG Artists
825 Seventh Avenue
New York, NY 10019
(212) 489-8300
www.imgartists.com

International Creative Management (ICM)
8942 Wilshire Boulevard
Beverly Hills, CA 90211
(310) 550-4000
No URL

International House of Blues Foundation
6255 Sunset Boulevard
Hollywood, CA 90028
(323) 769-4901
www.ihobf.org

Monterey Peninsula Artists
901 18th Avenue
Nashville, TN 37212
(615) 321-4444
No URL

Nashville Entertainment Association (NEA)
PO Box 121948
1105 16th Avenue South, Suite C
Nashville, TN 37212
(615) 327-4308
www.nea.net

National Association for Campus Activities
    (NACA)
13 Harbison Way
Columbia, SC 29212-3401
(803) 732-6222
www.NACA.org

New Audiences Productions, Inc.
155 West 72nd Street
New York City, NY 10023
(212) 595-5272
www.newaudiences.com

Reed MIDEM Organization
125 Park Avenue South
New York, NY 10017
(212) 370-7470
www.reedmidemorg.com

Rhythm and Blues Foundation
1555 Connecticut Avenue NW, Suite 401
Washington, DC 20036-1111
(202) 588-5566
www.rhythm-n-blues.org

South by Southwest Music & Media
Conference
PO Box 4999
Austin, TX 78765
(512) 467-7979
www.sxsw.com
    North by Northeast
    185A Danforth Avenue, 2nd Floor

Toronto, Ontario Canada M4K 1N2
(416) 469-0986
www.nxne.com

North by Northwest
PO Box 4999
Austin, TX 78765
(512) 467-7979
www.nxnw.com

Young Audiences
115 East 92nd Street
New York, NY 10128-1688
(212) 831-8110
www.youngaudiences.org

Young Concert Artists, Inc.
250 West 57th Street, Suite 1222
New York, NY 10019
(212) 307-6655
www.yca.org

William Morris Agency, Inc.
1325 Avenue of the Americas
New York, NY 10019
(212) 586-5100
www.wma.com

INDUSTRY DIRECTORIES

Billboard Directories
1695 Oak Street
PO Box 2016
Lakewood, NJ 08701
(800) 344-7119
www.billboard.com/store/directories
    Billboard International Buyer's Guide
    Directory

*Billboard International Latin Music
  Buyer's Guide Directory*
*Billboard International Talent and Touring
  Directory*
*Billboard International Tape/Disc
  Directory*
*Billboard Nashville 615/Country Music
  Sourcebook*
*Billboard Radio Power Book: Directory of
  Music Radio and Record Promotion*
Billboard Record Retailing Directory

Music Directory Canada
CM Books
23 Hannover Drive, Unit 7
St. Catharines, Ontario
Canada L2W 1A3
(905) 641-3471
www.musicdirectorycanada.com

The MBI World Report 2002
The Music Group
CMP Information Ltd
Ludgate House
245 Blackfriars Road
London SE1 9UR
0207 579 4123
www.musicweek.com

The Music Business Registry
7510 Sunset Boulevard #1041
Los Angeles, CA 90046-3400 USA
(800) 377-7411
www.musicregistry.com

The Musician's Atlas
Music Resource Group
PO Box 682
Nyack, NY 10960
(845) 353-9303
www.musiciansatlas.com

Music Yellow Pages
United Entertainment Media, Inc.
6 Manhasset Avenue
Port Washington, NY 11050
(516) 944-5940
www.musicyellowpages.com

*Performance International Touring Talent
  Publications*
203 Lake Street, Suite 200
Fort Worth, TX 76102-4504
(817) 338-9444
www.performancemagazine.com
  *The Black Book: Entire Performance
    Guide Series*
  Concert Production
  Equipment and Personnel
  Facilities
  Talent Buyers
  Talent Management
  Transportation Guide

Pollstar, USA
4697 W. Jacquelyn Avenue
Fresno, CA 93722-6413
559-271-7900 Voice
559-271-7979 Fax
www.pollstar.com
  PollstarOnline.com
  Agency Rosters
  Talent Buyer Directory
  Concert Venue Directory
  Concert Support Services Directory

Recording Industry Sourcebook
Artist Pro
236 Georgia Street, Suite 100
Vallejo, CA 94590
(707) 554-1935
www.artistpro.com/Sourcebase.cfm

NOTES

Concert Promotion and Arts Administration

* * *

THE BUSINESS OF CONCERT PROMOTION

**ARTS ADMINISTRATION AND
THE CULTURAL ARTS**

INTERVIEW HIGHLIGHT
Julie Lokin, Cofounder,
New Audiences Productions, Inc.

RESOURCE HIGHLIGHTS
The Association of Performing Arts Presenters
The National Endowment for the Arts
The International House of Blues Foundation

RESOURCES

The Business of Concert Promotion

Buyers of entertainment (concert promoters) present live performances of artists in many types of venues. There are three main groups.

One buys popular entertainment as their major source of generating revenue. There are large conglomerates, such as Clear Channel Entertainment, Inc. that put on more than 26,000 events annually in the United States. And there are smaller companies that put on a special folk, jazz or bluegrass festivals once a year; student associations that present all the popular music shows for colleges and universities; and individuals that present raves and other small shows. These buyers are known as concert promoters.

The second group, known as arts presenters, puts on cultural art events—symphony orchestras, operas, classical and chamber music concerts, choral groups, dance, musical theater, multimedia events—in major concert venues, such as the Kennedy Center in Washington, D.C. and Carnegie Hall in New York and at universities and in smaller concert venues throughout the United States and Canada. Many of these presenters are non-profit organizations that receive contributions that help underwrite their shows. (See the article "Arts Administration and the Cultural Arts" later in this segment.)

Concert promoters and arts presenters have the same essential challenge: to bring in paying audiences to see their events.

The third group uses live entertainment as an ancillary to another activity that is expected to bring in the majority of the income. This group includes promoters of events such as trade conventions, rodeos, balloon festivals, stock car races and the owners of bars and nightclubs. While music may be important at these venues, it is not the main revenue generator.

THE ROLE OF MUSIC UNIONS

In order to ensure standard pay, working conditions and benefits in various industry segments, music-related unions negotiate collective bargaining agreements with businesses that hire their members. These include talent agencies, buyers of live performances, motion picture companies, television producers, casinos, opera companies and record companies. These companies, termed signatory companies, agree to abide by union conditions and to hire only union members, pay them the wages and benefits established in their agreements and use union-approved contracts.

The relationships between unions and businesses that have collective bargaining agreements are governed by the National Labor Relations Board, an independent federal agency created in 1935 to enforce the National Labor Relations Act.

These agreements help prevent employers from taking unfair advantage of union members by establishing fair employment practices. There is monetary protection if employers fail to pay or cancel or cut short engagements and arbitration procedures for settling contractual disputes between employers and union members. Unions sign separate agreements with concert promoters and nightclubs. The wages that are specified for each group differ.

Unions have offices called "locals" in various cities. These abide by the rules and regulations set by national executive boards, but otherwise act independently to set wages and standards that are appropriate to their particular location.

If union members are employed by nonsignatory companies, such as nonunion nightclubs or independent record labels, they are in violation of union rules and generally receive less than union approved pay (scale). In so doing, they undermine the bargaining strength of the union and its members and jeopardize their own membership.

Nonsignatory buyers of entertainment include small coffeehouses, bars and small concert (under 500 people) promoters, located in small towns, which hire start-up talent and bands that do not command enough draw or earn enough money to be union members.

Professionals that work in the entertainment industry can join a union by paying an initiation fee and annual dues, participating in an indoctrination program and abiding by the rules and regulations.

Union members pay a percentage of their wages as work dues. These monies are used to fund various services, such as health and welfare funds and pension funds.

HOW CONCERT PROMOTERS AND ARTS PRESENTERS MAKE MONEY

Concert promoters and arts presenters make money by producing events that bring in money from ticket sales and ancillary sources. However, many events the are promoted by arts presenters

THE MUSIC PERFORMANCE TRUST FUND

The Music Performance Trust Fund is an important AFM fund that collects more than $12 million annually from signatory record companies that earmark a percentage (.20375%) of the suggested retail price of each recording sold. The Fund is used to hire union musicians to play free live concerts and finance music appreciation programs. In 2001, the Fund presented more than 25,000 free concerts in parks, senior citizens' homes, veterans' hospitals, schools and other public places to more than 15 million people throughout the United States and Canada.

receive charitable donations from private donor, nonprofit organizations and state and federal arts organizations.

THE IMPORTANCE OF DRAW

The greater the artists' draw, the greater the chance that buyers will fill the performance venues.

If talent is purchased for an event that already has a captive audience or where music is ancillary to the main event, it is less important to book talent that has great draw.

If music is the main source of income, then artists' draw is paramount. Artists with draw will also help boost attendance at other events. For example, if attendance at a symphony or an opera is declining, artists that have draw can help reverse the trend.

INCOME AND EXPENSE

Draw determines what an artist will be paid and what ticket prices will be.

To determine potential profits, promoters and

arts presenters deduct the projected expenses and concession fees from projected ticket sales. Expenses include—

- Fees to acts

- Costs of contract riders (free tickets, limos, refreshments, equipment rentals)

- Ticket printing and distribution

- Box office accounting

- Facility rental, maintenance and related personnel

- Security

- Production construction and rentals (sound, lights, special stage construction)

- Production personnel (stagehands, electricians, stage manager, etc.)

- Insurance (personal liability, property damage, etc.)

- Promoter's direct concert expenses

- Promotion and advertising

- First aid

- Overtime

Promoters do not customarily pay travel and lodging expenses for acts.

When promoters own or lease facilities, they have annual costs, such as facility maintenance, leasehold improvements, insurance and payments to performance rights organizations.

Concert promotion is a high-risk business. Even the most successful promoters can make mistakes in estimating an event's draw, which can result in large losses. They can overestimate what audiences will pay; or put on a show when there are too many competing events; and so on.

Promoters that anticipate less than 100% sell-outs may give away blocks of unsold tickets to schools or nonprofit organizations to help fill the seats (papering the house). They deduct those tickets' value as a charitable contribution.

Fee Arrangements

Fee arrangements with acts depend on whether draw is a factor in making money; what the income projections are; whether the promoter has agreements with music-related unions; whether the concerts are underwritten by nonprofit funding or sponsored by commercial businesses and the promoter's expenses. Here are typical arrangements—

- Flat fee (straight guarantee). An agreed-on fee paid to the act, regardless of how much income the promoter brings in.

- Percentage of ticket sales. Promoter pays a specified percentage of the gross income of ticket sales.

  Example: The promoters offer an act 60% of gross income from ticket sales and the concert has a gross income of $100,000. If that occurs, the act will gross $60,000. If only $60,000 worth of tickets are sold, the act will gross only $36,000.

- Flat fee plus percentage. A guarantee is agreed upon. After that amount is reached, the act earns a percentage of what is taken in over that amount.

  Example: Promoter offers an act $15,000 plus 80% of gross receipts over $60,000. The concert has a gross income of $100,000. The act grosses $15,000 plus $32,000 (80% of $40,000) total of $47,000.

- Flat fee versus percentage, whichever is greater. Both the fee and the percentage are set prior to the performance.

  Example: The promoter offer the act a flat fee of $25,000 versus a percentage of 50% of gross income. If a concert where they anticipated gross income of $100,000 ends up to be $40,000, the act will take the flat fee.

Contractual arrangements between talent agents and promoters specify how ticket income is accounted for. Usually, a member of the act's management team will be the person who verifies the promoter's accounting for receipts from ticket vendors and cash, checks and credit card payments. Once this is done, the amount to be paid to the act is calculated and a final check written. Usually this takes place during, not after, the performance.

Most promoters specify "kill dates" to cancel concerts. This is done in case income from ticket sales does not reach a specified amount by a specified date. Talent agents specify "kill fees" that are paid to acts in the event of cancellations.

Talent agents that represent nonheadline acts that have draws in particular cities will try to persuade promoters to put them on bills with headliners to increase the chances of a sellout concert. When headliners can virtually guarantee sellout concerts, agents will ask promoters to hire unknown acts to provide them with opportunities to increase their draw.

CONCERT PROMOTION CONTRACTS

The contracts between concert promoters and acts can be as simple as the performance agreement provided below or as complex as those required by name acts. Some contracts have many pages in riders that specify things such as the size of the stage, the name brand of acoustic piano and tuning requirements, size of the mixing platform, personnel needed for loading and unloading equipment, the brand names for food and drinks, number of free tickets for guests and security requirements. The promoter must calculate the costs of providing what the acts require as part of their expenses in promoting the concert and

MUSIC-RELATED UNIONS

The major union for musicians is the American Federation of Musicians of the United States and Canada, AFL-CIO, CLC (AFM) with more than 15,000 members. Musician members are instrumentalists, band leaders, recording session contractors, orchestrators, copyists, music librarians, arrangers and proofreaders. They work in all mediums of music including live performance, network radio and TV, educational TV, cable and pay TV, TV films, movies, documentary films, traveling musical productions, music videos and recording.

The American Federation of Television and Radio Artists, AFL-CIO (AFTRA) members are singers, sound effects artists, actors, announcers and narrators that work in radio, television and recording.

The American Guild of Musical Artists (AGMA) represents singers and dancers in the fields of opera, classical music and ballet.

The Screen Actors Guild (SAG) represents vocalists that sing in motion pictures.

The American Guild of Variety Artists (AGVA) represents singers and other entertainers that perform at casinos, resorts and fairgrounds.

figure in those expenses when negotiating fees.

Contracts must build in the costs of adhering to union requirements, particularly with regard to stagehands, electrical technicians, etc., because they get extra pay for overtime.

Promoters that do not own venues have to make contracts with venue owners. These contracts specify fees, insurance, personnel, concession and parking arrangements, and so on. The bigger the facility, the longer and more complex the contract.

SAMPLE PERFORMANCE AGREEMENT

Agreement made as of _____, 20__ , between the parties identified below.

1. Artist_____

2. Purchaser_____

3. Place of engagement_____

   Name_____

   Street Address _____

   City, State, Zip _____

   Telephone _____

In consideration for the following covenants, conditions, and promises, the Purchaser agrees to hire the Artist to perform an engagement and the Artist agrees to provide such performance services, under the following terms and conditions:

4. The dates, time, duration of show, and sound check time are as follows:

   Dates _____Time _____ AM/PM

   Number of Sets _____Duration of Each Set____

   Sound Check Time_____

5. The consideration to be paid shall be

   (a) Guaranteed Fee of $_____

   (b) Percentage _____ (gross/net of door)

   (c) Workshop Fee of $ _____

   (d) Meals/Lodging _____

   (e) Transportation _____

       (i) Air _____

       (ii) Ground _____

   (f) Materials _____

   (g) Total _____

   (h) Advance Payment of $ _____

       due on _____(Date)

   (i) Balance of Payment of $ _____

       due on _____(Date)

6. Further consideration to Artist by Purchaser is provided in the Rider of Additional Terms attached to this Agreement.

7. Sound and/or lighting equipment to be provided by Purchaser shall be as described in a separate Sound Reinforcement and Lighting Agreement.

8. This Agreement constitutes the entire agreement between the parties and supersedes all prior and contemporaneous agreements, understandings, negotiations, and discussions, whether oral or written. There are no warranties, representations, and/or agreements among the parties in connection with the subject matter of this Agreement,except as specifically set forth and referenced in this Agreement. This Agreement shall be governed by [insert your State's name] law; is binding and valid only when signed by the parties below; and may be modified only in a writing signed by the parties. If Artist has not received the deposit in the amount and at the date specified in subsection 5(h), then Artist thereafter at anytime shall have the option to terminate this Agreement.

9. The persons signing this Agreement on behalf of Artist and Purchaser each have the authority to bind their respective principals.

10. If you have any questions, please contact our home office at _____

AGREED TO AND ACCEPTED

Purchaser _____

By Date _____

Artist _____

By Date _____

Name and Title (an authorized signatory)

_____

Name and Title (an authorized signatory)

_____

PRINCIPLE JOB RESPONSIBILITIES

While booking talent that will draw is important, repeat business is essential for successful concert promoters. They must work with talent agents and book acts that consistently ensure profits and satisfy their audiences; produce events that are enjoyable; and promote those events successfully. During events, promoters work with many kinds of people—superstars, musicians, road managers, stage hands, electricians, parking attendants, concessionaires, security—and related vendors, such as ticket brokers, printers (tickets, promotional brochures, ads, etc.) and sound and lighting companies. Coordinating the jobs of these people is a major task, and unexpected problems can arise. Problem solving skills and making and keeping good working relationships are a necessity.

Concert Promoters' Relationship to Talent Agents

Solid relationships with talent agents ensure that promoters have access to the talent that can make their events profitable. They must work together to calculate draw and expenses and negotiate fees and other contractual requirements. Talent agents want assurances that concerts will be well produced and promoted. They will provide the promotional materials that will help the promoters do so. This is particularly important when concerts or tours are helping to support the releases of recording.

Concert Production

A good show is at the heart of customer satisfaction: and that begins with a good production.

Here are the critical areas that promoters oversee—

- *Sound reinforcement:* Being able to hear performances is paramount. Acts can bring in their own equipment and operators; they can require promoters to provide equipment by specifying their needs in con-

tracts. Promoters that own venues and have installed permanent sound reinforcement equipment may need to rent extra equipment and have the equipment set up and operated by some acts' professional sound operators. Some acts ask promoters to provide people trained in sign language to translate for deaf members of the audience.

- *Lighting:* Sometimes acts bring their own lighting equipment and operators; sometimes they ask promoters to rent the equipment. Promoters that own venues generally install permanent lighting equipment and may agree to have it operated by the hired acts' professional sound operators. Acts may bring in separate light shows.

- *Security:* Promoters must provide environments in which acts can put on good shows. Problems with crowd control, violence, drugs and alcohol must be swiftly and unobtrusively taken care of. Riders in artist contracts often specify security requirements for artists and their audiences. Depending on the nature of the event, promoters can hire a combination of private and city police and may have trained in-house staff to manage minor problems. For a venue of 15,000 people, 300 to 500 security people are hired.

  Backstage, artists need to be ensured of their privacy; on-stage, they need to be assured that members of the audience are not going to jump on the stage and disturb the performance.

- *Equipment loading:* Promoters must provide safe places to load and unload equipment and private entries for famous entertainers and adequate time to set up and test sound and lighting equipment. Depending on the venue, personnel to help unload equipment and set it up will be provided by union stage hands and electrical technicians.

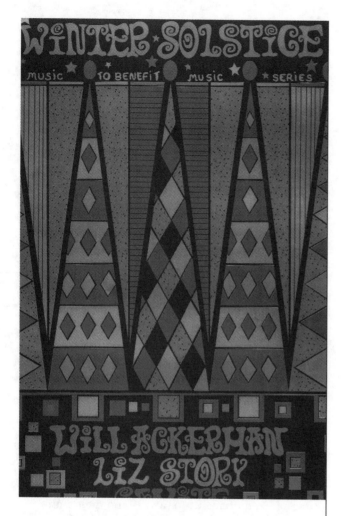

For particularly heavy and cumbersome equipment, fork lift operators will be hired.

- *Parking:* Parking attendants are hired to help efficiently route traffic to parking spots.

- *Amenities:* Adequate water and toilet facilities are minimal requirements. Food and drink help performers relax during intermissions.

- *Dressing room(s):* Acts need places to relax before and between acts and change costumes.

- *Stage monitors:* Vocalists and musicians need to hear themselves on stage to play and sing in sync with each other. Monitoring systems can be as simple as a few speakers turned towards the musicians; or as elaborate as in-ear monitors and radio headsets.

- *Sound and lighting check:* Acts need adequate time before a performance to make sure equipment is working and to test monitoring and sound reinforcement systems and lighting.

Promoting Concerts

If no one knows about a concert, no one will come. Understanding the types of acts that appeal to particular audiences is very important. Rock concerts are promoted differently from classical ones.

Promotion includes developing relationships with advertising salespeople, newspaper and magazine writers and business sponsors so that they will help promote events.

A promotional campaign will include some or all of the following—

- Mailed or emailed announcements to lists of attendees and subscribers to past concerts, sometimes with offers of ticket discounts

- Announcements on Web sites

- Purchase of special interest group mailings lists to target markets and mailings or emailings to them

- Press releases to newspapers, magazines and special interest newsletters

- Persuasion of print, radio and television media to conduct interviews with artists

- Print, radio and television advertisements

- Free tickets to potential reviewers, radio program directors and other media personnel

- Posters and fliers posted in prominent locations

Finding Sponsors

Linking concerts and artists with companies that sell beverages, alcohol, cigarettes, clothing and other goods and services is a popular form of business advertising. The acts and the companies help each other promote their names and brands. Some companies are interested in the sheer number of people (impressions) that see a concert; others feel it is more important to ensure that there is social and emotional congruence between the acts and their products.

Sponsorship can take many forms. Businesses pay artists to appear in television, radio and print advertisements. Payments to promoters and acts for these types of branding depend on the number of people that see or hear the ad, perceived name values and to some extent the brand value of the sponsoring company.

Businesses sponsor entire concert series in return for being mentioned in all concert advertisements and having their banners displayed in prominent locations during the concerts. Because sponsors take over some of the jobs of concert promotion (hiring acts and providing advertising support), promoters and sponsors have to work out how expenses are to be allocated.

CAN ACTS PROMOTE THEIR OWN CONCERTS?

Artists can rent halls and put on their own shows. They decide how to meet expenses, how to split profits and what to do if their concerts lose money. Artists that do this get a good understanding of the job of a concert promoter.

COLLEGE AND UNIVERSITY PROMOTERS

Colleges and universities hire performing artists in many genres, throughout the school year. Most have concert facilities, sound and lighting equipment and able personnel to run them.

The major promoters of concerts in colleges and universities are student/campus activities offices. Their budgets range from under $5000 to more than $500,000 and are largely derived from student fees. Budgets and bookings are generally administered by students that get valuable train-

CLEAR CHANNEL ENTERTAINMENT: AN ENTERTAINMENT GIANT

In 1997, SFX, Inc. bought up most all major independent promoters in the United States. In 2001, Clear Channel Entertainment bought SFX, Inc. It is the world's largest diversified promoter, producer and presenter of live entertainment events. Clear Channel owns or controls more than 135 live entertainment venues, owns over 1200 US radio stations in 300 major markets and 37 TV stations and owns or controls 900 Web sites, including sites that allow visitors to listen to music online and a subscription service that offers limited downloads (MusicNow). In 2001, more than 72 million people attended approximately 26,000 Clear Channel events and generated approximately 70% of concert ticket revenues in the United States. 2001 revenues were $7.97 billion, compared to $5.35 billion in 2000.

ing and experience and often go on to work in other music business jobs.

They have wide latitude in hiring talent because they do not have to make a profit. Many college and university promoters attend talent showcases sponsored by the National Association for Campus Activities (NACA). (See Resource Highlight about the NACA in Segment 6, Talent Agents.)

Individual departments have their own budgets for bringing in relevant presentations. And some work with nonprofit arts presenters to bring in artist residency programs that include performances. Music departments bring in musicians

SWARMS OF FANS JOCKEY BACK AND FORTH FROM CLUB TO CLUB AT SHOWCASES SPONSORED BY SOUTH-BY-SOUTHWEST'S 2002 MUSIC EDUCATION CONFERENCE AND FESTIVAL.

for special workshops; woman's studies departments bring in female performers; environmental departments may hire protest songwriters, etc.

College and university clubs, sororities and fraternities also have budgets for hiring talent.

PROMOTERS OF BENEFIT CONCERTS

Benefit concerts are presented to raise money and promote all kinds of political, social, environmental organizations and causes. To be successful, they must hire performers that draw enough people. Many promoters and well-meaning advocates of good causes have lost considerable money by assuming that the righteousness of their cause would, by itself, draw large audiences.

SHOWCASES

The word "showcase" in the music business means to audition an act for a specific audience. Many music business organizations and nonprofit organizations sponsor showcases at annual and regional conferences for people that hire artists.

Artists' managers hire clubs in New York, Los Angeles, Nashville, Montreal and Toronto in order to showcase their clients for entertainment industry professionals (record company executives, concert promoters, producers, publishers, etc.).

CONCLUSION

Buying entertainment, bringing in paying audiences to see their events and putting on a good show is the concert promoters job. It is a complex business that demands skill at managing and directing, audience development, problem solving and relationship building with artists, media and community leaders.

Arts Administration and the Cultural Arts

Classical music, opera, choral groups, dance troupes and Broadway theater are often referred to as the cultural arts, or arts, to distinguish them from entertainment arts and pop culture. Arts presenters put on cultural arts events and most are nonprofit organizations, which enables them to apply for grants and receive private donations.

Some presenters specialize in one type of event, such as musical theater or chamber music. Others hire a variety of talent, which may include jazz and folk artists, modern ballet troupes and classical pianists. Some presenters bring in events for extended stays in public and private schools (art residency programs) that include workshops and lectures.

Few people that work in the cultural arts can clearly define the difference between cultural art and pop entertainment. But many are quick to say that unless the cultural arts are made more accessible, less elitist and more entertaining to their audiences, that attendance and interest will decline. Many say that there are areas in which the distinction between art and entertainment blur. For example, some arts presenters present jazz and folk artists in series with classical concerts. Some pop artists are classically trained and are as talented as classical artists. The distinction between art and entertainment becomes important, however, because nonprofit businesses need to use their profits to further charitable, religious, scientific, social, literary or educational purposes. Few entertainment promoters meet that criteria.

ARTS PRESENTERS INCOME

According to the Association of Performing Arts Presenters (APAP), approximately 7000 organizations bring cultural arts events to more than 6 million people weekly and generate more than $5 billion annually. According to the American Symphony League, in 2000, $1.2 billion was generated by American orchestras.

A portion of arts presenters and performing group income is derived from ticket sales and a portion from business and government grants and private donations.

Some arts presentations are inherently expensive. A symphony orchestra, by definition, has 101 players that earn union scale. But if they are 101 great players, larger salaries are negotiated. To attract a major soloist that will help with draw, such as violinist Itzhak Perlman, is to pay fees that can be equivalent to a pop entertainer. If ticket prices were based entirely on ticket sales, attendance would be limited only to the very wealthy. Grants and charitable contributions help make up deficits.

Unless the cultural arts are made more accessible, less elitist and more entertaining to their audiences, that attendance and interest will decline.

PRINCIPLE JOB RESPONSIBILITIES

The chief operating officers (CEOs) of arts presenters are called arts administrators; the CEOs of performing groups are called executive directors.

Although many of the job responsibilities are similar to those of concert buyers, arts administrators and executive directors have additional responsibilities: they must ensure the continued vitality of the arts they are presenting by meeting the following challenges—

- Lack of music programs in the public schools

- Decreased grants for the cultural arts

- Competition from the entertainment sector

- Decreased media coverage for the cultural arts

Because arts administrators work in the nonprofit sector, they must work closely with the organization's board of directors, who may feel differently about how to balance the cultural missions of their organizations with financial realities.

ARTISTIC MISSION

The better organizations can define their missions, values and visions, the better able they will be to focus on plans to achieve them. Administrators and directors used to think that their jobs were to pick events and programs, mar-

ket them and sell tickets. They became less and less able to differentiate their organizations from commercial entertainment concert buyers and were increasingly lured out of working in the nonprofit sector by the lucrative opportunities in the entertainment arts.

Here are some of the questions arts organizations are trying to answer in honing their missions—

- What aesthetic values drive our choices of programs and events?

- What leadership role should our organization take in the arts community? In the community-at-large?

- What educational roles should our organization be taking on?

- What noncommercial goals do we wish to foster?

- What is our obligation to bring in international arts events?

- Why do we want to compete with entertainment arts?

- Why should we be concerned with ethnic diversity?

Answering these questions will help them to survive and successfully meet the challenges that threaten the continued vitality of the cultural arts.

FUNDING

The cultural arts have always derived a portion of their income from government and business grants and private donations. Arts administrators and executive directors must be adept in grant-writing and fund-raising.

Grant organizations want to know how their funds will achieve specific goals or foster significant change in their communities and they will evaluate outcomes after the grant period is over. Grant organizations have fewer funds to spread among increasing arts organizations and want to be assured their money is being wisely spent. In the past it was acceptable to show that attendance at concerts increased in a given period. Now, grant organizations want to know what else arts presenters did to make those concerts a more meaningful experience or whether audiences were drawn from more ethnically diverse sectors of society.

AUDIENCE DEVELOPMENT

There has been a steady decline of music education in the public schools since the 1980s. Many children went to schools that lacked these programs and grew up with little, if any, exposure to the cultural arts and have no vocabulary for thinking about it and appreciating it. They did, however, have a great deal of exposure to pop entertainment and culture. Now, the cultural arts must compete with our culture's predispositions to pop entertainment and the lack of education in the cultural arts.

Many arts administrators and executive directors are taking on the job of audience development to help people find their way into the cultural arts sector and educate them about what they are see and hear.

Audience development can take many forms—

- Artists and conductors introduce the works and discuss them before they are played

- Visual aids during performances translations of foreign language operas, background videos and photographs that complement performances and light shows

- Educational materials displayed in performance hall lobbies

- Music workshops in schools and in ethnically based community organizations

SAN DIEGO SYMPHONY RECEIVES MULTIMILLION-DOLLAR GIFT

According to Douglas Gerhart, San Diego Symphony president and CEO, in 2002 the San Diego Symphony's New World Endowment Campaign, will receive a gift that may be as much as $100 million from longtime supporters Joan and Irwin Jacobs. It is expected to be the largest individual donation ever given to a U.S. symphony orchestra. The gift will help place the organization's endowment near the top 10 of U.S. orchestras and help secure its financial future.

- Artists and conductors that lecture at schools, businesses, community organizations

- Forums on specific topics and chat rooms on arts presenters' Web sites

- Composer, artist biographies and other information posted on arts presenters' Web sites

- Work with parents to encourage school administrators to fund cultural arts programs

- Work with teachers to help them introduce cultural arts into current nonarts curriculums or special school programs

Arts administrators are trying to bring in more ethnically diverse audiences to their events. They must figure out what in their programs will appeal to particular audiences and why. Bringing in artists from countries of origin may draw audiences from those artists' cultures. Arts presenters could introduce programs of varied symphonic music in public schools and ask children to fill

Nerve Endings

The Oregon Symphony Orchestra's *Nerve Endings* series presents classical music in a nontraditional manner, through the inclusions of film, visuals, actors and interaction with the audience. The series has been enormously successful in attracting new friends to the Oregon Symphony Orchestra.

In 2001, the series featured a concert of Aaron Copeland's *Appalachian Spring* and a video of Martha Grahams choreography of the work as the piece was played. During a concert of Copeland's *Third Symphony,* the audiences were given a feeling of how Copeland was threatened by the McCarthy hearings by having actors on stage re-create dialogues between Copeland and the prosecutors before each symphony movement to give them a context for understanding what they were hearing.

out questionnaires about what they did and did not like.

This new job responsibility means that arts presenters must become arts educators and reach out to their communities rather than just expect people to show up at events. They must enhance the knowledge of people that already have a love of the cultural arts so that they can share it with friends and neighbors. Presenters must learn how their programs can touch the needs and concerns of people that are new to the arts and provide something that is of lasting value in their lives.

To help administrators meet this need, seminars are presented in audience development, through umbrella organizations, such as the Association of Performing Arts Presenters

(APAP). These seminars share information about what organizations throughout the country are doing in this arena.

Artists and conductors are taught how to present educational lectures to students, business people and nonarts community organizations.

WORKING WITH UNIVERSITIES

Universities play a role in educating their communities about cultural arts and then present events that bring in diverse audiences. Most university events draw audiences from outside the university—up to 75%. These events fulfill part of universities' roles as intellectual and cultural leaders within their communities, committed to ethnic and social diversity.

Arts residency programs are ubiquitous at universities. Grants for residency programs are increasingly available and residency programs help fill concert halls. These programs can be as simple as bringing in artists for two days and asking them to present a few lectures in public schools in addition to their performances or asking musical groups to spend 6 to 8 weeks in residency and give workshops to other musicians in and outside of the university, in addition to their performances. These nonperformance activities help bring in new audiences.

CONCLUSION

The survival of the cultural arts is a major challenge that faces many arts presenters that compete with the dominance of pop entertainment culture in the media and reductions in school cultural art programs. Many arts presenters take on the role of educators in order to entice new and more ethnically diverse audiences to their events.

Julie Lokin:
Cofounder, New Audiences Productions

New Audiences Productions, Inc., a concert production company based in New York City, produces over 20 concerts and events per year in such venues as Carnegie Hall, Lincoln Center, Town Hall, and the Beacon Theatre. The company is known for its ability to pair artists from different genres and consistently attract a cross-section of their representative audiences. In recent years they have produced smooth jazz concerts with Fourplay, Boney James and The Rippingtons; flamenco guitarist Paco de Lucia; and contemporary folk artists Dar Williams and David Bromberg. They have presented the CD 101.9 Jazz Wednesday Series at the World Trade Center, including Joe Sample and Angela Bofill; Joan Baez, Spyro Gyra and Sonny Rollins at the Beacon Theater; the Colors of Christmas with Roberta Flack and Peabo Bryson at Carnegie Hall; Loreena McKennitt and Ladysmith Black Mambazo at Town Hall; and Indigo Girls at Central Park Summerstage. They have also presented concerts in Washington D.C., New Haven, Philadelphia and Baltimore.

New Audiences was founded in 1971 by JULIE LOKIN and Art Weiner, members of the Jazz Society of Hunter College. The great Charles Mingus was New Audiences' first concert presentation. The concert was an unqualified success: it reignited Mingus' recording and performing career and inspired Lokin and Weiner to revive

COURTESY NEW AUDIENCES PRODUCTIONS

the New York jazz scene by forming a concert production company. Up until 1995, when larger concert promotion companies began competing with them, New Audiences presented virtually every major jazz concert in New York City.

In 1997, *Pollstar Magazine* named New Audiences as "Independent Promoter of the Year."

Today, New Audiences has diversified to include many other facets of the music business, including personal management, tour management and concert advertising and marketing.

* * * * * * * *

Rapaport: What are some of the problems you encounter during shows?

Lokin: The difficulties include union regulations, which require that the running time of the show be kept to three hours. Any time over that and the promoter is charged an overtime fee. This means that you must get the bands to agree to set lengths and schedules and stick to them.

Then there are unexpected difficulties that you encounter during the show. For instance, during a show with Grover Washington, Jr. at the Beacon, the belt from an under-stage exhaust fan caused a lot of smoke. The audience thought there was a fire. Grover saved the day by telling the people not to panic and generally cooling them out. The program went long, but we didn't get billed for overtime. And then there are artists that have to overcome stage fright before they go on or band members that are playing New York for the first time and are unfamiliar with how long it can take to get anywhere. So one of the requirements for being a concert promoter is to be a problem solver.

Rapaport: How do you feel about contract riders?

Lokin: When we first started out, artists were very happy when there was a pitcher of water and a bowl of fruit in the dressing room. Now, artists and managers have gotten very particular about what they include on contract riders, including specifying brands of vitamins and specific rare wines.

We try to make artists understand that riders add to the cost of production and reduce the actual profits that all of us can make. We also know that if the artists are happy, they'll put on a good show. If that means providing coffee that is grown in areas where the growers have not cut down the shade trees for the songbirds to roost, we do it. The only thing we don't do in New York is provide hotels or transportation.

Rapaport: How do you feel about tour and concert sponsorship by brand name companies?

Lokin: When we started New Audiences, concerts helped get a media buzz going and helped major labels sell new releases. Record companies underwrote some radio and print advertising, set up displays in key record stores, and on special occasions bought tickets and threw back stage parties for media. Today, record companies have limited the spending of advertising dollars, except for huge names. They are finding different ways to sell records, such as the Internet, in-store promotions, etc. And large companies, like Nike and Budweiser, have taken over sponsorship of concert tours to promote their brand. They deal directly with the bands.

The hope was that sponsorship would help bring ticket prices down; but the fact is that they continue to go up. What bands say is that prices would be even higher if they didn't have those sponsorship dollars.

The first time we had a commercial sponsor was in 1985 when we did a music series on a boat that cruised the Hudson River. Anheuser Busch helped with the advertising budget in return for "pouring rights"—the right to sell their beer on the boat. The synergy between promoter and advertiser was that direct.

Brand sponsorship can be a touchy area for many artists because it implies the endorsement of products, so, although sponsorship might help promoters offset advertising costs, they have to be careful not to be associated with a company that will offend the artists. That is why the content of radio and print promotion is dictated by the bands. Ten years ago, sponsors would have dealt with the promoters that would then promote their names in any advertising. Today, the promoter has to take the band AND its sponsor. There is no choice.

Rapaport: What other major changes have you seen in the concert promotion business in the last decade?

Lokin: There have been more changes in the concert promotion and record business in the last 4 or 5 years than in the last fifty. The biggest change is the consolidation of concert promoters into megapromoters, like Clear Channel Entertainment, House of Blues and Concerts West that now own or control the major live venues in large cities as well as radio and television stations.

The synergy here is obvious: radio and TV are major advertising mediums for concerts; advertising is a major part of a concert promotion budget. So promoters that also own radio stations have a "clear channel" for lots of guaranteed promotion of a show and the marketing costs can virtually disappear. Radio stations are restricted as to the number of ad minutes they can sell; but if they are advertising their own events, they not only do not have to pay for advertising, they have virtually unlimited airtime to promote them. And they can mention other advertisers on their spots as a value-added incentive. *(Rapaport note: Radio stations sell advertising: advertising spots to be played so many times a day at specified times for a particular price. But they also sell or guarantee extra promotion by way of radio station-sponsored announcements to give away free tickets or mentions that the radio station is sponsoring the concert. This nonadvertising time is either sold as some of the "value" in buying paid advertising, or is actually sold as an addition to advertising. And sometimes the radio station will demand that in return for this added value that the bands prominently display company posters or banners at the concert.)*

What this means is that virtually all the major talent that comes through New York and other large cities will be promoted by

Entertainment today is dominated by pop culture and that reality is the saddest change of all. Fewer and fewer people are in the music business for the art.

large conglomerates. There is no way a small independent concert promoter like me can compete for the well-known acts. We used to do shows with Dire Straits, Bonnie Raitt, Little Feat, Stephen Stills, etc. No more.

It means that talent agents can call up one of the large conglomerates and with virtually no haggling, secure dates for their artists. Artists are often overpaid to insure that their venues are filled. And talent agents can sell them a relatively unknown act because promoters want to insure a grip on the acts when they get big. They will risk a loss because they have a lock on the market for the major acts. If promoters gross hundreds of millions of dollars a year, they can afford to lose $10,000 on a few concerts. The upside is that the unknown acts get exposure in cities where they need to build draws so that the next time around, they can make a profit for the promoter. The net result is that ticket prices continue to skyrocket.

It used to be that that when small promoters like us took a chance on an unknown act and lost money, they were known as "the promoter of record." When the act got more famous, it was an unwritten courtesy that the first option for a concert was given to that promoter. That concept is pretty much out the window.

In the long run, it's a no-win situation for

the bands and their audiences. For a while the acts will earn bigger fees, but as competitors fall away, they will be at the mercy of the megapromoter, and ticket prices will continue to escalate.

Another change is that radio stations are promoting concerts, such as the "Smooth Jazz" series on CD101.9 and the WAVE in Los Angeles. The artists don't want to turn them down because they are afraid of losing airplay. That means that a promoter who has built up an artist in a particular market may lose the act to a radio station. I feel that it is unfair competition. And so is a situation when you have a non Clear Channel radio station wanting to promote a show. If the bands accept, they fear being shut out of airplay on Clear Channel stations.

Rapaport. So how have you dealt with these changes?

Lokin: I dig out the shows other promoters don't care about and try to stay under the radar screen. We're doing fewer shows, making them count for more, and marketing them better.

Today we do fewer and fewer straight ahead jazz concerts. We do blues, a little classical, some world music, more folk and smooth jazz. One of our most unusual shows was the Shaolin Warriors from China. Usually something like that would be part of subscription performance arts series. It was the first time we tried something that different. We were approached by a classical agent who gave me a very favorable deal for taking a chance. It was an opportunity to learn to market to a very diverse audience. We advertised in Chinese language papers as well as in the New York Times. We got posters and flyers to all the dojos where martial arts were taught. We did mailings to our New Audiences list. And lo and behold, we virtually filled a 2800 seat hall with a very mixed audience. It was a great show.

We also take the skills and knowledge we have developed as concert promoters and use them in other ways. For instance, we took on artist's management for French jazz pianist Claude Bolling and, for a brief time, the Firesign Theater. We have acted as consultants to European jazz festival promoters, including the Umbria Jazz Festival in Italy and the Vienna Jazz Festival

Rapaport: Does New Audiences promote fewer jazz concerts because they don't draw?

Lokin: Straight-ahead jazz is definitely not selling as well in concerts as it used to, especially in New York. There's a lot of debate about why this is happening, but I think it's a combination of many factors.

First, here in New York, many clubs feature the jazz artists in intimate club settings. If a jazz artist has played the New York clubs three times in a year, it is not likely that a concert will draw.

Second, jazz, and for that matter, classical music is very challenging to listen to. I don't think audiences want to be challenged. Although the Ken Burns jazz series on TV got a lot of publicity and resulted in record sales for jazz artists like Louis Armstrong and Miles Davis that aren't alive anymore, the jury is out about whether there will be a trickle-down effect for sales of jazz concerts and recordings by newer artists.

Third, major labels are signing fewer and fewer jazz artists. They're putting much more money into packaging the greats from many years ago. New talent needs to be nurtured and challenged by audiences, producers, concert promoters, record companies, etc. They are not nurturing new talent.

But there are some interesting new trends. Jazz artists are being booked on classical subscription series to try and increase attendance and make the concerts more palatable to a more varied audience. For instance you might see Wynton Marsalis or Herbie Hancock playing with a classical symphony orchestra.

Jam bands like like Beyla Fleck, Modeski, Martin and Good and Livesoul are attracting more fans. While the music they play can't really be called jazz, some jam band artists are being signed by Blue Note, formerly a traditional jazz label, because of their appeal to younger audiences.

And then you have the stars of the current jazz world going out on the road together. For example, in the Fall of 2001, Michael Brecker, Herbie Hancock and Roy Hargrove went on tour to do a Miles Davis tribute. Their combined draw helped fill concert halls.

Entertainment today is dominated by pop culture and that reality is the saddest change of all. Fewer and fewer people are in the music business for the art. When I started out as a concert promoter, I wanted to be in the music business. I loved the music; I loved interacting with the artists. I wasn't just a businessman who could sell anything from ladies garments to computers to concerts. After 30 years, I know how to do business, but that's not why I got into it. Today, many of the people running the record companies and concert promotion companies could care less about the music. It is just business—a place to make a lot of money.

www.newaudiences.com

The Association of Performing Arts Presenters

The Association of Performing Arts Presenters (APAP) is an organization for nonprofit arts presenters of the cultural arts: classical and choral music, opera, dance, musical theater, etc. The APAP actively supports more than 1400 member organizations with grants and educational programs to help them put on events, diversify and expand event audiences and help artists develop their careers. Their annual national conference has 450 artist show-cases and provides educational workshops and exhibition booths. Continuing education seminars on specific topics are presented at various locations throughout the year to increase knowledge among arts presenters, agents and managers. A few examples of 2002 workshops include: Presenting the Performing Arts, a nuts and bolts course on how to put on and promote an arts events, and Classical Music Connections, a five-day workshop to broaden appreciation of classical music and successfully present classical music events.

The National Endowment for the Arts

The National Endowment for the Arts (NEA) is the largest single source of funds for the nonprofit arts sector in the United States. The NEA awards grants for exemplary projects in the arts, including dance, design, folk and traditional arts, literature, media arts (film, television, video, radio, audio), music, musical the-ater, opera, theater, visual and multidisciplinary works.

The NEA has awarded more than 113,000 grants to arts organizations and artists in all 50 states and the six U.S. jurisdictions. The public investment in the nation's cultural life has result-ed in new and classic works of art that reach every corner of America.

Nonprofit, tax-exempt U.S. organizations may apply for grants. Applicants may be arts organiza-tions, arts service organizations, federally recog-nized tribal communities and tribes, official arts units of state or local governments and other organizations that help advance the mission of the NEA.

The International House of Blues Foundation

The International House of Blues Foundation (IHOBF) is a nonprofit organization dedicated to promoting cultural understanding and creative expression through music and art. The foundation celebrates diversity by bringing art and music to schools and communities and highlights African American cultural contributions.

Three days a week, the foundation hosts the Blues SchoolHouse, a special program created for students in grades 5-12 that are held at six venues owned by House of Blues Entertainment, Inc. This multidisciplinary performance teaches blues, folk art and African American history and offers students the opportunity to speak directly with musicians and artists. Thousands of students and teachers attend the program annually.

Each year, the foundation awards Blues Ambassador scholarships to college-bound high school seniors that have demonstrated interests and achievements in the arts or have shown leadership in promoting understanding among people of diverse backgrounds.

RESOURCES

American Choral Directors Association (ACDA)
502 SW 38th Street
Lawton, OK 73505
(580) 355-8161
www.acdaonline.org

Association of Performing Arts Presenters (APAP)
1112 16th Street NW, Suite 400
Washington, DC 20036
(202) 833-2787
www.artspresenters.org

American Symphony Orchestra League (ASOL)
33 West 60th Street
New York, NY 10023-7905
(212) 262-5161 phone
www.symphony.org

Blues Music Association (BMA)
PO Box 3122
Memphis, TN 38173
(901) 572-3842
www.bluesmusicassociation.com

Chorus America
1156 15th Street NW, Suite 310
Washington, DC 20005
(202) 331.7577
www.chorusamerica.org

Clear Channel Entertainment, Inc.
650 Madison Avenue
New York, NY 10022
(212) 838-3100
www.clearchannel.com

Creative Artists Agency (CAA)
9830 Wilshire Boulevard
Beverly Hills, CA 90212
(310) 288-4545
www.caa.com

Fischoff Chamber Music Association
PO Box 1303
South Bend, IND 46624-1303
(219) 237-237-4871
www.fishoff.org

The Foundation Center
79 Fifth Avenue
New York, NY 10003
(212) 620-4230
www.fdncenter.org

House of Blues Entertainment, Inc.
6255 Sunset Boulevard
Hollywood, CA 90028
(323) 769-4600
www.hob.com

International Creative Management (ICM)
8942 Wilshire Boulevard
Beverly Hills, CA 90211
(310) 550-4000
No URL

National Assembly of State Arts Agencies
1029 Vermont Avenue NW
Washington, DC 20005
(202) 347-6352
www.nasaa-arts.org

National Endowment for the Arts
1100 Pennsylvania Avenue NW
Washington, DC 20506
(202) 682-5400
www.Arts.endow.gov

New Audiences Productions, Inc.
115 West 72nd Street
New York, NY 10023
(212) 595-5272
www.newaudiences.com

North American Folk Music and
   Dance Alliance
1001 Connecticut Avenue NW, Suite 501
Washington, DC 20036
(202) 835-3655
www.folk.org

Opera America,
1156 15th Street NW, Suite 810
Washington, DC 20005
(202) 293-4466
www.operaamerica.org

South by Southwest Music & Media Conference
PO Box 4999
Austin, TX 78765
(512) 467-7979
www.sxsw.com
   North by Northeast
   185A Danforth Avenue, 2nd Floor
   Toronto, Ontario Canada M4K 1N2
   (416) 469-0986
   www.nxne.com

North by Northwest
PO Box 4999
Austin, TX 78765
(512) 467-7979
www.nxnw.com

RESOURCES: STATE ARTS COUNCILS

A complete list of State Arts Councils are
available on the National Endowment for the
Art's website, *www.nasaa-arts.org*

RESOURCES: UNIONS

American Federation of Musicians (AFM)
1501 Broadway
Paramount Building, Suite 600
New York, NY 10036
(212) 869-1330
www.afm.org
    AFM-Hollywood
    1777 Vine Street, Suite 500
    Hollywood, CA 90028
    (213) 461-3441

American Federation of Television & Radio
Artists (AFTRA)
(Offices in major music markets)
260 Madison Avenue
New York, NY 10016
(212) 532-0800
www.aftra.com
        AFTRA-Hollywood
        6922 Hollywood Boulevard
        Hollywood, CA 90028
        (213) 461-8111

American Guild of Musical Artists (AGMA)
1727 Broadway at 55th Street
New York, NY 10019
(212) 265-3687
www.musicalartists.org

American Guild of Variety Artists (AGVA)
184 5th Avenue
New York, NY 10010
(212) 675-1003
No website

International Alliance of Stage and
    Theatrical Employees (IASTE)
1430 Broadway
New York, NY 10018
(212) 730-1770
www.iatse.lm.com

Screen Actors Guild (SAG)
5757 Wilshire Boulevard
Los Angeles, CA 90036
(323) 954-1600
www.sag.org
    SAG-New York
    1515 Broadway
    New York, NY 10036
    (212) 944-1030

INDUSTRY DIRECTORIES

Billboard Directories
1695 Oak Street
PO Box 2016
Lakewood, NJ 08701
(800) 344-7119
www.billboard.com/store/directories
    Billboard International Buyer's Guide
    Directory

Billboard International Latin Music
  Buyer's Guide Directory
Billboard International Talent and Touring
  Directory
Billboard International Tape/Disc
  Directory
Billboard Nashville 615/Country Music
  Sourcebook
Billboard Radio Power Book: Directory of
  Music Radio and Record Promotion
Billboard Record Retailing Directory

Music Directory Canada
CM Books
23 Hannover Drive, Unit 7
St. Catharines, Ontario
Canada L2W 1A3
(905) 641-3471
www.musicdirectorycanada.com

The MBI World Report 2002
The Music Group
CMP Information Ltd
Ludgate House
245 Blackfriars Road
London SE1 9UR
0207 579 4123
www.musicweek.com

The Music Business Registry
7510 Sunset Boulevard #1041
Los Angeles, CA 90046-3400 USA
(800) 377-7411
www.musicregistry.com

The Musician's Atlas
Music Resource Group
PO Box 682
Nyack, NY 10960
(845) 353-9303
www.musiciansatlas.com

Music Yellow Pages
United Entertainment Media, Inc.
6 Manhasset Avenue
Port Washington, NY 11050
(516) 944-5940
www.musicyellowpages.com

Performance International Touring
  Talent Publications
203 Lake Street, Suite 200
Fort Worth, TX 76102-4504
(817) 338-9444
www.performancemagazine.com
  The Black Book: Entire Performance
    Guide Series
  Concert Production
  Equipment and Personnel
  Facilities
  Talent Buyers
  Talent Management
  Transportation Guide

Pollstar, USA
4697 W. Jacquelyn Avenue
Fresno, CA 93722-6413
559-271-7900 Voice
559-271-7979 Fax
www.pollstar.com
  PollstarOnline.com
  Agency Rosters
  Talent Buyer Directory
  Concert Venue Directory
  Concert Support Services Directory

Recording Industry Sourcebook
Artist Pro
236 Georgia Street, Suite 100
Vallejo, CA 94590
(707) 554-1935
www.artistpro.com/Sourcebase.cfm

Record Companies

* * *

THE BUSINESS OF RECORD COMPANIES

INDEPENDENT RECORD LABELS

INTERVIEW HIGHLIGHT
Marco Cardenas: Nasty Boy Records

RESOURCE HIGHLIGHTS
Recording Industry Association
of America

The Foundation to Assist
Canadian Talent on Records

RESOURCES

The Business of Record Companies

Record companies make and sell recordings in many formats—vinyl (7-inch 45s, 12-inch extended play records (EPs) and long-playing records, LPs), analog cassettes, compact discs (CDs), minidiscs (MDs), digital videodiscs (DVDs) and digital downloads. Approximately 300,000 titles are available for sale annually. According to the Recording Industry Association of America (RIAA), in 2001, U.S. consumers purchased $13.7 billion in recordings. This was a 4.2% decrease from the $14.3 billion in recordings purchased in 2000. CDs continue to be the format of choice (91% of all units shipped). Globally, sales of recordings decreased 5% to $33.7 billion, according to the International Federation of the Phonographic Industry (IFPI).

The RIAA and the IFPI say a large factor that contributed to decreased sales was online piracy.

The RIAA also reported an increase in DVD music videos: a 138% increase to 7.9 million units shipped in 2001. DVD music videos represented a $190 million market in 2001 and an $80.9 million market in 2000.

RECORDING LABELS

There are two categories of record companies: major labels and independent labels. Each segment makes important contributions to the national entertainment industry and to regional economies.

Major Labels

Major recording labels are consolidated into five companies, each integrated into larger multinational conglomerates: Warner Music Group (AOL Time Warner, Inc.-United States), EMI Recorded Music (EMI Group-Great Britain), Universal Music Group (Vivendi Universal-France), Sony Music Entertainment (Sony Corporation-America-Japan) and BMG Entertainment (Bertelsmann-Germany). These companies release approximately 6000 recordings annually in the United States and account for approximately 85% of the retail sales. The United States is also the largest producer and consumer of entertainment products, accounting for 60% of the world's consumption of music.

These conglomerates own subsidiaries that enable them to control all aspects of manufacturing and marketing. Once artists are signed, their music is manufactured and packaged in the conglomerates' manufacturing and printing facilities; marketed through their distribution subsidiaries, which sell products directly or through subdistributors and wholesalers to record stores and large department store chains, Internet outlets and other retailers; and promoted through media subsidiaries. Joint ventures between conglomerates enable the major labels to dominate and control the marketing and promotion of music worldwide.

Independent Labels

Independent labels in the United States are not subsidiaries of major labels and are not distributed through companies that are owned by major labels. However, in Canada, many independent labels are distributed by major label subsidiaries.

Some independent labels make distribution and promotional deals with major labels that provide distribution through their subsidiaries, as well as through independent distributors that reach niche markets. The major labels provide the independents with access to media exposure they would not otherwise have, which helps independent artists to become more successful.

Independent labels release approximately 30,000 recordings annually in the United States and account for approximately 15% of the retail sales. The independent label industry has no leader, no dominant label or artist with multiple platinum sales, no recording epicenter and only sparse exposure on major network radio and television. Some independent labels are owned by artists that put out recordings and sell them at performances and by mail order. Other artists record for independent labels that release the recordings of many artists. Independent labels have been profitable with sales of less than 5000.

Many independent labels were started to breathe life into niche genres that were largely ignored by major labels, such as bluegrass, zydeco, gospel, Christian, new age and so on. They enrich the spectrum of music that is available to the public.

Some artists start their own labels because their artistry or followings have not developed enough for larger labels to sign them. Their records help them gain experience in recording, marketing and sales; act as demos that help introduce their work to entertainment buyers and publishers; and satisfy their fans. Some artists leverage their successes into recording deals with larger independent or major labels; and some become successful without any affiliation, such

PIRACY AND DECREASING RECORD SALES IN 2001

"This past year [2001] was a difficult year in the recording industry, and there is no simple explanation for the decrease in sales," said Hilary Rosen, President and CEO of the RIAA. "The economy was slow and 9/11 interrupted the fourth quarter plans, but a large factor contributing to the decrease in overall shipments last year is online piracy and CD-burning. When 23% of surveyed music consumers say they are not buying more music because they are downloading or copying their music for free, we cannot ignore the impact on the marketplace."

According to recent surveys among a total of 2,225 music consumers between the ages of 12 and 54, commissioned by the RIAA and conducted by Peter Hart Research Associates, 23% of those music consumers surveyed said that they did not buy more music in 2001 because they downloaded or copied most of their music for free.

The same survey found an explosive growth in the copying of that downloaded music onto a burned CD or a portable Mp3 player. Over 50% of the music fans that downloaded music for free made copies of it. Just two years ago, only 13% did so.

The survey also found that ownership of CD burners nearly tripled since 1999: in 2001, 40% of music consumers owned a CD burner compared to only 14% in 1999.

"Global piracy on the physical side costs the recording industry over $4 billion a year. That doesn't even include losses online. While the physical piracy problem is not new, our markets continued to expand. Now that consumer purchasing is threatened as well, the impact of all piracy is greater," concluded Rosen.

Major labels are attempting to reduce piracy by building in copy-protection systems into CDs.

Courtesy RIAA

CONSOLIDATION OF RECORD LABELS: MAJOR HOLDINGS

WARNER MUSIC GROUP: Warner Bros. Records, Atlantic, Elektra and London-Sire. *www.wmg.com*

UNIVERSAL MUSIC GROUP: A&M, Decca Record, Deutsche Gramophone, Geffen, Interscope, Island, Def Jam Music Group, Jimmy and Doug's Farmclub.com, MCA, Mercury, Motown, Philips, Polydor, Polygram, Universal and Verve. *www.umg.com*

EMI GROUP: Abbey Road Studios, Angel, Blue Note, Capitol, Chrysalis, Java, Narada, Real World, Toshiba EMI and Virgin. *www.emi-group.com*

BMG: Ariola, Arista, BMG Funhouse, RCA, Windham Hill and Zomba. *www.bmg.com*

SONY MUSIC: Columbia, Epic, Harmony, Legacy, Loud and Masterworks. *www.sonymusic.com*

as Ani diFranco (alternative rock) and Stephen Halpern (new age).

Independent labels and artists use various sales outlets to reach consumers—direct sales at performances, fairs, craft shows and educational workshops; mail-order promotions to fan lists; museums; artists' Web sites; record stores and nonrecord store chains; specialty music mail-order catalogues; and wholesale gift shows.

Although many independent distributors place records in large retail stores, most independent labels cannot afford to take advantage of the promotional opportunities that those stores offer, such as in-store record play, wall space for posters and co-op ads for in-store retail magazines. Fees to feature recordings in the listening posts of major chain retail stores range from

$500 for three months to many thousands of dollars monthly.

With only rare exceptions, independent labels receive no exposure in print media that is owned by the conglomerates. They receive virtually no exposure on major AM and FM radio stations. This means they must develop alternative promotional resources that serve niche music genres. These include independent magazines; college, community, Web and public radio stations that are not owned by conglomerates; video programs that are receptive to new music and participation in trade organizations that serve their interests. Some have been so successful at developing niche markets that major labels have purchased them. BMG bought Windham Hill, a label that specializes in new age instrumental music.

LEGAL REQUIREMENTS

There are no state or federal certifications or licenses required for record companies. They must, however, abide by the worldwide laws and agreements that govern the intellectual property rights of composers and record companies. Labels that are signatories to union agreements must abide by their terms, including the wages set for recording sessions.

California has imposed a seven-year limitation on the terms of personal service contracts (California Labor Code, Section 2855). According to the law, no one can be forced to sign a personal service contract for a period longer than seven years.

However, the law directly conflicts with standard record company practices (and all U.S. major label record contracts originate in California). Most record contracts obligate artists to deliver 2 to 7 recordings within this period, an obligation difficult for most artists to comply with. In order to enable record companies to extend the time period, the RIAA persuaded the California legislature to pass an amendment that enables the record companies to break the seven-year rule with recording artists and sue their artists for "future lost earnings" if the artists break the contract. Today, it is standard procedure for record companies to give artists extensions, which can last fifteen years or more, and impose penalties when artists do not meet delivery dates. These penalties are commonly imposed by reducing the amount of advances for subsequent albums.

HOW RECORD COMPANIES MAKE MONEY

Record companies make money by selling recordings. It is a high-risk business.

According to the RIAA, approximately 90% of the records that are released by major recording labels fail to make a profit. The successes must pay for the failures to make the labels (and their artists) profitable.

Independent labels have to be more careful in their choices and in their allocation of expenses because they do not have the resources to cover many failures. However, they can succeed with far fewer sales. They can make and promote records for far lower costs than major labels and be profitable with far fewer sales.

The budgets for making and selling recordings are tied to what labels estimate they will sell. Manufacturing costs cannot be calculated without knowing in advance how many CDs, cassettes, etc., will be produced. Knowing how many recordings might be sold makes it possible to budget recording costs.

Experience counts. Most profitable labels have histories of selling and promoting that enable them to estimate gross income.

Record companies bear these major costs —

- Manufacturing

- Some promotion

- Distribution

- Royalties

- Administration

VIVENDI TROUBLES REFLECT CHANGE IN INVESTORS' HOPES FOR BIG MEDIA

Vivendi Universal, the trouble French media company, is expected to put parts of the company up for sale... The corporate ambitions and market forces that spurred Vivendi and other media companies like AOL Time Warner to collect company after company in the pursuit of a digital future have been transformed.

The media conglomerates are now loaded with debt. The high-tech dreams of easy money from delivering all manner of media over the Internet or wirelessly have faded...

The heyday for media mergers is over," said Harold Vogel, an independent media analyst...

Universal Music, the world's largest record company, whose artists include Enrique Iglesias, Luciano Pavarotti, U2 and Eminem, would surely be attractive to another major record company like Time Warner. But analysts doubt that the music business could be sold because of likely European antitrust objections. Resistance from the European Union's antitrust regulators, they note, prevented both Time Warner and later Bertelsmann from acquiring the EMI Group of Britain in the last two years."

Steve Lohr
The New York Times
July 3, 2002

Artists bear these costs, which are advanced to them by record companies:

- Recording
* Some promotion
* Touring

RECORDING COSTS

Recording costs are borne by artists, not record companies. Record companies commonly make loans to artists (advances) for these costs and recoup them from royalties. In the case of artist-owned labels, artists usually obtain funds from friends, family, banks and investors.

With the exception of jazz and classical artists, new major label artists can spend between $100,000 and $500,000 to make a record. Recording budgets of one million dollars and more are not uncommon for famous artists. Many independent artists will spend less than $10,000. The business of recording is addressed in Segment 10, Audio Services.

Manufacturing Costs

Manufacturing includes replicating recorded material and packaging. The costs depend on the number to be manufactured. The more product that companies order, the less the cost per unit. Manufacturing costs are generally borne by recording labels and are not recouped from artists' royalties, although labels try to deduct packaging costs from the base price on which they pay these royalties.

Major labels that own CD replication and packaging facilities sell excess time to independent labels. Otherwise, independent labels buy replicating services from independent CD replicaters such as Sanyo, Cinram and Zoomas and from brokers, such as Disc Makers and Oasis CD Duplication. Most vinyl record manufacturers, such as Record Technology Inc., are independently owned and operated.

Major labels pay approximately $.50 to $.55 per CD. Independent labels that order more than 100,000 CDs a year pay approximately $.65 per CD. Labels that buy less than 10,000 CDs a year pay approximately $1.20 per CD. These costs include the printing of 4-page package inserts and tray cards.

Royalty Costs

Record labels pay two royalties: The first is a record royalty to the performing artist; the second is a mechanical royalty to composers and publishers. Some companies pay record royalties on a percentage (8% to 16%) of the suggested list retail price (SLRP) less a packaging cost, generally 15%

to 25% of the SLRP. Others base royalties on the wholesale price to distributors. For a CD with an SLRP of $16.98, the packaging deduction at 25% is $4.25 and the amount paid to the artist will be calculated as a percentage of $12.73. Thus, at a 10% royalty, artists will receive $1.27; at a 14% royalty rate, $1.78.

Royalties are paid within a contractually agreed on amount of time after the record companies collect the money from their distributors and stores.

Record labels pay composers and publishers mechanical royalties. They try to cap mechanical royalty budgets at ten songs payable at 75% of the statutory rate ($.80 per song in 2002), which equals $.60 per song under the controlled composition clauses of recording contracts.

Promotional Costs

Major labels budget approximately 20% of annual gross income for promotion and selectively allocate the funds according to sales projections for each artist. Independent labels generally budget 10% of projected gross sales.of all recordings annually and selectively allocate that budget.

Promotional costs include designing and printing promotional and packaging materials for recordings; press kits and Web sites; and advertising, radio promotion, videos, public relations and mailing costs. Some or all the costs for video production and radio promotion may be recouped from artists' royalties, depending on their contractual agreements.

Distribution Costs

The record companies decide on the suggested list retail price (SLRP) of each format. The SLRP helps stores to determine the discount price they charge customers and helps performers determine the price to charge to fans at gigs and by mail order.

The price at which distributors buy from recording companies (distributor wholesale price)

PHOTO: NICKEL CREEK

IN 2001, NICKEL CREEK'S FIRST RECORDING FOR SUGAR HILL RECORDS, AN INDEPENDENT LABEL OWNED BY THE WELK MUSIC GROUP, WAS CERTIFIED GOLD. THE BAND'S LUCKY BREAK WAS EXPOSURE OF THEIR VIDEOS ON COUNTRY MUSIC TELEVISION.

is also set by the record companies. This is commonly 50% to 55% off the SLRP. If the volume is high enough, the discount can go to 60%.

The price at which stores buy from record distributors (store wholesale price) is determined by the distributors. This is commonly 55% to 65% of the SLRP. Stores return unsold product at 100% of their cost.

The price at which record stores buy from record companies that own their own distribution warehouses is approximately 75% of the SLRP.

Administration Costs

In addition to the expenses of making individual recordings, recording labels bear administrative

GOLD, PLATINUM AND DIAMOND RECORDINGS

GOLD recordings are those that sell 500,000 units.

PLATINUM recordings are those that sell one million units.

DOUBLE PLATINUM recordings are those that sell two million units.

DIAMOND recordings are those that sell ten million units.

These figures must be certified by the RIAA.

According to SoundScan, of 35,516 recordings released in 2000, only 88 sold more than a million copies; and only 114 were certified gold.

costs (salaries, buildings and equipment). Depending on the scale of operations, administration costs range from 10% to 40% of annual gross income.

PRINCIPLE JOB RESPONSIBILITIES

The principle job responsibilities for people that work in record companies are—

- *Administration:* Handle legal matters (contracts); mergers and acquisitions; restructuring; and royalty administration and accounting

- *Artists and Repertoire (A&R):* Scout for new artists; sign artists; career development; input on creative aspects (selection of songs, producers). Oversee recording budgets and progress; coordinate with sales and promotion departments when recordings are finished to select which songs will be singled out for airplay and in what markets. Liaison between artist and all other record company departments

- *Creative:* Graphic design and photography for all packaging and promotional materials, advertising, merchandising materials, etc. New media: Create and produce music videos. Support, create and oversee Web sites, online sampling and streaming technologies

- *Marketing:* Budget and design marketing campaigns. Coordinate plan with sales, promotion and public relations departments. Expand existing markets and develop new ones

- *Promotion:* Execute budgets and implement plans for getting radio airplay for artists

- Public relations: Execute budgets and implement plan for editorial and print coverage for artists

- *Sales:* Work with distributors, retail company branches and rack jobbers to place records and in-store advertising in retail venues

- *Manufacturing:* Schedule and coordinate work with manufacturers and printers

- *Publishing:* Work with subsidiary publishing companies to maximize publishing and licensing revenues

GETTING RECORD DEALS: MAJOR LABELS

Major labels sign artists that perform music in the most popular music categories or that have sold many records in a niche genre.

Consumers need to hear music to want to buy it. Exposure of artists' music on radio and televi-

THE RECORDING INDUSTRY ASSOCIATION OF AMERICA

2001 Consumer Profile

Phone: 202/775-0101

Web: www.riaa.com

	#	#	#	#	#	#	#	#	#	#		Total U.S. Dollar Value
ROCK	31.6	30.2	35.1	33.5	32.6	32.5	25.7	25.2	24.8	24.4	%	The figures below (in millions)
POP	11.5	11.9	10.3	10.1	9.3	9.4	10.0	10.3	11.0	12.1		indicate the overall size of the
RAP/HIP-HOP[1]	8.6	9.2	7.9	6.7	8.9	10.1	9.7	10.8	12.9	11.4		U.S. sound recording industry
R&B/URBAN[2]	9.8	10.6	9.6	11.3	12.1	11.2	12.8	10.5	9.7	10.6		based on manufacturers'
COUNTRY	17.4	18.7	16.3	16.7	14.7	14.4	14.1	10.8	10.7	10.5		shipments at suggested list prices.
RELIGIOUS[3]	2.8	3.2	3.3	3.1	4.3	4.5	6.3	5.1	4.8	6.7		
JAZZ	3.8	3.1	3.0	3.0	3.3	2.8	1.9	3.0	2.9	3.4		1992 $9,024.00
CLASSICAL	3.7	3.3	3.7	2.9	3.4	2.8	3.3	3.5	2.7	3.2		1993 $10,046.60
SOUNDTRACKS	0.7	0.7	1.0	0.9	0.8	1.2	1.7	0.8	0.7	1.4		1994 $12,068.00
NEW AGE	1.2	1.0	1.0	0.7	0.7	0.8	0.6	0.5	0.5	1.0		1995 $12,320.30
OLDIES	0.8	1.0	0.8	1.0	0.8	0.8	0.7	0.7	0.9	0.8		1996 $12,533.80
CHILDREN'S	0.5	0.4	0.4	0.5	0.7	0.9	0.4	0.4	0.6	0.5		1997 $12,236.80
OTHER[4]	5.4	4.6	5.3	7.0	5.2	5.7	7.9	9.1	8.3	7.9		1998 $13,723.50
												1999 $14,584.50
												2000 $14,323.00
FULL LENGTH CDS	46.5	51.1	58.4	65.0	68.4	70.2	74.8	83.2	89.3	89.2	%	2001 $13,740.89
FULL LENGTH CASSETTES	43.6	38.0	32.1	25.1	19.3	18.2	14.8	8.0	4.9	3.4		
SINGLES (ALL TYPES)	7.5	9.2	7.4	7.5	9.3	9.3	6.8	5.4	2.5	2.4		
MUSIC VIDEOS/VIDEO DVDS[5]	1.0	1.3	0.8	0.9	1.0	0.6	1.0	0.9	0.8	1.1		
VINYL LPS	1.3	0.3	0.8	0.5	0.6	0.7	0.7	0.5	0.5	0.6		Methodology
10-14 YEARS	8.6	8.6	7.9	8.0	7.9	8.9	9.1	8.5	8.9	8.5	%	
15-19 YEARS	18.2	16.7	16.8	17.1	17.2	16.8	15.8	12.6	12.9	13.0		
20-24 YEARS	16.1	15.1	15.4	15.3	15.0	13.8	12.2	12.6	12.5	12.2		
25-29 YEARS	13.8	13.2	12.6	12.3	12.5	11.7	11.4	10.5	10.6	10.9		
30-34 YEARS	12.2	11.9	11.8	12.1	11.4	11.0	11.4	10.1	9.8	10.3		
35-39 YEARS	10.9	11.1	11.5	10.8	11.1	11.6	12.6	10.4	10.6	10.2		
40-44 YEARS	7.4	8.5	7.9	7.5	9.1	8.8	8.3	9.3	9.6	10.3		
45+ YEARS	12.2	14.1	15.4	16.1	15.1	16.5	18.1	24.7	23.8	23.7		
RECORD STORE	60.0	56.2	53.3	52.0	49.9	51.8	50.8	44.5	42.4	42.5	%	
OTHER STORE	24.9	26.1	26.7	28.2	31.5	31.9	34.4	38.3	40.8	42.4		
TAPE/RECORD CLUB	11.4	12.9	15.1	14.3	14.3	11.6	9.0	7.9	7.6	6.1		
TV, NEWSPAPER, MAGAZINE AD OR 800 NUMBER	3.2	3.8	3.4	4.0	2.9	2.7	2.9	2.5	2.4	3.0		
INTERNET[6]	NA	NA	NA	NA	NA	0.3	1.1	2.4	3.2	2.9		
FEMALE	47.4	49.3	47.3	47.0	49.1	51.4	51.3	49.7	49.4	51.2	%	
MALE	52.6	50.7	52.7	53.0	50.9	48.6	48.7	50.3	50.6	48.8		

The figures below (in millions) indicate the overall size of the U.S. sound recording industry based on manufacturers' shipments at suggested list prices.

Peter Hart Research conducts a national telephone survey of past month music buyers (over 3,000 per year). Data from the survey is weighted by age and sex, and then projected to reflect the U.S. population age 10-and-over. The reliability of the data is +/- 1.8% at a 95% confidence level. With respect to genre, consumers were asked to classify their music purchases; they are not assigned a particular category by Hart Research.

Permission to cite or copy these statistics is hereby granted as long as proper attribution is given to the Recording Industry Association of America.

[1] "Rap": Includes Rap (9.1%) and Hip-Hop (2.3%).

[2] "R&B": Includes R&B, blues, dance, disco, funk, fusion, Motown, reggae, soul.

[3] "Religious": Includes Christian, Gospel, Inspirational, Religious, and Spiritual.

[4] "Other": Includes Ethnic, Standards, Big Band, Swing, Latin, Electronic, Instrumental, Comedy, Humor, Spoken Word, Exercise, Language, Folk and Holiday Music.

[5] 2001 is the first year that music video DVD was recorded separately.

[6] "Internet": Does not include record club purchases made over the Internet.

Courtesy RIAA

sion fulfills that need. Most commercial media deliver six major categories of music: rock, pop, Rap/Hip-hop, R&B/urban (includes rhythm & blues, blues, dance, disco, punk, reggae, soul and Motown) and country. Major labels sign artists whose music fits the programming needs of these stations. (The business of record promotion—how record labels get artists' music to be played on these stations—is discussed in Segment 9, Marketing and Selling Records.)

When seeking record deals with major labels, the question that artists and their managers must be able to answer is this: Why should record companies risk the money, time and effort to sign them?

Although talent plays a part in that answer, other factors are equally compelling—

- The music's appropriateness for commercial radio and television programming needs

- The effectiveness of the teams that work with artists (attorneys, talent agents, managers) and their contacts within the record companies

- The willingness of artists to tour

- Artists' effectiveness in increasing fan bases with performances and recordings and their willingness to participate in media campaigns designed by their record companies

- Artists' potentials for commitment, longevity, stability and sustained creativity

Many of these factors are proven in the marketplace. A fan base that has grown to many thousands in a year's time is evidence of an artist's capacity to excite fans. An artist that has put out a recording of his or her own music and sold ten thousand records in three states provides evidence that a recording label with more marketing and promotional muscle may sell hundreds of thousands of recordings.

GETTING RECORD DEALS: INDEPENDENT LABELS

Independent labels look for artists that fit the genre of music they specialize in. Because they are devoted to their genres and committed to helping their artists achieve success, talent is a major component of their decisions.

The second major component is artists' willingness to perform live and tour. Because exposure on major media radio, television and print is sparse, many consumers first hear independent label artists at live performances. Performances help create the excitement (buzz) that is needed for alternative radio stations to play recordings and for reviewers to write about them.

CONTRACTS BETWEEN RECORD COMPANIES AND ARTISTS

Recording contracts between record companies and artists are complex. Managers and artists must find attorneys that are well-versed in negotiating these contracts. The greater the artists' proven value in the marketplace during negotiations, the better the negotiation will go, particularly with regard to controversial issues, such as which promotional costs will be recouped from artists' royalties.

Most recording labels combine advances and recording costs in an all-inclusive recording fund (all-in). The fund provides incentives for artists to minimize recording costs to maximize the amount of available cash for payments to managers, lawyers and band members. The record companies recoup the entire amount from artists' royalties.

Major labels pay 12% to 18% of the suggested retail price (SLRP) for recordings sold in retail stores and independent labels pay 8% to 12%, less packaging (container) costs. However, payments to producers are part of artists' recording budgets and are expected to be paid out of advances and, depending on the artists contracts with producers, a percentage of artists' royalties. If artists negotiate a 12% record royalty and contract to pay producers a 2% record royalty, the artists net a 10% royalty.

Attorneys may settle on a lower royalty rates for new artists and ask for progressively higher royalty rates when sales reach agreed-on amounts. Labels try to negotiate discounts for packaging and other costs. Royalties for sales in new technology mediums (such as limited digital downloads) are evolving.

No label guarantees the amount of money it will put into promotion, even though the expenditures of many promotional costs, such as the production of videos and radio promotion, is recouped from artists' royalties by the record companies. This issue is particularly controversial in the area of video production, where artists are asked to repay 50% to 100% of costs that can exceed entire recording budgets.

The release of approximately 6000 major label recordings a year means that the labels must prioritize and budget marketing campaigns. Simultaneous releases of artists from subsidiaries that serve similar audiences compete with each other. Who gets what promotional support depends on many factors, among them the stature of the artists; previous sales histories; whether new recordings contain what the key executives consider will be hit songs; and the clout of the attorney/management team and the allies artists and their managers have within the record companies.

Few contracts guarantee to release recordings of new artists or reveal the amount of recordings to be manufactured—information that would be useful to managers, talent agents and artists because it would reveal the nature of the labels' marketing commitments.

Here are some of the most contested points of record contract negotiation—

- *Terms and recording commitment:* How many recordings must artists deliver to the

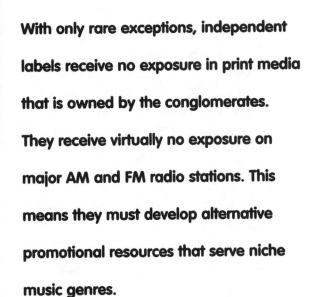

With only rare exceptions, independent labels receive no exposure in print media that is owned by the conglomerates. They receive virtually no exposure on major AM and FM radio stations. This means they must develop alternative promotional resources that serve niche music genres.

label and what are the expected delivery dates? Major labels generally ask for five to seven recordings, deliverable within seven years; independent labels ask from one to three recordings. If the artist cannot fulfill that obligation, the record label can opt to extend the life of the contract. Some contracts impose penalties for late delivery.

- *Creative control:* Who has final say in the selection of producer and control over creative content? Major labels want to ensure that producers have the experience and stature to deliver albums that can be commercially exploited and that the recordings will contains songs that can garner airplay. Artists pay producers out of their royalties and want creative control.

- *Promotional expenses:* What promotional expenses will be recouped from the artists' royalties? In the case of videos, who controls the budget and makes decisions about their creative content? If record companies are in the business of financing the sale and promotion of recordings, there seems

POTENTIAL PROFITS: INDEPENDENT LABELS

Independent labels can profit with substantially fewer sales than major labels by keeping recording and promotional costs down and marketing to niche audiences.

EXAMPLE 1.

An independent label signs a new artist and projects that it will sell 5000 CDs at a distributor wholesale price of $7.19. Of these, 1500 will be purchased by the artist at $7.19 to sell at gigs. Some contracts allow artists to buy at a lower price, with the stipulation that they not be royalty bearing. The label manufactures 25% more CDs (1250) than it anticipates it will sell for promotional giveaways and in anticipation of returns from stores.

The artist receives an advance of $7500 that is used for recording.

Projected gross income from sales

5000 CDs at a distributor wholesale price of $7.19 (5000 x $7.19)	$35,950.00

Expenses

Manufacturing ($.75 x 6250)	($4687.50)
Promotion (10% of projected sales of $35,950)	($3595.00)

Record royalties

10% of $16.95 SLRP less packaging ($1.27 x 5000)	($6350.00)
Publishing royalties at full statutory ($.80)	($4000.00)
Total record company expenses	($18,632.50)
Projected gross profit for the record company:	$17,317.50

The record label makes a gross profit of $17,317.50. The label also recoups $6350 of the $7500 advance it made to the artist. The artist still owes $1150 to the record label, which will be recouped from future royalties when sales exceed 5000 and new recordings are manufactured.

The artist will earn money by selling recordings that they purchased from the record label at their gigs. If the artist writes all the songs and owns their own publishing company he or she will receive the publishing royalties; if not, the publishing royalties will be split between the publisher and the writers.

POTENTIAL PROFITS: INDEPENDENT LABELS

EXAMPLE 2:

An independent label estimates it will sell 50,000 recordings. Because of volume sales they receive a wholesale price per unit of $7.49. The label anticipates returns on large-volume sales and adds promotional giveaways. It manufactures 25% more CDs (12,500) than it anticipates it will sell. (Stores return unsold product at 100% of their cost.)

The artist receives an advance of $50,000 and does not purchase records for sales at gigs, because the record company feels that will compete with store sales.

Projected gross income from sales

50,000 CDs at a at a distributor wholesale price of $7.49 (50,000 x $7.79)	$374,500

Expenses

Manufacturing ($.75 x 62,500)	($46,875)
Promotion (20% of projected sales of $374,500)	($74,900)

Record royalties

10% of SLRP of $16.95 less packaging ($1.27 x 50,000)	($63,500)
Publishing royalties at 75% of statutory ($.60 x 50,000)	($30,000)
Total expense	($215,275)
Projected gross profit for record company	$159,225

The label and the artist profit if the record company sells 50,000 recordings. The label will recoup the money it advanced the artist and the artist will receive an additional $13,500 ($63,500 record royalties - $50,000 advance). If the artist writes all the songs and owns their own publishing company he or she will receive the publishing royalties; if not, the publishing royalties will be split between the publisher and the writers.

POTENTIAL PROFITS: MAJOR LABELS

Major labels generally do not make a profit until sales exceed 100,000 units, a goal rarely reached without substantial airplay on commercial radio and television.

Here are two examples of projected income and expense that are applicable to major label deals.

EXAMPLE 1.
The record company estimates it will sell 200,000 recordings. Because the record company will use its parent companies' distribution system to get recordings into major retail record chains, it will receive approximately $10.00 per recording. Because it contracts to manufacture more than a million recordings a year, it pays $.50 per CD. The company anticipates returns on large-volume sales and adds promotional giveaways. It manufactures 25% more CDs (50,000) than it anticipates it will sell. (Stores return unsold product at 100% of their cost.) The artist royalty is 14% of the SLRP less packaging costs. The record company spends $200,000 making a video and another $200,000 on other marketing and promotional costs. It will recoup 50% of these costs from artists' earnings.

The artist receives an all-in advance of $250,000.

Projected gross income from sales ($10.00 x 200,000 units)	$2,000,000
Expenses	
Manufacturing ($.50 x 250,000)	($125,000)
Promotion 50% of $400,000	($200,000)
Record royalties	
14% of SLRP of $16.95 less packaging ($1.78 x 200,000)	($356,000)
Mechanical royalties at 75% of statutory ($.60 x 200,000)	($120,000)
Total record company expense	($801,000)
Gross record company profit	$1,199,000

The record company makes a gross profit of $1,199,000 and recoups its all-in recording fund advance of $250,000 and $200,000 of its promotional costs.

The artist has a total debt of $450,000 (all-in advance plus 50% of promotional costs).

Although the artist earns $356,000 in record royalties, he or she owes the record company $94,000. If the artist wrote all the songs and owns their own publishing company, the record company may recoup the debt from the publishing royalties (cross-collateralization).

POTENTIAL PROFITS: MAJOR LABELS

EXAMPLE 2.
The record company estimates that it will sell 1,000,000 recordings.

    The record company receives $10.00 per recording. It pays $.50 per CD. It manufactures 25% more CDs (250,000) than it anticipates it will sell. The record company spends

$500,000 making a video, $1,000,000 getting airplay and $500,000 in additional marketing and promotional costs. It will recoup 50% of these costs from artists' earnings ($1,000,000).

    The artist receives an all-in advance of $1,000,000.

Projected gross income from sales ($10,000 x 1,000,000 units)	$10,000,000
Expenses	
Manufacturing ($.50 x 1,250,000)	($625,000)
Promotion (50% of $2,000,000)	($1,000,000)
Record royalties	
14% of SLRP of $16.95 less packaging ($1.78 x 1,000,000)	($1,780,000)
Publishing royalties at 75% of statutory ($.60 x 1,000,000)	($600,000)
Total expense	($4,005,000)
Gross profit	$5,995,000

The record label makes a gross profit of $5,995,000 and recoups its all-in advance of $1,000,000 and another $1,000,000 in promotional costs.

    The artist has a total debt of $2,000,000 (all-in advance plus 50% of promotional costs). Although the artist earns $1,780,000

in record royalties, he or she still owes the record company $220,000. If the artist wrote all the songs and owns their own publishing company, the record company may recoup the debt from the publishing royalties (cross-collateralization).

POTENTIAL PROFITS: ARTISTS

The profitability of major label contracts with artists is a sore point. Since 90% of major label artists fail to make a profit on their first recording, those artists cannot repay their advances. This means that it is difficult for those artists to get released from their contracts and, at the same time, record companies are reluctant to commit money to promote new recordings. When the companies do promote their new recordings, the artists have already compounded their debt, which makes it harder for them to profit from their new venture.

Some artists make little or no profit even when sales of recordings are substantial. Out of advances and earnings, artists must pay managers, lawyers and producers and bear all the costs of recording and some costs of video production and radio promotion. Some artists feel that the difference between the labels' and artists' gross profits are too heavily weighted in favor of the record companies. Why attorneys and managers allow artists to sign such contracts has begun to be questioned in court by artists that signed them and by numerous artists' advocacy groups.

EXAMPLE: MAJOR LABEL

Units sold	200,000	1,000,000
Gross income from royalties	$356,000	$1,780,000
Expenses		
Manager: 20% of gross	($71,200)	($356,000)
Lawyer: 5% of recording fund advance	($12,500)	($50,000)
Producer: 4% of artists' royalties	($14,240)	($71,200)
Recording	($150,000)	($250,000)
Video production	($100,000)	($250,000)
Radio promotion	($100,000)	($750,000)
Total expenses	$447,940	$1,727,200
Artist gross profit:	$(91,940)	$52,800
Record company gross profit	$1,199,000	$5,995,000

to be little justification in asking artists to finance some or all promotional costs.

- *Rights to the masters and artwork:* Who owns the masters and for how long? If artists pay for recording costs, why would they not own the masters and artwork once their advances have been repaid?

- *Ownership of artists' Web sites:* Who owns the name of the Web site and controls creative content? Can artists develop their own Web sites and sell recordings and other merchandise?

- *Packaging costs:* Costs have dropped substantially in the past decade. Many contracts deduct $3 to $4 in packaging costs, even though real costs seldom exceed $1.

- *Publishing:* Many recording companies ask for a percentage of artists' publishing or that artists make exclusive-term song writing agreements with labels' publishing subsidiaries. Most ask that mechanical licenses be at controlled mechanical rates.

- *Circumstances under which labels cancel contracts:* Why should companies hold on to artists that are not profitable? What happens when extensions for the delivery of records exceed 7 years?

Distribution and Production Deals

There are alternatives to recording contracts that sign artists directly to record companies—

- *Distribution deals:* Independent labels deliver an agreed amount of manufactured and packaged recordings to larger recording labels, which agree to distribute them. The larger labels contract directly with stores and deal with networks of distributors. The smaller labels pay for recording, manufacturing, marketing and promotion. The larger labels pay the smaller ones 70%

to 80% of the monies they receive from distributors and stores.

- *Pressing and distribution (P&D) deals:* Independent record labels deliver masters to larger labels that manufacture, distribute and promote the recordings. The larger labels pay 14% to 18% of the suggested retail price to the smaller ones.

- *Production deals:* Artists sign with producers that own production companies. Some producers have ongoing commitments to provide labels with certain amounts of recordings per year; others are production companies that only hope to make deals with labels. The royalties that artists receive depend on whether the production companies have existing deals with recording labels and what their contracts provide.

Production contracts with artists are as complex as record deals, particularly when production companies have existing contracts with record companies. In these contracts, producers are intermediaries between the record companies and the artists.

CONCLUSION

The recording industry provides artists with many opportunities to make and sell recordings at levels that are commensurate with their popularity in the marketplace. Artists that are just beginning to perform sometimes make and sell recordings on their own labels to gain experience in recording and to make money at gigs. Artists that perform regularly and have larger followings can approach independent labels that have histories of success in promoting and selling music in various categories. Artists that record popular music categories and have success at selling thousands of recordings on independent labels and garnering airplay and promotional support can approach major labels.

Independent Recording Labels

Virtually every town in America and Canada has at least one artist or band that puts out their own CDs. Artists that have with local and regional followings sell as many as 5000 recordings a year at performances. Additional recordings are sold to record stores, churches, health food stores, museums, etc. Artists that have followings in several states can sell many more recordings.

There are thousands of record labels that focus on particular genres of music: reggae, children's, folk, bluegrass, blues, jazz, mariachi, classical, Cajun, Zydeco, Celtic, rap, industrial rock, world beat, Klezmer, etc. These labels have catalogues of many artists and gross incomes of up to several million dollars a year.

Each year, indie recordings win increasing amounts of market share from major labels. According to SoundScan, a company that tracks sales of recordings at retail record outlets, sales of indie product in the United States accounted for 16.3% of the market from January to June 2000. According to statistics published by the Recording Industry Association of America (RIAA), that represents $1.009 billion dollars (total sales for that same six-month period were $6.194 billion).

The actual income generated by sales of indie recordings may be much higher. Many indies do not bar code their recordings because they sell them at performances, by mail order to fans and

PHOTO: IRENE YOUNG

STEPHEN HALPERN HAS RELEASED 50 RECORDINGS ON HIS LABEL INNER PEACE MUSIC AND SOLD 4 MILLION RECORDINGS WORLDWIDE. HE IS ONE OF THE MOST INFLUENTIAL NEW AGE RECORDINGS ARTISTS AND CONTEMPORARY SOUND-HEALING PIONEERS.

on the Internet. And, SoundScan statistics do not include sales generated in nonrecord retail stores, such as at health food stores, motorcycle shops, toy stores, museums, national parks, outlets that are particularly receptive to independent product appropriate to their customers' tastes.

If you add consumer purchases of concert tickets for indie performances, promotional merchandise, such as t-shirts, posters, bumper stickers-and sales of musical equipment and recording gear to musicians-it is easy to realize that indie recordings are a multibillion dollar industry.

This success is due to a synergy of factors: the tenacity, imagination and perseverance of the artists; affordable recording and computing technology; the availability of music information and audio education for musicians; the continuing growth of promotional and distribution networks that serve niche music genres, especially the Internet; and increased memberships in trade organizations, such as the Association For Independent Music (AFIM), Folk Alliance and Gospel Music Association.

Indie labels have spurred a music renaissance. They have revitalized music by enriching and widening the spectrum that is available to the public. They have enfranchised musicians. Indie labels have been a big boon to music business and audio education, to the technology industry and to the revitalization of regional economies.

TRAINING GROUND FOR MAJOR LABELS

Indie labels are the training grounds for the majors. Artists, such as Loreena McKennitt, bands like Pearl Jam, and whole labels, such as Windham Hill and Interscope have signed deals

with major labels. Indie labels have spurred major labels into marketing genres of music they previously spurned, such as hip-hop, cowboy, ambient electronica and Latin.

CONTROL OF ARTISTS' CAREERS

Artists that make and sell their own recordings study business and technology to profit from their careers, without surrendering their passion and artistic control. Many successful indie artists serve as mentors and inspire others to learn business and seize control of their careers.

REVITALIZATION OF REGIONAL ECONOMIES

Every time an independent recording business opens, employees are hired, services are contracted from local vendors and musical and audio equipment is purchased from local retailers. As artists expand sales beyond their communities, they import money, which further increases their economic base. Instead of money being funneled into corporate and global pockets, indie artists draw money into their communities.

INDIES UNDER SIEGE

However, for all its successes, the indie record industry is increasingly under siege.

Competition for the Leisure Dollar
Consumers are bombarded with advertising, largely from business giants, for an array of entertainment and leisure products, which compete for their leisure dollars. Indie recordings have difficulty competing for consumer attention. The glut of products makes it extremely difficult to find and separate the great from the mediocre

Control of Access to Popular Media
The large conglomerates that own major labels, television networks, popular magazines, publish-

ing companies and many heavily trafficked Internet sites are exercising increasing control over popular entertainment media.

Many people are exposed only to the music and videos that these conglomerates own. Major labels get national radio airplay for their artists, interviews on popular television shows and articles in national print media simultaneously.

Music from independent labels is rarely heard on popular AM and FM commercial radio stations and rarely reviewed in popular print media. As independent radio stations get swept into conglomerates, indies have fewer and fewer stations that play their music.

The control of access to popular media by major conglomerates is tightening and threatens to strangle the indies.

Retail Store Consolidation

The increasing consolidation of retail stores into superstores and the loss of mom-and-pop stores make it increasingly difficult for indie artists to have their products available. Moreover, major labels pay stores for floor, wall and bin space and for selections featured in-store play and listening booths and for posters to be hung. Few indies can afford to pay the prices.

Because of the poor economic climate in 2001-2002, indie labels face increasing difficulties in getting their music into chains that carry records and getting paid on time, if at all, by distributors.

Unless artists have powerful distributors and a steady flow of product, they are up for tougher times. Many successful indie labels are very concerned.

Here is how Stephen Hill, founder of the label Hearts of Space, analyzes the problem.

The evidence we are seeing, aside from a steady increase in the percentage of returns, is a decrease in the time-in-the-bins period for selling records. What once averaged 18 to 24 months is now down to less than nine months. This essentially means that the window of opportunity for retail sales is now as short for

indie as it is for major label product, but without the massive national promotion, advertising and video exposure that drives the customers into the stores to buy the mainstream hits. The prognosis is for lost sales and higher returns for the independent titles. Many indie titles, unlike major label ones which are hit oriented, take a long time to take off, but after they do, profit from being able to be sold year after year. On top of this are the substantial increases in the cost of in-store marketing programs. Very shortly, indies will be driven out of the already marginalized position they have been occupying for the last 15 or so years. I would go so far as to say that eventually ALL independent and niche genre product, as well as virtually all but the strongest selling back catalog, whether indie or major, will sooner or later be scaled out of Big Retail. This is due to the intrepid economics of consolidation, which favors the large over the small. Simply put, it is a game only elephants will be comfortable playing.

The consolidation of retail record stores has, in some cases, meant that indie labels are unable to collect the money owed to them by a store that has been bought up. Collection of money is a chronic problem: distributors have difficulty collecting from retailers and indies have difficulty collecting from distributors.

In 2001, five major distributors (Valley Media Inc., Pacific Coast One-Stop, Northeast One-Stop, Campus One-Stop and Music Merchandisers) went out of business. This bankruptcy of Valley Media was particularly hard on independent labels. It left 171 labels with few distribution options and monies owing that are difficult to collect.

THE INTERNET: A NEW ALLY

The Internet provides new sources of distribution and promotion and is an ideal medium for serving niche interests. It offers easy access to hundreds

VIRTUOSO MANDOLINIST DAVID GRISMAN HAS RELEASED 47 ALBUMS ON HIS ACOUSTIC DISC LABEL AND SOLD 2 MILLION RECORDINGS WORLDWIDE. MANY RECORDINGS FEATURE GRISMAN COLLABORATING WITH SUCH PREMIER ACOUSTIC MUSICIANS AS JERRY GARCIA OF THE GRATEFUL DEAD, FOLK ARTIST DOC WATSON, JAZZ GUITAR MASTER MARTIN TAYLOR AND JAZZ KEYBOARD VIRTUOSO DANNY ZEITLIN. *The Grateful Dawg*, THE NEW MOVIE RELEASED IN OCTOBER 2001 BY SONY PICTURES CLASSICS, CELEBRATES DAVID'S LONG FRIENDSHIP WITH JERRY GARCIA. THE MOTION PICTURE SOUND TRACK WAS SIMULTANEOUSLY RELEASED ON ACOUSTIC DISC AND INCLUDES SOME OF THE TRADITIONAL MUSIC THAT INSPIRED THEM. DAVID WAS PRODUCER AND MUSICAL DIRECTOR.

of genres. This accessibility feeds a public that is increasingly interested in music that is not available on popular, large entertainment mediums.

Almost all Web music-related sites—artist Web sites, artist community sites, on-line stores, online radio stations, etc.—provide people with a means to get information and sample the music of artists they are curious about. This is revolutionizing niche radio programming and the greater access encourages exploration and sales.

Marketing reports from Forrester Research show that total sales of recordings on the Internet are increasing (over $1 billion in the United States in 2000). Sales of recordings in niche genres often top sales in retail stores. For example, Internet sales of jazz records represented 12.7 percent of sales in all genres as compared with 2.8 percent of sales through traditional retail outlets. Many indies say that Amazon.com is a savior because it carries indie records and provides indie labels with the equivalent of Web sites.

The Internet provides alternatives for consumers. They can pay for a selection of cuts from a variety of CDs to be downloaded to their computer hard drives or MP3 players or have it sent to them on CD-R. Subscription services offered by indie sites, comparable to mail-order record clubs, offer subscribers such incentives as free downloads, first access to new releases, reduced prices, etc.

Getting Lost in Cyberspace

Although there is a great deal of hope that the Internet will compensate for the increasingly con-

solidation of retail stores and help recoup the sales indies will lose, there are some potential pitfalls.

The proliferation of Web sites means that indie artists and labels must find methods for getting people to them and returning. A site can easily get lost in cyberspace. The incredible competition for audience share on the Internet and the increasing presence and dominance of large sites by major entertainment conglomerates does not make getting visitors an easy task for independent artists.

CONCLUSION

The sides in this ongoing battle are clearly drawn: corporate conglomerates and big money on one side and small, decentralized groups of independent musicians on the other. While the major label industry continues to homogenize and narrow its focus to only a few musical genres, the independent label industry has diversity, vitality and creativity.

The advantages that indies have are their decentralization, flexibility and small scales of operation. Nevertheless, new strategies must be adopted to maintain and increase the gains they have made, particularly in the areas of exposure, promotion and distribution. By taking steps to counter the new challenges that confront them, independent bands and artists can continue to prosper.

Marco "Magic" Cardenas: Nasty Boy Records

This is an American Dream story. It started with Marco Cardenas, a 14-year-old Hispanic kid from the projects that walked into Avondale, Arizona's town hall and talked the city clerk into letting him use a neighborhood park for free Thursday night rap parties. Their popularity led to him being a paid DJ at weekend parties. "I was probably the only kid my age supporting a mom and six sisters," he said.

When he was 16, Cardenas started going to swap meets, where he made and sold personalized songs—tens of thousands of them over a period of fifteen years. "Someone would come up and ask for a birthday song for their sister, a song for their jailed cousin, their sick Grandmother," Cardenas said. "They gave me six or seven facts and I'd improvise a rap song and cut a cassette. It gave me skill, a following, the stage names 'DJ Magic' and 'Magic' and the seed money to start my label."

In 1997, Marco released his first CD. "Tha 1st Chapter" under the name Nastyboy Klick. One cut featured Roger Troutman, a singer who was recording for Warner Brothers. "Troutman asked for permission to appear on my recording and they granted it. It added prestige to the project and a name people could recognize," said Magic. The project cost $10,000.

Six months before that release, Magic had cultivated a friendship with Don Parker, program director for KKFR-FM, a successful Phoenix rap/R&B crossover station. Magic hired some very well known rap and R & B groups to put on a concert called The Old School Super Jam. When he had lined up the artists, he asked Parker whether his station would be the exclusive concert presenter. Parker said yes and retitled the show Super Snakes 5 th Anniversary Birthday Bash. The concert was a huge success and gave Magic the "in" he needed.

When his CD was finished, Magic asked Parker if he would listen to one of the songs. "We went into the production room and soon he was saying, 'Wow, I think you might have something here.'"

KKFR started playing the song "Down for Yours." Within two weeks, it became the station's number one requested song. The news got to the record labels. Here was a rapper getting more airplay than their million-dollar records and selling like wildfire at local record stores. Magic got a personal call from Daniel Glass, head of Mercury Records: "Hey, Magic, I hear you've got a hot record. Please don't talk to anyone before you talk to me." He got another call from Doug Morris, Chairman of the Board at Universal Music Group.

First, he went to see Morris. "The visit kind of spooked me," Magic said. "It was too much like a movie—sitting in this huge office on the 18th floor, Morris in a suit and tie behind a big desk,

NB RIDAZ

We can do much better selling half a million on our own than two million for a major. I don't want to be another write-off, another rapper that gets shoved in the background when the record company gives the priority nods to their main stars.

smoking a cigar. He offered me $200,000 and I hedged by saying I had to talk to my lawyer. Then I went to see Glass. I was much more comfortable. When he offered me $250,000 and a nonrecoupable bonus of $50,000, I signed."

Although the single "Down for Yours" peaked at Number 10 on the Billboard charts and sold over 115,000 singles, it was not enough for Mercury to renew the contract.

Magic's second CD, "Tha Second Coming," was made for an independent label, Upstairs Records. It had a hit song, "Lost in Love" that got airplay all over California. But Upstairs did not have the distribution muscle to stock the record in enough quantities to make it a sales hit. Magic and Upstairs parted amicably.

In the fall of 2001, Magic put out NB RIDAZ on his own Nastyboy label. When the single "Runaway" started getting airplay in Phoenix, the owner of Upstairs called and asked for another chance. Magic agreed. By the end of December 2001, "Runaway" was getting 1100 spins a week on over 50 stations all over the country and the

major independent distributors were doing a good job at stocking the stores.

The major labels are beating on DJ Magic's door. Fred Davis, record mogul Clive Davis' son, offered to broker a deal and came in with an offer for $600,000. But Magic has refused to sign for less than an advance of $2.5 million. "Right now our profit margins are good. We can do much better selling half a million on our own than two million for a major. I don't want to be another write-off, another rapper that gets shoved in the background when the record company gives the priority nods to their main stars. I know that if a label gives us that kind of money, they'll push our record. In the meantime, I'm making a living making the music I love."

Nasty Boy Records
3622 W. Charter Oak Road
Phoenix, AZ 85029
(602) 843-3150
No URL

The Recording Industry Association of America

The Recording Industry Association of America (RIAA) is a nonprofit trade association. Their membership consists of all major labels and a few independent labels. They account for 90% of the recordings that are created and manufactured in the United States.

It is a major lobbying organization that supports members' intellectual property rights and First Amendment freedoms. In this regard, the RIAA spearheaded the passage of the Digital Performance Right in Sound Recordings (DPRSR) Act. It is currently negotiating with members and with other nonprofit associations about which entity will establish the fees and collect and distribute them. The RIAA also spearheaded the lawsuit against Napster.

The RIAA surveys the entire music marketplace: retail outlets; record clubs; rack jobbers; and ancillary markets to track and compile sales and marketing data on music trends in the United States. It compiles, analyzes and reports on how many recordings are sold annually by format (e.g., CD, cassette), market segment (e.g., rock, jazz).

One of the RIAA's primary missions is to investigate the illegal production and distribution of pirated sound recordings. According to the RIAA, piracy costs the music industry hundreds of millions of dollars a year. It has an enforcement team of investigators and lawyers, which ferrets out and sues violating companies, has pirated products confiscated and works with international copyright organizations to combat piracy in other countries.

The RIAA administers the Gold, Platinum and Diamond Awards, which are given to recognize the success of recording artists and their producers as measured by the number of recordings they sold.

The Foundation to Assist Canadian Talent on Records

FACTOR is dedicated to providing assistance toward the growth and development of the Canadian independent recording industry. In 2001 FACTOR's revenues were $7.5 million and $5.5 million was made available in loans and awards.

Funding is received from the contributions of 16 sponsoring broadcasters and three of the six components of the Department of Canadian Heritage's Sound Recording Development Program.

The funds assist Canadian recording artists and songwriters in having their material produced, their videos created and their international tours supported. FACTOR provides support for Canadian record labels, distributors, producers and engineers-facets of the infrastructure that must be in place for artists and the Canadian independent recording industry to succeed in the global marketplace.

FACTOR also supports seven regional affiliates, The Music Industry Association of Newfoundland & Labrador; the Music Industry Association of Nova Scotia; the Manitoba Audio Recording Industry Association; the Saskatchewan Recording Industry Association; the Alberta Recording Industry Association; the Pacific Music Industry Association; and the Recording Arts Industry Yukon Association.

RESOURCES

ORGANIZATIONS AND TRADE ASSOCIATIONS

Association For Independent Music (AFIM)
1158 26th Street, #505
Santa Monica, CA 90403
(310) 453-6932
www.afim.org

The Blues Foundation
49 Union Avenue
Memphis, TN 38103
(901) 527-2583
www.blues.org

Blues Music Association (BMA)
PO Box 3122
Memphis, TN 38173
(901) 572-3842
www.bluesmusicassociation.com

Canadian Country Music Association (CCMA)
3800 Steeles Avenue West, Suite 127
Woodbridge, Ontario
Canada L4L 4G9
(905) 850-1144
www.ccma.org

Canadian Recording Industry Association
890 Yonge Street, Suite 1200
Toronto, Ontario
Canada M4W 3P4
(416) 967-7272
www.cria.ca

Children's Entertainment Association (CEA))
75 Rockefeller Plaza
New York, NY 10019
(212) 275-1605
www.kidsentertainment.com

Country Music Association (CMA)
1 Music Circle South
Nashville, TN 37203
(615) 244-2840
www.countrymusic.org

Country Music Society of America
1 Country Music Road
PO Box 2000
Marion, OH 43306
(800) 669-1002
No URL

The Foundation to Assist Canadian Talent
    on Records (FACTOR)
125 George Street
Toronto, Ontario
Canada M5A 2N4
(416) 368-8678
www.factor.ca

Folk Alliance
North American Folk Music and
    Dance Alliance
1001 Connecticut Avenue NW, Suite 501
Washington, DC 20036
(202) 835-3655
www.folk.org

Fischoff Chamber Music Association
PO Box 1303
South Bend, IND 46624-1303
(219) 237-4871
www.fischoff.org

Gospel Music Association (GMA)
1205 Division Street
Nashville, TN 37203
(615) 242-0303
www.gospelmusic.org

International Association of African American
    Music
413 South Broad Street
Philadelphia, PA 19147
(215) 732-7744
www.IAAAM.com

International Association of Jazz Educators
    (IAJE)
PO Box 724
Manhattan, KS 66505-0724
(785) 776-8744
www.iaje.org

International Bluegrass Music Association
(IBMA)
1620 Frederica Street
Owensboro, KY 42301
(270) 684-9025
www.ibma.org

The International Federation of the
    Phonographic Industry (IFPI)
IFPI Secretariat
54 Regent Street
London W1B 5RE
United Kingdom
+44 (0)20 7878 7900
www.ifpi.org

RESOURCES CONTINUED

National Association of Recording
Merchandisers (NARM)
9 Eves Drive, Suite 120
Marlton, NJ 08053
(856) 596-2221
www.narm.com

Pacific Music Industry Association (PMIA)
404-3701 Hasting Street
Burnaby, British Columbia
Canada V5C 2H6
(604) 873-1914
www.pmia.org

Rap Coalition
111 East 14th Street, Suite 339
New York, NY 10007
(212) 714-1100
www.rapcoalition.org
www.rapcointelpro.com

Recording Arts Coalition (RAC)
(No address and phone at this time)
www.recordingartscoalition.com

Recording Industry Association of America
   (RIAA)
1330 Connecticut Avenue NW, Suite 300
Washington, DC 20036
(202) 775-0101
www.riaa.com

Rhythm and Blues Foundation
1555 Connecticut Avenue NW, Suite 401
Washington, DC 20036-1111
(202) 588-5566
www.rhythm-n-blues.org

Society for the Preservation of Bluegrass
Music of America (SPBGMA)
PO Box 271

Kirksville, MO 63501
(660) 665-7172
www.spbgma.com

Soundscan
1 North Lexington Avenue
White Plains, NY 10601
(914) 328-9100
www.home.soundscan.com

Young Concert Artists, Inc.
250 West 57th Street, Suite 1222
New York, NY 10019
(212) 307-6655
www.yca.org

INDUSTRY DIRECTORIES

Billboard Directories
1695 Oak Street
PO Box 2016
Lakewood, NJ 08701
(800) 344-7119
www.billboard.com/store/directories
   Billboard International Buyer's Guide
      Directory
   Billboard International Latin Music
      Buyer's Guide Directory
   Billboard International Talent and Touring
      Directory
   Billboard International Tape/Disc
      Directory
   Billboard Nashville 615/Country Music
      Sourcebook
   Billboard Radio Power Book: Directory of
      Music Radio and Record Promotion
   Billboard Record Retailing Directory

The MBI World Report 2002
The Music Group
CMP Information Ltd
Ludgate House
245 Blackfriars Road
London SE1 9UR
0207 579 4123
www.musicweek.com

The Music Business Registry
7510 Sunset Boulevard #1041
Los Angeles, CA 90046-3400 USA
(800) 377-7411
www.musicregistry.com

Music Directory Canada
CM Books
23 Hannover Drive, Unit 7
St. Catharines, Ontario
Canada L2W 1A3
(905) 641-3471
www.musicdirectorycanada.com

The Musician's Atlas
Music Resource Group
PO Box 682
Nyack, NY 10960
(845) 353-9303
www.musiciansatlas.com

Music Yellow Pages
United Entertainment Media, Inc.
6 Manhasset Ave
Port Washington, NY 11050
(516) 944-5940
www.musicyellowpages.com

*Performance International Touring Talent
   Publications*
203 Lake Street, Suite 200
Fort Worth, TX 76102-4504
(817) 338-9444
www.performancemagazine.com
   *The Black Book: Entire Performance
     Guide Series*
   Concert Production
   Equipment and Personnel
   Facilities
   Talent Buyers
   Talent Management
   Transportation Guide

Recording Industry Sourcebook
Artist Pro
236 Georgia Street, Suite 100
Vallejo, CA 94590
(707) 554-1935
www.artistpro.com/Sourcebase.cfm

RECORDING CATALOGS

PhonoLog
Muze Inc.
304 Hudson Street
New York, NY 10013
(800) 404-9960
www.muze.com

All Music Guide (AMG)
Alliance Entertainment Group
301 East Liberty, Suite 400
Ann Arbor, MI 48104
(734) 887-5600
www.allmediaguide.com

Marketing and Selling Records

* * *

MARKETING RECORDS

**CREATING A STORY:
THE RADIO AIRPLAY BANDWAGON**

INTERVIEW HIGHLIGHT
Wendy Day: Founder, Rap Coalition

RESOURCE HIGHLIGHTS
National Association of Recording
Merchandisers

Association for Independent Music

RESOURCES

Marketing and Sales

Marketing consists of strategic campaigns to advertise and sell products. Before campaigns are designed, research is conducted to try to determine consumer preferences and purchasing abilities.

MARKET RESEARCH

Market research is an effective and proven tool for planning marketing campaigns.

Market research for recordings seeks answers to these questions—

- Who buys recordings in particular genres (demographics)?

- How do consumers hear music and get information about the recordings they buy?

- What other products are purchased by the target audience?

Similar questions are asked by radio and television companies to confirm who is listening or watching their programs in order to better target advertising sales.

This kind of market research is conducted by several nonprofit recording organizations, such as the Recording Industry Association of America (RIAA), and independent marketing organizations, such as Arbitron.

The information they provide enables companies to spot trends in buying habits and tastes in music and target their marketing towards particular audiences.

Characterize the Audience

Record companies must characterize the audiences of their artists by age, sex, social and political interests, occupation, financial status, lifestyle interests, hobbies and tastes in music and art. Isolating special interests can open unusual avenues about what merchandise (T-shirts, coffee mugs, decals, etc.) to offer, unusual places to perform and other businesses to partner with (cobranding).

Here is an example of the type of market research information that is provided by the RIAA.

"Although people under the age of 30 account for 45% of all music purchasers, growth amongst this largest consumer segment of the marketplace has been declining for the past decade. In 2000 music purchases by teens and 20-somethings were flat. However, the 45-year-old and over segment more than doubled its share of the market since 1990, rounding out the decade with a 23.8% market share. And again in 2000, while record stores continue to be the outlet of choice for consumers, more and more music purchasers are shopping at mass merchandisers like Wal-Mart and Best Buy as the changing lifestyles of consumers dictate where they purchase their music." (*Courtesy: RIAA*)

Analyze the Competition

Record companies routinely assess the strengths and weaknesses of their artists by comparing them to their competition.

They must be able to answer these questions—

- What differentiates their artists from others?

- Why is someone going to buy their recordings?

Record companies and marketing organizations look at how other artists are marketed. They examine where they perform, get airplay and editorial coverage (reviews, articles, etc.) and they look at the other promotional elements that contributed to success. They analyze the images and messages other artists convey in their marketing materials. They survey consumer groups.

Analyze the Genres of Music

Record companies need to know how well particular genres of music are selling. This information is valuable to help determine which new artists to sign, to spot declines and increases in music trends and so on. Analyses often include demographic breakdowns. Here is an example:

"Rock continues to be the mainstay of the industry, but Rap/Hip-Hop made the biggest move of 2000. There were many other notable increases in the popularity of some music genres over the previous year. Alternative/Modern Rock is the category in which we find the largest increase (+11%) in the proportion of music consumers who rank this genre as one of their favorites-a 24 point increase has occurred in the share of teenagers who rank it as one of their favorite (57% in '00 vs. 33% in '99). Rap/Hip-Hop is now among the favorite genres of 29% of music consumers, up six points from the previous year. Dance music is the genre of choice for 33% of music consumers, a six-point increase from '99. African Americans (+14 points.) and women age

MAJOR SOURCES OF MARKETING INFORMATION

- **BROADCAST DATA SYSTEMS (BDS) AND GAVIN**–Track radio airplay weekly on commercial and noncommercial radio stations.

- **MEASURECAST**–Tracks Internet radio airplay daily and provides information on audience demographics and ratings of 50 stations.

- **NATIONAL ASSOCIATION OF RECORDING MERCHANDISERS (NARM)**–Tracks sales of all entertainment products in retail stores.

- **NIELSON MEDIA RESEARCH**–Provide information about how many and what type of viewers watch particular television programs in particular regions.

- **RECORD INDUSTRY ASSOCIATION OF AMERICA (RIAA)**–Provides sales statistics for each major genre of music and medium and conducts consumer surveys.

- **SOUND INQUIRY RESEARCH AND CONSULTING**–Marketing organization that specializes in digital music distribution and delivery.

- **SOUNDSCAN**–Tracks retail sales by store and genre, weekly.

19 to 29 (+12 points) have experienced the greatest increase in fans of this genre." (*Courtesy RIAA*)

Analyze Sales of Other Entertainment Products

Competition among manufacturers of entertainment products is strong. Record companies need to know what other entertainment products their target audiences purchase so they can better plan

GROSS DOLLAR VOLUME

Retail Comparisons For Music

Music Sales	Grand Total of All Segments					
	2000	1999	1998	1997	1996	1995
Increased	49%	80%	73%	66%	46%	34%
Decreased	51%	18%	11%	12%	39%	44%
No Change	–	2%	16%	22%	15%	22%

Album Sales

	2000	1999	1998	1997	1996
Overall Top 200	35.1%	34.7%	34.0%	32.1%	31.7%
Releases During The Year	37.8%	40.9%	37.1%	36.2%	34.6%

Note: Albums can be included in both categories.

Data in this section provided courtesy of Soundata.

Product Category

	2000	1999	1998
Currents*	65.6%	66.4%	64.0%
Catalog	34.4%	33.6%	36.0%

*Currents are defined as sales taking place within 15 months of release date.

Data in this section provided courtesy of Soundata.

Music

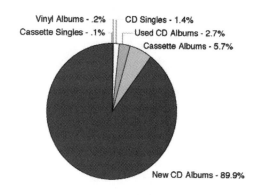

Vinyl Albums - .2%
Cassette Singles - .1%
CD Singles - 1.4%
Used CD Albums - 2.7%
Cassette Albums - 5.7%
New CD Albums - 89.9%

Video

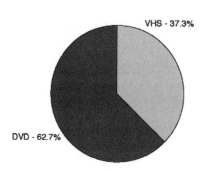

VHS - 37.3%
DVD - 62.7%

Average Music Returns

2000	1999	1998	1997	1996
16.4%	14.1%	15.2%	16.4%	18.1%

Average Video Returns

2000	1999	1998	1997	1996
14.3%	17.2%	18.1%	17.1%	18.2%

All data in this section is weighted.

2000 Results Annual Survey

CONSUMER PROFILE

Genre

	2000	1999	1998	1997
Rock	24.8	25.2	25.7	32.5
Rap/Hip Hop[1]	12.9	10.8	9.7	10.1
Pop	11.0	10.3	10.0	9.4
Country	10.7	10.8	14.1	14.4
R&B/Urban[2]	9.7	10.5	12.8	11.2
Religious[3]	4.8	5.1	6.3	4.5
Jazz	2.9	3.0	1.9	2.8
Classical	2.7	3.5	3.3	2.8
Soundtracks	0.7	0.8	1.7	1.2
Oldies	0.9	0.7	0.7	0.8
New Age	0.5	0.5	0.6	0.8
Children s	0.6	0.4	0.4	0.9
Other[4]	8.3	9.1	7.9	5.7

[1] "Rap" includes Rap (10.3%) and Hip Hop (2.6%).
[2] "R&B" includes R&B, Blues, Dance, Disco, Funk, Fusion, Motown, Reggae, and Soul.
[3] "Religious" includes Christian, Gospel, Inspirational, Religious, and Spiritual.
[4] "Other" includes Ethnic, Standards, Big Band, Swing, Latin, Electronic, Instrumental, Comedy, Humor, Spoken Word, Exercise, Language, Folk, and Holiday Music.

Outlet

	2000	1999	1998	1997
Record Store	42.4	44.5	50.8	51.8
Other Store	40.8	38.3	34.4	31.9
Tape/Record Club	7.6	7.9	9.0	11.6
Internet	3.2	2.4	1.1	0.3
Other[1]	2.4	2.5	2.9	2.7

[1] "Other" includes TV, Newspaper, Magazine Ad, or 800 Number.

Age

	2000	1999	1998	1997
10-14 Years	8.9	8.5	9.1	8.9
15-19 Years	12.9	12.6	15.8	16.8
20-24 Years	12.5	12.6	12.2	13.8
25-29 Years	10.6	10.5	11.4	11.7
30-34 Years	9.8	10.1	11.4	11.0
35-39 Years	10.6	10.4	12.6	11.6
40-44 Years	9.6	9.3	8.3	8.8
45+ Years	23.8	24.7	18.1	16.5

Gender

	2000	1999	1998	1997	1996
Male	50.6	50.3	48.7	48.6	50.9
Female	49.4	49.7	51.3	51.4	49.1

Total U.S. Dollar Value

RIAA figures (in millions) indicate the overall size of the U.S. sound recording industry based on manufacturers shipments at suggested list prices.

2000	1999	1998	1997
$14,323.0	$14,584.5	$13,723.5	$12,236.8

All data on this page is provided by the Recording Industry Association of America and is reprinted with its permission, 2000.

Each figure represents a percentage of that year s total U.S. dollar value.
Totals may not add up to 100% due to "Don t Know/No Answer" responses.

Annual Survey 2000 Results

But most news about entertainers is managed and provided to the press by public relations' people in the form of press releases and written interviews.

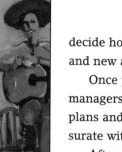

how to compete. A new trend is for major chain record stores to carry electronic products, such as DVDs, videos, games and portable music devices.

SCHEDULING AND ALLOCATING PRIORITIES FOR RECORD LABEL RELEASES

Labels set up record release schedules based on the input artists' managers and producers provide about their artists' recording plans and on information the labels have learned about optimum release dates.

Every month, major labels release recordings in each of the most popular music genres and some in specialty genres. Some may also release special compilation packages of artists that were previously popular and recordings that feature the music of popular films (sound tracks).

Major labels release records by their top-selling artists, artists that have had promising sales (over 250,000 recordings) and new artists. The labels' goal is to identify which artists have the best chance of selling gold, platinum and diamond recordings and to assign promotional budgets accordingly.

Meetings are held among recording company presidents and the A&R, marketing, sales and promotion executives to decide which artists to promote. They review the touring, sales and promotional histories of the artists; the strength of their management teams; the stability of the acts, etc. They evaluate past marketing campaigns and

decide how to best market midselling and new artists.

Once priorities are assigned, artists' managers are apprised of the labels' plans and asked to book tours commensurate with those plans.

After recordings have been mixed, record company presidents and the A&R, marketing, sales and promotion executives listen to them and review marketing allocations. Independent promoters may be asked to provide opinions on which cuts will make the best singles for various radio markets. Once the singles are selected, budgets are allocated for music videos that will feature them.

This is a critical time, particularly for midselling and new artists, because if the companies do not like what they hear, budget allocations will change and some recordings that may have had generous allocations will only be minimally promoted. Alternatively, some artists that record companies previously discounted may be given priority status.

Once the budgets and marketing plans are finalized, marketing executives inform all the people in the company that work in marketing about the artists and their music, so they can do their parts in implementing the campaigns. Regional sales and radio promotion offices are sent recordings and press kits and told about priorities and budget; graphics departments are assigned jobs; advertising agencies and public relations firms are hired, etc.

Artists' managers add to record companies' efforts by meeting with marketing, sales and promotion staff. They discuss tour plans, hype and offer to help in any way they can to implement campaigns.

MARKETING MATERIALS

Visual materials are used to complement the recordings, provide information, attract attention and make artists' names and images memorable. These materials are often released before recordings and music videos are aired.

These materials can help persuade people to play recordings, air music videos and hire artists for performances. They provide the information that writers need to review recordings, interview artists and write articles about them. They help create excitement among fans.

Marketing materials are designed to provide the information that is most required by fans and business people, including—

- The genre of music
- Instruments played
- Performance history
- Recording history
- Biographies

Designs for marketing materials are provided by in-house creative departments, independent graphic designers, photographers and advertising agencies. The primary task is to differentiate artists from their competitors.

Designers incorporate artists' images into everything that audiences see, hear and read about them. The elements of design—words, typography, paper, photographs, drawings, colors, shapes and lines—are skillfully related so they visually present the music, image, ideas and emotions that artists convey. Design themes are used to establish clear, consistent and memorable identities throughout all materials. The skillful execution of ingenious visual ideas is as demanding an art form as creating memorable music.

Marketing materials are incorporated into every element of marketing campaigns. When a variety of printed materials are assembled and sent in one package, it is referred to as a press kit. These are sent to radio stations, booking agents, magazine editors and writers, concert promoters, etc.

Marketing materials include—

- Recording covers and booklets
- Music videos
- Web sites
- Biographies
- Publicity photographs
- Sell sheets for retailers (two-sided sheets that concisely describe the recording and backgrounds of the artists)
- Posters
- Brochures
- Advertisements
- Reviews

MARKETING CAMPAIGNS

Marketing campaigns expose artists to the widest number of people within a targeted sector, motivate people to buy the artists' recordings and increase name recognition. They are designed to hit as many entertainment mediums as possible.

It is not by chance that within three months of a major label recording being released, an artist is on tour in 25 major cities; has his her own single simultaneously played many times a day on major AM and FM radio stations; is seen on the cover and has articles and interviews in national and regional entertainment and news magazines; is featured on prominent radio and television talk and interview shows; has their music video played on MTV and other syndicated entertainment shows; and their recordings are the first to be seen and heard when consumers walk into retail stores.

Marketing campaigns include the following elements—

- Radio promotion and radio appearances
- Television appearances

DOLLY PARTON PUBLICITY MATERIALS

SUGAR HILL

Dolly Parton In Her Own Words On

<u>Little Sparrow</u> – I picked this title because I thought it
and my Daddy used to call me his little songbird. I als
<del>ght</del> *Little Sparrow* represen

SUGAR HILL

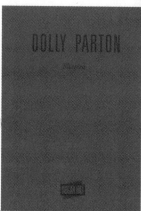

DOLLY PARTON

Every year it gets a littl

In 2001, pop country star Dolly Parton chose to record *Little Sparrow,* an all-acoustic blue grass album, for independent recording label Sugar Hill. It sold over 200,000 records. "This is the music I would have been doing all along, if I could have made a living at it," said Parton. The GRAMMIES awarded Dolly her 3rd "Best Country Female Country Vocal Performance."

RollingStone ®

★ ★ ★

Dolly Parton
Little Sparrow
SUGAR HILL/BLUE EYE
Parton sparkles without the glitz

A LL THE MAKEUP IS GONE
on *Little Sparrow:* After a
long spell as a bubbly Hol

- Performances (tours)

- Convention appearances

- Record release parties

- Public relations efforts

- Internet promotions

- Fan clubs

- Media advertising

- Retail store campaigns

- Miscellaneous marketing elements (testimonials, charity appearances, merchandise, etc.)

The most expensive campaigns include all marketing elements and are carried out in a concentrated period of time to provide maximum exposure to artists' target audiences.

Independent record companies use the same elements in their marketing campaigns, but the scale of operations differs, as does how and where their marketing efforts are directed.

Radio

The key element of major label campaigns is radio airplay of singles. People want to hear recordings before they buy them. Most record companies can reasonably estimate how many albums people will buy based on the amount of times singles are played on particular radio stations.

There are approximately 10,700 commercial and 2,500 noncommercial (college, community and publicly owned) radio stations in the United States. Of these, music is the primary focus for about 6300 commercial stations and 1900 noncommercial stations.

Many stations worldwide provide programming on the Internet, which makes it possible for people to listen to radio stations from all over the world. There are a growing number of Internet-only stations.

Many large commercial radio stations are owned by conglomerates. Programming is centralized (singles are chosen by one person to be played on numerous stations) and is accomplished by an intricate system of coordination between independent record promotion companies, major label marketing executives and the conglomerate's director of programming. Airplay for commercial stations that are not owned by conglomerates and do not have centralized programming is chosen by program directors (PDs). Airplay for noncommercial stations is chosen by PDs and disc jockeys.

It is the job of independent radio promotion companies to introduce recordings and persuade directors of programming, PDs and disc jockeys to play singles.

Some independent promotion companies specialize in getting airplay for major- label artists. These companies have established long-term relationships with PDs, have track records for knowing station preferences and consistently pick hits. Record companies pay dearly for their expertise. Some music business experts estimate that the cost of getting a charted hit for an artist in a popular format is $1 million.

Other independent promotion companies get airplay for independent labels. They target noncommercial radio stations and the commercial stations that are ignored by major labels, primarily college radio, community and publicly owned stations and independently owned commercial stations.

Independent record labels pay record promoters up to $5000 a month, depending on how many stations are covered.

However, radio is not the key element of most independent label campaigns because the opportunities for airplay are sparse and the cost of hiring independent promoters is high.

It is the job of regional record company personnel, independent promoters, artists' managers and public relations firms to arrange radio interviews for artists that are receiving airplay.

DELBERT MCCLINTON'S NOTHING PERSONAL ALBUM NOMINATED FOR GRAMMY® FOR "BEST CONTEMPORARY BLUES ALBUM"

LOS ANGELES, Calif. - Delbert McClinton's critically acclaimed, commercially, successful album Nothing Personal (New West Records) was nominated for a Grammy® Award in the category of "Best Contemporary Blues Album." Delbert is a previous Grammy Award winner, having won "Best Rock Performance by a Duo or Group" in 1991 with Bonnie Raitt for their duet "Good Man, Good Woman." He was also nominated in 1988 in the "Best Contemporary Blues" category for his album Live In Austin.

The 44th annual Grammy Awards will be announced and televised on Wednesday, February 27, 2002, from the Staples Center in Los Angeles.

2001 was a watershed year for Delbert, who made his New West label debut with Nothing Personal on March 6, only to receive accolades in the media ranging from Rolling Stone to the Wall Street Journal and on to national TV.

A brief recap of the album's achievements follows:

- "No. 1 Americana Album of the Year" on the Album Network Americana Roots chart, spent 12 weeks at No. 1 (beating out the prior record for longevity set by Steve Earle)

- Delbert and Nothing Personal ranked Billboard's No. 5 blues artist and No. 3 blues album in the magazine's year end issue.

- Chosen "Album of the Week" by The New York Times

- Cited as "Mr. McClinton's best recording ever" by The Wall Street Journal

- Appeared on "Saturday Night Live," "The Late Show with David Letterman," "The Late Late Show with Craig Kilborn," "Austin City Limits" (to be shown during the week of January 5th) and "Mountain Stage" (PBS)

- Featured on NPR's "Weekend Edition," "World Cafe," "E Town," "Mountain Stage" and "A Prairie Home Companion"

Among the excerpts from major reviews—

"Typically, the most you can expect from even a gifted journeyman this far down the line is punch-the-clock competence and occasional flashes of fire. But this Texan comes roaring out of the gate on Nothing Personal."—Rolling Stone

"Here the singer and multi-instrumentalist deliver a tears-and-tequila-stained CD drenched in pure Tex-Mex soul."— People

"McClinton's first new album in three years finds the king of ripsaw vocals exploring every greasy corner of his roadhouse sound, from sly Texas 'tonk and swamp boogie to Memphis moaners and elegant uptown blues."— Entertainment Weekly

"This is the second coming of Delbert McClinton." ****—Pulse

And now, in 2002, there are no signs of slowing down. Delbert will soon embark upon the eighth annual "Delbert McClinton Sandy Beaches Tour" (http://www.delbert.com) from January 12-19 featuring a compendium of legendary country, blues, Americana and rock musicians. He will be featured on "Austin City Limits" on the PBS series' episode that airs during the week of January 5. He will also record a new album set for release later in the year and will tour extensively.

Courtesy: Mark Pucci Media and New West Records

Tracking Airplay. Record labels track what music is getting airplay and where, from reports provided by Gavin and Broadcast Data Systems (BDS). These companies provide information to publications that compile charts (rankings of artists according to how much airplay they received in what markets and for how many people). The recording that reaches the most people in any week is Number 1. Charts are compiled for all genres. *Billboard Magazine* publishes charts for commercial radio stations. *College Music Journal* (CMJ) publishes charts for noncommercial stations.

Record companies compare the data from these reports to weekly retail sales information from SoundScan and adjust shipments to retail stores accordingly.

Radio Station Income. Radio stations make money by selling advertising. What they can charge depends on how many people listen. Market research firms, such as Arbitron, provide this information. Survey results are used by stations to persuade advertisers that they will reach their targeted audiences.

The challenge radio stations have is to keep current listeners and attract new ones. This is done by maintaining a consistent sound and identity and by designing marketing campaigns (promotions) that increase name recognition and attract new listeners. These promotions can be live broadcasts from advertising venues, such as car dealerships and sports events, free tickets to concerts and other events, merchandise giveaways and so on.

Record labels have a stake in helping stations maintain and increase their listenerships and they contribute money for radio station promotions. These contributions are not considered payola because they are not slated for any particular artist and there is little attempt to direct how radio stations spend these monies. And since all major labels contribute money for radio station promotions, it is difficult to say whether stations favor any particular label over another.

DELBERT McCLINTON

Payola is the payment of cash or its equivalent to a program director or other staff to persuade them to play the record of a particular artist. Payola is illegal.

Television

Network television and cable stations reach many more people than does radio. The exposure of artists on national television has potent effects on sales.

The primary means of exposure is the playing of music videos on popular entertainment shows, such as MTV. Almost all the music videos shown on network and cable television are by artists that record for major labels. The competition for these spots is very high.

Other methods of television exposure are for artists to give interviews or perform live. Some television shows are owned by the conglomerates that own the record companies, which makes it easy for them to book appearances for their artists. But some are owned by independent companies that do not own record companies. Artist appearances on these shows are arranged by talent agencies.

Appearances on network television shows are usually reserved for the artists that record companies have allocated the most promotional dollars and whose campaigns are coordinated with other promotional elements, such as national tours, radio airplay, coverage in major music magazines and ads in music trade magazines.

As with radio, television stations make profits primarily from advertising. Market research is provided by Nielson Media Research and survey results are used by television stations to persuade advertisers that they will reach their targeted audiences.

Performances

Live performance is a major component of a marketing campaign. Performances generate the excitement that leads to airplay, sales, reviews and articles. Live performances are the primary way for independent artists to introduce their music to audiences.

For established major and independent label artists, talent agents book appearances and tours, with the guidance of record company marketing executives and artists' managers. Managers work with regional record company personnel to coordinate such other campaign elements as retail store support, editorial coverage in local newspapers and magazines and interviews on radio stations.

Release Parties

Record companies hold record release parties in cities where their artists perform. They invite newspaper and magazine writers, program directors, television producers and retail sales people. These parties help to build excitement about the release and establish rapport among artists, labels and guests.

These parties can be held at rented venues or backstage after key performances.

Conventions

Appearances by artists at major record company and music association conventions insure that influential business people are introduced to and hear their music. Conventions present great opportunities for artists' and their managers to meet and get to know the personnel that will be responsible for artists' marketing campaigns.

Major labels hold annual conventions of their own to bring together local, regional, national and international personnel from their companies.

Major and new acts perform. Conventions are a convenient and effective method to introduce promising new artists to the entire company and to signal record companies' marketing and promotion personnel where priorities lie. The artists that are selected to perform are virtually guaranteed to have large marketing budget allocations when their recordings are ready.

Industry conventions held by such associations as BMI, ASCAP and NARM and award ceremonies, such as the Grammies, bring together key recording and media people and they showcase performers. Those appearances help artists to build name recognition and establish their value and status in the industry.

Independent labels do not hold their own conventions. They and their artists attend conventions sponsored by nonprofit associations in particular genres, such as the Gospel Music Association or the Folk Alliance, or associations that represent many independent recording artists, such as the Association for Independent Music (AFIM) and South-by-Southwest. Conventions provide opportunities for artists and labels to introduce their work at performance showcases and award ceremonies.

Public Relations

Public relations (PR) is the art of raising consumer awareness via editorial coverage in newspapers and magazines (print media), fan newsletters and Internet sites. Another task is to keep unfavorable stories out of the news. This job is handled by recording labels' public relations' offices and independent PR firms.

Editorial coverage is highly sought after because, in the eyes of the public, writers provide unbiased information that is considered to be more credible than advertising. But most news about entertainers is managed and provided to the press by public relations' people in the form of press releases and written interviews.

Public relations people also arrange for interviews on radio and television news shows. They coach artists about what information to provide during interviews in order to maintain the consistency of the artists' messages and images that has been established.

Press Releases

Press releases are universally used by entertainment and other businesses to provide news and other information to print, radio, Internet and television personnel. Press releases are factual mini-istories that capsulize information and tell who, what, where, when and how. They anticipate questions and answer them. They often include quotes from prominent newspapers and magazines. They are organized so the most important information comes first and the least important last.

Information provided in press releases is used to create news stories, articles, announcements and reviews and to entice media writers to conduct interviews.

Internet Promotion

The Internet contains a vast music world where consumers and business people can listen to, buy and exchange information about virtually any musician and composer in the world. People can read artist biographies and histories, reviews of their works, articles and interviews; hear and download music samples, streaming broadcasts and live concert Webcasts; download music, buy recordings and associated merchandise and communicate with artists via emails and chat rooms. Journalists can download photographs and other information for use in their stories.

Label sites are designed by the record labels' creative staff or by advertising agencies and include graphics and other marketing materials, such as biographies, posters, merchandise, etc. Artists' sites may be designed by the record labels or by designers chosen by the artists, depending on their contractual arrangements. Record companies offer free downloads of selections from new recordings as incentives for people to listen and buy.

Information and music is provided to the following—

- Paid-for Internet subscription services (streaming and downloads)

- Independent record promoters

- Internet broadcasters and streaming sites

- Internet fanzines

- Internet retailers, such as *www.Amazon.com* and *www.CDBaby.com*

- Information sites for artists and composers

- Music bulletin boards, such as Velvet Rope, which is sponsored by *www.Starpolish.com*

- Artist collectives, such as Internet Underground Music Archives, *www.IUMA.com*

- Internet newsletters and columnists, such as *Leftsetz@aol.com and JPNotes@aol.com*

In 1999, Loreena McKennitt released a special two-CD live album on her independent label Quinlan Road and donated the profits to The Cook-Rees Memorial Fund for Water Search and Safety. Her innovative creative talents, independence, humanistic depth and extraordinary sense of business inspire musicians and music professionals to attain higher creative and professional standards.

Search engines provide links to sites where artists are mentioned and where there are articles and reviews.

Free file-sharing of music occurs globally on a massive scale. Currently there is no credible information on whether these sites help or hinder the sale of music.

Fans

Marketing efforts are geared towards developing and increasing followings of fans because they are loyal and enthusiastic promoters of music. They follow artists from gig to gig and bring their friends; they buy recordings and talk them up. Fans include consumers, radio station programmers, critics, retailers and writers that have favorite artists and take whatever opportunities they can to promote them.

When fans become known, special care is taken to keep them and repay their enthusiasm. They are often the first to know about gigs and new CDs, sometimes with offers of discounts. They are kept up to date about artists' activities via newsletters and emails. Media friends are given free tickets to shows, free recordings and merchandise.

Paid Advertising

Paid advertising in entertainment magazines and other media features artists and provides information about the availability of records and concert appearances.

Record companies advertise recordings in trade magazines, such as Billboard and CMJ to increase awareness of them by radio and television station personnel and retail store buyers and to communicate that the labels are spending major marketing dollars to promote them.

Retail Store Campaigns

Chain record stores make money by selling records and in-store advertising, and some experts say that the latter accounts for more profits. Record labels purchase wall, bin and floor space to stack and rack records and put up posters and mobiles. They pay for the use of listening booths that feature the recordings that have priority allocations; and for the choices that stores make about which recordings are played throughout the store. Record labels also buy advertising in record stores' promotional publications.

Because of the high prices record stores charge, major labels buy the majority of in-store advertising.

Miscellaneous Marketing Elements

Record labels use a variety of other elements to increase name recognition. These include—

- Exposure of artists' work in other entertainment mediums, such as films and video games

- Licensing of compositions for other artists to record

- Merchandise that features artists' names, such as t-shirts, coffee cups, posters and so on

- Appearance of artists in advertisements of other products, such as beverages, clothing, sports events, etc. (testimonials)

- Guest appearances at sporting, political, charity and other events

- Guest appearances on recordings of other prominent artists

SELLING RECORDS

Today, customers can purchase recordings from a variety of traditional (brick and mortar) and Internet stores. These include—

- Chain record stores

- Chain electronic stores

- Independent record stores

- Discount retail chain stores

- Department stores

- Variety retail stores (grocery stores, drugstores, minimarts)

- Record label Web sites

- Internet record stores

- Other (live performances, mail-order catalogs, record clubs, etc.)

The suggested retail price of recordings (SLRP) is set by the recording label. The actual price stores charge consumers for recordings is set by the store owner and depends on volume sold and any special discount incentives that record labels offer to help move product. Stores and distributors can return unsold product to record labels for 100% of the wholesale price.

Major Label Distribution

Major labels own distribution subsidiaries. They sell recordings directly to large chain stores, including record, electronic and department stores.

Generally, the higher the volume of purchases and the fewer the returns, the better the price that chains can purchase recordings from record labels, and, to some extent, the better the discount prices they can offer in their stores. This also means that chain stores can decide to offer some music as loss leaders and discount some titles to just above the wholesale price.

Major label subsidiaries also sell to one-stop distributors and rack jobbers. One-stops stock a variety of products and sell them to independent retail stores, some retail chain stores and specialty stores, such as health food stores and truck stops.

Rack jobbers stock, maintain and control an inventory of music and other products in stores. They rent space in stores and stock them with what they think customers will buy. Some rack only the charted artists in a particular genre; some rack only recordings of top charted artists; some rack a mix of recordings and other entertainment products. Rack jobbers service many grocery and drugstore chains.

Sales of recordings that have bar codes are tracked weekly by SoundScan, which makes it easy for record companies to evaluate the effectiveness of their marketing campaigns and get recordings quickly to stores where sales are highest.

Independent Label Distribution

A number of national and regional independent distributors carry the music of independent labels and sell to the same stores as major label distributors, to independent record stores and to one-stops. Rack jobbers seldom buy independent label product, unless it becomes a charted hit. A few large independent record companies handle distribution in-house and have their sales force work directly with retail accounts.

Distributors of independent labels ask that product be bar coded so that sales can be tracked weekly by SoundScan. Sales at performances and festivals are also tracked, but the record companies must send SoundScan sales figures.

Chain Record Stores

Major labels stock chain record stores in amounts that are based on marketing campaign budgets and on actual sales figures generated weekly by SoundScan. Because these labels buy wall, bin and floor space from record stores, they control the type and quantity of product that is stocked and where it is displayed, what customers hear when they walk in the doors and what they select to listen to in listening booths. Stores pay for what is actually sold and return unsold product, so overstocking is not a large concern.

Weekly reports about airplay from Broadcast Data Systems and sales from SoundScan tell marketing staff whether airplay is generating sales and whether there is sufficient quantity at particular stores to meet demand. Product displays and product stock are shifted accordingly.

Chain record stores allocate some space for independent label recordings that have regional and national independent distributors. However, independent labels are generally stocked by genre in the back bins. Stores generally carry no more than five recordings for each independent artist they stock. Restocking time for independent recordings can take as much as two months.

Retail Stores

Retail stores that carry a variety of products often allocate space for entertainment products and hardware. Generally, because space is limited, only charted hits and well-known artists are stocked.

Independent Record Stores

There are several hundred independent record stores in the United States, such as New World Record, in Buffalo, New York and Zia Records in Phoenix, Arizona. Most buy major label recordings from one-stops and independent recordings from independent record distributors.

Record Label Web Sites

Major labels do not currently sell recordings on their Web sites, music subscription Web sites or to artists to sell at gigs because they do not want to compete with store sales. Most major label contracts do not allow their artists to sell recordings at artist-owned Web sites.

Both major label sites and artist Web sites sell related merchandise, such as T-shirts, posters.

Most independent labels sell their recordings at their Web sites because of the difficulty in stocking chain and independent record stores with enough product to meet demand. They sometimes offer discount prices and provide loyal customers with specials, such as one free recording for every ten purchased.

Many online subscription services offer permanent downloads. These constitute record sales that generate royalties for performers and composers.

At this time, online subscription services that offer streaming and temporary downloads do not provide links to Web sites that sell recordings. Since there is a correlation between the number of times that consumers hear a recording and decide to buy it, these services are expected to provide such links in the near future. There is fear, however, that these links will radically reduce sales in non-Internet stores.

Internet Stores

The variety of Internet stores that sell recordings is astonishing. It ranges from sites that sell recordings from chain record and general retail stores to Internet only record stores, such as *www.Emusic.com*, *www.CDBaby.com* (indies only) and *www.CDNow.com*, to sites that sell entertainment and other products, such as *www.Amazon.com*, to online bookstores that sell recordings, such as *www.barnesandnoble.com*, and to global online superstores, such as *www.buy.com*. Some buy direct from record labels; others from distributors. Some sell CDs, others sell MP3s; some sell both.

The Internet is changing the manner in which consumers hear and buy music. Internet sales are proliferating. Some expected changes are—

- Links to sites where consumers can purchase music that is placed on the subscription sites that offer streaming and temporary downloads

- Major record labels and the conglomerates that own them will offer direct online sales.

- In-store kiosks will have CD burners. Consumers can listen to music offerings from MP3 sites and select the compositions they want to burn.

Other Record Sales Opportunities

Major record companies utilize other sales opportunities, such as record clubs and the licensing of recordings to independent and foreign labels, particularly of recordings in their back catalogues and of artists that have been dropped from their labels. They also have mail-order record clubs that sell recordings of noncurrent releases at excellent discounts.

The majority of independent label artists sell their recordings and related merchandise at performances, some at prices well below those offered by chain record stores. Independent record labels that have rosters of many artists routinely sell recordings to their artists at deep discounts.

Independent label artists also sell recordings by mail order to fans and through mail-order specialty catalogs. Some independent labels only make their recordings available on the Internet.

One of Canadian artist Loreena McKennitt's business strengths is the amount of recordings that she sells at performances and by mail order. She was one of the first major label artists to win this concession in her recording contract. "Being able to sell your CDs at performances helps to maintain cash flow. Many fans purchase older recordings that may be unavailable at stores," Loreena said.

CONCLUSION

Market research is used to select and target audiences for particular products and to establish what will motivate them to buy. Marketing campaigns raise audience awareness about particular recordings, build name recognition for artists and sell recordings.

The entertainment giants own distribution centers and control distribution in the large retail chain stores. They can pay high prices for in-store advertising, rental of floor and wall space and determine which records are played in the stores and in listening booths. They control what music is stocked and in what amounts.

The giants control access to popular media, giving them added leverage to coordinate marketing and sales campaigns.

Independent recordings are distributed by independent distributors, one-stops and rack jobbers. Their records are stocked in fewer numbers and most cannot afford in-store advertising. The records are seldom played on popular radio stations and reviewed in national print media.

The Internet is changing buying habits and offers buyers wider choices than most retail stores and the chance to listen to music in a variety of genres.

Creating a Story: The Radio Airplay Bandwagon

BRYAN FARRISH, INDEPENDENT RECORD PROMOTER

When working with the mass media (radio, TV, papers, magazines), one thing to keep in mind is that they are just that... MASS.

Commercial radio wants to build stars, whose songs are played all across the country during a particular time period. Radio wants to be part of the other media efforts that are taken to build these stars and does not want to be left off the bandwagon.

The job of a radio promoter is to build a story that convinces radio stations that enthusiasm for an artist's music is building and that the artist is becoming a star. The goal is to increase the number of spins that the artist receives daily and weekly and to induce radio stations that are not yet playing the artist to jump on the bandwagon. In radio parlance this is called "creating a story."

A single station, or even two or three stations, cannot build a star, no matter how much they play an artist. It takes a group of stations, across the country, playing the same artist many times a day.

Radio promoters make daily phone calls to program directors (PDs) to inform them about which other stations have added an artist. "Add" information is SO important that it is often the ONLY thing that is talked about, especially in the early stages of a radio campaign. Nothing in commercial radio happens without the add. It might start out like this: "We have adds last week in Tacoma, Austin, Orlando, Fresno, Wichita Falls and Dearborn and commitments from Miami, Seattle, Dallas and Chicago."

Next, radio promoters inform PDs about how many spins their artists are receiving at these stations and at what time of day, starting with the highest (or most exciting) recordings and providing additional information about where else radio action is developing. The radio promoters' rap is designed to make the station want to jump on the bandwagon.

The promoter also provides the PD with favorable comments from other stations, such as "Mary's record is getting great calls!" or "The XYZ song is moving into power...it's strong females for us!"

As the campaign progresses, the promoter might tell the PDs what other stations are doing by way of giveaways (concert tickets, CDs, merchandise, etc.), conducting artist's interviews, or anything else that convinces stations that a star is being built.

The promoter will remind PDs of upcoming artist appearances in their cities and remind them that the concert promoters are station advertisers; feed them news about concert attendances and reviews in other cities; provide them with sales figures from retail stores in the area and from other cities around the country; and quote from reviews and other favorable editorial coverage.

Each week, the promoter will call PDs at all the radio stations he is attempting to convince to play the artist's music.

Copyright 2001 by Bryan Farrish. Reprinted with permission.

Bryan Farrish has informative articles on radio promotion on his website: www.radio-media.com

Wendy Day:
Founder, Rap Coalition

Rap Coalition, founded by Wendy Day in 1992, is a nonprofit organization that is dedicated to the support, education and protection of rap artists. Its main goal is to keep artists from being unfairly exploited.

Since 1992, Rap Coalition has had an impact on the urban music industry by helping, for free, thousands of artists, DJs and producers individually, as well as through monthly panel discussions, seminars, demo listening sessions, rhyming (cipher) sessions, showcases and fair-deal negotiations. Rap Coalition helps artists break unfair, oppressive contracts with record labels, production companies and managers; teaches the business side of the music industry to thousands of artists and industry hopefuls from around the country; offers health care and dental benefits; coordinates panels at most of the major urban music conventions; has instituted a mentoring program that combines up-and-coming artists with established ones; and helps set up artist-owned record labels.

Some of the accomplishments of the Rap Coalition include—

- Obtained the release of artists from their recording contracts, including Dasez Tempo from Def Jam (1992), Killah Priest from Geffen/MCA Records (June 1998), Twista from production company Creator's Way Associated Labels (June 1999), Artifacts from Big Beat/Atlantic Records (January 1998), Tragedy from V1 (June 2000), Fiend from No Limit (March 2000), Nicole Rey from Electra (January 2002) and Big from Cash Money (April 2002).

- Negotiated better record deals, including a distribution deal for Cash Money Records with Universal Records, which included artists Juvenile, BG, Big Tymers, Hot Boyz and Lil Wayne. (April 1998); and an artist deal for Fiend at Ruff Ryders/Interscope (December 2000).

- Organized and produced educational panels for rap artists, including 23 panels for 360 Degrees Black (the first hip hop seminar) in July 1993, Anniversary Celebration for the Universal Zulu Nation in 1993 and 1994, Philadelphia Music Conference (1995 and 1996), the Detroit Music Mecca (1997), NARAS Chicago Chapter (1996, 1997 and 1998), Boston's Can We Talk (1997 and 1998), CUMA at Columbia College in Chicago (1996 and 1997), City of Dreams (1998), Next Level Conference at Harvard University (1999), University of Wisconsin Music Conference (1999), The Rock and Roll Hall of Fame Hip Hop Exposition (1999), How Can I Be Down Convention (the first two years) and monthly rap coalition panels in New York City (1993-1999, 2002).

- Organized "summits" between artists from all over the world to instill unity and create dialog and opportunities with all rappers. Participated with Minister Louis Farrakhan's Nation of Islam Hip Hop Summit in 1997.

- Organized the first RAPOLYMPICS in Los Angeles (October 1998), which Eminem publicly credits as helping him to get his deal at Aftermath/Interscope.

- Organized a training program for rap managers called Visionary Management.

- Publishes information on www.rapcointel pro.com for artists that want to make their own records.

* * * * * * *

Rapaport: How did you get the idea of founding the Rap Coalition?

Day: I was attending an eight-week class taught by Bert Padell, a music business accountant, at the New School in New York. I had just come out of a job in corporate America and knew I didn't want to go back. I wanted to do something that would help people. It makes me happy to help people. I'm not good at dealing with corporate greed or at being told what to do. I have two master's degrees, one in African American studies and an MBA in business. I knew I wanted to combine these somewhere in the nonprofit sector and I wanted to own my own company. So I decided to take three or four months off to see what my next venture was going to be. The class at the New School was fascinating to me because of how the music biz was run—there were so many practices within the biz that just didn't make sense to me.

The idea for Rap Coalition—an advocacy organization that would be based on stopping injustices in the music business-came to me in a flash during one of the classes. I knew what I was hearing in class wasn't fair to many artists. The class was based on pop music, which in turn was based on what radio stations were playing, which was slowly becoming more rap inclusive. It was not focusing on other music. I was a fan of rap and I knew there was an opportunity to help those artists with my tenacity and my ability to seek justice and fairness. At that time, I thought urban artists were more unfairly pimped in the business than their rock counterparts, and I wanted to be able to at least equalize the urban music world with the rock music world. Now I understand that all artists are prostituted equally. So right after class, I asked Bert, "If I put together business plan for this business idea I have, would you look at it." Then I stayed up all night writing it and took it to Bert the next morning. He loved it.

Rapaport: Where did you get the money?

Day: I started with half a million dollars of my own money. I cashed in my entire stock portfolio, sold my condo and BMW, cashed in everything. I was willing to do this even if it turned out there would be no market for this idea. I also thought that if I were to lose money, it would be my own. The risk didn't faze me. I don't focus very much on money. I have that ability to make money. In life, we choose to do things. If they're important, we find the money. Money was never a concern. Maybe I'm naïve. I figure out what needs to be done. Then I go get the money.

Rapaport: How did you go about making a community with rap artists? What was it about your idea that resonated with them and made them want to be a part of the Rap Coalition?

Day: It was difficult at first, especially because I was white and female and didn't have a track record. I started going to all the shows. Any event where rappers were, I was there. I also started doing educational panels. ASCAP gave me space for free. For six years, once a month, nine months a year, I organized panel discussions. I would get eight or nine people in the music industry to talk on a given subject. Afterwards, the artists could network with them and with each other. A few years after starting RC, I started pulling rappers out of bad record deals.

Two big breakthroughs came in 1996. First, I did a deal with an artist from Chicago called Twista who called me and said, "I'm putting out a record, would you shop me a deal?" After spending time breaking deals I thought, "I've seen so many bad contracts, I'd like to put together a good contract." But first I said to Twista, "Most of the record company presidents are my enemies because I've been getting artists out of deals. I don't want that to ricochet in making a deal for you." Twista said, "I'm going to be so important that they will have to deal seriously with you." I said, "Okay, but if at any time I feel that my past relationships are going to adversely affect this deal, I will get out." Twista did exactly what he said and blew up his record independently in Chicago by working radio and retail himself. So then we did a joint venture with Atlantic. After that, I was taken seriously as a power broker by artists and labels.

In that same year, Tupac Shakur talked me into having a board of advisors for Rap Coalition. I was so against this because I had been brought up not to talk about what and who you know; not to talk about money, not to brag, etc. He said, "You have to have an advisory board. Just try it for six months." So I assembled a group of artists, led by Tupac, and did it. He supported me 1000 percent. What I realized is that the rap industry cares very much about who you know, what money you make. They care about the facade and how you look. It's kind of sad, but it makes all the difference in the world.

[Rapaport note: The 2001 advisory board of Rap Coalition is a veritable "who's who" in the rap music industry: Chuck D from Public Enemy, Vinnie from Naughty By Nature, David Banner from Crooked Lettaz, Keith Murray, Yungbuk from PsychoDrama, Gipp from Goodie Mob, Sticky Fingaz from Onyx, Too Short, Ras Kass, Do Or Die, Killah Priest, Twista, Fiend, Pimp C from UGK, Easy Mo Bee, KLC from Beats by the Pound, Shinehead, C-Murder, 8Ball, EA Ski, Canibus, Shorty from Da Lench Mob, Evil Dee from Black Moon, Brotha Lynch Hung, Freddie Foxxx, Bizzy Bone, Cold 187um from Above The Law, Keith Murray, Big, Schoolly D and Kool Kim from UMC.]

Rapaport: Why did Tupac do this?

Day: Tupac loved my accomplishments, the fact that I was helping artists without being asked to help and risking my own financial safety. He really liked that I was real. And he was just as real to me. Since Tupac passed, I haven't found that quality of realness he had. It's a quality that is rare to find. People have parts of it, but not the complete package. Most people didn't know what he was like. He was antimedia and so the media spun the negative qualities—his spitting at cameras, giving the finger to news teams—that's the image they loved to cultivate. But he was one of the most warm, giving, funny and intelligent human beings I knew.

Rapaport: Tell me about the first meeting you held with artists that had beefs with each other?

Day: I did Twista's deal for free, but in return I asked that he sit down with Naughty by Nature, a group who had been tossing barbs with him back and forth on records, because the relationship had gotten out of hand. Once Twista's record blew up, I didn't want him to worry about being in the same city with Naughty. The beef had to do with a picture of them together in a Rap magazine shaking

It didn't cross my mind that record labels would want to keep the status quo. Part of me wanted to believe that the oppressive contract clauses were there because no one offered a better solution. In some cases they were there because the record labels wanted them to be there.

hands and a lyric that came out at the same time on Treach's album that said, "Take your tongue twisting ass back to Chicago." That line offended Twista. Then they started "dissing" each other back and forth, then it escalated to threats back and forth. I felt that Twista and Naughty had similar personalities and that if they could sit down and spend time with each other, they would like each other. So I arranged a meeting at a New York restaurant. Twista had to come because that was part of our deal. Naughty did it because I was gaining power in the industry and I guess they thought well, "We'd better humor that bitch." Once Naughty realized why Twista was upset, they apologized and explained what was meant by the song's lyric line. When that was accomplished, they all realized that the problem was just egos blown out of proportion.

Rapaport: What was the first summit you participated in to help "instill unity and create dialogue and opportunities with all rappers."

Day: It was the Universal Zulu Nation anniversary in 1994 and 1995, which up until then had been no more than a three-day party. I thought it would be cool for networking and education to have panels. The anniversary attracts pioneers of urban music and dedicated artists and fans from all over the world. Artists came from all countries and all walks of life— Europe, Africa, Japan. There were established artists and up-and-coming ones. Some of the established groups had lost their publishing rights and served as mentors to new groups, telling them what to do and what not to do. I organized the panels. The summit created unity because of the vibe of the event: it was a party atmosphere, not stiff like usual convention panels. People were sitting on the floor, lounging around. It started me on a rampage of organizing panels at every convention that existed in the urban arena. I became synonymous with panel discussions. They helped establish Rap Coalition as a beacon of education in rappers' minds.

Rapaport: How did you get involved with Minister Louis Farrakhan's Nation of Islam Hip Hop Summit in 1997? What did that summit accomplish?

Day: I received a phone call from one of Farrakhan's associates who was putting together a hip hop summit. I offered to help get artists there. I am relatively supportive of Farrakhan. I honestly believe very much in his love for black people. He really embraces the underclass, people that don't have money to give him or have the power to vote for him. It seems like he gives love to people who can't give it in return. No matter what the criticism, he helps people regardless. Some black leaders only help others when the cameras are rolling, but the minister helps black people all the time, even when its not convenient for him to do so. At the summit, hip hop people got together, said they would curse less, have more positive lyrics, be less misogynistic, be more unified, be less violent. Farrakhan offered to start a company that would put out an album under Interscope that would embody these ideals. But it never happened due to the industry executives he chose to team up with. What did happen was that summit was an excellent opportunity for people to interact. A lot of artists got together that normally wouldn't. Commercial artists talked with street artists.

Rapaport: How did the idea of the RapOlympics come to you? What did it accomplish?

Day: There was already an established tradition of MC (emcee) battles. This is where rappers get to flex their lyricism in a nonaggressive way. It's where two artists are given a word to "rap" off of and then they go head to head for 30 seconds. Selected panels or the audience decides who was best. You have to be an excellent lyricist and you must work well under pressure. Ninety percent of the rappers choke. I wanted to do something where signed recording artists could showcase their skills. So I asked nationally known artists to put together teams of rappers and called the competition RapOlympics. The leaders would control the teams so they didn't escalate into violence or aggression. Five teams were put together. I put one together too, and, unlike the other teams that included only rappers from one city, I included artists from all over the country—Detroit, Chicago, LA, New York, etc.

My team happened to include Eminem who was not very well known at that time. Instead of just having one round—just rapping off of one word—we did eight different rounds. One was to rhyme off the top of the head; in another, we drew a word out of a bag, like dog, cat, soccer and asked the teams to rap off of the word; in another, inspired by Raz Tazz, one of the premier rap artists, each tag team had 30 seconds to rhyme off the last word of the previous rapper's rhyme. What was cool about this was that the trick was to

end with a word that would be difficult for the opposing team to start with. In another round, we picked some CDs—reggae to rock and roll to blues—and the artists would be blindfolded and asked to pick out a CD cover. When the blindfold was taken off, the rapper would have to make a rhyme linking all the song titles together and it had to make sense. This one was so much fun. It got the crowd really hyped. Some of the raps were really funny. It was covered by all the RAP magazines, and even MTV and *Rolling Stone*. I did a swap with *Rap Sheet Magazine*. I organized their convention's MC battle and in exchange for my hard work, they found us the venue and flew my team to LA. We had a great time. My team won and they got to do the "Sway and Tech" radio the next night, as part of the prize. Dr Dre happened to be listening to the radio show and when he heard Eminem, he got in his car, came down to meet him and signed him on the spot. To this day Eminem credits me and the RapOlympics with his record deal. Eminem's special skill is that he is able to say things in a very catchy way; he is a skilled lyricist. That was a lot of fun. I really enjoyed doing it.

Rapaport: How do rap artists learn their skills?

Day: It's an inborn skill and then they add practice. It comes out of the African oral traditions and out of Jamaican toasting at funerals and parties (chatting). Rappers are always running lyrics in their head. Just like Michael Jordan practices eight hours a day, so rappers are rhymin' their entire day. It's something they can do with just their brain, in a shower, walking down the street, dressing. Rap Coalition tries to help them hone their skills by holding cipher sessions. This is where rappers get together in a giant circle and rhyme against each other one at a time. It gets them going and inspires them to do better than the last person.

Rapaport: What were some of the obstacles in forming Rap Coalition that you didn't anticipate?

Day: The biggest one was peoples' attitudes. It didn't cross my mind that record labels would want to keep the status quo. Part of me wanted to believe that the oppressive contract clauses were there because no one offered a better solution. In some cases they were there because the record labels wanted them to be there. Then there was the attitude of artists. Some felt that they didn't deserve a fair deal. They had the beat-me-down victim syndrome—I don't need to learn about the business, leave me alone, let me sign this, if I don't sign, nothing else will come along, I'll lose my opportunity, etc. Then they end up in my office three years later asking me to get them out of the contract. I feel that it's easier to educate artists in the first place than to go back and try to break a contract. No one should ever sign a contract out of desperation.

Rapaport: Did you have trouble because you were white and female?

Day: In the past ten years, there have only been a handful of people that have had attitude, not because I'm female, but because I'm white. Some have verbally attacked me in public. Ironically it has been only two black women that have told me that a white person shouldn't be running an organization that helps black people. But that's not sexism. It's racism. I don't argue with people that feel that way. I usually make a joke, "Hey, if someone's gotta do it, at least I'm glad it's me because at least I know where my heart is." There's no way to counter that statement. One woman was so critical of my "whiteness" on a panel that I got frustrated listening to her. I felt it was wasting the time of hundreds of people that were there to get information. To me it was a nonissue. So finally, I offered to let her come to my office, give her my Rolodex and all my con-

nections, and told her she could run Rap Coalition, but reminded her that like me, she would have to work for free. It absolutely shut her up. I was surprised by that. She never did come by my office to take me up on my offer. Today, six years later, she's a struggling publicist trying so hard to be a force in hip hop. She has made money off the backs of artist, something years ago she said she was against, and has made a tremendous amount of enemies just by being herself. I'd like to say that I've learned from these attacks, but the fact is, I don't pay much attention to them. Maybe some people would think they are difficult to handle, but for me, they are nonissues. It says something about the reality of what I choose to pay attention to. Racism and sexism may have slowed me down, but if it did, I didn't pay any attention to it. It may have been there, I didn't put energy into it. I don't notice things that try to slow me down. I just notice real problems and then I solve them.

Rapaport: So how does the organization make money?

Day: From the deals I do. For instance, when I do distribution deals for artists, I take five percent of the upfront money and donate it back to Rap Coalition. I don't make a living from the organization. I'm a volunteer. I work for free.

Rap Coalition does have a membership fee of $100, but it's not a prerequisite for coming to meetings, getting information, etc. We have never stressed the money part. I personally make money by writing business and marketing plans for rap artists; and I manage a handful of artists as well, but that activity takes less than two hours a day. What doesn't go to my rent and food gets dumped right into Rap Coalition.

Rapaport: Is there a lot of violence associated with rap? Have you been threatened?

Day: There's so little of that, it's not worth talking

about. It's mostly the media that plays up that rap is violent. The fact is that rap shows have the same incidence of injuries as rock shows. But because most of the media is white, they don't understand people of color. It's their way of playing up a difference between themselves and rappers, heightening the racism. Rappers are not more violent. But push any human being to an extreme and they're going to react, myself included.

Rapaport: What is the future of Rap Coalition?

Day: When I started the organization, I wanted to run it myself for 10 years. Five years ago, I chose a successor, David Banner. I did it because I knew I would get to this point. This made it possible to spend time with him and train him. When I started this, he was still going to Southern University and was president of his class. He's very relaxed and easy going. He's an artist and has the same passion and belief in Rap Coalition I do or close to it. He's passionate and outspoken about artists' rights. And he has initiated other programs that help people. For instance, he started a literacy program in Jackson Mississippi, just because there was a need. And then he spent more time teaching people to read and write than doing his own music. He's also somebody who is not driven by money. I have taught him to put out his own record so that he can make money for himself. I don't think he will be corrupted. But because he is an artist (and I am not) maybe only 60% of his time will go into Rap Coalition

www.rapcoalition.org

The National Association of Recording Merchandisers

The National Association of Recording Merchandisers (NARM) is a nonprofit trade association whose nearly 1000 member companies represent the retailers, wholesalers and distributors of prerecorded music in the United States. Their members include such familiar companies as Best Buy (Musicland, Sam Goody), Wherehouse, TransWorld Entertainment (Camelot, Coconuts, Record Town, Specs, Strawberries, The Wall, Waxie Maxie, FYE), Borders Books and Music, Target, Newbury Comics, Waterloo Records, CDNow and Amazon.

- NARM offers a range of programs and services that include a member directory, a newsletter, educational materials on merchandising, loss prevention and operations and a database of product offerings

- NARM sponsors an annual convention and other conferences and seminars throughout the year, which provide networking, selling and educational opportunities to members. In 2001, NARM and AFIM partnered to present their annual conventions.

- NARM gathers, commissions and disseminates research and information on annual sales figures and trends, used CDs, listening stations, record clubs, and digital distribution.

- NARM sponsors merchandising campaigns for seven major televised awards shows including the Grammy's, the MTV Awards and Soul Train. NARM originated the "Give the Gift of Music" campaign to promote music sales at Christmas, for Valentine's Day, birthdays and graduations. NARM offers low-cost CD samplers for classical and jazz (some have topped the Billboard charts) along with music teaching guides for use in schools.

- NARM's advocacy efforts have helped to forge industry consensus and support on a range of issues.

Association For Independent Music

The Association For Independent Music (AFIM) is a nonprofit organization that has approximately 1200 members that include independent record labels, distributors, retailers, manufacturers, mastering facilities and recording studios.

The AFIM works to improve communication among its membership; identify and promote cooperative activities that benefit the independent recording industry; and publicize the achievements and activities of the industry. Specific goals include—

- Provide opportunities for independent artists and distributors to thrive. This includes discounts from suppliers and advertising in industry publications and retail stores.

- Facilitate the participation of its membership in industry conventions such as Canadian Music Week, MIDEM, etc.

- Partner with the National Association of Recording Merchandisers (NARM) to hold an annual convention. The convention provides opportunities for independent labels to meet with distributors and introduce them to their recordings; map out promotional and sales campaigns; visit with successful labels to find out what works and what does not; share information about promotional and touring opportunities; and research information about distributors, manufacturers and other related businesses. Special interest groups within the organization focus on specific genres of music so people can work together to promote their particular genres.

- Facilitate the marketing of special interest genres.

- Further the education of and coordinate information between independent artists, labels, retail stores and distributors through convention panels, the AFIM Web site and AFIM directory.

- Advocate for the health of the independent music industry. Work closely with other nonprofit industry organizations, such as RIAA, AIM, CIPRA, NARAS, NARM and others.

The AFIM convention's highlight is the presentation of the Indie Awards for the best independent recordings released during the year in about 40 categories.

The annually updated *AFIM Directory,* which includes listings for all AFIM members, the Resource and Reference Guide and Independent Distribution Guide is free to all members and can be purchased by nonmembers as well.

RESOURCES

Arbitron
142 West 57th Street
New York, NY 10019-3300
(212) 887-1300
www.arbitron.com

Association For Independent Music (AFIM)
1158 26th Street, #505
Santa Monica, CA 90403
(310) 453-6932
www.afim.org

Broadcast Data Services (BDS)
1 N. Lexington Avenue
White Plains, NY 10601
(914) 684-5600
www.bdsonline.com

Bryan Farrish
Independent Radio Promotion
14230 Ventura Boulevard, Suite A
Sherman Oaks, CA 91423
(818) 905-8038
www.radio-media.com

Clear Channel Entertainment, Inc.
650 Madison Avenue
New York, NY 10022
(212) 838-3100
www.clearchannel.com

Gavin
United Business Media, Inc.
460 Park Avenue South
New York, NY 10016
(212) 378-0400
www.uemedia.com/divisions/gavin/html

Infinity Broadcasting
40 West 57th Street
New York, NY 10019
(212) 314-9200
www.infinityradio.com

Intercollegiate Broadcasting System (IBS)
367 Windsor Highway
New Windsor, NY 12553-7900
(845) 565-0003
www.ibsradio.org

MeasureCast, Inc.
921 SW Washington Street, Suite 800
Portland, Oregon 97205
(503) 889-1248
www.measurecast.com

National Association of Broadcasters (NAB)
1771 N Street NW
Washington, DC 20036-2891
(202) 775-2550
www.nab.org

National Association of Recording
    Merchandisers (NARM)
9 Eves Drive, Suite 120
Marlton, NJ 08053
(856) 596-2221
www.narm.com

National Federation of Community
    Broadcasters (NFCB)
Fort Mason Center, Building D
San Francisco, CA 94123
(415) 771-1160
www.nfcb.org

Nielson Media Research
A subsidiary of VNU
299 Park Avenue
New York, NY 10171
(212) 708-7500
www.nielsonmedia.com

Rap Coalition
111 East 14th Street, #339
New York, NY 10003
(212) 714-1100
www.rapcoalition.org
www.rapcointelpro.com

Society of Broadcast Engineers
9247 North Meridian Street, Suite 305
Indianapolis, IN 46260
(317) 946-9000
www.sbe.org

Sound Inquiry Research & Consulting
P.O. Box 25025
Albuquerque, NM 87125-5025
(877) 572-8525
www.soundinquiry.com

Soundscan
1 North Lexington Avenue,
White Plains, NY 10601
(914) 328-9100
www.home.soundscan.com

TRADE PUBLICATIONS AND DIRECTORIES
INDUSTRY DIRECTORIES

Billboard Directories
1695 Oak Street
PO Box 2016
Lakewood, NJ 08701
(800) 344-7119
www.billboard.com/store/directories
> *Billboard International Buyer's Guide*
>   *Directory*
> *Billboard International Latin Music*
>   *Buyer's Guide Directory*
> *Billboard International Talent and Touring*
>   *Directory*
> *Billboard International Tape/Disc*
>   *Directory*
> *Billboard Nashville 615/Country Music*
>   *Sourcebook*
> *Billboard Radio Power Book: Directory of*
>   *Music Radio and Record Promotion*
> *Billboard Record Retailing Directory*

Directory of Artists
Association of Performing Arts Presenters
(APAP)
1112 16th Street NW, Suite 400
Washington, DC 20036
(202) 833-2787
www.artspresenters.org

The MBI World Report 2002
The Music Group
CMP Information Ltd
Ludgate House
245 Blackfriars Road
London SE1 9UR
0207 579 4123
www.musicweek.com

Music Directory Canada
CM Books
23 Hannover Drive, Unit 7
St. Catharines, Ontario
Canada L2W 1A3
(905) 641-3471
www.musicdirectorycanada.com

The Musician's Atlas
Music Resource Group
PO Box 682
Nyack, NY 10960
(845) 353-9303
www.musiciansatlas.com

The Music Business Registry
7510 Sunset Boulevard, #1041
Los Angeles, CA 90046-3400 USA
(800) 377-7411
www.musicregistry.com

Music Technology Buyer's Guide
United Entertainment Media, Inc.
460 Park Avenue South
New York, NY 10016
(212) 378-0400
www.uemedia.com/divisions/mtbuyer/shtml

Music Yellow Pages
United Entertainment Media, Inc.
6 Manhasset Avenue
Port Washington, NY 11050
(516) 944-5940
www.musicyellowpages.com

Performance International Touring Talent
    Publications
203 Lake Street, Suite 200
Fort Worth, TX 76102-4504
(817) 338-9444
www.performancemagazine.com
    The Black Book: Entire Performance
        Guide Series
    Concert Production
    Equipment and Personnel
    Facilities
    Talent Buyers
    Talent Management
    Transportation Guide

Pollstar, USA
4697 W. Jacquelyn Ave.
Fresno, CA 93722-6413
(559) 271-7900 Voice
(559) 271-7979 Fax
www.pollstar.com
    PollstarOnline.com
    Agency Rosters
    Talent Buyer Directory
    Concert Venue Directory
    Concert Support Services Directory

Recording Industry Sourcebook
Artist Pro
236 Georgia Street, Suite 100
Vallejo, CA 94590
(707) 554-1935
www.artistpro.com/Sourcebase.cfm

RESODRCES

TRADE PUBLICATIONS

Acoustic Guitar Magazine
String Letter Publishing
255 West End Avenue
San Rafael, CA 94901
(415) 485-6946
www.acousticguitar.com

Acoustic Musician
PO Box 1349
New Market, VA 22844
(540) 740-4006
www.shentel.net/acousticmusician

The Album Network
120 North Victory Boulevard
Burbank, CA 91502
(818) 955-4000
www.musicbiz.com

Audio Engineering Society (AES) Journal
60 East 42nd Street, Room 2520
New York, NY 10165-2520
(212) 661-8528
www.aes.org

Bass Player
United Entertainment Media, Inc.
The Music Player Group
2800 Campus Drive
San Mateo, CA 94403
(650) 513-4400
www.bassplayer.com

Billboard
BPI Communications, Inc.
1515 Broadway
New York, NY 10036
(800) 745-8922 or (212) 764-7300
www.billboard-online.com

Bluegrass Unlimited
PO Box 771
Warrenton, VA 20188-0771
(800) 258-4727 or (540) 349-8181
www.bluegrassmusic.com

Blues Revue
Rt. 1, Box 75
Salem, WV 26426
(304) 782-1971
www.bluesrevue.com

Cadence Magazine
The Review of Jazz & Blues
Cadence Building
Redwood, NY 13679
(315) 287-2852
www.cadencebuilding.com/cadence/cadence
magazine

Canadian Musician
23 Hannover Drive, Suite 7
St. Catharines, Ontario
Canada L2W 1A3
(905) 641-3471
www.canadianmusician.com

CCM: Contemporary Christian Music
104 Woodmont Boulevard
Nashville, TN 37205
(615) 312-4246
www.ccmcom.com

Christian Musician
4441 South Meridian, Suite 275
Puyallup, WA 98373
(253) 445-1973
www.christianmusician.com

Circus
6 West 18th Street
New York, NY 10011
(212) 242-4902
www.circusmagazine.com

College Music Journal
CMJ New Music Monthly/
CMJ New Music Report
151 West 25th Street
New York, NY 10001
(917) 606-1908
www.cmj.com

Country Music Live
PO Box 128502
Nashville, TN 37212
(615) 595-0799
www.countrymusiclive.com

Crawdaddy!
PO Box 232517
Encinitas, CA 92023
(760) 753-1815
www.cdaddy.com

Dirty Linen
PO Box 66600
Baltimore, MD 21239
(410) 583-7973
www.dirtynelson.com/linen/

DMA (Dance Music Authority)
7943 Paxton Avenue
Tinley Park, IL 60477
(516) 767-2500
www.dmadance.com

Down Beat
102 North Haven Road
Elmhurst, IL 60126
(630) 941-2030
www.downbeatjazz.com

Electronic Musician
PRIMEDIA Business Magazines & Media Inc.
6400 Hollis Street, Suite 12
Emeryville, CA 94608
(510) 653-3307
www.emusician.com

EQ
United Entertainment Media, Inc.
The Music Player Group
2800 Campus Drive
San Mateo, CA 94403
(650) 513-4400
www.eqmag.com

The Gavin Report
United Business Media Inc
460 Park Avenue South
New York, NY 10016
(212) 378-0400
www.uemedia.com/divisions/gavin/html

Gig
United Entertainment Media, Inc.
The Music Player Group
2800 Campus Drive
San Mateo, CA 94403
(650) 513-4400
www.gigmag.com

Guitar Player
United Entertainment Media, Inc.
The Music Player Group
2800 Campus Drive
San Mateo, CA 94403
(650) 543-5400
www.guitarplayer.com

Guitar World/Guitar World Acoustic
1115 Broadway
New York, NY 10010
(212) 807-7100
www.guitarworld.com

Home Recording Magazine
6 East 32nd Street
New York, NY 10016
(212) 561-3000
www.homerecordingmag.com

Hollywood Reporter
5055 Wilshire Boulevard
Los Angeles, CA 90036
(323) 525-2000
www.hollywoodreporter.com

International Musician
American Federation of Musicians
1501 Broadway, Suite 600
Paramount Building
New York, NY 10036
(212) 869-1330
www.afm.org

JazzTimes
8737 Colesville Road
Silver Spring, MD 20910
(301) 588-4114
www.jazztimes.com

Keyboard
United Entertainment Media, Inc.
The Music Player Group
2800 Campus Drive
San Mateo, CA 94403
(650) 513-4400
www.keyboardmag.com

Mix
PRIMEDIA Business Magazines & Media Inc.
6400 Hollis Street, Suite 12
Emeryville, CA 94608
(510) 653-3307
www.mixonline.com

Modern Drummer
12 Old Bridge Road
Cedar Grove, NJ 07009
(973) 239-4140
www.moderndrummer.com

Music Connection
4215 Coldwater Canyon
Studio City, CA 91604
(818) 755-0101
www.musicconnection.com

Music Educators Journal
Music Educators National Conference (MENC)
1806 Robert Fulton Drive
Reston, VA 20191
(703) 860-4000
www.menc.org

The Music Trades
80 West Street
PO Box 432
Englewood, NJ 07631
(201) 871-1965
www.musictrades.com

Musico Pro
Music Maker Publications, Inc.
5412 Idylwild Trail, Suite 100
Boulder, CO 80301
(303) 516-9118
www.recordingmag.com/mumak/Pro

Onstage
PRIMEDIA Business Magazines & Media Inc.
6400 Hollis Street, Suite 12
Emeryville, CA 94608
(510) 653-3307
www.onstagemag.com

The Performing Songwriter
2805 Azalea Place
Nashville, TN 37204
(615) 385-7796
www.performingsongwriter.com

Pro Sound News
460 Park Avenue South
New York, NY 10016
(212) 378-0400
www.prosoundnews.com

Radio And Records
10100 Santa Monica Boulevard
Los Angeles, CA 90067
(310) 553-4330
www.rronline.com

Recording
Music Maker Publications, Inc.
5412 Idylwild Trail, Suite 100
Boulder, CO 80301
(303) 516-9118
www.recordingmag.com

Remix
PRIMEDIA Business Magazines & Media Inc.
6400 Hollis Street, Suite 12
Emeryville, CA 94608
(510) 653-3307
www.remixmag.com

Rolling Stone
1290 Avenue of the Americas
New York, NY 10104
(212) 484-1616
www.rollingstone.com

Sing Out!
PO Box 5253
Bethlehem, PA 18015
(610) 865-5366
www.singout.org

Sound & Communications
25 Willowdale Avenue
Port Washington, NY 11050
(516) 767-2500
www.soundandcommunications.com

Sound & Video Contractor
PRIMEDIA Business Magazines & Media Inc.
6400 Hollis Street, Suite 12
Emeryville, CA 94608
(510) 653-3307
www.svconline.com

RESESOURCES CONTINUED

The Source
215 Park Avenue South
New York, NY 10003
(212) 253-3700
www.thesource.com

Strings Magazine
String Letter Publishing
255 West End Avenue
San Rafael, CA 94901
(415) 485-6946
www.stringsmagazine.com

Tape Op
PO Box 14517
Portland, OR 97293
(503) 239-5389
www.tapeop.com

URB
1680 North Vine Street #1012
Hollywood, CA 90028
(323) 993-0291
www.urb.com

Variety
5700 Wilshire Boulevard, Suite 120
Los Angeles, CA 90036
(213) 857-6600
www.variety.com

Vibe
215 Lexington Avenue
New York, NY 10016
(212) 448-7300
www.vibe.com

Victory Review
PO Box 2254
Tacoma, WA 98401
(253) 428-0832
www.victorymusic.org

NOTES

Audio Services

* * *

THE AUDIO INDUSTRY

INTERVIEW HIGHLIGHT
Leslie Ann Jones: Director of
Music Recording and Scoring at
Skywalker Sound, A Division of
Lucas Digital, Ltd. LLC

RESOURCE HIGHLIGHT
The Audio Engineering Society

RESOURCES

The Audio Industry

The wide variety of entertainment products that contain music has spurred the growth of the recording industry and forced an increase in the number of replicating facilities. The digital revolution has encouraged the design and manufacture of a vast array of new equipment and software.

There are more than 1500 commercial recording facilities, 5000 project studios and 40 major CD and DVD replicating facilities in the United States and Canada. Thousands of sound reinforcement companies install sound systems and rent equipment and supply operators and many offer live recording services. Hundreds of audio manufacturing facilities produce equipment and software for composing, recording, editing, mixing and mastering music.

According to the International Music Products Association's (NAMM) Statistical Review of the Music Products Industry (2001), sales of computer music software in 1995 were $66 million; in 2000 they were $171.8 million.

RECORDING STUDIOS

Regardless of their size and sophistication, all recording studios are equipped to record (capture and store) sound; play back what was recorded; and improve, alter and edit sound (processing).

The source of recorded sound can be analog-musicians playing acoustic and electric instruments or singing. And it can be digital-musicians composing with samplers, tone generators, MIDI sequencers, etc.

Analog sounds are captured with microphones and pickups. In the digital domain, composers and performers use keyboards and sequencers to generate MIDI signals and audio files.

The sound (signal) is captured by recorders or contained in audio files that store sound so it can be heard, altered by signal processing equipment, blended with other sounds in mixing systems and finalized into a coherent piece of music. Recorders can be analog or digital, standalone computerized systems, such as digital audio workstations (DAW) or computers that use recording and editing software and processing plug-ins.

An excellent digital tape recorder can cost as little as $500; a digital audio workstation as little as $1200. High-quality recordings can be made with minimal equipment and processing; or with an unlimited degree of sound and rhythmic combinations, processing and mixing.

Analog or Digital; Compressed or Uncompressed Files

Engineers, musicians and producers continue to debate about whether to record music on analog or digital equipment and whether compressed digital files for MP3 format is degrading professional audio quality.

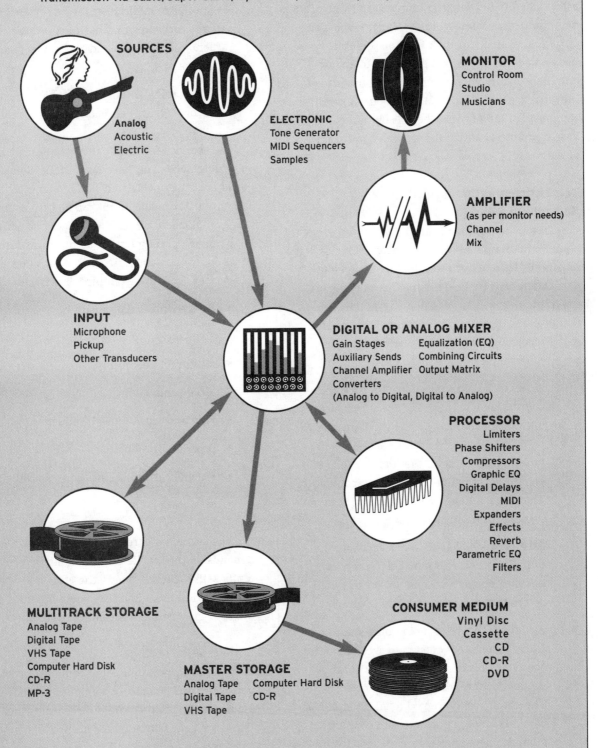

BASIC RECORDING PATH

Transmission via Cable/Super Cable, Optic Fiber, Radio Frequency, Satellite and Infrared.

SOURCES

Analog
Acoustic
Electric

ELECTRONIC
Tone Generator
MIDI Sequencers
Samples

MONITOR
Control Room
Studio
Musicians

AMPLIFIER
(as per monitor needs)
Channel
Mix

INPUT
Microphone
Pickup
Other Transducers

DIGITAL OR ANALOG MIXER

Gain Stages	Equalization (EQ)
Auxiliary Sends	Combining Circuits
Channel Amplifier	Output Matrix
Converters	

(Analog to Digital, Digital to Analog)

PROCESSOR
Limiters
Phase Shifters
Compressors
Graphic EQ
Digital Delays
MIDI
Expanders
Effects
Reverb
Parametric EQ
Filters

MULTITRACK STORAGE
Analog Tape
Digital Tape
VHS Tape
Computer Hard Disk
CD-R
MP-3

MASTER STORAGE

Analog Tape	Computer Hard Disk
Digital Tape	CD-R
VHS Tape	

CONSUMER MEDIUM
Vinyl Disc
Cassette
CD
CD-R
DVD

The choices are matters of personal preference and depend on what people have been accustomed to hearing and how well they have been trained to listen critically. Many people prefer digital formats for their inherent quietness (no hiss) and convenience. Others prefer to analog and high-quality vinyl manufacturing because they like the warm tones. Many like urban and rap music in MP3 formats because it boosts the bass frequencies and reduces the dynamic range of the music.

The Business of Commercial Recording Studios

Commercial studios make profits by renting time, equipment and personnel. The successful ones have well-defined purposes that are aimed at particular client bases. The type and purpose of the music that will be recorded guides the selection of the equipment, the personnel that operate it, the recording environment and the fees. Here are some examples—

- A 48-track studio specializes in rock and country music. They can record basic tracks and vocals and many vocal and instrumental overdubs. They have two staff composers and engineers that bands use to add electronics, rhythms and arrangements. They have an engineer that is skilled in sound processing and mixing.

- An advertising agency has a small studio that uses a recordist/arranger to record, edit and mix advertisements entirely with computerized equipment and programs.

- A film producer has a recording studio with a room large enough to accommodate symphony orchestras and large choral groups that are hired to play film scores. The studio can be rented to add symphonic arrangements to pop, rock and country albums. The engineers are skilled at working with classical instruments.

- A sound reinforcement company provides live recording for acoustic musicians. They specialize in direct-to-two track analog tape recording and use one to three excellent microphones and an engineer skilled in live mixing.

- A recording studio sends out engineers to record lectures and convention seminars.

Full-service facilities can accommodate most recording needs and have large staffs. Some facilities only offer specialized skills, such as arranging, producing or mastering. Some studios have stages that can accommodate large orchestras: they provide grand pianos and other instruments and supply such amenities as hot tubs and masseuses. Here are examples of services—

- Postrecording digital editing and mixing

- Two-track recording

- Multitrack recording

- MIDI production

- Film and video music production

- Broadcast production

- Remote recording (location recording)

- Mastering

The success of a recording studio business depends on repeat clients. The ability to consistently satisfy clients' needs, the atmosphere of the studio environment and the personableness of the staff provide the basics needed for success.

Corporate Recording Studios

Many large corporations—telecommunications, petroleum and chemical companies and advertising agencies, etc., now contain recording facilities. These are generally used for preproduction, arranging and editing and for the preparation of training videos and other marketing materials.

Project Studios

Project studios (home studios) are owned and operated by one or more persons for specific business purposes or as creative tools by hobbyists that do not have businesses.

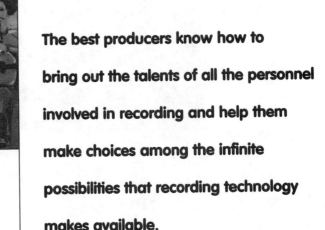

Although some end products may be commercial (CDs, video games), project studios do not rent time to others. They serve the specific purposes of their owners. Here are some examples—

- Music hobbyists

- Bands that arrange and record their own music

- Composers that create and arrange their own music

- Composers that create and arrange music for film, TV, advertisements or video games

- Producers that create mixes for dance clubs and records

- Engineers that edit music for broadcast and film

RECORDING PERSONNEL

What ultimately produces good recordings is operator skill, experience and creativity.

Recording is a partnership among many different people and each makes important contributions. The recording team may include an engineer, a producer, an arranger, an electronic instrument composer, studio musicians and the main artist or band. All of these people influence the sound and character of the music and shape its artistry.

Recording teams that work well together and balance each others skills are as important to success of the recordings as is building effective business teams.

The best producers know how to bring out the talents of all the personnel involved in recording and help them make choices among the infinite possibilities that recording technology makes available.

Studio Managers

Studio managers book time, negotiate and collect fees, purchase equipment and hire, fire and manage employees. They liaise between clients and other studio personnel. They are responsible for whether clients have comfortable (or uncomfortable) studio experiences and whether personnel are rewarded and acknowledged for their work.

Producers

Producers facilitate and direct the making of creative and business choices that are involved in recording and mastering. They help clients make good-sounding recordings efficiently and within budget. They direct recording sessions so they proceed smoothly and creatively and they take responsibility for making decisions regarding the final mix. They help focus arrangements toward their intended audiences and help select recording methods and studios that are appropriate for the music and the experience of the musicians.

Producers must be experienced in working with different styles of music, recording methods, studio environments, recording personnel and musicians. The best producers know how to bring out the talents of all the personnel involved in recording and help them make choices among the infinite possibilities that recording technology makes available.

A NEW FIELD FOR RECORDING ENGINEERS AND PRODUCERS IS SURROUND SOUND FOR RECORDINGS, DVDS AND MOVIES.

MUSICIAN, PRODUCER AND SOUND ENGINEER MIKE SOKOL IS A RECOGNIZED SURROUND SOUND EXPERT. SINCE 2000, HE HAS GIVEN DOZENS OF SEMINARS AND WORKSHOPS ACROSS NORTH AMERICA AT RECORDING SCHOOLS, UNIVERSITIES AND AES AND NARAS CHAPTERS ON MIXING MUSIC FOR SURROUND SOUND. HE IS A CONTRIBUTING EDITOR TO *Electronic Musician, On-Stage* AND *TV Technology* MAGAZINES AND THE AUTHOR OF *The Acoustic Musician's Guide to Sound Reinforcement & Live Recording.*

Producers are the objective conscience of projects: they can step back from the music and the personalities of the musicians and say what does and does not work. Objectivity is essential in deciding which songs to record, which arrangements work, when the musicians are properly rehearsed and ready to begin recording, which takes are satisfactory, what editing needs to be done and when the mix is complete. Objectivity is needed for mediating group conflicts and smoothing tensions. Detachment and impartiality can help avoid mistakes that would hurt quality.

Producers are responsible for the recording budget, for hiring studio musicians and arrangers and contracting for specialized services. They must balance the creative desires of musicians with their skills, their recording experience and their budget.

Producers are important liaisons between artists, managers and record labels. They must understand how recordings fit into companies' marketing and promotion plans.

Some producers are superstars in their own right. They have produced many records that are certified gold, platinum and diamond. Some freelance; others have production contracts with major labels and are allowed to sign artists. Other producers contract their services on a freelance basis and scout for talented groups. They invest time and money to record demos that they hope to sell to record companies.

Sometimes, professional producers are hired on an hourly basis as consultants. They can provide advice about studios and personnel that can save artists time and money. Some can be hired on an hourly basis to direct rehearsals, conduct complex overdubbing sessions or direct final mixes.

Producers can be paid by the hour: for a flat fee for the entire recording; or with an advance against a percentage of record royalties (2% to 5%). The amount depends on the producer's opinion of sales potential (derived from record label A&R staff), past recording sales, the amount of recording advances and their fame and track record. Rates for professional producers are seldom less than $75 an hour.

Engineers

Recording engineers work at the direction of producers. They select, set up and operate the equipment; execute the final mix; and prepare the final mix for mastering. They can spend hours of time and lots of money to get the sound that producers demand. Their skill determines the sound quality of the final recording.

Engineers' recording experiences are extremely helpful to musicians that are new to studio procedures. Often, musicians get their first inkling of really good sound quality and professional studio discipline from engineers.

Engineers do not try to correct musical errors

or make aesthetic judgments about the nontechnical aspects of recordings unless specifically instructed to do so by producers. They are trained to take and follow direction when working with producers and professional musicians.

Musicians that cannot afford professional producers can rent time in recording studios that have skilled engineers. They can help organize and direct sessions efficiently, make clear what options are available and foster a professional attitude among the musicians. They can be extremely talented at organizing and directing sessions.

Because of their experience in working with diverse groups and instrumentation, engineers can often double as producers and provide production skills. Usually their weakness is helping arrange the music. If that skill is needed, artists can hire experienced arrangers to provide direction during rehearsals or sessions.

Most engineers, unless they are hired on a freelance basis, are paid by the recording studio and their services are included in the basic hourly rate.

Arrangers

Arrangers adapt music for recording, simplify arrangements to make room for additional instrumental or vocal parts, score those additional parts and score new arrangements for compositions. They work at the direction of producers.

Some arrangers specialize in particular kinds of music or instrumentation and most have distinctive styles. Many arrange and play parts on electronic instruments.

Editors are specialized arrangers: they add processing effects to finished tracks—compression, echo, special effects and so on. They work with computer software and musical and computer keyboards to accomplish this.

Arrangers' fees are computed on the length of the arrangements and the number and kinds of instruments involved. When arrangers provide electronic arrangements, their payment is by the arrangement.

Most professional arrangers belong to the American Federation of Musicians (AFM), which sets minimum fees. Arrangers that are not affiliated with the AFM may agree to work for less, either to gain experience or to do musicians favors. Producers negotiate these fees on behalf of the artists.

Studio Musicians

Studio musicians and vocalists are hired for their skill at playing arrangements that are scored or at improvising arrangements during recording sessions.

Most belong to the AFM or the American Federation of Television and Radio Artists (AFTRA), which set minimum fees.

Musicians and record companies that do not belong to the unions set fees by agreements among themselves, often at hourly rates. Alternatives to hourly rates are flat session fees or fee-per-song (including rehearsals) or arrangements. The latter options are ideal because they allow musicians to predict recording expenses more accurately.

Session musicians are not paid a percentage of the profits, no matter how famous they are.

Mastering Engineers

Mastering is the last step before manufacturing. It is the preparation of the final product that is given to a manufacturer.

Mastering engineers are specialists. They are aware of technical requirements and have the equipment for creating proper masters, premasters and documentation for all manufacturing processes. These requirements differ for vinyl, cassette and CD manufacturing.

CD, cassette and vinyl mastering engineers work on digital workstations and high-resolution monitoring systems so they can make accurate judgments about levels and the "sound" of a project. They can hear any extraneous sounds in a project that were missed during final mixdown.

The mastering engineer will communicate with the artists and recording producers and engineers about their artistic views. Mastering engineers lend "fresh ears" to projects that may have been worked on for months.

Disc-mastering is discussed in the section on manufacturing vinyl records.

REPLICATION SERVICES

Artists have the choice of making analog cassettes, vinyl records, compact discs (CDs), MiniDiscs (MDs) and Digital Video Discs (DVDs). Vinyl records, cassettes and digital products are manufactured in different facilities because of the different processes and equipment that are used. Most facilities supply printing for packaging materials and collate and shrink-wrap product.

CD Manufacturing

CDs and DVDs are polycarbonate discs that are coated with a reflective metal and sealed in plastic. The digital information is arranged in a continuous spiral on one side of the disc. The information is read by a laser beam in the compact disc player while the disc rotates. The digital signal is processed and amplified through an audio playback system.

CD and DVD manufacturers must meet the manufacturing standards (Red Book) established by Sony and Philips to ensure that they will play in any player or drive.

The manufacture of CDs and DVDs requires a combination of lasers, robotics and high standards of quality control and cleanliness. Numerous steps in the manufacturing process occur in cleanrooms, since even the smallest dust particles will affect the final product. Each step of the process is carefully checked for flaws.

Most manufacturing facilities do a final quality control check by reading selected discs for defects, playing them on high-speed test equipment and listening in real time.

CD Recordable (CD-R)

Affordable small-quantity CD duplication systems (CD-Recordable or CD-R) are now available as stand-alone systems, integral parts of computers or as separate CD-R drives for computers. The advantages to using them are quick turnaround and the opportunity to create smaller runs than most manufacturers will accept.

These systems use lasers to record data on the heat-sensitive dye layers of blank CD-R discs to form the equivalent of the pits and lands in manufactured compact discs. The discs can be played on any CD player, CD drive or CD-ROM drive.

Blank CD-R discs (called blanks, gold worms, gold discs and one-offs) are easily recognized by their colors: gold or silver on one side; and blue-green or bright blue on the other. They are more fragile than manufactured CDs and are susceptible to damage from extremes in light, temperature and humidity, as well as scratches and dirt.

Manufacturing Cassettes

Producers have two manufacturing options: real-time and high-speed.

In real-time duplication, master tapes are duplicated at the speed they were recorded. Because the frequency response and dynamic range of the master tape are transferred almost exactly, real-time duplication produces the best tapes when high-quality tape is used. It is the most expensive duplication method, often double or triple the price for high-speed duplication. Every tape deck used must be regularly calibrated to ensure that there are no variations between tapes.

In high-speed duplication, the master tape and the duplicate cassettes are run at speeds up to 64 times the playing speed. The greater the speed, the greater the loss in high-frequency information and the greater the hiss. Cassette manufacturers that reproduce music of wide dynamic range or much high-frequency information will seldom duplicate at such speeds. Most use ratios of 8:1 or 16:1 and claim the audible differences are minimal compared with real-time duplication.

Manufacturng Vinyl

Manufacturing records involves four processes: disc-mastering, plating (matrixing), pressing and packaging.

Disc-mastering (disc-cutting) is the process of transferring the music from masters to grooves on

MASTERING COMPANIES, MANUFAC-TURERS AND MANUFACTURERS' BROKERS CAN BE FOUND IN— *The Billboard International Buyers' Guide, Mix Magazine Annual Directory of Manufacturers* **and the** *Recording Industry Sourcebook.*

a disk. The masters are played through disc-cutting consoles (lathes) that convert the music to mechanical motion. The lathes can be operated by analog or digital equipment. A stylus cuts grooves, which are analogous to the electrical signals of the music on the master tape. A separate master is cut for each side.

Engineers that specialize in this service can make adjustments and add equalization to make cuts "hotter," adjust stereo separation and make special copper masters for producers that want high-quality audiophile recordings.

Plating (matrixing) is a three-step electroplating process that makes the stampers (molds) that place the grooves on vinyl records. Each stamper can turn out 1500 to 2000 records.

Vinyl comes in different grades. The better the quality, the lower the surface noise on the final recordings.

A different manufacturing method and material-polystyrene, notvinyl-are used for manufacturing 45 rpm singles. These records wear out quickly and tend to produce greater background noise.

Brokers

Many firms that advertise they manufacture CDs, cassettes and vinyl are brokers or middlemen, not actual manufacturing firms. They offer their services to independent record companies and contract with replictors. Because the price for replicating drops as volume increases, brokers generally guarantee to buy large numbers of finished products annually to get the best prices.

sounds together with mixing boards and project them towards the listeners via speakers. Sound may be acoustic, electric or electronic.

Enjoyment of musical events and other large events is directly related to the quality of sound-for the audience and for performers.

Performers need to hear themselves to play in synch with each other. The part of a sound reinforcement system that accomplishes this is the stage monitoring system. This separate sound reinforcement system is provided so that performers can listen to a mix of instruments and vocals that they are most comfortable with. Monitor speakers are placed onstage facing the performers, or the performers wear headphones or in-ear systems that are linked to offstage amplifiers and mixing boards.

Set up and operation of sound reinforcement equipment is a skilled profession. Some operators learn their skills by working with artists, before apprenticing with sound reinforcement companies; others learn these skills in audio technology schools and intern with artists and sound reinforcement companies.

Many artists travel with their own sound systems and operators to ensure audio consistency throughout their tours.

AUDIO TECHNOLOGY MANUFACTURING

The vitality of the audio and sound reinforcement industry is due to the continuing evolution of products brought about by technological innovation and the vibrancy and growth of the entertainment industry.

Brokers offer a service. To stay in business they must develop reputations for delivery of quality products to their clients.

SOUND REINFORCEMENT SERVICES

Sound reinforcement companies install sound systems, rent systems and supplementary equipment and provide skilled personnel to operate them.

According to NAMM's *Statistical Review of the Music Products Industry* (2001), U.S. companies brought $431.0 million worth of sound reinforcement systems in 1990; in 2000, it was $901.8 million.

Sound reinforcement systems capture sound from microphones and pickups, alter sound with processers, make it louder via amplifiers, mix

- New audio manufacturing and replicating facilities are constantly being built to accommodate new technology.

- Digital audio workstations (DAWs) and computer-based recording and editing are prevalent.

- Musicians use keyboards, MIDI, sequencers and variety of available sound samples to emulate instruments and experiment with arrangements and sound processing.

- Equipment that is used for signal processing, such as effects, reverb, equalizers, compressors, etc., is available as computer software "plug-ins."

- Increasing sales of entertainment products that contain music—CDs, DVDs, videos, video games, etc.,—have stimulated the growth of audio and sound reinforcement services to meet production demands.

These technologic changes have given performers and composers new tools to help them to explore and stimulate creativity. The creators of audio products have incentives to continually bring innovative products to the marketplace; which in turn stimulates the retail sector to continuously change its marketing focus to introduce and sell the technologies. These symbiotic relationships underscore the necessity of all segments of the industry to work together to stimulate growth and profitability.

ONE OF THE HALLMARKS OF DIGIDESIGN'S SUCCESS IS THE PASSION FOR AUDIO THAT THEIR EMPLOYEES BRING TO THEIR JOBS. MANY ARE MUSICIANS, PRODUCERS OR SOUND ARTISTS THEMSELVES AND HAVE A PERSONAL INTEREST IN THE EXCELLENCE OF THE COMPANY'S PRODUCTS. HERE MARK PAPPAKOSTAS AND LISA LANE WORK WITH PROTOOLS AS PARTICIPANTS IN THE COMPANY'S INTERNAL TRAINING AND EDUCATION PROGRAM.

CONCLUSION

Audio services in the music industry encompass the recording and manufacturing of products that contain music and services that ensure that live performances can be heard by their audiences and by performers. There is a wide diversity of jobs available for people that have the skills and commitment to meet the demanding needs of this evolving and sophisticated industry.

Leslie Ann Jones:
Director of Music Recording and Scoring at Skywalker Sound, a Division of Lucas Digital, Ltd.LLC

PHOTO: BEATRICE COLL

LESLIE ANN JONES has more than 25 years of experience as a recording engineer and sound mixer. She has been an artist's manager and worked in artist relations at several record companies. The scoring stage at Skywalker Sound has been the recording studio of choice for many rock, pop, classical and jazz clients. Scores for such films as *Inspector Gadget, Sky Kids* and *Titanic* have been recorded there.

$$* \quad * \quad * \quad * \quad * \quad * \quad *$$

Rapaport: What do you do at Skywalker?

Jones: I have two jobs. One is to book the scoring room and manage the people that work here. The second is to be a recording engineer and producer for the outside clients that come in to record at Skywalker Sound.

Rapaport: What are some of the projects you have worked on?

Jones: I've been working with the Kronos Quartet, Rosemary Clooney and the sound track record for *Requiem for a Dream.*

Rapaport: What is your job in the scoring room?

Jones: This room was especially designed for medium and large orchestras that provide music for movie scores. I am the scoring engineer and mixer for many of these projects. Many orchestras are recorded live to stereo two-track, not multitrack. This requires helping set up the musicians in the room and helping conductors get a proper balance. The skills that are required are different from recording pop and rock music.

Rapaport: How did you get our job at Skywalker?

Jones: I was working at Capitol Records as a recording engineer and did not want to do it full time. I wanted to combine engineering with my administrative and marketing experience, not be nailed to working 14 hours a day. I read an article in one of the trade magazines on Gloria Borders, who at that time was the vice-president and general manager. The arti-

cle mentioned that Skywalker was putting increased attention and budget into their scoring stage. So I called her. She was looking for someone that was familiar with the scoring world and could bring in more music scores to Skywalker. She was not looking for another recording engineer. For her, marketing a scoring room and being an engineer were two different jobs. I helped convince her of the advantages of combining those skills.

Rapaport: Did you start with a dream of being in the music business?

Jones: Music was in our family. My father was Spike Jones, whose band was famous for comedy recordings including "Cocktails For Two," "You Always Hurt The One You Love," and "All I Want For Christmas Is My Two Front Teeth." My mother was a singer. I was involved with music at an early age, played a guitar and sang in folk bands as a teenager.

Rapaport: How did you get involved in the technical end?

Jones: I bought a sound system for one of the bands I played in. When the band broke up, I started renting and operating the system for others. I found that I enjoyed sound engineering and mixing as much as performing.

Rapaport: How did you get involved in recording?

Jones: In the mid-Seventies, I bought one of the first TASCAM semiprofessional recorders, put a 4-track studio in my basement and started recording band demos. I was self-taught. But I began to have dreams about combining artist management and producing. I really liked the creative involvement in making records. I knew that I needed to study with someone that knew more about recording than I. Then when I became a producer/manager like Peter Asher, I would know what an engineer did.

I got a job working in the publicity and artist relations departments of ABC Records and I began taking courses at Sherwood Oaks

An engineer has to be adept at quickly determining what part of the technical palette to use for a particular style of music.

Experimental College, coincidentally from an engineer that recorded one of my old bands.

Rapaport: What was your first studio job?

Jones: I applied for a position at ABC Studios. The studio manager had reservations about the difficulties I would face because, at that time, there were very few other women engineers, and most of them worked in the classical music field. He gave me a job as a production engineer. My job was to make EQ and cassette copies for foreign companies that had licensing agreements to manufacture records. EQ copies replicate all the processing of the record master. That's how I spent my first few months.

Then, a new project had a sudden change of schedule that the ABC assistant engineer couldn't accommodate and I got the job. My job was to set up the microphones for the session and set up and run the tape recorders. I ran as many sessions as possible and asked lots of questions. I went about my job and because I was good at it got moved up the ladder.

Rapaport: What other skills besides technical competence are important for recording engineers?

Jones: Not every project needs the same skills. An engineer has to be adept at quickly determining what part of the technical palette to use for a particular style of music. And have a personality that can go with the ebb and flow of a

wide range of clients. You have to know when to be invisible and when to give input and how to mediate artist conflicts. Sometimes you do what the client wants; other times, clients don't really know that they want or producers are vague about their directions and you have to interpret them.

Rapaport: What is the job of a producer?

Jones: Producers have two roles. The first is a creative one: helping artists with song selection and musical and vocal arrangements; knowing how to get the best performances out of artists; knowing when to stop sessions and go home; recognizing when parts aren't being played properly and so on. The second role is working with record labels on the recording budget and ensuring that artists don't exceed them, or, when justified, negotiating for more budget.

Rapaport: Was being a woman in this field a hindrance?

Jones: I don't think so. There have only been three instances in 25 years where I know for a fact that my gender had something to do with someone's perception of my performance. And in my early days working for ABC, a few people would come in asking me where the assistant engineer was. But once I proved I was capable that vibe would disappear. Discrimination is hard to prove and I will never know how many jobs I did not get.

I succeeded because I was competent technically and had good people skills. I loved being in a room when music was being made and was always ready to admit what I did not know. People appreciated that.

Rapaport: Do you have any volunteer jobs?

Jones: I've been a voting member of The Recording Academy (NARAS) for many years and in that time have served in a volunteer capacity as a Governor and President of the San Francisco Chapter, a Trustee from the Los

Angeles Chapter, and as Vice-Chair. I recently completed a two-year term as Chair of the Board of Trustees, which took about a day a week of my time. During the GRAMMIES, I'm down in Los Angeles for the entire week. Because a lot of my peers and clients are involved with The Recording Academy, it's a way of socializing outside of the work environment, plus it's a great way to give back to the music community. I'm also on the advisory board of Expressions School in Emeryville, CA (a new media school) as well as the Entertainment Studies program at the UCLA Extension.

I've also mentored students that want to be engineers at workshops given by the Audio Engineering Society. So many are learning at home or at school these days on computerized equipment and they have a real quandary about which skills to learn first and how to effectively use the glut of choices they have. Our job as mentors is to help them see a bigger technical and creative picture and help them understand that they need administrative and people skills.

I think it is important for women that want to work in executive or technical positions in the music industry to have role models. When I was starting out, there were so few. And I prefer to volunteer my time in areas where I am treated as an equal because it is important for men and women to recognize that equality can be a reality in this business.

The Audio Engineering Society

The Audio Engineering Society (AES) is the only professional society devoted exclusively to audio technology. Its international membership of 12,000 includes audio engineers, producer and sound reinforcement specialists, product designers, audio manufacturing executives, scientists and other audio professionals.

The AES serves its members, the industry and the public by stimulating and facilitating advances in the constantly changing field of audio. It encourages and disseminates new developments through annual conventions and exhibitions of professional equipment and through its 10-month a year Journal of the Audio Engineering Society, a professional, technical audio publication.

The AES has 47 sections (branches) and many student sections in various universities and audio schools throughout the United States, Canada, Europe Latin America and Asia. They regularly hold meetings to keep members up-to-date with new developments and offer workshops on specialized audio topics.

Conventions are held annually in the United States and Europe. The sites chosen for these meetings are in, or close to, high-density membership areas to afford large groups of members the opportunity of attending. Each meeting has valuable educational opportunities, including a full program of technical papers, seminars and workshops that cover current research and new concepts and applications. An integral part of each convention is a comprehensive exhibit of professional equipment. These conventions provide a valuable avenue for the exchange of ideas and experiences with other professionals and can further career advancement.

The society's members are involved in such diverse areas as—

- Research and development in audio and acoustics. Design, manufacture and operation of components and systems for production, pickup, recording, transmission or processing of sound or for controlling the acoustical environment.

- Marketing or installation of audio, acoustical and related equipment for commercial, institutional, broadcast or other entertainment use.

- Education in sciences and engineering basic to audio and acoustics.

Member benefits include free subscription to the Journal; discounted registration fees to all AES conventions and conferences; and discounted rates for AES publications and papers.

The AES offers the following memberships—

- *Member—$80/year*. Anyone active in audio engineering or acoustics that has an academic degree or the equivalent in scientific or professional experience in audio engineering and its allied arts and is familiar with the application of engineering principles and data in that field.

- *Associate member—$80/year.* Anyone that has an interest in audio engineering and in the society objectives, but who does not yet have the degree or the equivalent in professional experience required of a Member. Associate membership includes all the privileges except voting, holding office or chairmanships.

- *Student member—$40/year.* Anyone interested in audio that is enrolled in a recognized school, college or university. Student members may not vote or serve on committees, except in a local chapter.

- *Sustaining membership—$800/year.* Available to organizations in communications, manufacturing, research and allied areas of the audio and acoustic fields. Sustaining members help to support the society through contributions and receive recognition in the Journal and at all AES technical meetings.

RESOURCES

Audio Engineering Society (AES)
60 East 42nd Street
New York, NY 10165-2520
(212) 661-8528
www.aes.org

Electronic Industries Alliance (EIA)
2500 Wilson Boulevard
Arlington, VA 22201
(703) 907-7500
www.eia.org

Canadian Independent Record Producers
    Association (CIRPA)
150 Eglinton Avenue East, #403
Toronto, Ontario
Canada M4P 1E8
(416) 485-3152
www.cirpa.ca

Canadian Recording Industry Association
890 Yonge Street, Suite 1200
Toronto, Ontario
Canada M4W 3P4
(416) 967-7272
www.cria.ca

Music & Entertainment Industry Educators
    Association (MEIEA)
PO Box 83
Loyola University New Orleans
6363 St. Charles Avenue
New Orleans, LA 70118
(504) 865-3975
www.meiea.org

The National Academy of Recording Arts and
    Sciences (NARAS)
3402 Pico Boulevard
Santa Monica, CA 90405
(310) 392-3777
www.grammy.com

RESOURCES

NARAS-Nashville
1904 Wedgewood Avenue
Nashville, TN 37212
(615) 327-8030

NARAS-New York
156 West 56th Street
New York, NY 10019
(212) 245-5440

Pacific Music Industry Association (PMIA)
404-3701 Hasting Street
Burnaby, British Columbia
Canada V5C 2H6
(604) 873-1914
www.pmia.org

Society of Professional Audio Recording
  Services (SPARS)
364 Clove Drive
Memphis, TN 38117-4009 USA
(901) 821-9111
www.spars.com

INDUSTRY DIRECTORIES

Billboard Directories
1695 Oak Street
PO Box 2016
Lakewood, NJ 08701
(800) 344-7119
www.billboard.com/store/directories
  *Billboard International Buyer's Guide
    Directory*
  *Billboard International Latin Music
    Buyer's Guide Directory*
  *Billboard International Talent and
    Touring Directory*
  *Billboard International Tape/Disc
    Directory*

  *Billboard Nashville 615/Country Music
    Sourcebook*
  *Billboard Radio Power Book: Directory of
    Music Radio and Record Promotion*
  *Billboard Record Retailing Directory
    Directory of Artists*

*Association of Performing Arts Presenters
  (APAP)*
1112 16th Street NW, Suite 400
Washington, DC 20036
(202) 833-2787
www.artspresenters.org

The MBI World Report 2002
The Music Group
CMP Information Ltd
Ludgate House
245 Blackfriars Road
London SE1 9UR
0207 579 4123
www.musicweek.com

Music Directory Canada
CM Books
23 Hannover Drive, Unit 7
St. Catharines, Ontario
Canada L2W 1A3
(905) 641-3471
www.musicdirectorycanada.com

The Musician's Atlas
Music Resource Group
PO Box 682
Nyack, NY 10960
(845) 353-9303
www.musiciansatlas.com

RESOURCES

The Music Business Registry
7510 Sunset Boulevard #1041
Los Angeles, CA 90046-3400 USA
(800) 377-7411
www.musicregistry.com

Music Technology Buyer's Guide
United Entertainment Media, Inc.
460 Park Avenue South
New York, NY 10016
(212) 378-0400
www.uemedia.com/divisions/mtbuyer/shtml

Music Yellow Pages
United Entertainment Media, Inc.
6 Manhasset Avenue
Port Washington, NY 11050
(516) 944-5940
www.musicyellowpages.com

Performance International Touring Talent
    Publications
203 Lake Street, Suite 200
Fort Worth, TX 76102-4504
(817) 338-9444
www.performancemagazine.com
    The Black Book: Entire Performance
        Guide Series
    Concert Production
    Equipment and Personnel
    Facilities
    Talent Buyers
    Talent Management
    Transportation Guide

Pollstar, USA
4697 W. Jacquelyn Avenue
Fresno, CA 93722-6413
(559) 271-7900 Voice
(559) 271-7979 Fax
www.pollstar.com
    PollstarOnline.com
    Agency Rosters
    Talent Buyer Directory
    Concert Venue Directory
    Concert Support Services Directory

Recording Industry Sourcebook
Artist Pro
236 Georgia Street, Suite 100
Vallejo, CA 94590
(707) 554-1935
www.artistpro.com/Sourcebase.cfm

NOTES

Manufacturing and Retailing

* * *

**MUSICAL INSTRUMENTS AND
AUDIO PRODUCTS**

INTERVIEW HIGHLIGHTS
Peter Gotcher:
Cofounder, Digidesign

Steven Wilson: Director of Sales and
Marketing, Music Sales, Omnibus Press
and Schirmer Trace Books

RESOURCE HIGHLIGHT
NAMM, The International Music
Products Association

RESOURCES

Musical Instruments
and Audio Products

Up to this point, this book has been about the commercial exploitation of composers and performers and the sales of their products. From the public's point of view, these are the most visible, creative, exciting and lucrative facets of the music industry. But the recording, publishing and performance industries are dependent on, and supported by, manufacturers and retailers of musical instruments and other audio products.

In 2000, according to NAMM, the International Music Products Association, $7,147.7 billion worth of musical products were sold, an increase of 4% over the previous year. No statistics are available on the sale of used products, although NAMM estimates that this is a "substantial market."

According to a Gallup poll commissioned by NAMM, the largest number of consumers in all sectors are amateur and professional composers and performers of music. A least two persons in 40% of all households in America, play a musical instrument, although the report shows a continuing decline in the proportion of players under the age of 35.

Guitars and other fretted products, represent the largest sales and growth sector, accounting for $1089.4 million. More than 800,000 electric guitars were sold in 2000, an increase of 35.3% over the previous year.

In 2000, according to NAMM, approximately $902 million worth of professional audio products were sold, such as sound reinforcement and recording equipment and related accessories, an increase of $18 million over 1999 sales. Of this, $143 million represents sales of computers and software for audio applications. These figures do not include the home audio products industry.

SALES

The continued growth and profitability of musical instrument and audio product sales are dependent on the number of people that learn to play musical instruments and operate new audio products; marketing and promotion of these products; an audio services industry to help create and disseminate entertainment products; and the stimulation of consumer demand for those products.

More than 8400 retail stores in the United States sell new and vintage musical instruments, sound reinforcement equipment, audio recording gear, sheet music and related music accessories. Of these, approximately 1/3 are specialty stores that focus on a major product category, such as keyboards or sound reinforcement and recording equipment.

MARKETING AND PROMOTION

Manufacturers of musical instruments and audio products make retailers and their consumers aware of their products by—

- Advertising their products in trade and entertainment magazines

- Pursuing editorial coverage in trade and entertainment magazines

- Displaying their products at regional and national trade shows

- Educating salespeople

- Providing discounts for in-store campaigns

- Getting testimonials from well-known industry professionals

- Sponsoring concerts and other events

- Partnering with other manufacturers that sell related products

- Having informational Web sites

- Providing customer support

BOB BROZMAN AND HIS COLLECTION OF STEEL GUITARS
MANY MUSICIANS PRIDE THEMSELVES ON THEIR COLLECTIONS OF VINTAGE INSTRUMENTS AND PLAY THEM IN CONCERT.

Advertising

Manufacturers depend on print ads in trade magazines to make consumers aware of their products and to provide marketing support to their retailers. The two largest owners of trade magazines for musical instruments, audio products and services are United Entertainment Media *(EQ, Prosound News, Guitar Player, Bass Player, Keyboard, Drums, MC2, GiG, Extreme Gear, Music Yellow Pages)* and Primedia Business Magazines and Media *(Mix, Remix, Onstage, Electronic Musician and Sound* and *Video Contractor)*.

These magazines make the majority of their profits by selling advertising to manufacturers of musical instruments and audio products.

Advertising prices are based on circulation.

The average price for a full-color ad in trade magazines with circulations of 50,000 is $5,000

LIMP BIZKIT'S "PUT YOUR GUITAR WHERE YOUR MOUTH IS TOUR" AT MANY GUITAR CENTERS MAY HAVE FOUND THE BAND A NEW GUITARIST AND BROUGHT THE STORES AND THE BAND A BUNCH OF NEW FANS. THE FIRST STOP WAS FRESNO, CALIFORNIA WHERE ALMOST 1,600 PEOPLE CAME TO HEAR MORE THAN 200 HOPEFUL GUITARISTS AUDITION.

THE TOUR WAS A GREAT PUBLICITY HOOK-FOR LIMP BIZKIT AND THE GUITAR CENTER. IN FRESNO, TWO TV CREWS, FOUR RADIO STATIONS, THE *Fresno Bee* NEWSPAPER AND GUITAR WORLD MAGAZINE SHOWED UP. AND GUITAR CENTER FRESNO MANAGER JASON WILLIAMSON APPEARED ON *Good Morning Fresno.*

per page. Most magazines contain more pages of paid advertising than articles. A 250-page audio magazine may have 100 pages of articles and product reviews and 150 pages of paid advertising. A large-circulation music magazine, such as *Rolling Stone,* that features recording stars and their products may have twice the number of paid advertising pages as editorial pages.

Manufacturers aggressively pursue editorial coverage in magazines in which they advertise. This can blur the line between editorial objectivity and advertising, as it is difficult to critique audio gear negatively when the manufacturers are major advertisers.

Conventions and Conferences

National and regional conferences and conventions, such as NAMM, The National Association for Music Education (MENC), Folk Alliance, AES, South-by-Southwest, provide excellent opportunities for manufacturers to display their products to retailers and consumers. The cost of renting booths at these conferences runs as high as $75,000 at large industry trade shows. This does not include the cost of designing, producing, shipping and mounting the display, which can run into many hundreds of thousands of dollars. Many manufacturers hire musicians to perform at their booths and also hire audio specialists to give educational seminars.

Many manufacturers increase their visibility at trade shows and conferences by sponsoring private parties and dinners, sometimes with live entertainment; renting private hotel suites for meetings and sales presentations; providing free workshops; becoming conference and event sponsors; and giving away tickets to events and activities in nearby communities. Often, greater visibility translates into increased sales and greater brand recognition.

Education of Sales People

The education of retail sales people, about new products, is a major thrust of the marketing efforts of manufacturers. They know that consumers need to talk with experts about equipment and have it demonstrated. Retailers must be able to talk knowledgably about the variations in instruments and be trained in new technologies so they can demonstrate how to operate digital audio workstations and how to set up and operate sound reinforcement systems.

Sales people are invited to manufacturing facilities for training sessions in the operation and use of equipment. Manufacturers often offer retailers special discounts on products to provide incentives to put extra efforts into selling the equipment.

In-Store Campaigns

Manufacturers combine national marketing and advertising campaigns with special pricing deals to retailers. In turn, retailers make consumers aware of their products by advertising in local media, mailings and by posting information on their Web sites. Many manufacturers help pay for the cost of these ads when their products are featured (co-op advertising). These campaigns stimulate interest and sales.

Manufacturers also present free workshops at retail stores and accompany them with special discounts, to help bring in customers.

Testimonials

The use of famous performers and professional audio specialists to endorse musical instruments and audio products is common. These endorsements are supposed to provide consumers with feelings of trust in the product and they play on the fact that some people like to brag that they use the same equipment as the most famous names in the industry.

Testimonial advertising by well-known professionals include—

- Using products in print or television ads or on merchandising materials, such as t-shirts, sometimes accompanied by words of praise.

- Using product(s) at concerts and other performances (cobranding)

- Making guest appearances at trade show booths of manufacturers

- Giving workshops and miniconcerts at retail stores, sometimes using instruments and audio gear sold at the store

Manufacturers of instruments and audio products sponsor concerts for bands. Manufacturers also increase awareness of their brands by donating equipment to colleges and universities.

COMPENSATION IN THE RETAIL INDUSTRY

The two major retailing jobs are that of store manager and salesperson. Store managers are typically paid salaries, plus year-end bonuses based on net profits or on percentages of sales. The higher the volume of store sales, the higher the compensation. Salespeople are paid salaries, plus commissions on what they sell and bonuses.

In 1998, according to NAMM, the average store manager earned approximately $35,000 annually, not including bonuses and worked an average of 46.7 hours a week. Salespeople averaged $35,000 annually (with commissions) and worked an average of 40 hours. The majority of stores provided medical insurance and sick leave with pay and such other perks as company cars.

Partnering

Manufacturers sometimes partner with other manufacturers that have compatible products to increase their visibility and branding among consumers, for example, Apple (Macintosh Computers) and Digidesign (ProTools). They cosponsor events; place two or more products in ads and product brochures; and share booths at conferences and conventions. Additionally, manufacturers are consolidating into larger entities with compatible product lines, such as Harman International, which carries an extensive product range of loudspeakers, amplifiers, tuners, digital signal processors, mixing consoles, microphones, headphones, DVD players, CD players and recorders, navigation systems for cars and video products.

Web Sites

Web sites have become important sales tools for manufacturers and retailers, and, for many, have replaced glossy brochures. They can be continuously updated to keep customers returning.

These sites offer—

- Manuals

- Newsletters

- Sales of new equipment

- Sales of used equipment

- Reprints of articles that feature products

- Links to sites of interest to visitors

- Contests

- Information on other topics

- Artist interviews

- Investor information

Customer Support

Customers must be educated about the use of products and they need people they can call for information, after they make purchases. Education of customers is important since new products and improvements to old ones are being introduced constantly. This education can take many forms: printed and online manuals; information specialists that are available by phone; and chat rooms on special topics that are hosted by product specialists.

MUSIC EDUCATION AND RETAILING

Music education and retailing are necessary partners. The greater the number of musicians, the higher the sales of musical instruments and audio products. Most manufacturers and retailers put effort and money into public relations efforts to stimulate and support music education and raise awareness of its value.

NAMBI

In 1978, NAMM founded a sister organization, the NAMM Affiliated Music Business Institutions (NAMBI), in response to the music products industry's need to hire and retain professional employees. Their mission is to encourage and support students that are enrolled in music business degree programs at colleges and universities across the country.

In 1995, NAMM University was launched to provide training and professional development to retailers and manufacturers in the music products industry. More than 50,000 members have attended their programs.

NAMBI's current membership consists of over 30 colleges and universities. It provides an exchange of services between educational institutions, student participants and NAMM member firms, including an intern program. NAMM supports NAMBI with the NAMM Scholarship. This generous scholarship is awarded yearly to each NAMBI member institution to present to an outstanding upperclass music business major that has chosen the music products industry as a career.

Manufacturers help to fund nonprofit organizations that are actively involved in music education, such the Coalition for Music Education, a partnership between NAMM, The National Association for Music Education, (MENC), The National Academy of Recording Arts & Sciences (NARAS) and the American Music Conference (AMC). Their goal is to ensure that every child receives a high-quality education in music and the arts. The coalition was instrumental in drafting a congressional resolution in support of music education in public schools.

JEROME HEADLANDS PRESS DESIGNS AND
PRODUCES BUSINESS BOOKS FOR MUSICIANS
AND MUSIC BUSINESS AND AUDIO PROFESSIONAL.
THE BOOKS ARE PUBLISHED BY PRENTICE-HALL.
ACCORDING TO FOUNDER DIANE RAPAPORT,
"MANY OF OUR BIGGEST FANS ARE MUSICIANS
WHO WANT TO LEARN ENOUGH ABOUT BUSINESS
TO TAKE CONTROL OF THEIR CAREERS AND
PROFIT FROM THEIR ART."

MUSIC BUSINESS AND AUDIO EDUCATION

Music business and audio education has become an industry in itself. More than 500 universities, colleges and private schools offer curriculums in music management, copyright and audio and sound reinforcement technology. Workshops, seminars and conferences are held by nonprofit music organizations, such as the Audio Engineering Society (AES), Folk Music Alliance, etc. Musician conventions, such as South-by-Southwest, draw thousands of musicians to participate in live music showcases and hear professionals discuss business and audio issues. Many manufacturers offer books, video and DVD tutorials to their customers. Over 300 books and magazines serve the music business and audio education sector.

During the nineteen nineties, two developments provided a catalyst to the audio education industry: the changeover to digital recording mediums and storage devices (CDs) and the introduction of computer-based recording, editing and sound processing systems. Musicians loved these technologies because they provided them with creative composing, arranging and editing tools. Those that become adept at using them effectively had the opportunity to earn income by providing their skills to others. Audio professionals loved the technologies because it added convenience and speed to many audio processes.

These technologies were not easy to learn. Many commercial studios now require a formal audio education in how to use modern technologies to compose, arrange, record, edit, mix and master. Students must be trained to distinguish between bad and good sound; to adapt what they learn to best serve their music or that of their clients; and to prioritize among the virtually infinite choices for recording and sound processing. Recording facilities no longer have the time to train employees in the use of these technologies in-house.

Many schools have developed relationships with commercial audio businesses and steer their best students towards internships, where they work for a specified period of time in a facility at low wages in exchange for a number of credit hours towards a degree.

Audio professionals are more than technicians. They must be comfortable in talking with and meeting their clients' needs. They must understand how the music business operates and how to deliver products for their clients that can be commercial successes.

CONCLUSION

The retailing of musical instruments and audio products helps support the recording, publishing and performance industries. Internet Web sites are used by many stores to communicate with their retail customers and provide new sales outlets. Selling techniques have embraced the use of well-known artists to demonstrate instruments and equipment at conventions and stores and provide testimonials in print, radio and television advertising.

Self-help learning tools and in-store seminars provides foundations for learning music and audio recording and editing and foster an appreciation of music.

Peter Gotcher: Cofounder, Digidesign

PETER GOTCHER is a cofounder of Digidesign, the developer and manufacturer of ProTools, the leading software platform for recording, editing, signal processing and mixing. After he sold the company to Avid Technology Inc. in 1996, he became involved in venture capital work and specialized in digital media businesses. Those firms are now involved in business processes that help to develop market leaders and make businesses succeed.

DigiDrums, Gotcher's first company started in 1984 as a partnership between Gotcher and Evan Brooks. They were two musicians trying to fund their band by programming drum chips.

* * * * * * * *

Rapaport: How did this idea come about?

Gotcher: I bought one of the early drum machines to a band rehearsal. After twenty minutes, the band asked me to turn it off. It was too sterile. But it gave Evan and me the idea of programming our own drum sounds for use by our band, using my percussion collection. Once we did, it did not take a big leap to think about selling drum chips to other musicians to use in digital drum machines.

We took samples to EMU, hoping they would buy some. During the presentation, the vice president walked out of the room. When he came back he told us we had orders for the drum chips from SamAsh and Manny's, major music stores in New York City.

Rapaport: How did you fund this idea?

Gotcher: We bootstrapped the venture with $10,000. We worked out of our apartments, stayed up all night programming and packing boxes for UPS and during the day worked at day jobs. When you are 23, you can do that.

Within six months, DigiDrums was our only job. We sold more than 100,000 drum chips at between $40 and $250 each.

Our biggest problem was cash flow. Because we had no working capital, we learned some very good habits in cash conservation and relationship building. Because the chips we used were expensive, had to be ordered in quantity and paid for up front, we would call vendors we knew were willing to pay COD and use their money to keep making enough product to sell. It was our boot camp training in business.

Rapaport: How did you and Evan divide up the workload?

Gotcher: Evan was a better programmer than I; and I had more natural business and people skills. I did not write code and he did not talk to customers. That is what made our business work: we valued each other's skills and understood our limitations. Putting together a business is not unlike a band that puts together a team of skilled musicians that play different instruments but have common goals.

New companies have the ability to drive some compelling change in this industry and provide a new music business that is not dominated by major labels, while giving the public wider access to music of all genres. I want to help with that evolution.

Rapaport: When did you decide to branch out into designing a sound editing system?

Gotcher: First, the bottom began falling out of the drum machine business. And virtually simultaneously, Apple came out with their first Mac and Fairlight came out with their expensive programmable music system. It inspired us to design a low cost sound editing system, which we called Sound Designer. But by this time, we were smart enough to know that this idea was too big to bootstrap.

Rapaport: How did you fund the idea?

Gotcher: We did our first business plan and approached Tim Draper, a venture capitalist, and Franklin Resources, a mutual fund company. They loved the idea and we did not have to look elsewhere. Tim Draper introduced me to Paul Lego, a man who had an MBA from Harvard, was a Baker scholar and had been through GE's management training program. We liked each other immediately and I asked him to be the chief operating officer in charge of finance and business functions. Lego had experience that I did not. He knew how to grow a big company. To me, the key to developing a sound business is to assemble a team of people that you respect.

Rapaport: What are the attributes of business leaders in technology companies you come in contact with?

First, they have to be self-aware enough to know what their skills are, where they can effectively provide leadership and when it is time turn over some of the reins to someone else. Many businesses that fail do so because their leaders are afraid to delegate and are afraid to give up what they perceive as personal power.

Second, they need to have excellent communication skills.

Third, they must take the time to state a clear vision to all employees. Since every employee is going to be making large and small decisions that affect that vision, it is absolutely necessary for everyone to be going in the same direction. Every employee must be able to answer the questions, "What do you do and why." That is the ultimate test of a good leader: for employees to know and be able to say what that base vision is.

Finally, a leader needs to create a defensible ownership position in the marketplace. Technology businesses are different than landscaping companies where you can establish market share and make a decent living. That model does not work for technology. Innovation constantly unseats. Companies are either growing or shrinking. A lot of companies do not make it through multiple product cycles. You need to keep the ability to innovate alive, or you self-cannibalize your own business until it is broke and start something else.

What we did at Digidesign, almost from the beginning, was to transition from making a product to creating a platform. That was a vision that was difficult to sell in our company and I can remember many debates. But I saw that if we were only just another digital audio workstation that the competition would eat us up in a few years. I was convinced that we had to build a long-term franchise. My models were computer software companies that offered platforms for others to build and create from. That is what ProTools became—a platform that gave other companies the opportunities to add innovative and compatible tools, plug-ins, as they now are called, networked media sharing and so on. Success in business is not riding on past successes but continually creating new ones. It is just like music. If all you can create is one song that you keep imitating, you cannot grow as an artist and continually please yourself and your audience.

Rapaport: What new dreams are driving you?

Gotcher: My goal is to help business that will provide widespread electronic distribution of music so that more artists can make a living from music. New companies have the ability to drive some compelling change in this industry and provide a new music business that is not dominated by major labels, while giving the public wider access to music of all genres. I want to help with that evolution.

The music business is in a sorry state. The majors have a stranglehold on distribution and most independent labels are in trouble because of it. Record company executives are more risk adverse than ever. Bands have to fit into only five or six profiles or they do not get signed, no matter how talented. It is a pretty narrow taste set to funnel to the public and it is not succeeding. If REM came along today, I doubt they could get a deal.

Rapaport: What problems do the independent labels have?

Gotcher: There is great music being released on independent labels that does not fit major label profiles. But the public isn't hearing it in enough numbers to help the labels make a profit. A vibrant indie industry is being squeezed out of big retail and out of the media by the big players.

The indies have two big problems. One is

The music business is in a sorry state. The majors have a stranglehold on distribution and most independent labels are in trouble because of it.

exposure. They do not get played on any major media stations. The second is that they have a fulfillment problem. When people do get excited, they cannot find the records in retail stores. The public has different but related problems. Access to music is constricted to what the major labels want it to hear; and less radio programming is available for nonmajor label music.

Rapaport: How can the Internet help solve those problems?

Gotcher: Programs like *MusicMatch.com,* which offer a variety of services, can help provide substantial information about audience tastes and help point them to new music that they might like. Audiences do not need to vote for bands of their choice. Nor will they have to wade through an incredible amount of music to get to the nuggets.

The databases that *MusicMatch* has created provide it with a sophisticated method for finding commonalities in the choices that people make. Trying to classify choices is a complex process—figuring out say why someone loves Miles Davis and REM. It works best if we can look at the behaviors of large populations, which *MusicMatch* is helping us do. When you can analyze billions of listening logs, you find clusters of musical tastes. It means *MusicMatch* can slice musical demographics very finely and recommend music to people that will be highly relevant for their taste.

And that is how we can begin to solve the exposure problem for indies and help them spend limited marketing dollars effectively.

Steven Wilson:
Director of Sales and Marketing, Music Sales,
Omnibus Press and Schirmer Trade Books

Music Sales is one of the largest publishers of print music in the world. It also publishes technical and reference books for music, audio and music business professionals. Omnibus Press and Schirmer Trade Books publish popular, jazz and classical music biographies and books on music theory and history.

* * * * * * *

Rapaport: How did you get into this business?

Wilson: When I completed my education in England, I thought I wanted to be involved in an international company that specialized in exports and imports. My first job was with an international air freight company and the second with a container leasing corporation. Both companies were involved in moving goods around the world. After 3 years I decided to take a sabbatical and started traveling around the world living for a while in South Africa. On returning to England, I started working for a scientific book & magazine publisher—Heyden & Son and was immersed in publicity, production and selling magazine advertising space. That's where I began to get a rounded experience of book and magazine sales distri-

bution and where the bug for publishing was implanted.

In 1979, I responded to an ad by Hal Leonard Publishing Corporation, an American publisher looking for someone to build a distribution network in England. I started as a sales rep, was promoted to sales manager within a year and held the position for the next 4 years.

At that time, Leonard's company for distribution in England was Music Sales. In 1984, I moved to Leonard's headquarters in Milwaukee and was promoted to International sales manager. I traveled extensively and conducted business in 60 countries. That took me back to my early dream of working and travelling, but in a business that was intrinsically more exciting than air freight or container leasing.

In 1989, I was promoted to national sales manager, responsible for all United States and Canadian sales and for overseeing the in-house sales force.

In 1991, I decided to leave Hal Leonard and see what else was out there. For two years I worked for companies outside the music publishing business. In 1994, I was hired by Music

Sales Corporation as Director of Sales and Marketing for the United States and Canada. It has proven to be a very happy job home for me. I get to use all the knowledge that I've accumulated and find creative ways to build our products distribution to our retailers and ultimately the consumers.

Rapaport: Where does Music Sales sell its print music and instructional books?

Wilson: We sell to more than 5000 retail stores, from large music retail chains to independent retail stores. The print music business is driven by people that play music for pleasure and by serious music students. There is also a generation of music professionals that are using computers to compose, edit and record. We publish some of the best instructional books to help teach how to effectively use these technologies.

Rapaport: What differentiates you from your competitors?

Wilson: When we decide to publish a product, especially in the instructional area, the quality is very high and the packaging is stellar. We are known for being very creative in the packaging and the content of our instructional materials for people that are teaching themselves to play. We live in a very visual age: many people that buy our products do so because they are initially attracted by the packaging.

In 2001, we introduced our instructional guitar deck series, innovative in concept and design. Two books, *The Guitar Chord Deck* and the *Guitar Scale Deck* were sold together in a box shaped like a guitar neck. It became the ultimate gift for the guitar player and a must for beginners.

We are constantly reinventing older successful products and always looking for new and unique ways to package products, while at the same time embracing new technologies. For example, we were among the first to com-

bine instructional books with CDs and video packages. Last year we released book and DVD versions of the same instruction series and plan more instructional DVDs in 2002 and 2003.

Rapaport: What differentiates print music publishing from book publishing?

Wilson: We can make very fast response to breaking artists: we can produce books and sheet music of artists' popular songs that we represent and have them in the stores within a few weeks. The traditional ramp-up time for books is often up to a year. We are very flexible and nimble in our sales and marketing approaches and take advantage of new trends. So often music that is hot is out of vogue a few months later, so we have mastered being able to move very fast to capture a new market fad.

Rapaport: But Music Sales embraces both worlds.

Wilson: Yes, we do, because of the synergy between music instruction and other types of music books. Being book publishers opened up many additional distribution channels for us.

Rapaport: How has consolidation of book chains affected your business?

Wilson: It has made our book publishing business more difficult. We had more outlets to sell into and more opportunity. Now, because of bankruptcies and consolidation, there are a few major chains servicing the book and record industries and they make increasingly stringent demands on publishers for discounts and for product advertising. It costs more money to get really high visibility, such as a book displayed in the window, or end caps. The major publishing houses will spend much more for in-store advertising and the media coverage that helps sell books. They will often take higher risks and often have high failure rates. We try to tread more carefully.

We are fortunate, however, that many of our books are sold in nontraditional stores,

such as music instrument retail stores and record stores; and we focus on the print music business, which NAMM valued at $471 million in 2001.

Getting books in the stores isn't the challenge: getting them to sell through is. And, the chains do not want to carry our books for extended times, which means we have to turn over product more often.

Rapaport: What can you do to effectively compete?

Wilson: We combine traditional and nontraditional approaches. An example of a traditional approach is to link up publication of some of our biographies with artist performance tours.

That is the time when artists are likely to be in the news, heard on the radio and seen on TV. People hear the songs and want to learn them; they want to learn about the artist. We make that possible. For example, one of our strongest sellers in 2001 was the 850-page *The Definitive Dylan Songbook*. That was the same year Dylan came out with his album *Love & Theft* and supported it with live performances. Personality books like that are draws that bring people into the retail stores. But once they are there, they become interested in some of our other books and instructional materials.

Another example of a nontraditional approach is the combination of packaging books with DVDs.

In 2002, we are branching out into books about other entertainment arts such as film, with the publication of *The Independent Film Producer's Survival Guide: A Business and Legal Sourcebook*.

Rapaport: How did 9/11 affect your planning?

Wilson: After 9/11, we decided that we needed to show a positive face, not just for ourselves, but for the entire industry. We did not retrench. Some of our reps traveled extensively in October and November when business went into a tailspin for everyone. Our dealers were very happy to see them and had a lot of respect for the efforts they made during that time. By the time we got to NAMM, many of our retailers knew we were expending our best efforts during a difficult time.

Rapaport: Is there a difference in the personalities involved in these businesses?

Wilson: This is an industry of good honest people that make a living trying to educate people. We're friendly with our competitors and have what I call a mutual admiration society. This is not the case in many other industries.

Rapaport: What are your principles for doing business?

Wilson: My mantra for life is based on honesty and trust. When I come home, I look in the mirror and ask myself if I did the very best I could that day.

I always put my best foot forward in every situation because you never get a second chance to make a good impression. And this business is filled with busy people that have many options of where they are going to do business.

Good companies build their image in the marketplace and build strong foundations based on honesty, quality of service and product and deals that benefit both parties equally. You must build a strong foundation and part of that is a foundation built on a good reputation and a belief that what you are doing is for a good cause. Companies that take the opposite path ultimately fail because they cannot sustain deals that were based on malpractices.

I believe in being loyal to people that have given you good service. When I started at Music Sales, I inherited three great sales "professionals" and they are still here. We have six field sales people in our organization, whose cumulative experience adds up to 110 years of service in this industry; two of them have 30+ years and I have over 22 years. That represents a huge knowledge base to deal from. I know many people in this industry that

Good companies build their image in the marketplace and build strong foundations based on honesty, quality of service and product and deals that benefit both parties equally.

have spent most of their professional lives in the print business. That says a lot about the industry.

People come back to Music Sales over and over because we have a very highly regarded sales force known for its refreshing honesty and good ideas.

Like me, people get into this business get caught by it and stay. So many of the publishers, buyers and retailers have been in this industry many years. That is why I said earlier that we have become a mutual appreciation society. We are in this business to help each other succeed. A win for Music Sales represents a win for our sales reps, our wholesalers, our retailers and ultimately our satisfied consumers.

www.musicsales.com

NAMM, The International Music Products Association

NAMM, the International Music Products Association, is the international voice of the music products industry. It represents approximately 7,700 retailers, manufacturers, wholesalers and publishers in 100 countries.

NAMM's most important annual events are the trade shows held in January in Southern California and in July in Nashville, Tennessee, which are open only to NAMM members and the press. There, manufacturers and publishers showcase their latest products to national and international retailers and wholesalers. Members also meet to discuss issues of importance to the organization. Tens of thousands of people attend the trade shows.

Membership is open to music product businesses. Annual dues are $195.

NAMM's mission is to help the music products industry by encouraging music education and funding market research that shows its value across a range of age, social and ethnic groups. For example, NAMM funded scientific research to explore the relationship between music making and wellness, and music making and the brain. Results have proven conclusively that positive benefits of music-making range from increased intelligence to more healthy lifestyles. These research results are attractively packaged and help retailers make effective presentations about these benefits to local school boards and senior centers. The packages include—

- *The Einstein Advocacy Kit*: Presents the results of music/brain research

- *Music Making and Wellness Kit*: Presents the results of a study that found that senior adults who participated in group music lessons reported significantly decreased feelings of depression, anxiety and loneliness and showed an increase in Human Growth Hormone (hGH).

- *The Sesame Street Music Works Kit*: Presents information about the value of early music education as a key to intellectual development, physical wellness, self-esteem and improved academic success.

NAMM has partnered with The National Association for Music Education MENC), The National Academy of Recording Arts & Sciences NARAS, and the American Music Conference (AMC) to form the National Coalition for Music Education. Their goal is to ensure that every child receives a high quality education in music and the arts. The National Coalition for Music Education was instrumental in drafting a Congressional Resolution (HR 266) in support of music education in schools.

RESOURCES

The American Music Conference (AMC)
5790 Armada Drive
Carlsbad, CA 92008
(800) 767-6266
www.amc-music.com

Arts Education Partnership (AEP)
One Massachusetts Avenue, NW, Suite 700
Washington, DC 20001-1431
(202) 326-8693

International Association of Jazz Educators
(IAJE)
P.O. Box 724
Manhattan, KS 66505-0724
(785) 776-8744
www.iaje.org

International Music Products Association
(NAMM)
5790 Armada Drive
Carlsbad, CA 92008
(760) 438-8001
www.namm.com

Music & Entertainment Industry Educators
Association (MEIEA)
P.O. Box 83
Loyola University New Orleans
6363 St. Charles Avenue
New Orleans, LA 70118
(50) 865-3975
www.meiea.org

Music Sales Corporation
257 Park Avenue South
New York, NY 10010
(212) 254-2100
www.musicsales.com

The National Academy of Recording Arts and
Sciences (NARAS)
3402 Pico Boulevard
Santa Monica, CA 90405
(310) 392-3777
www.grammy.com

NARAS-Nashville
1904 Wedgewood Avenue
Nashville, TN 37212
(615) 327-8030

NARAS-New York
156 West 56th Street, No. 1701
New York, NY 10019
(212) 245-5440

National Association for Music Education
(MENC)
1806 Robert Fulton Drive
Reston, VA 20191
(703) 860-4000
www.menc.org

National Association of Music Merchants
(NAMM)
see International Music Products Association

NOTES

RESOURCES

FEDERAL AGENCIES

Copyright Arbitration Royalty Panel (CARP)
PO Box 70977
Southwest Station
Washington, DC 20024
(202) 707-8380
www.loc.gov/copyright/carp

National Endowment for the Arts
1100 Pennsylvania Avenue NW
Washington, DC 20506
(202) 682-5400
www.Arts.endow.gov

Service Core of Retired Executives (SCORE)
409 3rd Street SW
Washington, DC 20024
(800)634-0245
www.score.org

U.S. Small Business Administration (SBA)
409 3rd Street SW
Washington, DC 20416
(202) 205-6770
www.sba.gov

United States Copyright Office
Register of Copyrights
Library Of Congress
101 Independence Avenue SE
Washington, DC 20559
(202) 707-3000 (Information)
(202) 707-9100 (Forms hotline-use this number if
you know which form[s] you need.)
www.loc.gov/copyright

United States Patent and
Trademark Office
2021 Jefferson Davis Highway
Arlington, VA 22202
(800) 786-9199 or (703) 308-4357
www.uspto.gov

United States Securities and Exchange
Commission (SEC)
450 Fifth Street NW
Washington, DC 20549
(202) 942-7040
www.sec.gov

ORGANIZATIONS AND TRADE ASSOCIATIONS

Agency for the Performing Arts (APA)
888 Seventh Avenue
New York, NY 10106
(212) 582-1500
No URL

American Arbitration Association
335 Madison Avenue
New York, NY 10017-4605
(212) 716-5800
www.adr.org

American Bar Association
750 North Lake Shore Drive
Chicago, IL 60611
(312) 988-5000
www.abanet.org

American Choral Directors Association (ACDA)
502 SW 38th Street
Lawton, OK 73505
(580) 355-8161
www.acdaonline.org

American Civil Liberties Union (ACLU)
125 Broad Street
New York, NY 10004
(212) 344-3005
www.aclu.org

The American Music Conference (AMC)
5790 Armada Drive
Carlsbad, CA 92008
(800) 767-6266
www.amc-music.com

American Society of Composers, Authors,
    and Publishers (ASCAP)
One Lincoln Plaza
New York, NY 10023
(212) 621-6000
www.ascap.com

> ASCAP-Los Angeles
> 7920 Sunset Boulevard, Suite 300
> Los Angeles, CA 90028
> (323) 883-1000

> ASCAP-Nashville
> 2 Music Square West
> Nashville, TN 37203
> (615) 742-5000

American Symphony Orchestra League (ASOL)
33 West 60th Street
New York, NY 10023-7905
(212) 262-5161 phone
www.symphony.org

Arbitron
142 West 57th Street
New York, NY 10019-3300
(212) 887-1300
www.arbitron.com

Arts Education Partnership (AEP)
One Massachusetts Avenue NW, Suite 700
Washington, DC 20001-1431
(202) 326-8693
No URL

Association For Independent Music (AFIM)
1158 26th Street #505
Santa Monica, CA 90403
(310) 453-6932
www.afim.org

Association of Independent Music Publishers
    (AIMP)
120 East 56th Street, New York, NY 10022
(212) 758-6157
www.aimp.org

Association of Performing Arts Presenters (APAP)
1112 16th Street NW, Suite 400
Washington, DC 20036
(202) 833-2787
www.artspresenters.org

Association for the Promotion of Campus
Activities (APCA)
1131 South Fork Drive
Sevierville, TN 37862
(800) 681-5031
www.apca.com

Audio Engineering Society (AES)
60 East 42nd Street, Room 2520
New York, NY 10165-2520
(212) 661-8528
www.aes.org

Black Promoters Association of America
5825 Glenridge Drive, Bldg. 2, Suite 214
Atlanta, GA 30328
(404) 303-7700
No URL

The Blues Foundation
49 Union Avenue
Memphis, TN 38103
(901) 527-2583
www.blues.org

Blues Music Association (BMA)
PO Box 3122
Memphis, TN 38173
(901) 572-3842
www.bluesmusicassociation.com

Bread & Roses
233 Tamalpais Drive, Suite 100
Corte Madera, CA 94525-1415
(415) 945-7120
www.breadandroses.org

Broadcast Data Services (BDS)
1 North Lexington Avenue
White Plains, NY 10601
(914) 684-5600
www.bdsonline.com

Broadcast Music Incorporated (BMI)
320 West 57th Street
New York, NY 10019
(212) 586-2000
www.bmi.com

    BMI-Los Angeles
    8730 Sunset Boulevard
    Hollywood, CA 90069-2211
    (310) 659-9109

    BMI-Nashville
    10 Music Square East
    Nashville, TN 37203-4399
    (615) 401-2000

Bryan Farrish
Independent Radio Promotion
14230 Ventura Boulevard Suite A
Sherman Oaks, CA 91423
(818) 905-8038
www.radio-media.com

California Lawyers for the Arts (CLA)
Fort Mason Center
Building C, Room 255
San Francisco, CA 94123
(415) 775-7200
www.calawyersforthearts.org

Canadian Arts Presenting Association
    (CAPACOA)
17 York Street, Suite 200
Ottawa, Ontario
Canada K1N 9J6
(613) 562-3515
www.capacoa.ca

Canadian Conference of the Arts
189 Laurier Avenue East
Ottawa, Ontario K1N 6P1
(613) 238-2631
www.culturenet.ca/cca

Canadian Country Music Association (CCMA)
3800 Steeles Avenue West, Suite 127
Woodbridge, Ontario
Canada L4L 4G9
(905) 850-1144
www.ccma.org

Canadian Independent Record Producers
    Association (CIRPA)
150 Eglinton Avenue East, #403
Toronto, Ontario
Canada M4P 1E8
(416) 485-3152
www.cirpa.ca

Canadian Mechanical Rights Reproduction
    Agency (CMRAA)
56 Wellesley Street, West, Suite 320
Toronto, Ontario
Canada M5S 2S3
(416) 469-3186
www.cmraa.ca

Canadian Music Week (CMW)
5399 Eglinton Avenue West, Suite 301
Toronto, Ontario
Canada M9C 5K6
(414) 695-9236
www.cmw.net

Canadian Recording Industry Association
890 Yonge Street, Suite 1200
Toronto, Ontario
Canada M4W 3P4
(416) 967-7272
www.cria.ca

Children's Entertainment Association (CEA))
75 Rockefeller Plaza
New York, NY 10019
(212) 275-1605
www.kidsentertainment.com

Chorus America
1156 15th Street, NW, Suite 310
Washington, DC 20005
(202) 331-7577
www.chorusamerica.org

Church Music Publishers Association (CMPA)
PO Box 158992
Nashville, TN 37215
(615) 791-0273
www.cmpamusic.org

Clear Channel Entertainment, Inc.
650 Madison Avenue
New York, NY 10022
(212) 838-3100
www.clearchannel.com

Country Music Association (CMA)
1 Music Circle South
Nashville, TN 37203
(615) 244-2840
www.countrymusic.org

Country Music Society of America
1 Country Music Road
PO Box 2000
Marion, OH 43306
(800) 669-1002
No URL

Creative Artists Agency (CAA)
9830 Wilshire Boulevard
Beverly Hills, CA 90212
(310) 288-4545
www.caa.com

Creative Music Coalition
1024 W. Wilcox Avenue
Peoria, IL 61604
(309) 685-4843
www.aimcmc.com

Electronic Industries Alliance (EIA)
2500 Wilson Boulevard
Arlington, VA 22201
(703) 907-7500
www.eia.org

Electronic Music Defense and Education Fund
   (EMDEF)
c/o The Lindesmith Center
4455 Connecticut Avenue NW
Washington DC 20008
(310) 450-9036
www.emdef.org

Fischoff Chamber Music Association
PO Box 1303
South Bend, IND 46624-1303
(219) 237-4871
www.fischoff.org

Folk Alliance
North American Folk Music and Dance Alliance
1001 Connecticut Avenue NW, Suite 501
Washington, DC 20036
(202) 835-3655
www.folk.org

The Foundation to Assist Canadian Talent on
Records (FACTOR)
125 George Street
Toronto, Ontario
Canada M5A 2N4
(416) 368-8678
www.factor.ca

The Foundation Center
79 Fifth Avenue
New York, NY 10003
(212) 620-4230
www.fdncenter.org

Future of Music Coalition (FMC)
601 13th Street NW
Suite 900 South
Washington, DC 20005
(202) 783-5588
www.futureofmusic.org

Gavin
United Business Media Inc
460 Park Avenue South
New York, NY 10016
(212) 378-0400
www.uemedia.com/divisions/gavin/html

Gospel Music Association (GMA)
1205 Division Street
Nashville, TN 37203
(615) 242-0303
www.gospelmusic.org

The Harry Fox Agency, Inc. (HFA)
711 3rd Avenue
New York, NY 10017
(212) 370-5330
www.harryfox.com

House of Blues Entertainment, Inc.
6255 Sunset Boulevard
Hollywood, CA 90028
(323) 769-4600
www.hob.com

IMG Artists
825 Seventh Avenue
New York, NY 10019
(212) 489-8300
www.imgartists.com

Infinity Broadcasting
40 West 57th Street
New York, NY 10019
212-314-9200
www.infinityradio.com

Intercollegiate Broadcasting System (IBS)
367 Windsor Highway
New Windsor, NY 12553-7900
(845) 565-0003
www.ibsradio.org

International Association of African American
   Music
413 South Broad Street
Philadelphia, PA 19147
(215) 732-7744
www.IAAAM.com

International Association of Jazz Educators (IAJE)
PO Box 724
Manhattan, KS 66505-0724
(785) 776-8744
www.iaje.org

International Bluegrass Music Association (IBMA)
1620 Frederica Street
Owensboro, KY 42301
(270) 684-9025
www.ibma.org

International Creative Management (ICM)
8942 Wilshire Boulevard
Beverly Hills, CA 90211
(310) 550-4000
No URL

The International Federation of the Phonographic
Industry (IFPI)
IFPI Secretariat
54 Regent Street
London W1B 5RE
United Kingdom
+44 (0)20 7878 7900
www.ifpi.org

International House of Blues Foundation
6255 Sunset Boulevard
Hollywood, CA 90028
(323) 769-4901
www.ihobf.org

International Intellectual Property Alliance (IIPA)
1747 Pennsylvania Avenue NW, Suite 825
Washington, DC 20006-4604
(202) 833-4198
www.iipa.com

International Music Products Association
   (NAMM)
5790 Armada Drive
Carlsbad, CA 92008
(760) 438-8001
www.namm.org

International Publishers Association (IPA)
Av. Sarriá 130-132
08017 Barcelona, Spain
+ 34 93 252 3701
www.ipa-uie.org

International Recording Media Association
   (IRMA)
182 Nassau Street, Suite 204
Princeton, NJ 08542-7005
(609) 279-1700
www.recordingmedia.org

International Trademark Association (INTA)
(Formerly, the U.S. Trademark Association)
1133 Avenue of the Americas
New York, NY 10036-6710
(212)768-9887

The Lindesmith Center- Drug Policy Foundation
4455 Connecticut Avenue NW
Washington DC 20008
(202) 537-5005
www.drugpolicy.org

MeasureCast, Inc.
921 SW Washington St., Suite 800
Portland, Oregon 97205
(503) 889-1248
www.measurecast.com

Monterey Peninsula Artists
901 18th Avenue
Nashville, TN 37212
(615) 321-4444
No URL

Music & Entertainment Industry Educators
  Association (MEIEA)
PO Box 83
Loyola University New Orleans
6363 St. Charles Avenue
New Orleans, LA 70118
(504) 865-3975
www.meiea.org

Music Managers Forum (MMF)
PO Box 444
Village Station
New York, NY 10014-0444
(212) 213-8787
www.mmf-us.org

Music Publishers' Association (MPA)
PMB 246
1562 First Avenue
New York, NY 10028
(212) 327-4044
www.mpa.org

Music Sales Corporation
257 Park Avenue South
New York, NY 10010
(212) 254-2100
www.musicsales.com

NAMM
See International Music Products Association

Nashville Songwriters Association International
  (NSAI)
1701 West End Avenue
Nashville, TN 37203
(800) 321-6008 or (615) 256-3354
www.nashvillesongwriters.com

Nashville Entertainment Association (NEA)
PO Box 121948
1105 16th Avenue South, Suite C
Nashville, TN 37212
(615) 327-4308
www.nea.net

The National Academy of Recording Arts and
  Sciences (NARAS)
3402 Pico Boulevard
Santa Monica, CA 90405
(310) 392-3777
www.grammy.com

  NARAS-Nashville
  1904 Wedgewood Avenue
  Nashville, TN 37212
  (615) 327-8030

  NARAS-New York
  156 West 56th Street, No. 1701
  New York, NY 10019
  (212) 245-5440

National Assembly of State Arts Agencies
1029 Vermont Avenue NW
Washington, DC 20005
202/347-6352
www.nasaa-arts.org

National Association of Broadcasters (NAB)
1771 N Street NW
Washington, DC 20036-2891
(202) 775-2550
www.nab.org

National Association for Campus Activities
   (NACA)
13 Harbison Way
Columbia, SC 29212-3401
(803) 732-6222
www.NACA.org

National Association for Music Education (MENC)
1806 Robert Fulton Drive
Reston, VA 20191
(703) 860-4000
www.menc.org

National Association of Recording Merchandisers
   (NARM)
9 Eves Drive, Suite 120
Marlton, NJ 08053
(856) 596-2221
www.narm.com

National Conference of Personal Managers
c/o National President
Gerard W. Purcell
46-19 220th Place
Bayside, NY 11361
(718) 224-3616
www.ncopm.com

National Federation of Community Broadcasters
   (NFCB)
Fort Mason Center, Building D
San Francisco, CA 94123
(415) 771-1160
www.nfcb.org

National Music Publishers Association (NMPA)
475 Park Avenue South
New York, NY 10016-6901
(646) 742-1651
www.nmpa.org

New Audiences Productions, Inc.
155 West 72nd Street
New York City, NY 10023
(212) 595-5272
www.newaudiences.com

Nielson Media Research
A subsidiary of VNU
299 Park Avenue
New York, NY 10171
(212) 708-7500
www.nielsonmedia.com

North American Performing Arts Managers and
   Agents (NAPAMA)
459 Columbus Avenue #133
New York, NY 10024
(888) 745-8759
www.napama.org

Opera America
1156 15th Street NW, Suite 810
Washington, DC 20005
(202) 293-4466
www.operaamerica.org

Pacific Music Industry Association (PMIA)
404-3701 Hasting Street
Burnaby, British Columbia
Canada V5C 2H6
(604) 873-1914
www.pmia.org

Pea Pod Music
2605 Barclay Drive
Nashville, TN 37206-1507
(615) 277-8195
www.writesongs.com

PEN Music Group, Inc.
1608 North Las Palmas Avenue
Los Angeles, CA 90028-6112
(323)993.6542
www.penmusic.com

Rap Coalition
111 East 14th Street, Suite 339
New York, NY 10007
(212) 714-1100
www.rapcoalition.org
www.rapcointelpro.com

Recording Arts Coalition (RAC)
(No address and phone at this time)
www.recordingartscoalition.com

Recording Industry Association of America
    (RIAA)
1330 Connecticut Avenue NW, Suite 300
Washington, D.C. 20036
(202) 775-0101
www.riaa.com

Reed MIDEM Organization
125 Park Avenue South
New York, NY 10017
(212) 370-7470
www.reedmidemorg.com

Retail Print Music Dealers Association (RPMDA)
13140 Coit Road, Suite 320, LB 120
Dallas, TX 75240-5737
(972) 233-9107
www.printmusic.org

Rhythm and Blues Foundation
1555 Connecticut Avenue, NW, Suite 401
Washington, DC 20036-1111
(202) 588-5566
www.rhythm-n-blues.org

Society of Broadcast Engineers (SBE)
9247 North Meridian Street, Suite 305
Indianapolis, IN 46260
(317) 946-9000
www.sbe.org

Society of Composers, Authors and Music
    Publishers of Canada (SOCAN)
41 Valleybrook Drive
Don Mills, Ontario
Canada M3B 2S6
(416) 445-8700
www.socan.ca

Society of Composers and Lyricists (SCL)
400 South Beverly Drive, Suite 214
Beverly Hills, CA 90212
(301) 281-2812
www.filmscore.org

Society for the Preservation of Bluegrass Music of
    America (SPBGMA)
PO Box 271
Kirksville, MO 63501
(660) 665-7172
www.spbgma.com

Society of Professional Audio Recording Services
    (SPARS)
364 Clove Drive
Memphis, TN 38117-4009 USA
(901) 821-9111
www.spars.com

SESAC, Inc.
55 Music Square East
Nashville, TN 37203
(615) 320-0055
www.sesac.com

    SESAC-New York
    421 West 54th Street
    New York, NY 10019
    (212) 586-3450

    SESAC-Santa Monica
    501 Santa Monica Boulevard, Suite 450
    Santa Monica, CA 90401-2430
    (310) 393-9671

Songwriters Association of Canada
31 Madison Avenue, Suite 202
Toronto, ON
Canada M5R 2S2
(416) 961-1588
www.songwriters.ca

The Songwriter's Guild of America (SGA)
1222 16th Avenue South, Suite 25
Nashville, TN 37212
(615) 269-7664
www.songwriters.org

    SGA-Hollywood
    6430 Sunset Boulevard, Suite 705
    Hollywood, CA 90028
    (323) 462-1108

    SGA-New York
    1560 Broadway, Suite 1306
    New York, NY 10036
    (212) 768-7902

Songwriter Universe
11684 Ventura Boulevard, Suite 975
Studio City, CA 91604
www.songwriteruniverse.com

Sound Inquiry Research & Consulting
PO Box 25025
Albuquerque, NM 87125-5025
(877) 572-8525
www.soundinquiry.com

Soundscan
1 North Lexington Avenue
White Plains, NY 10601
(914) 328-9100
www.home.soundscan.com

South by Southwest Music & Media Conference
PO Box 4999
Austin, TX 78765
(512) 467-7979
www.sxsw.com

    North by Northeast
    185A Danforth Avenue, 2nd Floor
    Toronto, Ontario
    Canada M4K 1N2
    (416) 469-0986
    www.nxne.com

North by Northwest
PO Box 4999
Austin, TX 78765
(512) 467-7979
www.nxnw.com

TAXI
5010 North Parkway Calabasas, Suite 200
Calabasas, CA 91302
(800) 458-2111
www.taxi.com

William Morris Agency, Inc.
1325 Avenue of the Americas
New York, NY 10019
(212) 586-5100
www.wma.com

World Intellectual Property Organization (WIPO)
2 United Nations Plaza, Suite 2525
New York, NY 10017
(212) 963-6813
www.wipo.org

World Trade Organization (WIPO)
Centre Wiliam Rappard
Rue de Lausanne 154
CH-1211 Geneva 21, Switzerland
+41 22 739 51 11
www.wto.org

Young Audiences
115 East 92nd Street
New York, NY 10128-1688
(212) 831-8110
www.youngaudiences.org

Young Concert Artists, Inc.
250 West 57th Street, Suite 1222
New York, NY 10019
(212) 307-6655
www.yca.org

UNIONS

American Federation of Musicians (AFM)
1501 Broadway
Paramount Building, Suite 600
New York, NY 10036
(212) 869-1330
www.afm.org

   AFM-Hollywood
   1777 Vine Street, Suite 500
   Hollywood, CA 90028
   (213) 461-3441

American Federation of Television & Radio Artists
   (AFTRA)
(Offices in major music markets)
260 Madison Avenue
New York, NY 10016
(212) 532-0800
www.aftra.com

   AFTRA-Hollywood
   6922 Hollywood Boulevard
   Hollywood, CA 90028
   (213) 461-8111

American Guild of Musical Artists (AGMA)
1727 Broadway
New York, NY 10019
(212) 265-3687
www.musicalartists.org

American Guild of Variety Artists (AGVA)
184 5th Avenue
New York, NY 10010
(212) 675-1003
No URL

International Alliance of Stage and Theatrical
Employees (IASTE)
1430 Broadway
New York, NY 10018
(212) 730-1770
www.iatse.lm.com

Screen Actors Guild (SAG)
5757 Wilshire Boulevard
Los Angeles, CA 90036
(323) 954-1600
www.sag.org

   SAG-New York
   1515 Broadway
   New York, NY 10036
   (212) 944-1030

TRADE PUBLICATIONS

Acoustic Guitar Magazine
String Letter Publishing
255 West End Avenue
San Rafael, CA 94901
(415) 485-6946
www.acousticguitar.com

Acoustic Musician
PO Box 1349
New Market, VA 22844
(540) 740-4006
www.shentel.net/acousticmusician

The Album Network
120 North Victory Boulevard
Burbank, CA 91502
(818) 955-4000
www.musicbiz.com

Audio Engineering Society (AES) Journal
60 East 42nd Street, Room 2520
New York, NY 10165-2520
(212) 661-8528
www.aes.org

Bass Player
United Entertainment Media, Inc.
The Music Player Group
2800 Campus Drive
San Mateo, CA 94403
(650) 513-4400
www.bassplayer.com

Billboard
BPI Communications, Inc.
1515 Broadway
New York, NY 10036
(800) 745-8922 or (212) 764-7300
www.billboard-online.com

Bluegrass Unlimited
PO Box 771
Warrenton, VA 20188-0771
(800) 258-4727 or (540) 349-8181
www.bluegrassmusic.com

Blues Revue
Rt. 1, Box 75
Salem, WV 26426
(304) 782-1971
www.bluesrevue.com

Cadence Magazine
The Review of Jazz & Blues
Cadence Building
Redwood, NY 13679
(315) 287-2852
www.cadencebuilding.com/cadence/cadence
magazine

Canadian Musician
23 Hannover Drive, Suite 7
St. Catharines, Ontario
Canada L2W 1A3
(905) 641-3471
www.canadianmusician.com

CCM: Contemporary Christian Music
104 Woodmont Boulevard
Nashville, TN 37205
(615) 312-4246
www.ccmcom.com

Christian Musician
4441 South Meridian, Suite 275
Puyallup, WA 98373
(253) 445-1973
www.christianmusician.com

Circus
6 West 18th Street
New York, NY 10011
(212) 242-4902
www.circusmagazine.com

College Music Journal
CMJ New Music Monthly/
CMJ New Music Report
151 West 25th Street
New York, NY 10001
(917) 606-1908
www.cmj.com

Country Music Live
PO Box 128502
Nashville, TN 37212
(615) 595-0799
www.countrymusiclive.com

Crawdaddy!
PO Box 232517
Encinitas, CA 92023
(760) 753-1815
www.cdaddy.com

Dirty Linen
PO Box 66600
Baltimore, MD 21239
(410) 583-7973
www.dirtynelson.com/linen/

DMA (Dance Music Authority)
7943 Paxton Avenue
Tinley Park, IL 60477
(516) 767-2500
www.dmadance.com

Down Beat
102 North Haven Road
Elmhurst, IL 60126
(630) 941-2030
www.downbeatjazz.com

Electronic Musician
PRIMEDIA Business Magazines & Media Inc.
6400 Hollis Street, Suite 12
Emeryville, CA 94608
(510) 653-3307
www.emusician.com

EQ
United Entertainment Media, Inc.
The Music Player Group
2800 Campus Drive
San Mateo, CA 94403
(650) 513-4400
www.eqmag.com

The Gavin Report
United Business Media Inc
460 Park Avenue South
New York, NY 10016
(212) 378-0400
www.gavin.com

Gig
United Entertainment Media, Inc.
The Music Player Group
2800 Campus Drive
San Mateo, CA 94403
(650) 513-4400
www.gigmag.com

Guitar Player
United Entertainment Media, Inc.
The Music Player Group
2800 Campus Drive
San Mateo, CA 94403
(650) 543-5400
www.guitarplayer.com

Guitar World/Guitar World Acoustic
1115 Broadway
New York, NY 10010
(212) 807-7100
www.guitarworld.com

Home Recording Magazine
6 East 32nd Street
New York, NY 10016
(212) 561-3000
www.homerecordingmag.com

Hollywood Reporter
5055 Wilshire Boulevard
Los Angeles, CA 90036
(323) 525-2000
www.hollywoodreporter.com

International Musician
American Federation of Musicians
1501 Broadway, Suite 600
Paramount Building
New York, NY 10036
(212) 869-1330
www.afm.org

JazzTimes
8737 Colesville Road
Silver Spring, MD 20910
(301) 588-4114
www.jazztimes.com

Keyboard
United Entertainment Media, Inc.
The Music Player Group
2800 Campus Drive
San Mateo, CA 94403
(650) 513-4400
www.keyboardmag.com

Mix
PRIMEDIA Business Magazines & Media Inc.
6400 Hollis Street, Suite 12
Emeryville, CA 94608
(510) 653-3307
www.mixonline.com

Modern Drummer
12 Old Bridge Road
Cedar Grove, NJ 07009
(973) 239-4140
www.moderndrummer.com

Music Connection
4215 Coldwater Canyon
Studio City, CA 91604
(818) 755-0101
www.musicconnection.com

Music Educators Journal
Music Educators National Conference (MENC)
1806 Robert Fulton Drive
Reston, VA 20191
(703) 860-4000
www.menc.org

The Music Trades
80 West Street
PO Box 432
Englewood, NJ 07631
(201) 871-1965
www.musictrades.com

Musico Pro
Music Maker Publications, Inc.
5412 Idylwild Trail, Suite 100
Boulder, CO 80301
(303) 516-9118
www.recordingmag.com/mumak/Pro

Onstage
PRIMEDIA Business Magazines & Media Inc.
6400 Hollis Street, Suite 12
Emeryville, CA 94608
(510) 653-3307
www.onstagemag.com

The Performing Songwriter
2805 Azalea Place
Nashville, TN 37204
(615) 385-7796
www.performingsongwriter.com

Pro Sound News
460 Park Avenue South
New York, NY 10016
(212) 378-0400
www.prosoundnews.com

Radio And Records
10100 Santa Monica Boulevard
Los Angeles, CA 90067
(310) 553-4330
www.rronline.com

Recording
Music Maker Publications, Inc.
5412 Idylwild Trail, Suite 100
Boulder, CO 80301
(303) 516-9118
www.recordingmag.com

Remix
PRIMEDIA Business Magazines & Media Inc.
6400 Hollis Street, Suite 12
Emeryville, CA 94608
(510) 653-3307
www.remixmag.com

Rolling Stone
1290 Avenue of the Americas
New York, NY 10104
(212) 484-1616
www.rollingstone.com

Sing Out!
PO Box 5253
Bethlehem, PA 18015
(610) 865-5366
www.singout.org

Sound & Communications
25 Willowdale Avenue
Port Washington, NY 11050
(516) 767-2500
www.soundandcommunications.com

Sound & Video Contractor
PRIMEDIA Business Magazines & Media Inc.
6400 Hollis Street, Suite 12
Emeryville, CA 94608
(510) 653-3307
www.svconline.com

The Source
215 Park Avenue South
New York, NY 10003
(212) 253-3700
www.thesource.com

Strings Magazine
String Letter Publishing
255 West End Avenue
San Rafael, CA 94901
(415) 485-6946
www.stringsmagazine.com

Tape Op
PO Box 14517
Portland, OR 97293
(503) 239-5389
www.tapeop.com

URB
1680 North Vine Street, #1012
Hollywood, CA 90028
(323) 993-0291
www.urb.com

Variety
5700 Wilshire Boulevard, Suite 120
Los Angeles, CA 90036
(213) 857-6600
www.variety.com

Vibe
215 Lexington Avenue
New York, NY 10016
(212) 448-7300
www.vibe.com

Victory Review
PO Box 2254
Tacoma, WA 98401
(253) 428-0832
www.victorymusic.org

INDUSTRY DIRECTORIES

Billboard Directories
1695 Oak Street
PO Box 2016
Lakewood, NJ 08701
(800) 344-7119
www.billboard.com/store/directories
    Billboard International Buyer's Guide Directory
    Billboard International Latin Music Buyer's
        Guide Directory
    Billboard International Talent and Touring Directory
    Billboard International Tape/Disc Directory
    Billboard Nashville 615/Country Music
        Sourcebook
    Billboard Radio Power Book: Directory of Music
        Radio and Record Promotion
    Billboard Record Retailing Directory

Directory of Artists
Association of Performing Arts Presenters (APAP)
1112 16th Street NW, Suite 400
Washington, DC 20036
(202) 833-2787
www.artspresenters.org

The MBI World Report 2002
The Music Group
CMP Information Ltd
Ludgate House
245 Blackfriars Road
London SE1 9UR
0207 579 4123
www.musicweek.com

Music Directory Canada
CM Books
23 Hannover Drive, Unit 7
St. Catharines, Ontario
Canada L2W 1A3
(905) 641-3471
www.musicdirectorycanada.com

The Musician's Atlas
Music Resource Group
PO Box 682
Nyack, NY 10960
(845) 353-9303
www.musiciansatlas.com

The Music Business Registry
7510 Sunset Boulevard #1041
Los Angeles, CA 90046-3400 USA
(800) 377-7411
www.musicregistry.com

Music Technology Buyer's Guide
United Entertainment Media, Inc.
460 Park Avenue South
New York, NY 10016
(212) 378-0400
www.uemedia.com/divisions/mtbuyer/shtml

Music Yellow Pages
United Entertainment Media, Inc.
6 Manhasset Avenue
Port Washington, NY 11050
(516) 944-5940
www.musicyellowpages.com

Performance International Touring Talent
    Publications
203 Lake Street, Suite 200
Fort Worth, TX 76102-4504
(817) 338-9444
www.performancemagazine.com
    The Black Book: Entire Performance Guide
        Series
    Concert Production
    Equipment and Personnel
    Facilities
    Talent Buyers
    Talent Management
    Transportation Guide

Pollstar, USA
4697 West Jacquelyn Avenue
Fresno, CA 93722-6413
559-271-7900 Voice
559-271-7979 Fax
www.pollstar.com
    PollstarOnline.com

Agency Rosters
Talent Buyer Directory
Concert Venue Directory
Concert Support Services Directory

Recording Industry Sourcebook
Artist Pro
236 Georgia Street, Suite 100
Vallejo, CA 94590
(707) 554-1935
www.artistpro.com/Sourcebase.cfm

RECORDING CATALOGS

All Music Guide (AMG)
Alliance Entertainment Group
301 East Liberty, Suite 400
Ann Arbor, MI 48104
(734) 887-5600
www.allmediaguide.com

PhonoLog
Muze Inc.
304 Hudson Street
New York, NY 10013
(800) 404-9960
www.muze.com

BIBLIOGRAPHY

THIS IS THE AUTHOR'S SELECTED LIST OF BOOKS ON THE
MUSIC INDUSTRY

88 Songwriting Wrongs and How to Right Them
Pete and Pat Luboff
Writer's Digest Books
Cincinnati, OH

12 Steps to Building Better Songs
Pete and Pat Luboff
Pea Pod Music
Nashville, TN

*The Acoustic Musician's Guide to Sound
Reinforcement and Live Recording*
Mike Sokol
Prentice-Hall
Upper Saddle River, NJ

All You Need to Know About The Music Business
Donald S. Passman
Simon & Schuster
New York, NY

The Billboard Guide to Home Recording
Ray Baragary
Billboard Books
Nashville, TN

The Billboard Guide to Music Publicity
Jim Pettigrew, Jr.
Billboard Books
Nashville, TN

Buzz Your MP3
Brian Freeman
Pigeonhole Press
E-books
www.pigeonholepress.com

The Craft and Business of Songwriting
John Braheny
Writer's Digest Books
Cincinnati, OH

The Craft of Lyric Songwriting
Sheila, Davis
Writer's Digest Books
Cincinnati, OH

The Entertainment Economy
Michael J. Wolf
Random House
New York, NY

*Exploding: The Highs, Hits, Hype, Heroes, and the
    Hustlers of the Warner Music Group*
Stan Cornyn
Harper Entertainment Group
Nashville, TN

Hit Men
Fredric Dannen
Vintage Books
New York, NY

How to Be Your Own Booking Agent
Jeri Goldstein
The New Music Times, Inc.
PO Box 1105
Charlottesville, VA 22902

How to Make Money Performing in Schools
David Heflick
Silcox Productions
PO Box 1407
Orient, WA 99160

How to Make and Sell Your Own Recording
Diane Rapaport
Prentice-Hall
Upper Saddle River, NJ

The Independent Musician's Contact Bible
Editor: David Wimble
Omnibus Press (Music Sales Corporation)
New York, NY

Making a Living in Your Local Music Market
Dick Weissman
Hal Leonard Publishing Corporation
Milwaukee, WI

Modern Recording Techniques
David Miles Huber and Robert Runstein
Focal Press (Butterworth-Heinemann)
Woburn, MASS

*Music Biz Know-How: Do-It-Yourself Strategies for
    Independent Music Success*
Peter Spellman
MBS Business Media
PO Box 230266
Boston, MA

Musicians and the Law in Canada
Paul Sanderson
Carswell
Toronto, Canada

Music, Money & Success
Jeffrey Brabec and Todd Brabec
Schirmer Books (Music Sales Corporation)
New York, NY

Music Publishing: A Songwriter's Guide
Randy Poe
Writer's Digest Books
Cincinnati, OH

The Musician's Business and Legal Guide
Editor: Mark Halloran
Prentice-Hall
Upper Saddle River, NJ

*The Musician's Guide to Making and Selling Your
    Own CDs and Cassettes*
Jana Stanfield
Writer's Digest Books
Cincinnati, OH

The Musician's Guide to Touring and Promotion
Billboard Books
Nashville, TN

Music is Your Business
Christopher Knab
FourFront Media and Music
Seattle, WA

Networking in the Music Business
Dan Kimpel
Hal Leonard Corporation
Milwaukee, WI

*Off the Charts: Ruthless Days and Reckless Nights
    Inside the Music Industry*
Bruce Haring
Carol Publishing Group
Secaucus, NJ

*Presenting Performances:
    A Basic Handbook for the Twenty-first Century*
Thomas Wolf
Association of Performing Arts Presenters (APAP)
Washington, DC 20036

Songwriter's Market
Writer's Digest books
Cincinnatti, OH

Songwriting: The Words, The Music and the Money
Dick Weissman
Hal Leonard Publishing Corporation
Milwaukee, WI

*Sound Check: The Basics of Sound and Sound
  Systems*
Tony Moscal
Hal Leonard Publishing Corporation
Milwaukee, WI

Sound Reinforcement Handbook
Gary Davis and Ralph Jones
Hal Leonard Publishing Corporation
Milwaukee, WI

*Star Tracks: Principles for Success in the Music
and Entertainment Business*
Larry E. Wacholtz
Thumbs Up Publishing
Nashville, TN

They Fought the Law: Rock Music Goes to Court
Stan Soocher
Schirmer Trade Books (Music Sales Corporation)
New York, NY

This Business of Music
M. William Krasilovsky, Sidney Shemel and
John Gross
Watson-Guptill Publishing
New York, NY

*Tim Sweeney's Guide to Releasing Independent
  Records*
Tim Sweeney and Mark Geller
TSA Books
Torrance, CA 90503

What's Going On in the Music Business
Frank Jermance and Dick Weissman
Hal Leonard Publishing Corporation
Milwaukee, WI

Writing Music for Hit Songs
Jai Josefs
Schirmer Trade Books (Music Sales Corporation)
New York, NY

You Can Hype Anything
Raleigh Pinskey
Citadel Press
Secaucus, NJ

ABOUT THE AUTHOR

Diane Sward Rapaport

Dᴀᴇ Sᴡᴀʀᴅ Rᴀᴘᴀᴘᴏʀᴛ is a music business pioneer. She began offering courses for musicians in music business management and publishing in 1974, after working for seven years as an artist's manager for Bill Graham's Fillmore Management. Her goal was to help musicians and songwriters make a living from their art.

In 1976, she cofounded, edited and published *Music Works-A Manual for Musicians,* a magazine hailed as a "bible for musicians" by the San Francisco Chronicle. It was the first magazine to feature music business and technology news.

In 1979 *How to Make and Sell Your Own Record,* her first book, was published by Putnam and now by Prentice-Hall. It has been called the "bible and basic text" that has helped revolutionize the recording industry by providing information about setting up new recording labels independent of major label conglomerates. It has sold more than 200,000 copies.

"This book has played a pioneering role in the long-overdue broadening of the avenues of the music industry... [It] has worked to reshape the way music is marketed, while helping to introduce ostensibly "uncommercial," innovative and truly special artists and their music to receptive audiences. More importantly, it has helped many of them realize their dreams." —Loreena McKennitt, from the foreword to *How to Make and Sell Your Own Recording.*

In 1988, Diane Rapaport founded Jerome Headlands Press, a company that produces and designs books for musicians and artists. Its current catalog includes *How to Make and Sell Your Own Recording; The Musician's Business and Legal Guide; The Visual Artist's Business* and *Legal Guide and The Acoustic Musician's Guide to Sound Reinforcement* and *Live Recording.* The books are published by Prentice Hall.

She has given numerous music business seminars for colleges, nonprofit music businesses and music conferences and served as an adjunct professor of music business at the University of Colorado, Denver.

CONTRIBUTING AUTHORS

MARK HALLORAN

Entertainment attorney Mark Halloran specializes in entertainment financing, production and distribution deals. He has acted as an expert witness in film, television and music litigation, for, among others, Kim Basinger, Muhammed Ali, ICM, Kevin Costner, Harold Ramis and Paramount. Mark has done production work for Universal, Paramount, Disney and Miramax and has sold distribution rights to Castle Rock ("Palmetto"), Universal ("Kissing A Fool"), USA Films ("Thick as Thieves"), Miramax ("Down in the Delta"), Sony Pictures Classics ("Bossa Nova") and Destination Films ("Ring of Fire" and "Drowning Mona").

Mark has co-authored three nationally published books on the entertainment industry, *Musician's Guide to Copyright* (with Gunnar Erickson and Ned Hearn), *The Musician's Business and Legal Guide* and *The Independent Film Producer's Survival Guide: A Business and Legal Sourcebook* (with Gunnar Erickson and Harris Tulchin).

Halloran cochaired the USC/Beverly Hills Bar Association Annual Entertainment Law Programs in 1989, 1990, 1994, 1995, and 1996, serves as a director of the USC Entertainment Law Institute and has taught classes on film finance at UCLA Extension.

EDWARD (NED) R. HEARN

Edward (Ned) R. Hearn is in private law practice, with offices in San Jose, California. Mr. Hearn's practice concentrates on entertainment, Internet and computer software businesses. He is a director of the California Lawyers for the Arts, an organization that provides legal assistance to musicians and other artists, board president of the Northern California Songwriters' Association, coauthor of *The Musician's Guide to Copyright* and a contributing author to *The Musician's Business and Legal Guide* and *How to Make and Sell Your Own Recording*. Mr. Hearn also lectures on music business and related legal issues.

GREGORY T. VICTOROFF

Gregory T. Victoroff has been an entertainment litigation attorney since 1979, representing clients in the music, film and fine art businesses in Los Angeles. He is a frequent author and lecturer on copyright and art law. Mr. Victoroff is editor and coauthor of *The Visual Artist's Business and Legal Guide* and a contributing author to *The Musician's Business and Legal Guide* and *How to Make and Sell Your Own Recording*. As an orchestral musician, he has backed such artists as Huey Lewis and the News, Santana and Bobby McFerrin.

INDEX

Act), 42
    mechanical licenses for digital phonorecord
        deliveries, 92–94
    protection of Internet transmissions by, 96
draws
    importance in concert promotion, 165
    for jazz concerts, 180–181
    understanding potential, 149
Drug Enforcement Administration (DEA), 133
drugs and controlled substances
        crackhouse law and, 134
        zero-tolerance attitude toward, 136
duration of copyrights, 33

E

Eames, Michael, 80–83
ecstasy prevention laws, 135
education
    audio education business, 278
    educating artists about contracts, 238
    music education and retailing, 276
EIA (Electronic Industries Alliance), 267, 292
Electronic Musician, 246, 301
EMDEF (Electronic Music Defense and Education
Fund), 133, 143, 144, 293
EMI Group, 190
Eminem, 237
engineers
    mastering engineers, 257–258
    as recording personnel, 256–257
entertainment conglomerates
    about, 1, 3
    concert promotion by, 179–180
    consolidation of record labels, 190
    control of popular media by, 205–206
entertainment industry
    entertainment conglomerates and, 1, 3
    music as part of, 1
entertainment vs. art, 156
EQ, 246, 301
equity, 9
ethics
    business principles for musicians, 15
    Code of Ethics for National Conference of Personal
    Managers, 131
    failure and admitting mistakes, 82
    honesty, 83
    standards for customer service, 112–113
    talent agents and, 157
    trust, 27, 284–285
exclusive term songwriter agreements, 71
expenses
    defined, 10
    shared by record companies and artists, 191–192

F

FACTOR (Foundation to Assist Canadian Talent on
Records), 5, 211, 212, 293
failures
    admitting, 82
    in business, 11
fair use
    as defense for sampling, 40–41
    landmark lawsuits over, 104
    Negativland sampling of U2 material, 104
    penalties for sampling, 105–106
    protection of expression of ideas and, 102–103
fans, 228
Farrish, Bryan, 232, 242, 291
FCC (Federal Communications Commission), 3
federal agency resources, 289
federal antibootlegging statutes, 103, 105
Federal Communications Commission (FCC), 3
fees
    arrangements with concert promoters, 166–167
    for artists' managers, 124–125
    attorneys' charges for services, 120–121
    buyouts and co-ownership, 107
    distribution of performance rights, 98
    for Form PA registration, 35
    for investigating copyright status of works, 40
    mechanical license fees
        for public performances, 95, 96–97
        rates for recorded songs, 89
    memberships
        AES, 266–267
        NMPA, 115
        NSAI, 62
        Rap Coalition, 238
        SGA, 84
        TAXI, 111
    for synchronization licenses, 99
    for talent agents, 146
    union overtime charged to promoters, 178
fictitious name certificates, 23
film
    recording studios for, 254
    synchronization licenses required for, 98–99
financial management
    artists' managers and, 126–127
    assets
        addressing in LLC operating agreement, 17
        defined, 8
    bookkeeping, 11
    business plans, 11, 12, 13
    coaccounting for collaborator/songwriter agreements,
    79
    financial statements, 8–9
    income and expenses in concert promotion, 165–167
    manager's role in, 141
    role of CPAs, 11
financial support for musicians, 5
Fischoff Chamber Music Association, 159, 184, 212, 293
FMC (Future of Music Coalition), 116, 117
Folk Alliance, 159, 212, 293
foreign performance rights, 96

M

ABOUT JEROME HEADLANDS PRESS

Jerome Headlands Press Inc., based in Jerome, Arizona, designs and produces business books for professionals that work in entertainment and the arts. It was founded by Diane Rapaport in 1990 with the goal to provide artists with access to business information and training to help them make a living and avoid costly mistakes.

How to Make and Sell Your Own Recording (revised fifth edition, 1999), by Diane Sward Rapaport, with a foreword by Loreena McKennitt, has been a friend and guide to more than 200,000 musicians, producers, engineers and owners of recording labels. It has helped revolutionize the recording industry by providing information about setting up independent record labels.

> *This book has played a pioneering role in the long-overdue broadening of the avenues of the music industry. . . [it] has worked to reshape the way music is marketed, while helping to introduce ostensibly "uncommercial," innovative and truly special artists and their music to receptive audiences. More importantly, it has helped many of them realize their dreams.*
> —Loreena McKennitt, from the foreword

The Musician's Business and Legal Guide, (revised third edition, 2001), a presentation of the Beverly Hills Bar Association Committee for the Arts, was compiled and edited by Mark Halloran Esq. In this book, prominent entertainment lawyers and business experts provide understandable information on vital legal and business issues. A unique characteristic is that current recording, publishing, production and management contracts are analyzed clause by clause.

> *Any musician who feels all at sea when confronting the business side of the job can get what he or she needs from this source.*
> —Billboard Magazine

The Acoustic Musician's Guide to Sound Reinforcement and Live Recording (1997) by Mike Sokol, tells how to set up and operate a sound system and describes the techniques that must be learned to provide good performance experiences for musicians and audiences.

> *A comprehensive guide to live sound and recording that makes very helpful readings for all giggers, regardless of genre.*
> —Gig Magazine

The Visual Artist's Business and Legal Guide (1994), a presentation of the Beverly Hills Bar Association Committee for the Arts, was compiled and edited by Gregory T. Victoroff, Esq. This comprehensive resource, written by prominent art lawyers, professionals and business experts, provides valuable legal and business information and can improve artists' chances for financial success.

> *This book will tell you how to protect your work, your integrity, your character and your rights to enjoy the returns of your own labor. . .gives artists' educators, managers and artists some important tools to avoid getting ripped off.*
> —Joan Jeffri, Director, Research Center for Arts and Culture, Columbia University

Jerome Headlands Press, Inc.
P.O. Box N
Jerome, Arizona 86331
jhpress@sedona.net